COMPANY CHARGES

COMPANY CHARGES

Spectrum and Beyond

Edited by

Joshua Getzler
Jennifer Payne

OXFORD
UNIVERSITY PRESS

OXFORD
UNIVERSITY PRESS

Great Clarendon Street, Oxford OX2 6DP

Oxford University Press is a department of the University of Oxford.
It furthers the University's objective of excellence in research, scholarship,
and education by publishing worldwide in

Oxford New York

Auckland Cape Town Dar es Salaam Hong Kong Karachi
Kuala Lumpur Madrid Melbourne Mexico City Nairobi
New Delhi Shanghai Taipei Toronto

With offices in

Argentina Austria Brazil Chile Czech Republic France Greece
Guatemala Hungary Italy Japan Poland Portugal Singapore
South Korea Switzerland Thailand Turkey Ukraine Vietnam

Oxford is a registered trade mark of Oxford University Press
in the UK and in certain other countries

Published in the United States
by Oxford University Press Inc., New York

First published 2006

British Library Cataloguing in Publication Data
Data available

Library of Congress Cataloging in Publication Data
Data available

Typeset by RefineCatch Limited, Bungay, Suffolk
Printed in Great Britain
on acid-free paper by
Biddles Ltd, King's Lynn, Norfolk

ISBN 0–19–929993–5 978–0–19–929993–5

1 3 5 7 9 10 8 6 4 2

FOREWORD

Company Charges

The history of company charges in England during the last 150 years is largely the history of the floating charge; and the history of the floating charge is a large part of the story of commerce and industry in England during that period.

The floating charge originated in England in a series of cases in the Chancery Division in the 1870s. But it was not created by the Chancery judges; it was the work of innovative transaction lawyers who were responding to the demands of their commercial clients. They wanted a form of charge which would afford them, by a single instrument, an effective and comprehensive security upon the entire undertaking of the debtor and its assets from time to time, while at the same time leaving the debtor free to deal with its assets and pay its trade creditors in the ordinary course of business without reference to them. Such a form of security is particularly attractive to banks and other loan creditors, and it rapidly acquired great importance in English commercial life.

Valuable as the new form of security was, it was not without its critics. One of its consequences was that it enabled the holder of the charge to withdraw all or most of the assets of an insolvent company from the scope of a liquidation and leave the liquidator with little more than an empty shell and unable to pay unsecured trade creditors. It was not recognized in the United States, where it was regarded as contrary to its fair dealing laws. It was seen by many judges as an injustice and by Lord Macnaghten as a great scandal. In *Salomon v A Salomon & Co Ltd*[1] he observed that the injustice of the case was not caused by the fact that a company is a distinct legal person separate from its members but by the excessive security conferred by a floating charge. He proposed that legislation should provide for unsecured trade debts incurred within six months of a liquidation to have priority over the debt secured by a floating charge.

By the end of the nineteenth century Parliament had intervened to require floating charges to be registered and to give preferential debts priority over the debt secured by a floating charge. Neither reform helped the ordinary trade

[1] [1897] AC 22, 53, HL.

creditors, whose debts were not preferential and who could not avoid giving credit to their customers in the ordinary course of business. In *Re London Pressed Hinge Co Ltd*[2] Buckley J observed that great mischief arose from the very nature of the floating charge which allowed a company to continue to trade and incur credit despite the existence of the charge. This put the ordinary trade creditors of the company at risk, even though they would not normally know of the existence of the charge; for the holder of the charge could step in without warning at any time and obtain priority over them. Such trade creditors would include the suppliers of goods which the charge holder could appropriate to the security and realize for its own benefit leaving the suppliers unpaid.

Until the end of the Second World War taxes and wages were relatively low, and the banks were content to take floating charges over circulating assets, though they were careful to take fixed charges over fixed assets such as land, plant, and machinery. But heavy wage and tax inflation after the war led the banks to explore ways of extending the scope of their fixed charges to cover book debts and other circulating assets.

It was soon established that the banks could take fixed charges over book debts provided that the proceeds were paid into a blocked account and rendered unavailable to the customer without the prior consent of the charge holder. But it was not practical to require the customer to seek permission every time it wanted to withdraw money from the account, and the banks did not want to monitor the bank account and be required to give their consent whenever the company wished to make a withdrawal. They wanted the best of both worlds. They wanted to have a fixed charge over the book debts while allowing the company the same access to the proceeds that it would have if the charge were a floating charge. With the first instance decision in *Siebe Gorman & Co Ltd v Barclays Bank Ltd*[3] they achieved this. Although the correctness of this decision was doubted by many practitioners, it was not challenged for more than 20 years. A further step was taken in *Re New Bullas Trading Ltd*,[4] where the Court of Appeal held that the distinction between a floating and a fixed charge was simply a matter of construction of the charge. The parties were free to make whatever agreement they liked; unless unlawful the intention of the parties, to be gathered from the terms of the debenture, must prevail.

This proved to be a step too far. Orthodoxy was restored by the Privy Council in *Agnew v IRC (Re Brumark Investments Ltd)*[5] which made it clear that the

[2] [1905] 1 Ch 576, 581, 583.
[3] [1979] 2 Lloyd's Rep 142.
[4] [1994] 1 BCLC 449, CA.
[5] [2001] UKPC 28, [2001] 2 AC 710.

distinction between a floating and a fixed charge, like that between a licence and a lease, was not simply a question of construction of the relevant document but a question of law. The object in construing the document is to ascertain the nature of the rights and obligations which the parties intended to grant each other in respect of the charged assets. Once these have been ascertained, the court can embark on the second stage of the process, which is one of categorization. This is a matter of law. It depends on the result of the first stage, not on the intention of the parties.

The Privy Council effectively overruled *New Bullas*, but it was not necessary to overrule *Siebe Gorman*, though it dropped a heavy hint that it thought that the case was wrongly decided on the facts. It was finally overruled by the House of Lords in *Re Spectrum Plus Ltd.*[6]

In the meantime Lord Macnaghten's proposal has at last borne fruit more than a century after it was made. In 1982 the Cork Committee recommended that 10 per cent of the proceeds of a floating charge should be made available to unsecured creditors; and while this was not implemented at the time a similar proposal was contained in the Enterprise Act 2002.

What the future holds is anyone's guess. The floating charge, never introduced into the United States, has been abolished in Australia and New Zealand. In 2005 a symposium was held at St Hugh's College in Oxford to discuss the implications of the *Spectrum* litigation and the subject of corporate securities in general. This book is the result. It should be required reading for anyone concerned with the future of the financing of commerce and industry. Only by studying the past can we avoid repeating its mistakes in the future.

The Right Honourable Lord Millett
March 2006

[6] [2005] UKHL 41, [2005] 2 AC 680.

PREFACE

On 22 September 2005 some 35 experts—lawyers, economists, practitioners, and academics—gathered at St Hugh's College in Oxford to discuss the decision of the House of Lords in *Re Spectrum Plus Ltd*,[1] handed down earlier that summer. This book is based on the lively exchange of views at the symposium, and explores the meaning of the *Spectrum* decision itself, and the various implications arising from it.

The issue at the heart of *Spectrum* was whether the charge given over book debts to the bank in that case was a fixed charge or a floating charge. The House of Lords decided, overruling the Court of Appeal,[2] that the charge should properly be characterized as floating. However, this seemingly simple decision creates a host of further issues for academics and practitioners. The decision has commercial consequences not only for the parties in the case but also for the business community at large. Many other transactions employing essentially the same terms as the contract in *Spectrum* awaited the outcome of the House of Lords' decision, and the *Spectrum* decision will not only have a retrospective effect but will also affect how secured lenders (in particular banks) will lend money in the future.

In particular the *Spectrum* litigation raises important questions regarding the fixed/floating charge divide, such as how that divide is determined, why it exists, whether it should be maintained at all, and if so in what format. The issue of fixed versus floating charges continues to be a vexing (and expensive) issue. As Roy Goode points out in his chapter in the past five years alone there have been 15 High Court decisions on floating charges of which six went to the Court of Appeal and three to the House of Lords—24 decisions and 48 judgments in all, which together must have involved millions of pounds in legal costs. The impact of the Enterprise Act 2002 on both secured and unsecured lending combines with the new test for characterization of collateral in *Spectrum* to change the terrain for administration of distressed companies. The *Spectrum* litigation thus connects to wider legal issues encompassing priority and control in insolvency law, and the proper divide between freedom of contract and

---

[1] [2005] UKHL 41, [2005] 2 AC 680.
[2] [2004] EWCA Civ 670, [2004] Ch 337.

mandatory regulation in the law of security. These issues are all reflected in the chapters gathered in this collection.

Gabriel Moss, who acted as lead counsel for the bank in *Spectrum*, provides some reflections on the House of Lords' decision. He suggests that the distinction between fixed and floating charges is based on fictions at the present time and that priority in insolvency should be based on rational policy choices rather than skill in drafting and fine distinctions. Roy Goode goes further and argues that the floating charge should be abolished altogether. This is an argument also made by Louise Gullifer and Jennifer Payne who explore the justifications for the fixed/floating distinction, and investigate the alternatives adopted by the United States, Canada, and New Zealand to deal with these issues. They suggest that these alternative approaches, and in particular that adopted in New Zealand, have much to recommend them as compared to the present English system. Sarah Worthington explores the implications of the House of Lords' decision for the future characterization of security agreements and also argues that although the approach of the House of Lords was perfectly proper, the statutory rule in the Insolvency Act 1986 that demands this approach is fundamentally misconceived, being both inefficient and ineffective. Nicholas Frome and Kate Gibbons consider why the *Spectrum* decision and some of its antecedents are likely to remain highly relevant for practitioners at least until the boundaries of the *Spectrum* decision have been clarified, and they suggest where those boundaries should be drawn.

Philip Wood considers *Spectrum* and its forerunner, *Agnew v IRC*[3] (also known as *Brumark*) in an international setting. He argues that these decisions should not be viewed with enthusiasm and that their ambit should be narrowed to facilitate lending on a secured basis. Robert Stevens explores the position of secured lenders in the light of both the *Spectrum* decision and the changes introduced by the Enterprise Act 2002. He argues that the suggested 'double whammy' to secured lenders of *Spectrum* and the Enterprise Act is not as devastating as sometimes suggested, and that in any case, secured lenders can avoid the effects of the Enterprise Act even after the *Spectrum* decision. Look Chan Ho examines the impact of the retrospective effect of the House of Lords' ruling in *Spectrum*, which means that many charges previously characterized as fixed were in fact floating. He argues that payments made in reliance on this characterization were payments made in reliance on a mistake of law and that charge holders who received such payments now stand the risk of having to disgorge their receipts. He considers the possibility of recovering the payments made to charge holders on the basis of unjust enrichment.

---

[3] [2001] UKPC 28, [2001] 2 AC 710.

John Armour asks whether the statutory policy of treating floating charges differently from fixed, which is given teeth through the characterization rules articulated in cases such as *Spectrum*, is appropriate. He uses the example of the floating charge to argue that statutory redistribution between claimants in corporate insolvency is generally undesirable. Joshua Getzler examines the historical origins of company charges, and suggests that the benefits of the floating charge in English corporate finance have been overplayed, and that the inimical effects of such charges have consistently been underestimated. Julian Franks and Oren Sussman address the criticisms made by economists of the English insolvency system. They investigate free-contract and regulatory models of insolvency procedure and ask how the *Spectrum* decision and the Enterprise Act might affect economists' assessments of rival insolvency systems. Michael Bridge concludes this collection with a consideration of the Law Commission's long awaited final report on the reform of security interests. He analyses the suggested reforms in close detail. While he concludes that reform in this area is long overdue, and he praises the work done by the Law Commission in this project, he also acknowledges the limitations, some substantial, in the final Report.

The symposium was initially planned at a time when only the more controversial Court of Appeal decision in this litigation had been handed down. The symposium was moved to a later date in order to follow the handing down of the House of Lords' decision. We are grateful to all those who adjusted their diaries to accommodate this change, and special thanks are due to Sarah Worthington who was involved in the initial planning of this symposium but was unable to be present at the reorganized date. We are very pleased that Sarah has nevertheless contributed a chapter to this book.

We would like to thank the Insolvency Service for sponsoring the symposium which began this project. Without its kind support the symposium would not have been possible. We would also like to express our gratitude to St Hugh's College for hosting the event and providing many forms of support, and to the editors at Oxford University Press who navigated the book through its stages with impressive speed. We must thank above all those who attended the symposium on 22 September 2005, especially those who wrote papers and have turned them into chapters. Special thanks are also due to Lord Millett who kindly agreed to write the Foreword to this collection, which explains admirably what is at stake in the law of company charges.

Joshua Getzler
St Hugh's College, Oxford

Jennifer Payne
Merton College, Oxford

31 March 2006

CONTENTS—SUMMARY

CONTENTS

LIST OF CONTRIBUTORS

John Armour, University Senior Lecturer in Law and Research Associate, Centre for Business Research, Cambridge University, and Fellow of Trinity Hall, Cambridge.

Michael Bridge, Professor of Commercial Law and Dean of the Faculty of Laws, University College London.

Julian Franks, Professor of Finance, London Business School and Centre for Economic Policy Research.

Nicholas Frome, Partner of Clifford Chance LLP, London.

Joshua Getzler, Reader in Legal History, University of Oxford and Fellow and Tutor in Law, St Hugh's College, Oxford.

Kate Gibbons, Partner of Clifford Chance LLP, London.

Sir Roy Goode, QC, Emeritus Professor of Law, University of Oxford and Emeritus Fellow of St John's College, Oxford.

Louise Gullifer, Lecturer in Law, University of Oxford and Fellow and Tutor in Law, Harris Manchester College, Oxford.

Look Chan Ho, Attorney-at-Law and Solicitor, Freshfields Bruckhaus Deringer, London.

The Right Honourable Lord Millett, formerly a Lord of Appeal in Ordinary, and Justice of the Court of Final Appeal of Hong Kong.

Gabriel Moss, QC, of 3/4 South Square, Gray's Inn, who acted as lead counsel for the bank in *Re Spectrum Plus Ltd.*

Jennifer Payne, Travers Smith Lecturer in Corporate Finance Law, University of Oxford and Fellow of Merton College, Oxford.

Robert Stevens, Barrister, Lecturer in Law, University of Oxford and Fellow and Tutor in Law, Lady Margaret Hall, Oxford.

Oren Sussman, Reader in Finance, Saïd Business School, University of Oxford and Fellow of Wadham College, Oxford.

Philip R Wood, Special Global Counsel, Allen & Overy LLP, Visiting Professor/

Distinguished Visiting Fellow at the Universities of Oxford, Cambridge, and London.

Sarah Worthington, Professor of Law and Deputy Director, London School of Economics.

TABLE OF CASES

TABLE OF LEGISLATION

UK LEGISLATION

Primary legislation

Secondary legislation

NATIONAL LEGISLATION

Australia

Canada

New Zealand

United States

EUROPEAN LEGISLATION

Directives

Regulations

1

FICTIONS AND FLOATING CHARGES: SOME REFLECTIONS ON THE HOUSE OF LORDS' DECISION IN *SPECTRUM*

Gabriel Moss QC

A. Introduction

In Jane Austin's *Emma*, members of an outing of idle gentry are given the alternatives of saying 'either one thing very clever . . ., or two things moderately clever or three things very dull indeed . . .'.[1] Considering the clever points made in the other chapters of this book, it seems that my role is to point out three very dull things. I will therefore divide the remainder of this chapter into three parts.

B. How Did We Get Here?

What follows is a very concise and highly subjective view of the history of the problem, entirely unsupported by the decided cases.

In the beginning, there were fixed charges. But if one wanted to create a fixed charge over an entire business there were problems. In particular, there were two related problems: (i) some assets would not yet exist; and (ii) some assets would be changing regularly. These problems were dealt with by equity. Logically, there could not be a *present* charge over property which did not yet exist. However, equity invented what was in effect a fiction, namely that you can *today* have an equitable charge over *future* property. A necessary allied fiction, in order to make the security effective, was that when the asset was born, it was born

[1] Penguin Popular Classics, 280.

already subject to the charge.[2] This meant that even if by the time the subject matter of the charge came to exist, the debtor company had gone into liquidation and beneficial title to its assets had passed to its creditors,[3] the security was still effective. Thus the *scintilla temporis* problem was resolved in favour of the secured creditor and against the general body of creditors. The secured creditor had the prior (fictitious) equitable interest. The underlying policy purpose was plainly to assist in the creation of valid, effective security over a business and its assets.

These two allied fictions enabled Slade J to say in the *Siebe Gorman*[4] case, and it remains true even after the House of Lords' decision in *Re Spectrum Plus Ltd*,[5] that *in principle* you can have a fixed charge today on future book debts as well as present book debts. The fact that the book debts may be turning over in the ordinary course of trade is also not a problem as long as you can specify the book debts sufficiently.

Where do floating charges come into this? In the nineteenth century it was thought to be a necessary corollary to there being a fixed charge over *all* of the assets for a trading company, that this would paralyse the business. This was because a fixed charge required the chargee's consent to any disposals. Thus the courts interpreted what looked like fixed charges over all the assets of a business to be in fact floating charges in order to avoid business paralysis and make the security work. This rationale is referred to in the case of *Agnew v IRC*[6] (alias *Brumark*). The logical consequence of this should have been that an apparent fixed charge was to be interpreted to be a floating charge if that interpretation was necessary to avoid business paralysis.

Neither the case law nor the subsequent statutes have ever provided a complete and conclusive definition of a floating charge. At the time of the original legislation at the end of the nineteenth century no such definition was required because the animal was instantly recognizable: it was a charge over all the assets of a trading business which looked fixed but had to be interpreted as floating in order to avoid business paralysis.

Accordingly, I would argue that a floating charge was thus yet another equitable fiction. It was a convenient fiction enabling present security to be taken over a shifting mass of present and future assets. The concept was a fiction because

[2] See *Tailby v Official Receiver* (1888) 13 App Cas 523, HL.
[3] *Re Oriental Island Steam Co* (1874) 9 Ch App 557, 560; *Ayerst v C & K (Constructions) Ltd* [1976] AC 167, 180, HL.
[4] *Siebe Gorman & Co Ltd v Barclays Bank Ltd* [1979] 2 Lloyd's Rep 142.
[5] [2005] UKHL 41, [2005] 2 AC 680.
[6] [2001] UKPC 28, [2001] 2 AC 710, para 7, per Lord Millett.

you could not point to any one asset within the circulating class of present and future assets and say that that particular asset (prior to crystallization and the turning of the floating charge into a fixed charge) belonged to the chargee in equity.

Given the fictitious nature of the floating charge, it should have come as no surprise that the courts were never able to find a satisfactory logical basis for the floating charge.[7] One theory was that a floating charge was a fixed charge combined with a licence to deal in the ordinary course of business. This I would suggest was a contradiction in terms: the existence of the licence to deal negated the existence of the charge. Since there was no charge over any particular asset, logically there could not be a charge over the whole collection of present and future assets. The rival theory was more or less that there was a real immediate charge in the usual sense but that it hovered over the entire class until crystallization. Something that hovers in that way is not really a charge at all. The *Spectrum* case does not resolve the conflict of theories.[8]

It might be objected to here that I am founding the allegation of 'fiction' on a basic misconception, namely that a 'charge' is only a real charge if certain preconceived criteria are met. It could be said against me that the courts are perfectly entitled to invent the concept of 'floating charge' by laying down rules of law which specify what is needed to constitute a 'floating charge'. It might be argued that for me to say that such a charge is not a real 'charge' is to indulge in metaphysics and to go against wisdom of HLA Hart in *The Concept of Law*.[9]

I fully accept that the courts have invented a new concept, namely a 'floating charge'. In the sense that it is a recognized legal concept, it is not a 'fiction'. However, the word 'fiction' is used in this type of context to denote something which rules of law identify as a concept but which concept is illogical and anomalous, however convenient and useful as a matter of policy it may be. I do not think it will be necessary for me to enter here into the debate whether it is analytically more revealing to refer to an illogical and anomalous invention as a 'fiction' or not. The courts certainly do not regard the 'floating charge' as a fiction but the thesis of this chapter is that the courts' failure to recognize the fictitious (in the sense of 'illogical and anomalous') nature of the concept lies at the root of their difficulties in dealing with it. It seems to me that to pretend that an illogical and anomalous concept is 'real' because it is backed by rules of law rather than 'fictions' obscures rather than clarifies the concept.

---

[7] The debate is summarized in Sir Gavin Lightman and G Moss, *The Law of Receivers and Administrators of Companies* (3rd edn, 2000) para 3–008 and is discussed further in this book in S Worthington, 'Floating Charges: The Use and Abuse of Doctrinal Analysis', ch 3, and L Gullifer and J Payne, 'The Characterization of Fixed and Floating Charges', ch 4 below.

[8] See Gullifer and Payne, ch 4 below.

[9] 2nd edn, 1994.

Since the invention of the floating charge, priorities issues have been raised both by statute and the case law. It has thus become necessary for courts to distinguish between fixed and floating charges. However, if I am right in calling the floating charge a 'fiction', *the courts have throughout been trying to distinguish between a reality and a fiction* and this was always going to put them in a very difficult position. Those who think that a floating charge should not be called a fiction can perhaps explain why the difference between fixed and floating charges has played such a huge role in UK jurisprudence and indeed in the work available to the Insolvency Bar.

C. Where Are We Now?

Knowledge of the present world, for clarity of analysis, needs to be divided into three 'Rumsfeld' categories: the 'known knowns', the 'known unknowns' and the 'unknown knowns'. These analytical categories were popularized by the well-known US Secretary of State for Defense, Donald Rumsfeld, at a Department of Defense news briefing on 12 February 2002.

1. The 'known knowns'

What do we *think* we know as a result of the House of Lords' decision in *Spectrum*? Lord Scott accepted that the *Re Keenan Brothers Ltd*[10] formula using a blocked account worked.[11] That was one way in which a valid fixed charge on the shifting class of present and future book debts could be created.

During the argument in the House of Lords, Lord Walker suggested that the operation of the customer relationship between the bank and the client using a blocked account could be arranged very simply and conveniently. One account could be the overdrawn account consisting of the bank's lending on overdraft to the customer. The other account could be a blocked account for receiving the proceeds of book debts subject to a fixed charge to the bank. Once a month, a relatively junior bank official could look at the two balances and decide whether or not to make a transfer. Unfortunately, this suggestion does not appear in Lord Walker's judgment. It is replaced[12] by a reference to Lord Millett's warning in the *Agnew* case at para 48 about the blocked account having to be operated as one in fact. Unless that was a reference to the usual rules relating to matters such as sham, variation, abandonment, etc, in other words recognized legal categories

[10] [1986] BCLC 242, Ire SC. [11] [2005] UKHL 41, [2005] 2 AC 680, para 117.
[12] ibid para 160.

which can be relied on as allowing subsequent events to affect the legal result,[13] it is difficult to know what it refers to.

2. The 'known unknowns'

What do we know to be a remaining mystery even after the House of Lords' judgment? One thing we do not know and can only guess at is what types of transfer, from the blocked account to the overdrawn current account, will be permitted for the blocked account to remain a blocked account operated as such in fact, etc.

If we descend from the lofty heights of the House of Lords and consider an ordinary business relationship between a banker and his corporate customer, we can image the conversation when the fixed charge on book debts is set up. The customer is happy to give a 'fixed' charge on book debts as long as he can use the proceeds in his business. The bank explains that the documentation requires the proceeds to go into a blocked account from which the bank may or may not release the proceeds into the current account. Everything, it seems, depends on what is said next. If the bank and the customer agree that there *will* be transfers, then there is no genuine blocked account. No doubt a nod or wink will also be fatal. It seems that the bank will have to insist that any transfer will be made in its discretion. I suppose the bank can indicate that as long as there were no financial difficulties it is likely to exercise that discretion in a particular way. One cannot tell how far any reassurance in that direction will be a step too far. No doubt liquidators and administrators will have fun cross-examining directors and bank managers on exactly what was said or, if people cannot remember, what 'would have been said'. The whole thing is, of course, wholly out of touch with any kind of commercial reality. Whether or not the bank manager uses the 'right' or 'wrong' form of words, the commercial deal is the same.

No wonder the Court of Appeal could not see what the fuss was about in banks being allowed to have the benefit of fixed charges on book debts which economically worked like floating charges. As Lord Phillips MR pointed out with practical commercial wisdom: 'Priorities in the event of insolvency should not turn upon the technical skill with which the bank accounting arrangements have been set up'.[14]

In addition to the great unknown as to what can or cannot be said at the start of the relationship, what do Lord Millett and Lord Walker mean about the blocked

13 These concepts are discussed further at Gullifer and Payne, ch 4, Part C below.

14 *National Westminster Bank v Spectrum Plus Ltd* [2004] EWCA Civ 670, [2004] Ch 337, para 99.

account, subsequently, having to be operated as a blocked account 'in fact'?[15] Lord Millett has retired from the House of Lords and although Lord Walker is still there, we may never get an explanation from their Lordships. It took over 25 years for the *Siebe Gorman* form of charge to get to the House of Lords, in *Spectrum*, so we may have to wait a long time for this puzzle to be clarified at the highest level. My own humble suggestion for this unknown is that the qualification only refers to the established categories by which ostensible transactions can be challenged, such as sham, variation, abandonment, etc.

3. The 'unknown knowns'

Everyone in the *Spectrum* case agreed that the question was one of legal categorization. The correct approach to legal categorization is absolutely fundamental and vital, not only in relation to this subject, but in relation to many forms of finance, which are often complicated and artificial.

There appear to be two lines of cases which at first sight seem contradictory. First, there are the cases which say that one starts by looking at the label that the parties have attached to the transaction and then seeing whether the terms of the transaction are inconsistent with that label.[16] Then there are other cases which focus on one key aspect which is said to distinguish one legal concept from another.[17]

In order to try to harmonize all the cases on this subject, I would suggest that the key word is 'touchstone'.[18] The starting point is whether the legal concept in question or the choice between two legal concepts depends on a 'touchstone'. If it does, then labelling is either irrelevant or of no significant weight. All that the court does is look at the rights and obligations of the parties as created by the terms of the contract and then sees how they match up to the touchstone. The most obvious example is the difference between 'lease' and 'licence', where the courts say that the 'touchstone' is exclusive occupation. By contrast, for example the difference between lending on security and outright purchase, using title as security has no such 'touchstone' and the label governs unless the terms agreed between the parties are inconsistent with it.[19]

---

[15] *Agnew v IRC* [2001] UKPC 28, [2001] 2 AC 710, para 48, per Lord Millett, *Re Spectrum Plus Ltd* [2005] UKHL 41, [2005] AC 680, para 160, per Lord Walker: '. . . Lord Millett did not expand on this point, which may raise difficult questions'.

[16] For example, *Welsh Development Agency v Export Finance Co* [1992] BCC 270, CA (hereafter *WDA v Exfinco*); *Orion Finance v Crown Financial Management* [1996] BCC 621, 625–7 CA, per Millett LJ.

[17] For example, *Street v Mountford* [1985] AC 809, HL; *Shell v Manchester Garages* [1971] 1 WLR 612; *Agnew v IRC* [2001] UKPC 28, [2001] 2 AC 710, per Lord Millett. This issue is discussed in detail in Gullifer and Payne, ch 4, Part C below.

[18] *WDA v Exfinco* [1992] BCC 270, 280B, CA, per Dillon LJ.

[19] *WDA v Exfinco* [1992] BCC 270, CA.

The reason why the *Agnew* case (also known as *Brumark*) was a key turning point for the present subject is that Lord Millett appears to have identified the difference between fixed and floating charges as being a 'touchstone' question, the 'touchstone' being the ability of the chargor to use the proceeds of the ostensibly fixed charge for his own purposes without the chargee's consent. In the case of book debts, for this purpose, the proceeds of book debts are identified with the debts and are treated as one subject matter, even though it is a matter of strict law, they could be separated.

We presented the House of Lords with what we hoped would be an insuperable difficulty in applying the touchstone test so as to hold the *Siebe Gorman* form of charge to be a floating charge. We pointed out that, as a matter of legal analysis, all the proceeds of the book debts subject to the fixed charge had to be paid to the bank and became the bank's money, whether or not the account was in credit. Therefore, the bank had total control over the proceeds. What the debtor took out was either a new loan if the bank account was overdrawn or the bank's moneys in satisfaction of the customer's chose in action if he had a positive balance. Even if the positive balance situation could somehow be regarded as the recycling of the proceeds to the debtor, on the basis that the proceeds could be traced through to the chose in action and then to the moneys paid out, this approach was legally impossible for an overdrawn account (the usual and mutually contemplated position in these cases, including the position in *Spectrum Plus* itself). Each drawing on an overdrawn account is undoubtedly a new loan by the bank of its own moneys and not the proceeds of the book debts. The proceeds cannot be traced through an overdrawn account and have therefore disappeared.

It may be that it was because of this argument that Lord Scott changed tack and stated that 'categorisation depends upon the commercial nature and substance of the arrangement, not upon a formalistic analysis of how the bank clearing system works'.[20]

However, every previous case on the subject had stressed or at least accepted that the court's inquiry was not into the 'commercial nature' or 'substance' in an economic sense of the arrangement but into its legal nature and substance. It seems, therefore, that Lord Scott in order to get around an apparently insuperable legal difficulty, resorted to economics when the previous case law told him to look at the law. For example, the House of Lords in *McEntyre v Crossley Brothers Ltd*[21] and the House of Lords in the case of *Lloyds & Scottish*

[20] [2005] UKHL 41, [2005] 2 AC 680, para 116.
[21] [1895] AC 457, 462–3, HL, per Lord Herschell, 467, per Lord Watson.

Finance Ltd v Cyril Lord Carpet Sales Ltd,[22] followed in turn by the Court of Appeal in *WDA v Exfinco*[23] all emphasized in their respective contexts that the question of categorization depended upon the legal effect of the terms and not their economic effect. The same point was made by Lord Walker himself when sitting as Walker J in the case of *Re Polly Peck International plc (No 4)*.[24]

The importance of the question of categorization stretches far beyond the issue of fixed and floating charges on book debts. The success of many huge transactions depends on having achieved the desired legal categorization of what has been agreed. If the House of Lords reserved to themselves the right to re-categorize such transactions in accordance with their commercial substance, then this could undermine in a fundamental way a number of significant transactions. It is interesting that the House of Lords did not overrule or disapprove of cases which endorsed extremely artificial transactions such as *WDA v Exfinco*.[25] It may well be, therefore, that Lord Scott's remarks must be restricted at least to 'touchstone' cases where the touchstone consists of some practical, physical, or economic effect. For example, one could argue that his reference to commercial substance is simply to the question of whether, as a matter of commercial substance, the chargor has access to the proceeds of the book debts without the consent of the chargee, regardless of the strict legal analysis. If that is correct, then at least Lord Scott's remarks can be limited so as to prevent damage to artificial structures which do not involve a 'touchstone', such as situations in which absolute title is transferred as part of what in economic terms is a security mechanism.

Lord Walker refers to the 'practical question'[26] as to whether a trader can continue to use his circulating capital, including any credit under an agreed overdraft. Lord Walker contrasted this version of the question with that of Lord Phillips in the Court of Appeal, who had approached the question of the proceeds as a question of tracing in equity.[27] Thus Lord Walker's approach appears to be consistent with the suggestion for limiting the effect of Lord Scott's remarks suggested above.

A very disturbing aspect of both the speeches of Lord Scott and Lord Walker is their apparent bias towards preferential creditors as parties favoured by statute. The previous cases had not shown any bias between the attempts of secured lenders to take ever more extensive fixed charges and the attempts of preferential creditors to have them re-categorized as floating charges. They had approached

22 [1992] BCLC 609, HL. 23 [1992] BCC 270, CA. 24 [1996] 2 All ER 433.
25 [1992] BCC 270, CA. 26 [2005] UKHL 41, [2005] 2 AC 580, para 155.
27 *National Westminster Bank Plc v Spectrum Plus Ltd* [2004] EWCA Civ 670; [2004] Ch 337, paras 87–91.

the question of characterization as a technical issue. The type of bias shown by the House of Lords, if picked up by the lower courts, suggests that the approach may no longer be a purely technical one and that therefore general danger of 're-characterization' may have become greater. A purely technical approach promotes legal certainty and the introduction of a policy bias may have introduced more uncertainty into the law than is commercially desirable.

D. Where Do We Go from Here?

1. Commercial substance

If a broad view of Lord Scott's remarks is taken, nothing is safe if the commercial substance is different from the legal substance. It is difficult to believe, however, that the courts will actually go down this road. If they did, we must remember that neither lawyers nor judges have any special training or qualifications to recognize commercial substance. However, if the question of commercial substance is only looked at in 'touchstone' cases where the touchstone consists of some commercial criterion, the damage can be limited and contained, although there will undoubtedly remain a considerable area of legal uncertainty and risk.

2. A prediction

My guess is that in practice the Crown will not challenge a blocked account operated in the way that Lord Walker suggested in argument. However, we can expect liquidators, if they have any funds, to look closely at the banking documents and where possible cross-examine directors and bankers in relation to the operation of blocked accounts. Any secured lender planning to operate a *Re Keenan Brothers Ltd*[28] or other blocked account will be wise to keep a good paper trail of the secured lender's decisions to allow transfers to the current account.

3. Bad for the economy

I would predict that in practice banks will make more use of factoring and invoice discounting, even though in economic substance they amount to lending on security.[29]

[28] [1986] BCLC 242, Ire SC.

[29] See N Frome and K Gibbons, '*Spectrum*: An End to the Conflict or the Signal for a New Campaign?', ch 5, and PR Wood, 'A Review of *Brumark* and *Spectrum* in an International Setting', ch 6 below.

In theory, it is even possible that these could be re-characterized as lending on security, but since the House of Lords made no adverse comment about the cases upholding such transactions, that seems unlikely.

The difference between a sale on complicated conditions on the one hand and lending on security on the other does not depend on a 'touchstone'. It *should*, therefore, be safe from re-characterization, notwithstanding Lord Scott's remarks. The net economic effect will be that borrowing will be more expensive and this will potentially damage the economy. Unfortunately, judges pay little or no attention to this type of factor. An alternative approach by the House of Lords might have been that since you can restructure a lending on security as an artificial sale there is no reason why a floating charge on book debts cannot be restructured as an artificial fixed charge, if that means that the lenders have better security and can lend more cheaply, to the benefit of customers and the economy. No doubt a suitable empirical study could test the generally accepted view of bankers that the old position was ultimately more beneficial to lenders, borrowers and the economy generally.

4. Conclusion: fiction and reality

It is high time that security, registration, and priorities were rationalized to accord with commercial substance and sweep away distinctions such as those between fixed and floating charges, which depend on fictions. Whilst the conversations in the novel *Emma* are fictitious, fixed and floating security interests should not be based on vintage fictions but should consist of a well-defined reality which accords with commercial substance. Priority in insolvency should be based on rational policy choices rather than skill in drafting and fine distinctions.

2

THE CASE FOR THE ABOLITION OF THE FLOATING CHARGE

Roy Goode

A. Introduction

The floating charge is one of equity's most brilliant creations. It has enabled financiers to advance large sums on the security of a company's inventory and receivables while leaving the debtor company free, within the limits set by the charge, to dispose of such assets in the ordinary course of business free from the security interest. Through its all-embracing nature it has facilitated, when used in conjunction with fixed charges, security over the entirety of the debtor's assets, and this in turn has enabled the chargee to stipulate for the power to appoint an administrative receiver to take control of the company for the benefit of the chargee, run the business, hive it down to a specially formed subsidiary or sell off the business or its assets. Moreover, though the receiver's agency power by which he can commit the company to contracts entered into in its name ceases when it goes into liquidation, the security rights remain exercisable despite the winding up, leaving the liquidator to stand on the sidelines until the receivership has been completed. Only the holder of a floating charge can appoint an administrative receiver and then only if, with any fixed charges, the security covers the whole or substantially the whole of the company's property.

Radical changes to the Insolvency Act 1986 introduced by the Enterprise Act 2002 have sharply limited the circumstances in which it is possible to appoint an administrative receiver, and in most cases this power has been replaced by the power to appoint an administrator, whose duty, however, is to protect the interests of all the creditors. So the function of the floating charge as facilitating management of the company for the benefit of the debenture holder has now all but disappeared. But the floating charge continues to be governed by special statutory provisions, including priority rules, and almost all the case law generated in recent years on priority issues in insolvency has centred on the floating charge. It is therefore timely to re-examine this instrument and to consider, in the light of the various decisions on the priority of the floating charge and of the Law Commission's wide-ranging proposals on company charges, whether the floating charge, popular as it remains, has not passed its sell-by date.

This chapter is concerned solely with the priority status of the floating charge and the question of its continued utility. It does not address the various statutory provisions for the avoidance of transactions altogether, for example as preferences or transactions at an undervalue. Such provisions are designed to reverse unjust enrichment of a particular creditor at the expense of the general body of creditors, not to regulate priorities of competing claims.

B. The Present Priority Status of the Floating Charge

It has long been established that a floating charge creates a present security interest, though it is an interest in a shifting fund of assets, not in individual items of property, and becomes enforceable only when an event has occurred that causes the charge to crystallize. At that point it confers a fully fledged property interest on the chargee which in principle has priority over unsecured claims and over subsequent security interests except, it is thought, a security interest granted to one who dealt with the company prior to crystallization and acquires his interest without notice of crystallization.[1] For policy reasons insolvency law has modified this priority. First, floating charge claims are subordinate to the claims of preferential creditors.[2] This rule goes back to s 2 of the Preferential Payments in Bankruptcy Amendment Act 1897, and it is based not on some general perception that the floating charge represented too much of a threat to preferential creditors but on a very precise identification of the kinds of asset typically covered by a floating charge and the need to protect workers whose labours produced them. The policy was stated with great clarity by Mr George Kemp in moving the Second Reading of the Bill in the House of Commons:

---

[1] For this latter point, see R Goode, *Legal Problems of Credit and Security* (3rd edn, 2003) para 5–50.

[2] Insolvency Act 1986, s 175(2)(b). There is also subordination outside insolvency where the debenture holder takes possession of any property comprised in the charge (Companies Act 1985, s 196(1), (2), as amended by the Insolvency Act 1986, s 439(1) and Sch 13) or appoints a receiver (Insolvency Act 1986, s 40).

> To make plain the incidence of the order of payment in the case of a company being wound up, he would take the case of a limited company, with, they would suppose, an ordinary share capital of £300,000, debentures to a similar amount, and weekly wages paid of £1,000. They would suppose, too, that there was a mortgage of £10,000 on the lands and buildings of the company. First in order of payment there came this mortgage of £10,000. Secondly, came the workpeople with their claims for their wages—if their wages were in arrears, say two weeks, £2,000—as against the debenture holders under a floating charge on the remaining assets of the company; then came the debenture holders, and fourthly came the ordinary shareholders.[3] What was the justice of this? First of all, the mortgagee got his money, because it was on the lands and buildings, which were not in any way affected by, nor did they affect, the work of the workpeople. Secondly, why should the workpeople come in priority to the debenture holders under a floating charge? For the reason that the raw material and the articles partly or wholly manufactured were part of the assets of the debenture holders. This raw material had benefited by the work of the workpeople to the extent of the time for which their wages were in arrear. Therefore it was only right and just that the workpeople should have the benefit of the enhanced value of these articles, which, as the law stood at the present time, would be first claimed by the holders of debentures or debenture stock.[4]

The policy became somewhat distorted as the statutory list of Crown preferences for taxes and the like expanded, since these too had priority over the floating charge claims. Originally the subordination was limited to preferential claims arising before crystallization of the floating charge, but this changed when the definition of 'floating charge' was altered to cover any charge which *as created* was a floating charge.[5]

Secondly, the preferential claims having been met, a prescribed part of the assets subject to a floating charge must be surrendered to the liquidator so as to become available to unsecured creditors.[6] This new provision, which resuscitates the idea of the 10 per cent fund recommended by the Cork Report,[7] is linked to

[3] Ordinary unsecured creditors should, of course, have been mentioned before shareholders; no doubt the omission was an oversight and was in any event not material to the illustration.

[4] HC Deb 10 February 1897, cols 72–73. The reasoning would not, it is true, have applied to raw materials still unprocessed at the time of winding up, but given what was then perceived to be the fractional amount of unpaid wages as a percentage of the debentures it would no doubt have been unnecessarily pedantic to treat these separately from the manufactured stock.

[5] See now Insolvency Act 1986, s 251.

[6] Insolvency Act 1986, s 176A; Insolvency Act 1986 (Prescribed Part) Order 2003, SI 2003/2097.

[7] *Insolvency Law and Practice: Report of the Review Committee* (Cmnd 8558, 1982) paras 1538 *et seq*. The origin of this recommendation is not generally known—even to members of the Insolvency Law Review Committee itself! It was the present writer who, while serving on the Legal Panel set up by the Committee, lightheartedly suggested it to a member of the Committee, as a means of taking the heat off the floating charge, while passing the time in conversation on the train home after cerebral stimulation in the shape of a couple of pints of beer at St Pancras Station. It was somewhat to the writer's astonishment that this idea featured as a recommendation in the Committee's report six months later!

the abolition of Crown preference[8] and the decision that the benefit of this should go to ordinary unsecured creditors rather than enhancing the assets subject to the floating charge. The prescribed part has been set at a level designed to secure this result.

Until recently it had been thought that floating charge claims were also subordinate to the expenses of the liquidation,[9] a result which at first sight seemed logical in that these have priority over preferential claims which in turn have priority over floating charge claims. However, as the House of Lords pointed out in *Buchler v Talbot*,[10] it was always the intention of the legislature that liquidation expenses should be paid only out of the assets of the company, and assets subject to a floating charge were not the assets of the company at all to the extent of the chargee's security interest. Though the decision is controversial[11] my view is that the analysis cannot be faulted. The decision does, however, create difficulties for liquidators in that in many cases it leaves them with no free assets with which to conduct the liquidation. Accordingly the Company Law Reform Bill contains a provision to restore the law to what had previously been thought to be, reversing the effect of *Buchler v Talbot*.

Finally, the floating charge has given rise to circularity problems in the ordering of priorities where a fixed chargee agrees to subordinate its interest to the holder of a floating charge and the debtor company goes into winding up with preferential debts.[12]

C. Do We Still Need the Floating Charge?

Many years ago Professor Robert Pennington published a much-cited article on the genesis of the floating charge.[13] Years later, as a contribution to a collection of essays in his honour, I ventured to suggest that the time had come to abolish the floating charge as a distinct security device on the ground that, useful though it had been, it had accumulated such a vast quantity of analytical baggage that its practical utility had become significantly impaired.[14]

[8] Enterprise Act 2002, s 251. [9] *Re Barleycorn Enterprises Ltd* [1970] Ch 465.

[10] [2004] UKHL 9, [2004] 2 AC 298.

[11] See, for example, RJ Mokal, 'Liquidation Expenses and Floating Charges—The Separate Funds Fallacy' [2004] LMCLQ 387, who contends that the House of Lords misunderstood the nature of an interest under a mere charge.

[12] See n 34 below.

[13] 'The Genesis of the Floating Charge' (1960) 23 MLR 630.

[14] 'The Exodus of the Floating Charge' in D Feldman and F Meisel (eds), *Corporate and Commercial Law: Modern Developments* (1996) 193. Anyone else wishing to engage in this biblical series will have to wrestle with Leviticus!

Moreover, the Americans, who had never possessed the concept of the floating charge, showed in Article 9 of the Uniform Commercial Code (UCC) that it was a wholly unnecessary device. English lawyers, like their American counterparts, had been much occupied with the question whether it was consistent with the existence of a security interest to allow the debtor company to deal with the charged assets as its own. Pre-Code American law said it was not; English law agreed that it was inconsistent with fixed security but invented the halfway house of the floating charge, a security in a shifting *fund* of assets which did not attach to specific assets until crystallization, thus leaving the debtor free to deal with the charged assets in the ordinary course of business, but nevertheless conferred a security interest that would attach on crystallization. In Article 9 the rule that the conferment of a dealing power was inconsistent with a fixed security was jettisoned, and a buyer in the ordinary course of business was protected by a priority rule to the effect that it would acquire an overriding title, even if taking with knowledge of the security interest and even if the latter had been protected by filing, unless the buyer knew that the disposition to it was in breach of the security agreement.[15]

What is interesting is that in Canada, where nine Provinces have enacted Personal Property Security Acts modelled on Article 9, lawyers and even the courts continued for some time to treat the floating charge as somehow still available as a distinct security device running in parallel with the Article 9-type security interest,[16] until eventually the courts very sensibly ruled that in the new regime the floating charge had no role to play. This does not appear to have had any adverse effect on the extension of business credit and few appear to have mourned the passing of the floating charge, which had become seen as an unnecessary complication in a modern personal property security law.[17] More recently New Zealand has followed suit.[18]

[15] See UCC §§ 9–201, 9–205, 9–320.

[16] See, for example, *Access Advertising Management Inc v Servex Computers Inc* (1993) 15 OR (3d) 635.

[17] See JS Ziegel, 'Floating Charges and the OPPSA: A Basic Misunderstanding' (1994) 2 Canadian Business Law Journal 470. Professor Ziegel's penetrating analysis, and his criticism of the decision in *Servex Computers*, was subsequently approved by Day J in *Credit Suisse Canada v Yonge Street Holdings* (1996) 28 OR (3d) 670, Gen Div. Similar decisions were given in other Provinces and it can now be taken as settled that the concept of a floating charge has no place in the Canadian Personal Property Security Acts.

[18] For further discussion of this issue, see L Gullifer and J Payne, 'The Characterization of Fixed and Floating Charges', ch 4, Part E below.

D. The Company Law Review

The wide-ranging Company Law Review, under its Steering Committee, established different groups to examine different facets of company law reform. One of these was a group tasked with examining the system for registration of company charges. Initially this group adopted a rather conservative approach, suggesting minor changes which would not have addressed long-standing problems. Fortunately Mr Jonathan Rickford, who was in overall charge as Project Director, responded enthusiastically to a suggestion of a seminar in Oxford to re-examine the whole subject. As the result of the ideas generated at the seminar the group was reconvened and its final report to the Steering Committee was altogether more forward-looking. The group drew attention to a number of deficiencies in the existing registration system, and the Final Report made a number of provisional proposals for significant reform,[19] recommending that the whole subject be referred to the Law Commission, which in due course it was.

E. The Law Commission's Consultation Papers

After the Lord Chancellor had made the reference to the Law Commission the team there headed by Professor Hugh Beale quickly realized that registration of company charges could not be dealt with in isolation from rules governing the creation, perfection, and priority of security interests and the impact of insolvency. The terms of reference were thus drawn widely enough to enable the Commission to proceed with the preparation of a new personal property security law, albeit one which had in the first instance to be limited to security given by companies. The Commission published three major documents, a consultation paper in June 2002,[20] a consultative report in August 2004 which incorporated draft regulations to be made under the forthcoming Company Law Reform Bill[21] and a final Report in August 2005.[22] The initial proposals were wide ranging. They adopted a functional approach to security along the

[19] *Modern Company Law for a Competitive Economy: Final Report* (2001) ch 12, available at <http://www.dti.gov.uk/cld/final_report>.

[20] *Registration of Company Security Interests: Company Charges and Property other than Land* (Law Com Consultation Paper No 164).

[21] *Company Security Interests: A Consultative Report* (Law Com Consultation Paper No 176). Both consultation papers can be found at <http://www.lawcom.gov.uk/closed_consultations.htm>.

[22] *Company Security Interests* (Law Com No 296, Cm 6654) <http://www.lawcom.gov.uk/lc_reports.htm>. For a detailed discussion of the Law Commission's proposals, see M Bridge, 'The Law Commission's Proposals for the Reform of Corporate Security Interests', ch 12 below.

lines of UCC Article 9 as recommended long ago by the Crowther Report[23] and the Diamond Report,[24] thus including conditional sales and certain leasing agreements as well as security in the traditional sense, and provided the first coherent framework for a modern personal property security law. The Commission's proposals as set out in the second of the above documents have been admirably described by Professor Beale elsewhere.[25] Suffice to say at this point that the intermediate consultative report was a superb document covering security in both tangible and intangible property, including investment securities, and tackling head on in satisfying detail the various issues raised by consultees, a number of whose submissions for change in the original proposals were accepted. In the consultative report the Commission, having decided to put title retention on the back-burner in the light of representations, proceeded to clarify its position as regards the floating charge. In essence, the new form of security interest, even if described as 'floating', would be a fixed security interest and the floating charge would disappear as a distinct security device. The label 'floating', if used by the parties, would thus be indicative of the shifting nature of the collateral rather than being treated as postponing attachment of the security interest. As under UCC Article 9 the conferment of a continued dealing power on the debtor company would not affect the fixed nature of the security, though there would be a special priority rule to protect buyers in ordinary course of business without their having to search the register of security interests and without being affected by such interests even if they did search unless they took with knowledge that the disposition to them was in breach of the security agreement. Moreover, the financier, holding a fixed security, would no longer be subordinate to subsequent security interests as it is at present, and the device of inserting a negative pledge clause and noting it in the registration particulars would no longer be necessary. The new security interest would thus have 'all the advantages of the floating charge without most of the disadvantages'.[26] The one important feature that was missing was the impact of the proposed changes on the rules of insolvency law governing floating charges, and in particular the subordination of floating charge claims to preferential debts. The consultative report indicated a potentially fruitful approach based on the New Zealand legislation and looking to the typical subject matter of a floating charge rather than the instrument itself, but said that further work would need to be done on it. The unfortunate effect of this, when coupled with time constraints, was to give a hostage to the opponents of the proposals. A factor that had led to this situation

[23] *Report of the Committee on Consumer Credit* (Cmnd 4596, 1971), ch 5 and App III.

[24] AL Diamond, *A Review of Security Interests in Property* (1989).

[25] H Beale, 'Reform of the Law of Security Interests over Personal Property' in J Lowry and L Mistelis (eds), *Commercial Law: Perspectives and Practice* (2005) ch 3.

[26] Law Com Consultation Paper No 176 (n 21 above) para 2.57.

was the Commission's hesitancy about trenching on insolvency law, on the basis that policy issues relating to insolvency were a matter for the Government, not the Law Commission,[27] a weak argument, because security interests are inseparably linked to insolvency law; indeed, the acid test of the efficacy of a security interest is whether it remains valid in the debtor's insolvency.

F. Responses to the Proposals on the Abolition of the Floating Charge

One might have expected that bankers in particular would welcome the replacement of the floating charge, with all the problems of characterization and priority issues it continued to generate, by a fixed charge which would substantially improve their position. But while they did not absolutely oppose this proposal they indicated that such a tried and trusted security device should not be abandoned without the most careful consideration. The reasons for this extreme caution are unclear. It may be that they did not fully understand the effect of the proposals; if they had, it is hard to see why they would not have urged their adoption. The Commission's own comment in its final Report was as follows:

> Responses to our proposals to change the distinction between fixed and floating charges were particularly difficult to analyse. First, it has been hard to gauge whether there is real opposition to our proposals when correctly understood. The floating charge is viewed as enormously important. Some respondents appeared to think that we were suggesting that it should no longer be possible to create floating charges. That was not at all our intention. The scheme proposed was designed to enable fixed and floating charges to be superseded by a new single form of charge that would be more flexible and give the lender better protection. We believe that in terms of the law of security there is a good case for this change.[28]

Similarly the Association of Business Recovery Professionals (R3) and the Financial Law Committee of the City of London Law Society (CLLS), whose members were highly experienced and knowledgeable practitioners, did not say that they were wholly opposed to the abolition of the floating charge,[29] rather that they were seriously concerned about the insolvency implications, particularly as regards the impact on the statutory provisions relating to preferential creditors and the surrender of the prescribed part, which they quite rightly felt had not been worked out. In fact, the problem of preferential claims was readily soluble.

[27] ibid para 2.60.

[28] *Company Security Interests* (Law Com No 296, Cm 6654, August 2005) para 3.164.

[29] Indeed, the separate Insolvency Law Committee of the CLLS strongly favoured abolition of the distinction between fixed and floating charges.

One had only to turn back to the parliamentary debates on the 1897 Act,[30] which showed that the rationale for the subordination of floating charges was that they concerned assets typically resulting from the labours of the workforce, that is, inventory and raw materials, to which one could add the receivables resulting from sale of inventory. So all that was necessary was to substitute for the reference to floating charges a reference to security in inventory and receivables. At the end of the day, the real stumbling block was not so much an entrenched opposition to the abolition of the floating charge as the inadequacy of the period for consultation permitted by the legislative timetable,[31] coupled with the innate resistance to change which has long been a characteristic of the banking and legal professions. In that connection it is worth recalling the words of the famous French scholar Professor René David, one of the world's greatest legal comparativists, in observing the same attitude towards the harmonization of law:

> International unification of law inevitably implies some reforms in the law of each country. Lawyers and businessmen are attached to the *status quo*, to the order of things which they know, and to which their behaviour and their ways of doing things have been adapted. They view all reform with suspicion, seeing primarily the trouble it will cause, rather than its beneficial effects and the progress which it is intended to produce. When the reform has been carried out, they will be reconciled and recognize that it may have improved matters. Until then, many circles will be against it on principle, even if no acquired right or vested interest is threatened or questioned.[32]

G. The Law Commission's Final Report

In its final Report *Company Security Interests* the Law Commission at last provided a solution. Unhappily, having done so, it then retreated from its proposal, offering the following explanation:

> 3.171 We believe there is a good case for including in our scheme the provisions that would remove the distinction between fixed and floating charges. We also think an adequate substitute test is available to determine which assets preferential creditors and the unsecured creditors fund should have priority over.
> 3.172 However we recognize that insolvency law has undergone significant changes in recent years, and that there is great unwillingness to see further changes in the immediate future. To maintain it means that the scheme will have to be more complex than we would like. It means that lenders will have to continue to use a 'cocktail' of fixed and floating charges when under the more radical approach

[30] See n 4 above and accompanying text.

[31] See M Bridge, 'The Law Commission's Proposals for the Reform of Corporate Security Interests', ch 12 below.

[32] 'The Unification of Private Law' in *International Encyclopaedia of Comparative Law*, vol II, ch 5, para 59.

> advocated in the CR [Consultative Report, Law Com Consultation Paper No 176] a single charge would have sufficed. However it does not make the scheme unworkable or prevent it being a substantial improvement on the current law.
> 3.173 In the light of this, we have decided not to recommend at present the changes proposed in the CR that would have had the result of removing the distinction between the fixed and the floating charge. The proposed rules should be considered again when insolvency law is next reviewed.

It has to be said that compared with the rigorous approach adopted in the consultative report this is feeble stuff. To swallow the camel of a major reform of rules governing attachment, perfection, and priorities, and of the registration system itself, while straining at the gnat of what would in fact have been a modest reformulation of the insolvency rules so as to refer to charges over inventory and receivables instead of floating charges is at first sight very puzzling. Moreover, since the Commission went on to recommend that floating charges, instead of being subordinate to subsequent fixed charges, should have priority according to the time of registration, thus obliterating the primary distinction between fixed and floating charges, the outcome is conceptual confusion.

What went wrong? Why did the Law Commission not stick to its guns and work with the professions to refine the insolvency proposals? The answer is not that the Commission was pusillanimous or had lost the stomach for a fight—a number of other proposals had been maintained despite some opposition—but that it was locked in by a very tight timetable. The entire programme had to be geared to the timing of the introduction of what is now the Company Law Reform Bill. From this two unavoidable but adverse consequences flowed. First, the period allowed for consultation on such a major exercise was too short, and consultees justifiably complained that they had not had adequate time to consider the detail and work out the implications. Secondly, there was simply no time to go on working over the insolvency effects of abolition of the floating charge if the final Report was to be ready by the time the Bill was introduced. The Law Commission was thus faced with a triple choice: to maintain its position and press ahead with its original proposal, risking lack of support from the Department of Trade and Industry because of the opposition that had been expressed; to continue discussions with the professions and lose incorporation of the regulation-making power in the Bill; or to withdraw its proposal to abolish the floating charge in order to accommodate the opposition and meet the parliamentary timetable. In such an unenviable situation it felt constrained to go for the last option. Ironically, the sacrifice has so far proved to be in vain, because in its present form the Bill still does not contain the regulation-making power that will enable the legislation proposed in the final Report to proceed.

H. Is the Floating Charge So Wonderful?

The constant refrain to the effect that the floating charge remains the greatest thing since sliced bread needs to be subjected to critical scrutiny. Corporate floating charges have now been with us for some 135 years—plenty of time, one might think, for the courts to have worked out in detail their nature and priority. Yet in the past five years alone there have been 15 High Court decisions on floating charges of which six went to the Court of Appeal and three to the House of Lords—24 decisions and 48 judgments in all, which together must have involved millions of pounds in legal costs. The majority of the cases centred on the crucial question of characterization. Was the charge fixed or floating? It is astonishing that after all this time we still extol the virtues of a security device which continues to generate controversy and differences of opinion among the judiciary as to its essential nature. Nor will the decision of the House of Lords in the *Spectrum* case resolve all the problems. One important one is mentioned below in Philip Wood's chapter, namely cascade clauses in financing agreements providing for payment of revenues generated by the company (1) to pay its operating expenses, (2) to service the debt, (3) to add to reserves, and (4) to pay dividends or subordinated shareholder loans.[33] As Philip Wood rightly points out, it is quite impracticable to require all revenues to go to the creditor, to which one might add that it is equally impracticable to require the debtor to get authority from the creditor every time it wishes to pay an operating expense. And all these difficulties stem from the single question of characterization. Add to that the continuing uncertainties as to certain aspects of the priority rules affecting floating charges,[34] and we can see very clearly the advantages of abolishing the floating charge as a distinct security device, as has happened throughout Canada and more recently in New Zealand. As holder of a fixed security the lender would have priority except as against those dealing

[33] See PR Wood, 'A Review of *Brumark* and *Spectrum* in an International Setting', ch 6 below.

[34] Including the circularity problem where A, holding a fixed charge, agrees to be subordinated to B, holding a floating charge, and the debtor company goes into liquidation with preferential creditors which rank above the floating charge but ordinarily below the fixed charge which by agreement is subordinate to the floating charge. I have suggested elsewhere that an equitable solution is provided by recourse to the doctrine of subrogation, by which the holder of the floating charge should be accorded priority over preferential creditors in right of the fixed chargee, which would give effect to the subordination agreement while leaving the position of the preferential creditors exactly as it would have been if that agreement had not been made. There seems no good reason why an *inter partes* agreement should give the preferential creditors a windfall. See R Goode, *Commercial Law* (3rd edn, 2004) 671–4. But this argument, the correctness of which had been conceded in *Re Woodroffes (Musical Instruments) Ltd* [1986] Ch 366, was rejected by Chadwick J in *Re Portbase Clothing Ltd* [1993] Ch 388. However, in its final Report the Law Commission considered the subrogation approach to be more satisfactory in terms of policy than the result reached in *Re Portbase Clothing Ltd* and recommended its adoption (*Company Security Interests* (n 28 above) paras 3.181 *et seq*).

with the company in the ordinary course of business without notice that the disposition to them was in breach of the security agreement. The reliance on the uncertain effects of registration of a negative pledge clause to preserve priority would become unnecessary. All the rules on crystallization, itself a subject continuing to attract litigation, could be jettisoned and there would no longer be any need to distinguish between fixed and floating charge assets in the security agreement. The insolvency provisions could be readily amended to substitute references to inventory and receivables for references to floating charge assets. It is true that the banks still hanker after the ability to take a priority-preserving fixed charge over receivables by stipulating for control over accounts as dictated by *Spectrum*, but in practice this will not happen, as few companies will be willing to subject themselves to a regime requiring them to open a blocked account and obtain approval for every withdrawal from their account. For most practical purposes the fixed charge over book debts is dead.

I. The Modernization of English Personal Property Security Law

There are two final questions. Are we really so complacent as to believe that a security device that evolved by judicial decisions in the nineteenth century is adequate to meet financing requirements of the twenty-first century? And are we so arrogant as to think that we can totally ignore not only the experience gained by financiers and lawyers in the United States, which has operated without a floating charge concept for over 50 years with no ill effects under Article 9 of the Uniform Commercial Code—adopted by every State in the Union including the civil law State of Louisiana—but also the similar experience of lawyers and financiers in Canada, which did have the floating charge but found that under the new regime it had no place and served no purpose? New Zealand too has found that all the objectives of the floating charge and more can be achieved by a fixed charge over shifting assets and has introduced legislation which effectively abolishes the floating charge as a distinct security device.[35] Have we nothing, then, to learn from the experience of 60 common law jurisdictions spanning a period of over half a century?

It is high time that we in England grasped the nettle and introduced a modern personal property security law along the lines recommended in the Law Commission's intermediate Report but extended to non-corporate security and to conditional sale and hire-purchase agreements and leases exceeding 12 months or some other specified period. We can no longer manage effectively with legal rules based on a mass of case law, much of it conflicting or unclear, on which are

[35] Personal Property Securities Act 1999, as amended.

superimposed the priority effects of registration provisions that were never designed for that purpose. Moreover, the abolition of administrative receivership outside exempted categories and its replacement by administration for the benefit of all creditors, not merely the all-assets debenture holder, has greatly attenuated one of the major advantages of the floating charge.

But the professions are entitled to say that they need adequate time to consider the implications of what is proposed and to suggest fine tuning that will overcome difficulties that may not yet have been identified. The introduction of a power for the DTI to make regulations to give effect to the new legal framework would provide all the time and opportunity that is needed to resolve any remaining problems and to alleviate the remaining concerns of industry and the professions, whose participation in the regulation-making process is the key to its success. Let us hope that they will all grasp the opportunity to see that this country is provided with a long overdue Personal Property Security Act that clarifies, modernizes, and simplifies the law, as recommended first by the Crowther Committee some 35 years ago.

3

FLOATING CHARGES: THE USE AND ABUSE OF DOCTRINAL ANALYSIS

Sarah Worthington

Perhaps predictably, this chapter does not challenge the detailed doctrinal analysis delivered by the House of Lords in *Spectrum*.[1] That is dealt with in several other chapters in this book. This chapter seeks to make two relatively discrete contributions to the learning and analysis in this area. The first concerns the implications of the House of Lords' decision for the future characterization of security agreements and for the theory that underpins their practical impact. This is the 'use' of doctrinal analysis. The second, which is somewhat shorter, addresses the controversial 'so what?' question. It suggests that although the approach of the House of Lords was perfectly proper—indeed, inevitable—in the circumstances, the statutory rule in the Insolvency Act 1986 that demands this approach is fundamentally misconceived. The regime is unnecessarily circuitous and costly given the benefits it is intended to deliver to secured and unsecured creditors; it is both inefficient and ineffective. This is the 'abuse' of doctrinal analysis. These issues are preceded by a short summary of the *Spectrum* decision itself.

A. The *Spectrum* Decision

The debenture in *Spectrum* provided security to the lender by way of a specific charge over all the borrower's present and future debts. The chargor was prohibited from charging or assigning the debts, and was required to pay the proceeds of collection into an account with the lending bank, but the debenture did not specify any restrictions on the chargor's operation of that account. The

1 *Re Spectrum Plus Ltd* [2005] UKHL 41, [2005] 2 AC 680 (hereinafter *Spectrum*).

issue was whether this charge was fixed or floating. This doctrinal characterization was required in order to determine who had priority to the secured assets on the company's insolvency. If the charge was fixed, the chargee would have priority; if the charge was floating, the preferred creditors would have priority.[2]

At first instance, Sir Andrew Morritt V-C found that the charge was floating.[3] He held, as a matter of law, that a charge over debts is necessarily floating if the chargor is entitled to use the proceeds of the debts in the normal course of business unless and until the chargee intervenes. Whatever the other restrictions on the chargor's dealings with the book debts, they cannot upset this verdict. This conclusion followed directly from his acceptance of the Privy Council's approach in *Agnew v IRC*[4] (better known simply as *Brumark*). Moreover, he held that the effect in law of the actual terms of the debenture was this. This second step effectively overruled the 25-year-old decision of Slade J in *Siebe Gorman & Co Ltd v Barclays Bank Ltd*,[5] where a clause in essentially the same terms had been upheld as a fixed charge.

Somewhat surprisingly, the Court of Appeal disagreed, and held that the charge was fixed. Lord Phillips MR gave the only reasoned judgment.[6] He considered the impact of contradictory Court of Appeal precedent,[7] the construction of the charge itself, and the relevance of the fact that banks had relied on the decision in *Siebe Gorman* for over 25 years. I have already commented critically elsewhere on the last two aspects of this analysis.[8] The House of Lords reversed the decision of the Court of Appeal and restored the Vice-Chancellor's judgment. The charge was thus characterized as a floating charge. It followed that the preferential creditors had priority over the lending bank.

---

2 Insolvency Act 1986, s 175(2)(b).

3 *Re Spectrum Plus Ltd* [2004] EWHC 9, [2004] 2 WLR 783.

4 [2001] UKPC 28, [2001] 2 AC 710 (hereinafter *Agnew*).

5 [1979] 2 Lloyd's Rep 142 (hereinafter *Siebe Gorman*).

6 Jonathan Parker and Jacob, LJJ simply agreed.

7 The Court of Appeal held that it was bound by its own earlier decisions (including *Re New Bullas Trading Ltd* [1994] 1 BCLC 485, CA (hereinafter *New Bullas*)), rather than by more recent Privy Council authority (*Agnew*). It has not always reacted in this way: see, for example, *Darayan Holdings Ltd v Solland International Ltd* [2004] EWHC 622, [2005] Ch 119, paras 75–86, per Lawrence Collins J. Also see H Bennett, 'Precedent and the Privy Council' (2005) 121 LQR 23–9.

8 S Worthington, 'An "Unsatisfactory Area of the Law"—Fixed and Floating Charges Yet Again' (2004) 1 International Corporate Rescue 175–84.

B. The Use of Doctrinal Analysis: Characterization and its Consequences

Characterization of a charge as fixed, rather than floating, carries with it many advantages. It enables chargees to avoid the statutory priority accorded to preferential creditors,[9] the 'ring-fencing' rules designed to benefit unsecured creditors,[10] and the risk that an administrator may dispose of the charged assets.[11] A floating charge holder is subject to all of these incursions. In addition, the rights of a floating charge holder are subject to more extensive registration requirements,[12] greater risks of loss of priority (as against other charge holders, purchasers, and other parties[13]), subordination to the costs and expenses of an administrator,[14] and the avoidance provisions directed at floating charges created not for new value in the period prior to insolvency.[15] Given all of this, it is easy to see why chargees scramble to have their security characterized as fixed rather than floating.

On the other hand, these enormous statutory advantages must be balanced against the powerful practical commercial disadvantages associated with fixed charges. Accepted orthodoxy holds that a chargor is not permitted to dispose of assets that are subject to a fixed charge without the consent of the chargee. This degree of chargee control is acceptable if the charge is secured against a borrower's fixed assets, but is unworkable if the charge is secured against a borrower's circulating assets: the resulting operational paralysis is commercially unacceptable, since obtaining the necessary consents is practically impossible. The floating charge emerged in the United Kingdom in response to the desire by lenders to have workable forms of security over all of a borrowing company's assets, including those that the company needed to dispose of in the ordinary course of business in order to operate.[16] But, of course, such a floating charge is subject to all of the statutory disadvantages outlined earlier.

Over the years, lenders have striven to construct debenture agreements that deliver the statutory advantages associated with fixed charges *and* the practical commercial advantages associated with floating charges. *Spectrum* is merely one illustration. It, and other cases like it, attempt to exploit deep doctrinal

---

[9] Insolvency Act 1986, ss 40, 175(2)(b), Sch B1, para 65(2).

[10] Insolvency Act 1986, s 176A.

[11] Insolvency Act 1986, s 15.

[12] Companies Act 1986, s 396 requires all floating charges to be registered, but not all fixed charges (for example, charges over shares and negotiable instruments need not be registered).

[13] See below, especially Section 5 of this Part: 'Consequences: theory and practice'.

[14] Insolvency Act 1986, s 19 (but not the general costs and expenses of a liquidator: *Re Leyland Daf Ltd sub nom Buchler v Talbot* [2004] UKHL 9, [2004] 2 AC 298).

[15] Insolvency Act 1986, s 245. A fixed charge is vulnerable only if it involves a preference.

[16] Contrast the permissive UK approach with the restrictive US approach in *Benedict v Ratner* 268 US 353 (1925), Sup Ct US. The Uniform Commercial Code, Article 9, now overcomes the problem.

uncertainties about the necessary degree of chargee control and confusions about the relevance of the relationship between assets and proceeds. Exactly how much control does a lender need to exercise over a borrower's use of the debts before a security slips from being a fixed charge to being a floating charge? Can a favourable fixed charge analysis be advanced successfully by explicitly separating the debt from its proceeds, creating a fixed security over the former while leaving the latter under the control of the borrower?[17] Finally, can floating charge doctrine supply an adequate answer to the question of what rights a chargee has in the charged assets prior to crystallization of a floating charge? All of these issues are considered in this chapter. The House of Lords in *Spectrum* appears to have provided a clear answer to the first of these questions (despite certain commentators' views to the contrary), a relatively clear answer to the second, and no assistance in relation to the third.

1. Characterization: fixed charges and chargee control

After *Spectrum*, the law appears clear.[18] The essential difference between a fixed and a floating charge turns upon the ability of the chargor to deal with the charged assets, *removing them from the ambit of the security without the consent of the chargee*. This, and this alone, provides the characterization test.[19] The charge is fixed if and only if the chargor is required to preserve the charged assets, or their permitted substitutes, for the benefit of the chargee (either absolutely, or as part of the pool of charged assets standing as security for the chargor's obligation). If this is not a requirement, then the charge is floating. In particular, the charge is floating if the chargor is free to remove the charged assets, and their permitted substitutes, from the scope of the security, and use them for its own benefit in the course of its business (at least until the charge crystallizes or the chargee intervenes to enforce the floating security). Put another way, the distinction is between fixed/non-fixed charges: the 'fixed' category is restrictively defined; all charges that fall outside this restrictive category, and into the 'non-fixed' category, are floating charges. This approach, rather than the approach that found favour in the Court of Appeal, is consistent with the historical development of floating charges in the United Kingdom.[20]

---

[17] See *Re New Bullas Trading Ltd* [1994] 1 BCLC 485, CA, followed by the Court of Appeal in *Spectrum*, but overturned on the appeal of *Spectrum* to the House of Lords.

[18] Despite claims to the contrary from interested members of the lending community.

[19] This is the necessary inference to be drawn from *Spectrum*: Lord Scott, para 107, Lord Walker, paras 138, 139.

[20] The Court of Appeal in *Spectrum* favoured categorization from the opposing starting point, ie on a 'floating/non-floating' basis: a charge is floating if and only if the chargor has complete freedom to deal with the charged assets in the ordinary course of business, at least until the charge crystallizes; any charge that does not meet this liberal use-requirement is a fixed charge. According

Moreover, every charge must inevitably be of one type or the other *as a matter of law*. The issue is not one of bilateral contracting between lender and borrower, where the intention of the parties may be material to the characterization. And there is no intermediate third category somewhere between fixed and floating charges.[21] The fixed/floating charge distinction is not one that assists in defining the relative rights of chargor and chargee (here a third category might be apt); it is one that defines the rights of non-contracting third parties to have access to the asset pool on insolvency. Either these third parties have access or they do not: only those two possibilities exist, and the choice between them must be determined as a matter of law, not as a matter of intention attributed to lender or borrower.

With this test as the key determinant in any characterization, certain distractions can be eliminated. The nature of the charged property is irrelevant in determining whether a charge is fixed or floating: tangible and intangible property, present and future property, can each be the subject of both fixed and floating charges.[22] The fact that the charged property is ordinarily dealt with in the course of the chargor's business, or not, is also irrelevant: a fixed charge may be taken over assets that are ordinarily dealt with (so long as the dealing is then exclusively for the benefit of the chargee), and a floating charge may be taken over assets that are ordinarily retained, not a dealt with, by the chargor (although such a practice is at odds with the chargee's interests, and delivers no practical benefit to the chargor).[23]

In applying the characterization test, the easy cases are at the extremes. If the debenture denies the chargor *any* freedom to dispose of the charged assets, and instead requires them to stand permanently as security for the discharge of the obligations owed to the chargee, then the charge is fixed. On the other hand, if the debenture gives the chargor *complete* freedom to dispose of the charged

---

to this test, most charges taken by lenders will be fixed charges (or very easily reconstructed as such): see *National Westminster Bank v Spectrum Plus Ltd* [2004] EWCA Civ 670, [2004] Ch 337 (hereinafter *Spectrum* CA). The House of Lords' 'fixed/non-fixed' test, by contrast, has the opposite impact: most charges taken over circulating assets will be floating charges, not fixed charges.

[21] In favour of such a category, see *Spectrum* CA, para 24 (Lord Phillips MR).

[22] For example, in *Re Bond Worth Ltd* [1980] Ch 288 the floating charge was over present tangible property (although contrast the comment in *Re Atlantic Medical Ltd* [1992] BCC 653, 658, that limiting a floating charge to present property would be 'very unusual indeed').

[23] For example, a floating charge over coal-washing machinery: *Re Cosslett (Contractors) Ltd* [1988] Ch 495, CA; a floating charge over land: *Welch v Bowmaker (Ireland) Ltd* [1980] IR 252. The only possible relevance that the type of assets can have is in implying permission to deal, or otherwise, into a debenture document which is silent on the matter. If assets are normally dealt with by the chargor in the ordinary course of its business, then the implication may be that this was intended to continue, and the charge will be floating, for example. See S Atherton and RJ Mokal, 'Charges over Chattels: Issues in the Fixed/Floating Jurisprudence' (2005) 26 Company Lawyer 10.

assets unless and until the chargee intervenes, and only then requires them to be made available to the chargee in priority to the other creditors, then the charge is floating.[24] It is the intermediate cases that cause difficulty, and, unfortunately, most debentures fall into the intermediate range. These are the debentures that impose *some* restrictions on the manner in which a chargor may dispose of the charged assets, but not a total embargo. *Spectrum* was just such a case. Is this type of charge fixed or floating?

The test adopted by the House of Lords provides a relatively easy answer to the question. To repeat, the charge is floating unless the chargor is barred from removing the charged assets, and their permitted substitutes, from the scope of the security, and using them for its own benefit in the course of its business. The prohibitions required to ensure that a charge is fixed, and thus of a form that is advantageous to the chargee, are often commercially and operationally unattractive to the chargor.

2. Charges over book debts

Elsewhere I have suggested that in the case of a charge over book debts there are only a limited number of ways to ensure that the charge is fixed.[25] The first is to prevent all dealings with the book debts so that they are preserved for the benefit of the chargee's security. This is unattractive, since the restriction has to include a ban on collection. Restrictions on other dealings are less problematic, and can be seen as the fair price for the commercial advantages of credit. The second method is to prevent all dealings other than collection, and to require the collected proceeds to be paid to the chargee in reduction of the chargor's outstanding debt. In this way, both the value of the security and the value of the outstanding obligation are reduced in tandem, and the security is effectively redeemed as the obligation is reduced. The third method is again to prevent all dealings other than collection, and to require the collected proceeds to be paid into a bank account with the chargee bank. This account must then be *blocked.* The purpose of this is not to expropriate the chargor's contractual chose in

[24] Indeed, this overstates the degree of freedom allowed to the floating chargor. Precedent indicates that the assumed freedom associated with a floating charge is confined to the right to deal with the charged assets *in the ordinary course of business.* To reinforce this, a floating charge will crystallize automatically once the chargor is unable to carry on its business in this way, even though no term in the debenture so provides: *Re Woodroffes (Musical Instruments) Ltd* [1986] Ch 366, 377–8, CA (Nourse LJ); *Re Brightlife* [1987] Ch 200, 212–15 (Hoffmann J). As charged assets are dissipated, it is assumed that any newly acquired assets matching the same description will be subjected automatically to the same charge.

[25] S Worthington, 'An "Unsatisfactory Area of the Law"—Fixed and Floating Charges Yet Again' (2004) 1 International Corporate Rescue 175.

action, as in the previous case.[26] This chose in action is a valuable asset and continues to belong to the chargor. Blocking the account merely ensures that this substitute asset is not at the free disposal of the chargor, to be dissipated at will, but is instead preserved for the benefit of the chargee's security. The preceding analysis, based on the orthodox definition of a fixed charge, suggests that this blocking requirement will be interpreted strictly.[27] The final method is, yet again, to prevent all dealings other than collection, and to permit the collected proceeds to be paid into a bank account with a third party bank. The chargee must then take a fixed charge over this account, or enter into a control agreement with the third party bank to ensure that the account is blocked. These controls are necessary for the same reasons that control is required over the account with the chargee bank. None of these options is commercially attractive, and it is easy to see why commercial parties and their advisers have sought alternatives that might deliver fixed charge security to the chargee and operational flexibility to the chargor.

In this context, post-*Spectrum* discussions in relation to book debts, and in particular in relation to the use of the collected proceeds of those debts, have questioned whether strategies such as collateral permissions, pre-agreement sweeper arrangements, payment waterfalls, or post-debenture permissions might deliver these ends.[28] Ignore for the moment the fact that these suggested arrangements may not be evident on the face of the debenture itself, and simply consider the substance of the entire arrangement between the parties. To the extent that these arrangements permit the chargor to remove the charged assets, or their substitutes, from the ambit of the charge and use them for the benefit of the chargor, not for the benefit of the chargee or the chargee's security, the charge ought to be classified as floating on the tests adopted by the House of Lords in *Spectrum*. In reaching this conclusion, it is immaterial that these arrangements do not allow the chargor complete freedom of access to the proceeds, but provide limitations based on quantum or timing. The fixed/non-fixed distinction does not depend on unqualified access; qualified access is nonetheless access, and is sufficient for characterization of the charge as 'not-fixed'. The bald fact is that the chargor is entitled to

[26] The analysis applies equally whether the chargor has a credit balance or an overdraft: see Worthington (n 25 above) 175–84.

[27] In particular, it is not met by an ability to control the account in the future (as in *Siebe Gorman*), nor, probably, by blocked accounts subject to an advance agreed facility or sweeper agreement (see below).

[28] See the detailed discussions in L Gullifer and J Payne, 'The Characterization of Fixed and Floating Charges', ch 4, N Frome and K Gibbons, '*Spectrum*: An End to the Conflict or the Signal for a New Campaign?', ch 5, and PR Wood, 'A Review of *Brumark* and *Spectrum* in an International Setting', ch 6 below.

withdraw (at least some part of' the charged assets, or their substitutes, from the ambit of the charge. This feature makes it impossible for the charge to be characterized as fixed.

Of course, this conclusion follows only if the collateral arrangements permit *removal* by the chargor of the secured assets from the ambit of the security. Not all do. Certain quantum and timing limitations are commonly inserted in charge documentation, regardless of whether the document creates a fixed or a floating charge. When charges are fixed, such conditions will not, of course, permit disposal of the secured assets, but will simply define more aggressively the circumstances in which the chargee can enforce the security (when valuations fall below a certain level, for example). When charges are floating, these conditions may perform this simple protective function, or they may further constrain the chargor's use of the charged assets or their substitutes in the ordinary course of business. These limitations do not require re-characterization of the charge; they merely provide the chargee with additional contractual protection against destruction or depletion of the security.

Of course, in considering these collateral arrangements, the analysis has to go further and explain why collateral, *non*-debenture arrangements should influence the interpretation of a debenture that, on its face, presumably purports to create a fixed charge over the debts. If the collateral arrangements are entered into before or at the same time as entry into the debenture, then the total package is clearly relevant in determining the substance of the rights operating between the parties. In *Agnew*, Lord Millett, on behalf of the Privy Council, indicated that 'it is not enough to provide in the debenture that the account is a blocked account if it is not operated as one in fact'.[29]

The real difficulty arises with *post*-debenture collateral arrangements. Recall that the construction of an agreement (and its characterization as a matter of law) is generally determined independently of the post-contractual conduct of the parties.[30] Nevertheless, there are several significant exceptions to this rule.[31] Post-contractual conduct may be examined in order to show that the debenture is a mere sham or a pretence, or that it has been effectively varied by the parties after its execution, or that certain terms have been waived, or that one party is estopped from asserting its rights. Each of these options requires a slightly different doctrinal analysis. In each case, however, the inevitable conclusion is

[29] [2001] UKPC 28, [2001] 2 AC 710, para 48.

[30] *Whitworth Street Estates v Miller* [1970] AC 583, HL.

[31] These are discussed in some detail in S Atherton and RJ Mokal, 'Charges over Chattels: Issues in the Fixed/Floating Jurisprudence' (2005) 26 Company Lawyer 10. Also see the discussion of this point in Gullifer and Payne, ch 4 below.

that the collateral arrangements such as those described above can certainly deliver operational benefits to the chargor, but only at a cost of re-characterizing the charge as floating. In commercial terms, this may or may not be a price worth paying.

3. Charges over other revenue-generating assets

Of course, post-*Spectrum* analysis has also focused on the potential impact of the House of Lords' decision on charges secured against assets other than book debts. It is unrealistic to suggest that the decision will not have this broader impact. Much of its analysis is clearly of perfectly general application.

First, some misconceptions in this area must be cleared away. *Spectrum* does not insist that an asset and its proceeds are a single unit, or that the right to use proceeds is equivalent to the right to deal with the asset, or, marginally more subtly, that a charge over an asset must be a floating charge if the chargor is entitled to use at will any proceeds that are generated by the asset. All of these assertions completely miss the point of the distinctions identified in *Spectrum.* The characterization test is simple. If, and only if, the rights and obligations between the parties are sufficient to ensure that the charged assets are preserved for the benefit of the chargee, then the charge is fixed. Otherwise it is floating. In particular, a charge is floating if the chargor can remove the charged assets from the ambit of the security and use them, or their permitted substitutes, for its own benefit, rather than preserving them for the benefit of the chargee.

Spectrum was a case about debts. How will the *Spectrum* test be used to characterize charges over other revenue-generating assets?[32] There are countless examples of assets that generate proceeds: land, shares, insurance contracts, contractual performance rights, equipment put out on hire, leasing agreements, to name only a few. If the chargor is entitled to use these proceeds at will, is the charge over the underlying asset properly characterized as fixed or floating? Some of these cases are easy. A charge over land, perhaps land on which a restaurant is built, will be a fixed charge notwithstanding that the income from the restaurant is at the disposal of the chargor, not the chargee. The same is true of a charge over a fleet of vehicles run by a car-hire company, or a charge over equipment (such as computers, televisions, furniture) that is hired out to customers. It is irrelevant that the equipment is subject to wear and tear, and at risk of destruction from such use. Insurance and other contractual constraints are

---

[32] cf analysis offered in Frome and Gibbons, ch 5 below.

used to preserve the chargee from risk, or to reduce the risk. The test of a floating charge is that the chargor can remove the *charged assets* from the ambit of the security and use them, or their permitted substitutes, for its own benefit, rather than preserving them for the benefit of the chargee. Here, the charged assets remain preserved for the benefit of the chargee even though the chargor is entitled to the benefit of the proceeds. It is only if the *charged asset* itself (the land or equipment) is at the free disposal of the chargor that the charge is floating.[33] The same approach is appropriate if the charge is over shares, even if the chargor is entitled to use the dividends at will.[34] In all of these cases, the *charged assets* are themselves preserved intact for the benefit of the chargee, so the charge is fixed.[35]

But these cases are not analogous to charges over the *lease agreements* that might be entered into in relation to the above equipment. In these cases, the correct analogy is with debts. If the charge is over the lease *agreement*, not the leased *equipment*, and the debenture entitles the chargor to the benefit of the revenue generated by the lease, then the secured asset *is* being removed from the ambit of the charge for the benefit of the chargor, not the chargee. In the case of debts, the removal is commonly effected in one fell swoop when the debt is collected and the proceeds become available for the benefit of the chargor. But it cannot really matter that the removal is instead effected in tranches, via periodic payments, so that at the end of a defined period and after a series of payments, the secured asset is wholly converted to cash proceeds, which proceeds have been used for the benefit of the chargor, not the chargee. The analogy between charges over debts and charges over lease agreements is obvious.[36] Similarly, a charge over contractual performance rights will be floating if the chargor, not the chargee, is entitled to the benefits of performance; and a charge over an insurance contract will be floating if the chargor, not the chargee, is entitled to use the insurance proceeds for its own benefit. It is

[33] *Re Cosslett (Contractors) Ltd* [1988] Ch 495, CA.

[34] *Arthur D Little (in admin) v Ableco Finance LLC* [2002] EWHC 701, [2003] Ch 217, ChD.

[35] And it is irrelevant that, once the security is *enforced*, the chargee, not the chargor, may become entitled to these revenue streams. Such entitlement follows from *ownership* of the charged asset, not from the security interest in it. When the charge is enforced, the chargee (or its receiver) acquires the right to sell the charged asset and used the proceeds for paying off defined debts. In the interim, the chargee/receiver is entitled to receive all of the ownership benefits/revenue streams, and use them for those same defined purposes.

[36] This suggests that the controversial decisions in *Re Atlantic Computer Systems plc* [1992] Ch 505, CA ('*Atlantic Computer*') and *Re Atlantic Medical Ltd* [1993] BCLC 485 ('*Atlantic Medical*') cannot be supported. In both cases, the assignments of chattel sub-leases and rental payments were held to be fixed charges even though the assignor was free to use the proceeds of the rental streams in its business. This outcome seems inconsistent with the *Spectrum* and *Agnew* decisions, and current analysis suggests the arrangements might be better characterized as floating in both cases. Also see n 37 below.

irrelevant that a charged asset may remain, and remain of high value, despite the delivery of these incidental benefits to the chargor: a security is not judged as fixed or floating depending upon whether it continues to exist and provide adequate value to support the underlying obligation; the sole test is whether the nominated assets are wholly reserved, preserved for the benefit of the chargee. If they are not, the charge is floating. This is the tough fixed/not-fixed boundary issue.

These potentially unwelcome conclusions about leasing contracts deserve further comment. Commercial parties often think that it ought to be possible to deliver fixed charge security over long-term leasing agreements even though the chargor takes the benefit of the ongoing rental stream. This pragmatic approach gives the chargee the benefit of a fixed charge over the asset and the chargor the benefit of the ongoing rental stream in circumstances where the value of the asset is such that it can fully protect both interests. But this wishful thinking is inconsistent with the definition of fixed and floating charges accepted in both *Spectrum* and *Agnew*. The chargee in these circumstances has a floating charge, not a fixed charge; it cannot be otherwise where the chargor, not the chargee, is entitled to remove the benefits, or value, of the secured asset from of the ambit of the security arrangement.

In reaching these conclusions, the 'tree/fruit' analysis so commonly relied upon may be confusing rather than helpful.[37] It is likely to lead to rather unproductive debates about whether the book debt and its proceeds are one and the same asset.[38] This, in turn, leads to the tendency to characterize the charge according to the nature of the property to which the charge relates, rather than according to the degree of control the chargor has to use the property for its own benefit.[39] This is unfortunate. The critical issue is whether, from the date on which the charge is created, the asset must be retained (a fixed charge), or can be used in the ordinary course of business

[37] Indeed, the risk of error is amply demonstrated in S Worthington, *Proprietary Interests in Commercial Transactions* (1996) 77–8, and my erroneous discussion of the *Atlantic Medical* and *Atlantic Computer* cases, subsequently recanted in various published works. See also R Stevens, 'Security After the Enterprise Act', ch 7 below.

[38] See R Goode, 'Charges over Book Debts: A Missed Opportunity' (1994) 110 LQR 592, suggesting that it is impossible to create separate security interests over book debts and their proceeds; contrast DW McLauchlan, '*New Bullas* in New Zealand: Round Two' (2000) 116 LQR 211. I remain of the view that book debts and their proceeds are two separate assets, but that a charge over uncollected book debts must be classified as floating if the chargor has the freedom to remove the charged assets from the security by collecting the proceeds and using them: S Worthington, 'Fixed Charges over Book Debts and Other Receivables' (1997) 113 LQR 563.

[39] As in *Re Atlantic Computer Systems plc* [1992] Ch 505, CA (A Berg, 'Brumark Investments Ltd and the "Innominate" Charge' [2001] JBL 532); *Re Atlantic Medical Ltd* [1993] BCLC 485.

for the benefit of the chargor (a floating charge). This was the analysis applied in *Spectrum* to the security over book debts. The reason for looking at the use of the proceeds is simply, and solely, to determine *who* has the benefit of the book debts that have been removed from the ambit of the security by their collection, nothing more, nothing less. Most assets, including book debts, can be used in a variety of ways. The benefit of a book debt is not simply its collected proceeds; book debts may also be assigned, factored, and so on, before their eventual collection/realization. All of these benefits are only obtained by removal of the book debt from the ambit of the security. The question is, if such removal is permitted, who benefits? If the benefit is retained as a security for the chargee, then the charge is fixed charge. If the benefit is available to the chargor for use in the ordinary course of its business, then the charge is a floating charge.

4. Fixed charges for the future

It is clear from the preceding analysis that fixed charges over book debts, inventory and other circulating assets will rarely arise in practice. The restrictions that must be imposed on the chargor in order to deliver this result are generally commercially unacceptable. The analysis also raises three important incidental issues. First, it cannot be emphasized too strongly that the characterization of charges is a matter of law. The arrangement between the parties must be construed to determine what rights and obligations have been agreed between the chargor and the chargee. If (and only if) these rights and obligations are sufficient to ensure that the charged assets are preserved for the benefit of the chargee, then the charge is fixed. Otherwise it is floating. In particular, a charge is floating if the chargor can remove the charged assets from the ambit of the security and use them, or their permitted substitutes, for its own benefit, rather than preserving them for the benefit of the chargee.[40] In making this assessment, it is irrelevant that the parties intended their agreement to be characterized differently;[41] or that the permissions given to the chargor to take particular benefits are only those agreed to by the chargee in the contract, not rights simply assumed by the chargor;[42] or, conversely, that the written agreement prohibits disposal by the chargor if in reality the parties operate differently;[43] or that the chargee allows the chargor to deal, but subject to termination of this permission at will by the chargee;[44] or, finally, that the chargee's economic position is not in

[40] *Agnew*, passim.
[41] *Spectrum* CA, para 33; *Agnew*, para 32. Contrast *Siebe Gorman* and *New Bullas*.
[42] *Agnew*, para 34, roundly criticizing the contrary finding in *New Bullas*, 491–3.
[43] *Agnew*, para 48.
[44] As in *Siebe Gorman*, now overruled by *Spectrum*.

fact made materially worse,[45] or even that it is not made worse at all, because the facts are such that as charged assets are removed by the chargor, new assets of the same description are acquired and subjected to the same security, so preserving the chargee's position.[46]

5. Consequences: theory and practice

For a few academics, myself included, one further aspect of floating charges has proved tantalizing. Given the doctrinal differences between fixed and floating charges outlined above, what sort of property interest does the floating chargee have in the charged assets prior to crystallization? How does this differ from the property interest of a fixed chargee? Perhaps surprisingly, the theoretical answer to such a fundamental question has an exceptionally limited practical function. Its chief relevance is in determining priorities between competing interests in those rare cases not dealt with explicitly by the Insolvency Act 1986.[47] In practice, the problem arises only in the potential competition between a chargee and third parties claiming set-off, execution, distress, or garnishment. If the chargee's interest is a fixed charge, the interest is immune from these potential incursions; if the chargee's interest is a floating charge, it may be vulnerable to such claims. This difference in result may (or may not)[48] turn on some difference in the proprietary interest of each charge holder.

---

[45] See *Spectrum* CA, para 51 (Lord Phillips MR), suggesting that it is possible to distinguish long-term and short-term debts on the basis that collection of the former, normally paid by instalments, does not remove [the bulk of] the charged asset from the ambit of the security, and so might be considered as readily meeting the requirement of a fixed charge, even though similar provisions permitting collection of short-term debts would be characterized as floating charges. This assertion is reminiscent of the decisions in *Atlantic Computer* and *Atlantic Medical*, and reflects similar errors in legal analysis. It is irrelevant that the value of the pool of charged assets *in fact* remains relatively constant despite the chargor's dealing for its own benefit. If the chargor can engage in such dealing, then the charge is floating. Characterization depends upon the rights to deal with *each item* of the charged assets, as granted by the parties' agreement, so that the charge can be characterized 'as created', not by virtue of some process of taking accounts during the course of the operation of the security. Take a practical example: a fixed charge over machinery (such as computers) will permit the chargor to use the machines for its own benefit, collecting rents and using these rents at will, so long as the machines themselves are preserved for the benefit of the chargee. If the charge is over the rental stream, however, then the charge is necessarily floating if the chargor is permitted to collect the rents and use the proceeds for its own benefit rather than preserving these substitute assets for the benefit of the chargee.

[46] Both fixed and floating charges can be drafted to attach to future assets: see *Holroyd v Marshall* (1862) 10 HL Cas 191 (fixed charges), and almost every authority on floating charges. The security in both cases may be enhanced, but this says nothing at all of the proper characterization of the charge. That depends solely upon whether charged assets can be *removed* from the ambit of the security at the will of the chargor: see *Agnew* and its precedents.

[47] Also see Gullifer and Payne, ch 4 below, arguing that the difference may also be relevant to decrystallization.

[48] See the analysis that follows.

The authorities themselves are not consistent,[49] nor are commentators' views on their significance.[50]

Nevertheless, the quest has continued. Predictably, different possibilities have been proposed which together span the logical range of alternatives.[51] At one extreme, the floating chargee, prior to crystallization, may have no proprietary interest at all in the charged assets.[52] Alternatively, the intermediate position is that the floating chargee may have a new inchoate type of proprietary interest, with characteristics that are undeniably proprietary but of a lesser order than the proprietary interest of a chargee with a fixed charge. Finally, at the other extreme, the floating chargee may have the same quality of proprietary interest as is recognized in the context of a fixed charge, but one that is far more precarious since it is subject to permitted dealings by the chargor with the charged assets.

The first and most restrictive possibility just described is inconsistent with a number of cases where the courts have indicated or assumed that some form of present proprietary interest does exist.[53] The intermediate view is potentially consistent with these judicial observations, but has a problem describing the nature and incidents of the intermediate proprietary interest that is proposed. On one view, the difference is simply that before crystallization the floating chargee's proprietary interest is in a *fund* of assets, and does not attach to any specific charged assets; this happens only after crystallization.[54] Perhaps mistakenly, this distinction is seen as delivering to the chargee a proprietary interest that is fundamentally different before and after crystallization. This is discussed later. The third view had, until recently, only one proponent: a decade ago I suggested that the proprietary interests held by a floating chargee are merely a modified, defeasible, form of fixed charge.[55] Nolan now argues that a better explanation is that a floating chargee holds an overreachable fixed charge.[56]

Which view is right? I continue to support the defeasible charge theory. On this view, a charge that is classified as floating gives the chargee the same quality of proprietary interest as a chargee with a fixed equitable charge, with the same equitable rights to protect those interests, except that the floating interest is

[49] See S Worthington, *Proprietary Interests in Commercial Transactions* (1996) 79–86.

[50] See R Goode, *Legal Problems of Credit and Security* (3rd edn, 2003) paras 4.03 and 4.06. Contrast WJ Gough, *Company Charges* (2nd edn, 1996) 97–9 and 132–4. Also see Worthington (n 49 above).

[51] See Worthington (n 49 above) 78–86.

[52] Gough (n 50 above) 97–101 and ch 13.

[53] For example, *Driver v Broad* [1893] 1 QB 744; *Wallace v Evershed* [1899] 1 Ch 891; *Re Dawson* [1915] 1 Ch 626; *Spectrum.*

[54] Goode (n 50 above) 114; *Spectrum,* para 139 (Lord Walker).

[55] Worthington (n 49 above) ch 4.

[56] R Nolan, 'Property in a Fund' (2004) 120 LQR 108.

defeasible while the fixed one is not. Defeasance will occur whenever and to the extent that a third party acquires an interest in the charged assets through a transaction that falls within the chargor's licence to deal.[57] Nolan has put forward a variation to this view.[58] I am not sure that there is much more than language or semantics separating these two versions. On one version, the chargee's interest 'defeases'; on the other it is 'overreached'. One uses the language of commercial law; the other the language of land law. But the underlying concept is not materially different in any manner that I can discern.

Further arguments in favour of the defeasible charge theory require an examination of some preliminaries. In what follows, it is necessary to consider, in turn, the similarities between fixed and floating charges, and, in particular, the degree of potentiality associated with both; the allegedly distinctive notion of an interest in a fund; and, finally, the various judicial pronouncements that suggest that a floating charge is not a fixed charge with a licence to deal.

First, security is based on property. If the contractual arrangement between the parties does not give the chargee an interest in the chargor's property, then no security is created. The proprietary aspects of security interests are subtle, however, and based on equity's jurisdiction to order specific performance of contractual agreements, or use constructive trusts to perfect agreements where the consideration is executed, and so protect the parties' rights in proprietary ways.[59] Consider a fixed charge. The chargee has an immediate, present, proprietary interest by way of charge over the charged assets. Helpfully, the agreement between the parties can be worded so as to embrace future property as well as property presently owned by the chargor. If this is done, then as soon as the chargor acquires property matching the description in the debenture it will immediately become subject to the fixed charge regime. Importantly, however, the practical benefits of the chargee's property rights can only be realized in strict compliance with the contractual provisions in the debenture document (as supplemented by statute or by orders of the court). Typically, rights can only be enforced if the chargor is in default. In other words, the property rights associated with a fixed charge contain an element of potentiality: the proprietary interest is there from the outset, but the practical benefits that the interest delivers can only be realized in defined circumstances. Despite this, we would not countenance saying that a fixed charge 'hovers' over the charged assets until the conditions for enforcement arise. The property right simply carries with it the rights and limitations contained in the debenture document, enhanced or constrained by statute or by court order.

[57] Worthington (n 49 above) 78–86. [58] Nolan (n 56 above).

[59] See S Worthington, *Equity* (2003) 73–7.

It is the same with floating charges. These, too, depend on property. Moreover, the chargee can only act to enforce its rights in strict compliance with the contractual provisions in the debenture document. Finally, here too the agreement can be worded so as to embrace future property. The difference between fixed charges and floating charges is that with floating charges the parties have agreed that the charged assets may be *removed* from the ambit of the security agreement, provided this is done in the ordinary course of business or in accordance with the terms of the debenture.[60] Does this alter the nature of the property interest accorded to the chargee?

On the face of it, there seems to be no good doctrinal reason to distinguish between the proprietary interests at issue in the two different cases. Once the UK judiciary gave support to the heretical[61] idea that it was possible to have a charge over assets that might be removed from the ambit of the security by the chargor without the consent of the chargee, they must be taken to have supported the idea that a chargee received proprietary protection under this form of arrangement. That is the essence of security. This does not of itself suggest that the property interest is the same as that accorded to other (fixed) charge holders, of course. But consider the practicalities. Statutory incursions aside, the mere possibility of *removal* of the charged assets from the ambit of the security does not affect the chargee's practical property rights once the circumstances are such that the floating charge can be enforced. With both fixed and floating charges, the chargee is typically entitled to collect in the secured assets, realize them, and use the proceeds to pay off the outstanding secured obligations (subject to any statutory preferences and priorities accorded to third parties). In circumstances where assets can be added to the pool of secured assets (as is possible with both fixed and floating charges) and removed from the pool (as is possible with floating charges), the problem is in defining which assets are caught by the security when enforcement is in contemplation. With fixed charges, we manage this process without any special terminology, even though the issue is a live one. With floating charges, we have adopted the terminology of crystallization: once the charge crystallizes,[62] further assets can be added to the pool of secured assets, but no assets can be removed from the pool. In both cases, however, the relevant pool of assets is then realized, and the proceeds distributed in accordance with

[60] With fixed charges, assets can only be removed from the ambit of the security in breach of the security, or by accident or act of God that destroys or damages the property. Where removal is the result of the chargor's breach, the law's remedial regime ensures that the chargee's security will be enforceable against any traceable substitutes received by the chargor in exchange for the wrongful dealing with the charged property. Notably, this remedial approach also applies to dispositions of *floating charge assets* by the chargor in breach of the terms of the floating charge debenture; only *permitted* dispositions escape this 'traceable substitutes' remedial regime.

[61] As noted earlier, the US judiciary would not countenance this possibility: n 16 above.

[62] Either as a matter of law, automatically, or by processes defined in the debenture deed.

the terms of the debenture and any relevant statutory provisions. *Before* this stage is reached, and before the pool is finally defined in this way, what property interests do chargees have? We are untroubled by the notion that fixed chargees have a 'fixed charge interest' in all the assets embraced by the charge. This is notwithstanding that some of those assets may have disappeared from the ambit of the security by the time the security comes to be realized (such disappearance being a result of either breach or accidental destruction). Put another way, the chargee's property rights depend upon the chargee's *potential* ability to effect enforcement according to the terms of the debenture document; they do not depend upon actual enforcement. This is the pattern of equity's delivery of proprietary interests. The parallels with floating charges are obvious. Before the floating charge security is enforced, there seems little reason to suppose that the floating chargee does not have an analogous 'fixed charge interest' in the pool of assets that are potentially available for enforcement of the security according to the terms of the debenture document. Of course, when the charge is actually enforced, the pool may well comprise a different set of specific assets. The object of the chargee's property interest will therefore change over time to embrace the relevant pool of assets as it exists at any given time. Finally, by way of stating the obvious, the precise attributes of the bundle of property rights indicated by the phrase 'fixed charge interest' are not set in concrete, nor defined entirely by law; they are, at least in part, defined by the agreement between the parties.[63] This is as true of fixed charges as it is of floating charges.

That is the doctrine. There is, however, a degree of resistance to the idea that a floating charge holder has the same sort of property interest in the secured assets as a fixed charge holder. The intermediate possibility, in the three possibilities outlined earlier, attempts to provide a more attractive alternative. There are suggestions that use of the fund concept delivers an analysis within the second and intermediate category. For example, Goode favours the idea that a floating chargee has some form of intermediate inchoate property right, and has suggested that the floating charge gives the holder a present interest in a *fund* of assets which the debtor is free to manage in the ordinary course of its

[63] This is not unusual. Whether we are discussing security interests, equitable ownership, or legal ownership, the answer to the question, 'What rights are involved?' is 'It depends': it depends upon the precise terms of the arrangement between the parties. 'Security', 'equitable ownership' and 'legal ownership' may give a flavour of the interests involved, but the precise compass is a matter for agreement. See S Worthington, *Equity* (2003) 62. This variety does not offend the *numerus clausus* theory, since the *types* of property interests remains limited; it is simply the precise specification of rights within any one broad category that might vary. In any event, the benefits of the *numerus clausus* theory may be overstated: see S Worthington, 'The Disappearing Divide Between Property and Obligation: The Impact of Aligning Legal Analysis and Commercial Expectation' in S Degeling and J Edelman (eds), *Equity in Commercial Law* (2005) ch 5, 93.

business.[64] The floating charge does not attach to any specific charged assets until the charge crystallizes. This insight is assumed to dictate that the nature of the proprietary interests held by the floating chargee before and after crystallization is fundamentally different. In particular, prior to crystallization the quality of the proprietary interest held by the floating chargee is different from, and less than, the interest held by the fixed chargee.

But is this right? Consider the analogy with a beneficiary's interest in a trust fund. The beneficiary has 'equitable ownership' of the 'fund', just as she might have 'equitable ownership' of trust assets held under a bare trust. The difference is that in the first case the trust agreement does not allow her to extract her interest from the fund until certain conditions are met, and, in the interim, the trustee can invest and reinvest the fund (so that the precise assets it encompasses will change). But we do not analyse these two situations and then suggest that there must be some new and intermediate form of equitable ownership. In both cases, the beneficiary is simply the 'equitable owner' of the trust fund. In asserting this conclusion, it is taken for granted that the precise bundle of rights associated with 'equitable ownership' will vary depending upon the detailed terms of the trust under which such equitable ownership is derived. It is the same with fixed and floating charges. With floating charges, the charged assets form a fund. The chargee cannot have access to the fund before the conditions set out in the charge agreement are met. In the meantime, the chargor can deal with the fund according to the terms of the agreement. During this period, there is not a new form of security interest; the interest is of the same character as a fixed charge.

The defeasible charge theory commonly attracts at least one further criticism. This is the objection, gleaned from various cases, that a floating charge is not a 'fixed charge with a licence to deal'. In substance, the defeasible charge theory (and the overreachable charge theory) both appear suspiciously like fixed charges with a licence (or right, or power) in the chargor to deal with the charged assets. The most forthright assertion comes from Buckley LJ in *Evans v Rival Granite Quarries Ltd*:[65]

> A floating security is not a specific mortgage of the assets plus a licence to the mortgagor to dispose of them in the ordinary course of his business, but is a floating mortgage applying to every item comprised in the security, but not specifically affecting any item until some act or event occurs or some act on the part of the mortgagee is done which causes it to crystallise into a fixed security.

[64] R Goode, *Legal Problems of Credit and Security* (3rd edn, 2003) 114. Also see *Spectrum*, para 139 (Lord Walker): 'The chargee has a proprietary interest, but its interest is in a fund of circulating capital, and unless and until the chargee intervenes (on crystallization of the charge) it is for the trader, and not the bank, to decide how to run its business.'

[65] [1910] 2 KB 979, 999, CA.

What is meant by this assertion? If attention is directed exclusively to the second part of this quotation, then nothing is said beyond the matters considered earlier in this chapter. Indeed, courts commonly make the obvious point that the practical benefits associated with a floating charge security can only be obtained in respect of those assets that remain within the pool after effective crystallization of the security.[66]

The real problem for the defeasible charge theory is seen to come from the words '[a] floating security is not a specific mortgage of the assets plus a licence to the mortgagor to dispose of them in the ordinary course of his business'. Superficially at least, this assertion refutes the defeasible charge theory. However, the words are equally consistent with judicial emphasis of the simple point that although a floating charge is a present security, it is not simply a *fixed* (specific) charge plus associated personal, contractual, rights. Put another way, a chargee cannot avoid all the statutory provisions relating to floating charges by insisting that the charge in question really *is* a *fixed* charge, not a floating charge, while at the same time claiming that the charge has associated with it, via collateral contractual arrangements, all of the commercial benefits commonly delivered only by floating charges.[67] This is absolutely correct, and the defeasible charge theory does not suggest that option.[68] What the defeasible charge theory suggests is that the fixed/floating charge distinction is drawn on the basis of the control and benefit test outlined earlier, but that floating chargees, despite being subjected to all of the statutory incursions into their security, nevertheless

[66] See *Illingworth v Houldsworth* [1904] AC 355, 358, HL (Lord Macnaghten): 'a floating charge . . . is ambulatory and shifting in nature, hovering over and so to speak floating with the property which it is intended to affect until some event occurs or some act is done which causes it to settle and fasten on the subject of the charge within its reach and grasp'. Modern cases are no different. See *Re Cosslett (Contractors) Ltd* [1998] Ch 495, 510, CA (Millett LJ): 'The essence of a floating charge is that it is a charge, not on any particular asset, but on a fluctuating body of assets which remain under the management and control of the chargor . . .'. Or *Spectrum*, para 111 (Lord Scott): 'in my opinion, the essential characteristic of a floating charge, the characteristic that distinguishes it from a fixed charge, is that the asset subject to the charge is not finally appropriated as security for the payment of the debt until the occurrence of some future event. In the meantime, the chargor is left free to use the charged asset and to remove it from the security.'; see also para 139 (Lord Walker).

[67] W J Gough, *Company Charges* (2nd edn, 1996) 368, appears alert to the same troubling possibility of evasion of the statutory regime. Gough insists that a fixed charge with an implied power in the chargor to deal with the security is a conceptual impossibility: the charge cannot be characterized as *fixed* in these circumstances, because such a power is simply inconsistent with the existence of a specific charge. If his focus is on *characterization* of the charge, then it is impossible to disagree. But if it is on whether a proprietary security interest can ever exist in these circumstances, then disagreement is likely. For the history of the common law's development in this area, see R Gregory and P Walton, 'Fixed Charges over Changing Assets—The Possession and Control Heresy' [1998] Company Financial and Insolvency Law Review 68.

[68] This was the distinction drawn between the defeasible charge theory and 'a fixed charge plus a licence to deal' in S Worthington, *Proprietary Interests in Commercial Transactions* (1996) 81.

have the same quality of proprietary interest as a chargee with a fixed charge, with the same equitable rights to protect those interests, except that the floating chargee's interest is defeasible while the fixed one is not. Defeasance will occur whenever and to the extent that a third party acquires an interest in the charged assets through a transaction which falls within the chargor's licence to deal.

For completeness, it is equally true that a chargee cannot avoid the statutory incursions into floating charges by insisting that the arrangement in question is not a charge at all, but is instead a mortgage or an assignment of the underlying assets on terms that provide the lender with adequate security, but allow the borrower ongoing commercial benefits. Characterization of the arrangement between the parties is, again, a matter of law. It is irrelevant that the parties describe their arrangement as a fixed charge, a mortgage, or an assignment. If the rights actually given to each of the parties are those described in the first part of this chapter, then, as a matter of law, the arrangement will be characterized as a floating charge. The defeasible charge theory does not seek to alter this conclusion at all. It simply seeks to describe the proprietary interest of a floating chargee in the period after creation of the charge but before the charge has crystallized. Cases that make the assertion that a floating charge is not a fixed charge with a licence to deal are usually directing attention to the first characterization issue, not to the second property rights issue.

Finally, consider the rare circumstances in which it is suggested that all this theory may have some practical impact. Take the example of execution creditors attempting to levy execution against assets that are subject to security. The generally accepted view is that if the asset is subject to a fixed charge, the execution creditor will be denied access; if the asset is subject to a floating charge, the execution creditor will be entitled to access. But this outcome does not depend on some subtle difference in the property rights of the two charge holders. In both cases, the execution creditor takes the asset subject to the prior equities. If the charge is fixed, the prior equity is a security interest in favour of the chargee that denies the chargor any right to deal with the asset; this prior equity therefore defeats entirely the purported interest of the execution creditor. If the charge is floating, the prior equity is a security interest in favour of the chargee that allows the chargor to deal with the asset in the ordinary course of business (and execution is deemed to occur in the ordinary course of business) until the charge crystallizes; this prior equity does nothing at all to stand in the way of the interests of the execution creditor. The distinction is not between different fundamental property interests, but between the different particular aspects or permissions to deal associated with those interests.

6. Summary

Part B of this chapter has advanced two relatively simple propositions. The first has the support of the House of Lords. The second has not been the subject of serious judicial comment,[69] and might be regarded as of academic interest only (using that expression in its less attractive sense); nevertheless, its answer provides an important piece of the puzzle in our understanding of property interests and their operation.

The first proposition concerns the fixed/floating charge distinction. A charge is fixed if and only if the chargor is required to preserve the charged assets, or their permitted substitutes, for the benefit of the chargee. If this is not a requirement, then the charge is floating. In particular, a charge is floating if the chargor is free to remove the charged assets, and their substitutes, from the scope of the security, and use them for its own benefit in the course of its business at least until the charge crystallizes or the chargee intervenes to enforce the floating security.

The second proposition concerns the proprietary interest of floating chargees prior to crystallization of their security interests. Various views have been advanced, but it is suggested here that a floating charge gives the chargee the same quality of proprietary interest as a chargee with a fixed equitable charge, with the same equitable rights to protect those interests, except that the floating interest is defeasible while the fixed one is not. Defeasance will occur whenever and to the extent that a third party acquires an interest in the charged assets through a transaction which falls within the chargor's licence to deal.

C. The 'Abuse' of Doctrinal Analysis: Insolvency Consequences

The analysis that follows considers the controversial 'so what?' question. As already noted, the approach of the House of Lords in the *Spectrum* case was both proper and indeed inevitable, given the issue that needed to be determined. Their Lordships were required to characterize a particular security as either fixed or floating. This step was essential in order to determine the order of payment out of the proceeds of realization of the charged assets. Realizations from assets subject to fixed security are distributed on a different basis from realizations derived from assets subject to a floating security.[70] In particular, if the lending bank in *Spectrum* could prove that it had a fixed charge security, it would be protected from distributions in favour of unsecured creditors; if it had only a floating charge security, the realizations would be subjected to the prior

[69] Although see Lord Walker in *Spectrum*, para 139: cited at n 64 above.

[70] See nn 9–15 above and associated text.

entitlements of various unsecured creditors. In the end, in *Spectrum*, the lending bank was found to be in this disadvantageous second position.

But why is this intermediate step required at all? Economists might dispute the entitlement of unsecured creditors to *any* preferential treatment, suggesting that security holders (whether fixed or floating) have purchased the benefit of their security, and priced the cost of protection into the transaction; they should therefore be protected, and statutory incursions should not be permitted to disrupt the efficient operation of the market. Whatever the merits of this argument, it has clearly not found favour with the UK legislature.[71] But even those who support some form of protection for unsecured creditors might wonder whether such a policy is best delivered by a regime based on discrimination between fixed and floating charge holders.

For a start, this differential treatment of fixed and floating charges drives a lot of costly but unproductive commercial activity.[72] Commercial parties and their lawyers invest enormous time and effort into attempts to draft agreements that will be characterized as fixed charges (thus avoiding various statutory incursions regarded as unwelcome by the chargee), while at the same time providing various practical and operational advantages to the chargor (regarded as essential for the efficient conduct of the chargor's business, which in itself is desirable if the secured obligation is to be satisfied). Witness the volume and vigour of discussion and debate generated amongst lawyers by the *Spectrum* decision itself. This, if nothing else, suggests that the issues are not finally settled, and therefore that costly efforts will continue to be invested.

Furthermore, not only has the boundary between fixed and floating charges proved difficult to define exhaustively, the theoretical justification for relying on such a boundary is neither self-evident nor convincingly explained. Little sustained attention has been directed at demonstrating why the interests of certain secured creditors (floating chargees) must make way for the interests of unsecured creditors, while the interests of other secured creditors (fixed chargees) may remain untouched. If such a theoretical justification were evident, then efforts to distinguish between the two classes of creditors might seem more worthwhile. To date there is nothing approaching a defensible justification for such discrimination. The inevitable conclusion is that we appear to have chosen a difficult and irrelevant tool to effect a poorly justified distinction between

[71] It is, however, the approach adopted in Article 9 of the Uniform Commercial Code.

[72] As noted earlier, there are other differences in the treatment of fixed and floating charges imposed by the Insolvency Act 1986, but it is the drive for statutory priority and commercial attractiveness that generates most of the efforts noted here. Statutory provisions designed to prevent the abuse of security and illegitimate avoidance of the *pari passu* regime are of a different order.

classes of secured creditors in order to advance policy goals that, however worthy, are unrelated to the means by which they are being pursued.

Although their Lordships in *Spectrum* addressed in great detail the issue of what constitutes fixed and floating security, the real issue is how the legislature then intervenes to make special rules for the insolvency distribution of the proceeds of sale of the secured assets. The present rules do not optimize commercial practice; indeed, they do not best favour the interests of either the lender, the borrower, or the general creditors. They are inefficient: too difficult to apply, too uncertain, and too costly in their demands for pre- and post-insolvency analysis and negotiation. Moreover, they utilize an inappropriate factor to determine who should have priority to the assets of an insolvent debtor. Against these arguments for change, it is simply not to the point to suggest that the present arrangements are attractive because our law is clearly defined by a sophisticated mass of UK precedent, or, alternatively, that if the law is not clear, the judges can be relied upon to exercise their discretion appropriately to deliver the 'right' result. Assuming there is a desire to maintain some form of mandatory sharing with preferred and unsecured creditors, is there a readily available new and better test?

Various models exist for some sort of privileging of unsecured creditors. The United States model is not one. In the United States, Article 9 of the Uniform Commercial Code expressly validates the concept of a 'floating lien'. This overcomes early case law,[73] and allows a chargee to take an effective security interest over certain types of collateral, such as inventory or receivables. But such security interests are then regarded as indistinguishable from other security interests permitted by the Code: neither the validity of the security nor its priority in insolvency depend on the nature of the collateral, the type of security, or the degree of control exercised by the chargor.

In New Zealand, statutory carve-outs in favour of preferential and general unsecured creditors are based on characterization of the assets covered by the charge, not characterization of the charge itself. Charges over inventory and receivables are subject to statutory carve-outs in favour of these protected creditors; charges over other assets are not. This approach may simplify the analysis, although that is not self-evidently the case. For example, a debt is clearly a receivable, but is a 12-month leasing agreement a 'receivable'? Is a 50-year leasing agreement a 'receivable'? In any event, even this approach adds an additional and seemingly unnecessary step to the essential analysis.

A pragmatist might suggest that if the goal is to protect the unsecured creditors, then the most straightforward approach is simply to provide for a statutory

[73] *Benedict v Ratner* 268 US 353 (1925), Sup Ct US.

carve-out that operates against *all* security arrangements. It is not beyond the wit of policy advisers to calculate the required carve-out to achieve the desired level of protection. Since a 10 per cent fund was once mooted as an appropriate carve-out against floating charge realizations, a 1 per cent or a 5 per cent fund might provide an equivalent and adequate carve-out if it operated against all security realizations. This simple and straightforward approach would deliver the policy objectives, eliminate unnecessary steps in the analysis, and, crucially, remove the costly need to distinguish between fixed and floating charges at the time when the security is enforced, or, more importantly (since this is the more costly exercise), at the time when such arrangements are contemplated by lender and borrower.

If history is any guide, this plea is likely to fall on deaf ears, but we must put some sustained effort into pursuing rational solutions to these insolvency problems. After *Spectrum*, we appear to be in a position where the conceptual shortcomings evident in earlier judicial decisions have been resolved, but the ensuing commercial result is not necessarily satisfactory. We have constructed and defined a boundary that is both inefficient in its operation and inappropriate in providing a mechanism for delivering agreed policy objectives. We ought to be able to design a regime that is not so circuitous or so costly in delivering the desired benefits to secured and unsecured creditors. To persist with current practices is an 'abuse' of doctrinal analysis.

The efforts of the Law Commission in its work on the registration of company charges was a substantial step in the direction of providing a more modern and functional security regime.[74] However, that project has all but bitten the dust. In the end, we appear likely to retain a great deal of our old system, improved by electronic filing but by little else. And all the while we resolutely continue to boast that our system of commercial law is clear, certain, accessible, and commercially attractive (notwithstanding the litigation in cases such as *Spectrum*, and all the pre- and post-litigation hand-wringing). In the meantime, the European Commission is likely, in the longer term, to impose on us a secured financing regime that is far less attractive than one we might have designed for ourselves. We have missed the opportunity to put the first draft on the table. The short-sightedness of this is astonishing.

D. Conclusion

We seem to be a position where, as English commercial lawyers, we have won the battle but are likely to lose the war. The Law Lords in *Spectrum* reached a

[74] Law Commission, *Company Security Interests* (Law Com No 296, Cm 6654, August 2005).

legal conclusion that I am predisposed to think is correct, and properly based on precedent and principle. But the consequences that flow from that decision are not consequences determined by the House of Lords. They are consequences determined by the legislature and delivered in the guise of the Insolvency Act 1986. This is where the problem begins. It has two aspects. The first is whether the system of determining priorities as delivered by the Insolvency Act 1986 is attractive and efficient. The second is an even larger question, whether the whole structure of the law of secured financing in the United Kingdom is in an ideal state. Views differ, but we might have been well advised to commit our preferred version of the law to statute in order to participate effectively in the making of European and international law. In both these arenas we are singularly silent, or at least noticeably ineffective.

4

THE CHARACTERIZATION OF FIXED AND FLOATING CHARGES

*Louise Gullifer and Jennifer Payne**

A. Introduction

A great deal of uncertainty surrounds the characterization of a charge as fixed or floating. This uncertainty remains even after the decision of the House of Lords in *Re Spectrum Plus Ltd.*[1] Although their Lordships have provided some guidance in relation to charges over book debts in that case, uncertainties remain; for example, exactly what amounts to a blocked account is still unclear. This uncertainty is not insignificant as many important consequences flow from the characterization of a charge as fixed or floating, for the parties *inter se* and for third parties, both pre-insolvency and, more importantly, post-insolvency. This uncertainty is anathema to commercial transactions.[2] In this chapter we examine the process of characterization of charges, and contend that the fixed/floating distinction is not the most appropriate trigger for these consequences. We then investigate and recommend possible alternative triggers.

In *Spectrum*, Spectrum granted a charge to NatWest over its book debts by a clause in a debenture which secured Spectrum's obligation to NatWest to repay borrowings under an overdraft facility. The debenture provided that the charge over the book debts was a fixed charge and required the company to pay the proceeds of the debts when received into the company's account and not otherwise

* We would like to thank Harry Sigman, Jacob Ziegel, and Mike Gedye for their help, particularly in relation to Part E of this chapter.

[1] [2005] UKHL 41, [2005] 2 AC 680 (hereinafter *Spectrum*).

[2] *The Scaptrade* [1983] 2 AC 694, 704, HL, per Lord Diplock ('the English courts have time and again asserted the need for certainty in commercial transactions'), adopting the language of Robert Goff LJ in the judgment of the Court of Appeal in that case: [1983] QB 529, 540, CA.

to deal with the debts. It was modelled on the debenture taken by Barclays Bank in *Siebe Gorman & Co Ltd v Barclays Bank Ltd*.[3] Spectrum's account was never in credit.[4] The proceeds of the book debts were paid into Spectrum's account with NatWest and Spectrum drew on the account as necessary. Spectrum went into liquidation. The liquidators collected the book debts but refused to account for them to NatWest. The question for the court was whether this charge could be characterized as fixed or floating. Morritt V-C characterized it as a floating charge, following the Privy Council's decision in *Agnew v IRC*[5] and declining to follow *Re New Bullas Trading Ltd*.[6] Somewhat to everyone's surprise the Court of Appeal allowed the appeal from this decision and decided that the charge could properly be characterized as fixed. The House of Lords allowed the appeal from this decision, overruled *Siebe Gorman* on the debenture issue and characterized the charge as floating.

The *Spectrum* litigation is a good example of the uncertainty that surrounds the characterization of a charge as fixed or floating. First, what was regarded by many as a standard term in a commercial transaction had to go all the way to the House of Lords for a decision as to its legal significance. Not only has a huge amount of time and money been expended on this issue but the decision in *Spectrum* has implications both for the commercial transaction in that case, and for all of the other transactions with the same or similar terms which have been awaiting the House of Lords' decision. The ruling in *Spectrum* has retrospective effect[7] and therefore many cases held up to await their Lordships' decision, including closed receiverships and liquidations, where preferential debts have not been paid on the strength of the decision in *Siebe Gorman*, will have to be reconsidered with a view to adjusting the rights of the parties involved. This point is not insignificant as many important distinctions flow from this distinction.

In broad terms the essence of the floating charge, and the factor which distinguishes it from the fixed charge, is that the chargor can continue to deal with the assets which are the subject of the security and can transfer them to third parties in the ordinary course of business unencumbered by the security. The

3 [1979] 2 Lloyd's Rep 142.

4 cf the account in *Siebe Gorman* which was sometimes in credit. This was the only material difference between the *Siebe Gorman* and the *Spectrum* debentures.

5 [2001] UKPC 28, [2001] 2 AC 710 (also known as *Brumark*).

6 [1994] 1 BCLC 485, CA.

7 Their Lordships discussed and unanimously rejected the possibility of giving only prospective effect to their decision although they did not rule out this option as a possibility in future litigation: [2005] UKHL 41, [2005] 2 AC 680, paras 39–43, per Lord Nicholls; para 45, per Lord Steyn; para 74, per Lord Hope; para 126, per Lord Scott; para 161, per Lord Walker; para 162, per Baroness Hale; and para 165, per Lord Brown.

boundary between the two is not rigid[8] but nevertheless the characterization of a charge as fixed or floating will affect the extent of the parties' authority to deal with the secured assets. Whether or not the chargor is in breach of contract for dealings with the secured assets, for instance, will depend substantially on whether the assets are secured by way of a fixed or floating charge. Characterization can, therefore, affect the rights of the parties *inter se* as well as the rights of third parties.[9] To that extent, characterization is a matter of contractual interpretation, and the guiding doctrine can be freedom of contract, subject to any kind of protectionist measures that are in force, implemented either by Parliament[10] or by the common law.[11]

For third parties, it is relevant whether a charge is fixed or floating because this affects the status and validity of subsequent actions dealing with the charged property. A floating chargor has authority to create any subsequent charge, fixed or floating, ranking in priority to that floating charge, unless it is a floating charge over the same assets as the first charge.[12] The floating chargor has a freedom to trade prior to crystallization so that dispositions to purchasers in the ordinary course of business will generally be effective.[13]

The distinctions between fixed and floating charges are particularly important on insolvency.[14] All floating charges need to be registered, whereas not all fixed

---

8 For example, as Lord Walker recognizes in *Spectrum*, not every restriction on a trader's freedom of action is a badge of a fixed charge: [2005] UKHL 41, [2005] 2 AC 680, para 140.

9 It may be worth clarifying that, of course, as regards the parties *inter se*, characterization has relevance for the default terms in the contract. The parties could always, regardless of the ultimate characterization vis-à-vis the legislation, provide for particular rights and obligations *inter se*. Characterization may not therefore be ultimately determinative of the rights as between the parties.

10 For example, Unfair Contract Terms Act 1977.

11 Parties to a contract do not have unlimited freedom to agree any terms they choose. In particular, the courts will not enforce contracts involving the infringement of the criminal or civil law or terms which are otherwise contrary to public policy or morals. Penalty clauses are likewise unenforceable to the extent that they provide the claimant with more than the amount of his loss (see GH Treitel, *The Law of Contract* (11th edn, 2003) ch 11; H Beale (ed), *Chitty on Contracts* (29th edn, 2004) ch 17).

12 *Re Benjamin Cope & Sons Ltd* [1914] 1 Ch 800, CA. A second floating charge over part of those assets can rank in priority to the original floating charge if the power to create such a charge is reserved in the earlier charge: *Re Automatic Bottle Makers Ltd* [1926] Ch 412. A subsequent fixed charge will take priority unless the original clause contains a negative pledge clause of which the subsequent chargee has actual notice: *English & Scottish Mercantile Investment Co Ltd v Brunton* [1892] 2 QB 700, CA. Notice of the negative pledge clause and not just of the charge is needed.

13 Although the chargor has no freedom to deal with the assets subject to the fixed charge, nevertheless third parties who are bona fide purchasers for value without notice in the ordinary course of business will probably take free of the chargee's proprietary interest.

14 One of the advantages of the floating charge used to be the ability to appoint an administrative receiver under a 'qualifying charge'. This was largely removed and replaced by the ability to appoint an administrator: Insolvency Act 1986, Sch B1, para 14 (as inserted by the Enterprise Act 2002, s 248 and Sch 16). However, the holder of a qualifying floating charge has first choice

charges do.[15] Preferential creditors[16] rank in priority to debenture holders with assets covered by floating, but not fixed, charges.[17] A floating charge is subordinated to the costs and expenses of an administrator[18] but it seems that a floating charge holder's claim is not postponed to the costs and expenses of the liquidator, despite the fact that these rank ahead of preferential debts.[19] A fixed charge is not subordinated in this way. The amendments to the Insolvency Act 1986 made by the Enterprise Act 2002 provide for a proportion of the assets subject to a floating charge to be made available for the claims of unsecured creditors.[20] Assets subject to a fixed charge are immune from this provision. An administrator can dispose of assets subject to a floating, but not a fixed, charge without court approval.[21] A floating charge created not for new value in the period prior to insolvency is subject to challenge, and may be set aside.[22] No equivalent provision exists for fixed charges, which can only be avoided if they involve a preference.[23]

There remains a great deal of uncertainty regarding the boundaries between fixed and floating charges. One thing that is unquestionably true today is that the characterization of a charge as fixed or floating is not left to the parties themselves,[24] a point emphasized by their Lordships in *Spectrum*.[25] Although both fixed and floating charges are consensual securities created by agreement between the parties, the parties' designation of the charge, if any, is merely a factor, and not a conclusive factor, in determining the proper classification of the charge.

---

in appointing an administrator. This is implicit in the fact that a company or its directors proposing to appoint an administrator must first give notice to any person entitled to appoint an administrator under a floating charge (see Insolvency Act 1986, Sch B1, para 26).

[15] Companies Act 1985, s 396, for example fixed charges over shares, negotiable instruments. The major significance of failure to register is felt on insolvency, although there are some consequences which arise outside the insolvency context, for example Companies Act 1985, ss 395(2), 399.

[16] Insolvency Act 1986, Sch 6, paras 8–12. Crown preference was abolished by the Enterprise Act 2002, s 251.

[17] Insolvency Act 1986, ss 40, 175(2)(b); Sch B1, para 65(2). A floating charge for these purposes is defined so as to include a charge which, although originally floating, has since become fixed, for example through crystallization (Insolvency Act 1986, ss 40(1), 251).

[18] Insolvency Act 1986, Sch B1, paras 70 and 99.

[19] *Buchler v Talbot* [2004] UKHL 9, [2004] 2 AC 298 (see n 172 below for discussion), cf *Re Barleycorn Enterprises Ltd* [1970] Ch 465, CA.

[20] Insolvency Act 1986, s 176A. For details of the prescribed proportion, see Insolvency Act 1986 (Prescribed Part) Order 2003, SI 2003/2097, art 3.

[21] Insolvency Act 1986, Sch B1, paras 70–71. This is subject to the chargee's priority being transferred to the proceeds acquired from the disposition of the charged property. Court approval is required for disposal of property subject to a fixed charge.

[22] Insolvency Act 1986, s 245. The period is two years prior to insolvency if the floating charge holder is a person connected to the company, and within 12 months of insolvency for any other person.

[23] Insolvency Act 1986, s 239.

[24] *Agnew v IRC* [2001] UKPC 28, [2001] 2 AC 710, PC.

[25] [2005] UKHL 41, [2005] 2 AC 680, para 141, per Lord Walker.

The final characterization of the charge as fixed or floating is not left to the parties, but to the courts.

While the *Spectrum* litigation is a good example of the difficulties faced by the courts when characterizing a charge as fixed or floating, it is hardly unique. This question has been litigated very regularly in recent years,[26] often ending up in the appeal courts and the amount of academic literature on this issue is voluminous. It is also clear that the decision of the House of Lords in *Spectrum* is not the end of the road for this issue. Their Lordships have not answered all of the outstanding questions surrounding fixed and floating charges and uncertainties still remain after that decision.[27] Given the significance of this issue, and the commercial importance of this distinction being clear to all the parties without the need for recourse to the courts, the current process of characterization of a charge as fixed or floating needs to be reassessed. This chapter will investigate this issue. Part B will examine the nature of floating charges. Part C will look at the process of characterization as it is conducted by the courts. Part D will examine whether, and on what basis, the courts' involvement in this issue can be justified. Part E will assess whether the current process of characterization undertaken by the courts is appropriate, and if not what alternatives may be available. In Part F we put forward some proposals for reform.

B. The Nature of Floating Charges

A fixed charge is an immediate proprietary interest in the secured property which 'without more fastens on ascertained and definite property or property capable of being ascertained and defined'.[28] Hence, the chargee can prevent the

---

[26] For example, *Quicksons (South and West) Ltd v Katz (No 2)* [2004] EWHC 2443, [2005] BCC 138, ChD; *Ashborder BV v Green Gas Power Ltd* [2004] EWHC 1517, [2005] BCC 634, ChD; *Arthur D Little Ltd (in administration) v Ableco Finance LLC* [2002] EWHC 701, [2003] Ch 217, ChD; *Agnew v IRC* [2001] UKPC 28, [2001] 2 AC 710; *Smith v Bridgend CBC* [2001] UKHL 58, [2002] 1 AC 336; *Re Cosslett (Contractors) Ltd* [1998] Ch 495, CA; *Royal Trust Bank v National Westminster Bank plc* [1996] BCC 613, CA; *Re New Bullas Trading Ltd* [1994] 1 BCLC 485, CA; *Re Cimex Tissues Ltd* [1994] BCC 626, ChD; *Re GE Tunbridge Ltd* [1994] BCC 563, ChD; *William Gaskell Group v Highley* [1994] 1 BCLC 197, ChD; *Re CCG International Enterprises Ltd* [1993] BCC 580, ChD; *Re Atlantic Computer Systems plc* [1992] Ch 505, CA; *Re Atlantic Medical Ltd* [1992] BCC 653, ChD; *Re Croftbell Ltd* [1990] BCLC 844, ChD; *Ex p Copp* [1989] BCLC 13, Ch; *Re Permanent Houses (Holdings) Ltd* (1989) 5 BCC 151, ChD; *Re Brightlife Ltd* [1987] 1 BCLC 485, ChD; *Re Armagh Shoes Ltd* [1984] BCLC 405, ChD; *Re Bond Worth Ltd* [1980] 1 Ch 228, Ch; *Siebe Gorman & Co Ltd v Barclays Bank Ltd* [1979] 2 Lloyd's Rep 142, ChD.

[27] A number of difficulties remain unresolved, and indeed 'are likely to persist for as long as the distinction between fixed and floating charges exists': C Hare, 'Charges over Book Debts: The End of an Era' [2005] LMCLQ 440, 445. See text to nn 82–89 below.

[28] *Illingworth v Houldsworth* [1904] AC 355, 358, HL, per Lord Macnaghten.

chargor from disposing of or destroying the property, and if the property is wrongfully disposed of the person acquiring the property takes subject to the charge unless he can demonstrate that he is a bona fide purchaser of the legal interest for value without notice. A definitive view of the nature of a floating charge has proved more elusive. This is perhaps not surprising. It is a present security interest[29] which, traditionally defined, means a proprietary interest held by the creditor in the debtor's property, yet the debtor remains generally free to deal with the assets as if they were unsecured.

Broadly, three different theories have been put forward.[30] First, Gough has argued that a floating charge, while a present equitable security, does not give the holder any equitable proprietary interest until crystallization.[31] On this view the floating charge gives rise to a deferred equitable interest and, prior to crystallization, the holder has a personal or 'mere' equity against the chargor. However, a number of cases seem to suggest that this is inaccurate, and that some form of present proprietary interest does exist.[32] The second theory, which has been more generally accepted, holds that an immediate proprietary interest in the property owned by the company arises, albeit one that does not attach specifically to any of the assets until crystallization. The difficulty with this theory has been to explain the precise nature of the proprietary interest held by the chargor prior to crystallization.[33] Goode has suggested that the floating charge gives the holder a present interest in a *fund* of assets which the debtor is free to manage in the ordinary course of its business.[34] The floating charge does not attach to any specific charged assets until the charge crystallizes. This analysis was adopted by Lord Walker in *Spectrum* who stated: 'The chargee has a proprietary interest, but its interest is in a *fund* of circulating capital, and unless and until the chargee intervenes (on crystallization of the charge) it is for the trader, and not the bank, to decide how to run its business.'[35]

[29] A floating charge is clearly a present security, not an agreement to create a security in the future at the time of crystallization: *Evans v Rival Granite Quarries Ltd* [1910] 2 KB 979, CA.

[30] It has been suggested that there is no single 'correct' theory: *Smith v Bridgend CBC* [2001] UKHL 58, [2002] 1 AC 336, paras 61–63, per Lord Scott. See also S Worthington, 'Floating Charges: The Use and Abuse of Doctrinal Analysis', ch 3 above.

[31] WJ Gough, *Company Charges* (2nd edn, 1996) 97–101 and ch 13.

[32] For example, *Driver v Broad* [1893] 1 QB 744; *Wallace v Evershed* [1899] 1 Ch 891; *Re Dawson* [1915] 1 Ch 626, CA. The House of Lords' decision in *Spectrum* supports the idea that the floating chargee has an immediate proprietary interest of some kind: para 139, per Lord Walker. Gough's view has attracted more favourable treatment by the courts in Australia, see *Lyford v Commonwealth Bank of Australia* (1995) 130 ALR 267, FCA; *Wily v St George Partnership Banking Ltd* (1999) 161 ALR 1, FCA.

[33] See E Ferran, *Company Law and Corporate Finance* (1999) 510.

[34] R Goode, *Legal Problems of Credit and Security* (3rd edn, 2003) 114; see also Lord Walker in *Spectrum*: [2005] UKHL 41, [2005] 2 AC 680, para 139.

[35] [2005] UKHL 41, [2005] 2 AC 680, para 139, per Lord Walker. However, in the same paragraph Lord Walker also cites with approval S Worthington's book (*Proprietary Interests in*

On the basis of either of these views the nature of the interest held by the chargee before and after crystallization is fundamentally different. In other words, fixed and floating charges are inherently different creatures. The quality of the interest held by the floating charge holder is different from, and less than, the interest held by the holder of a fixed charge. However, other theories have advanced the view that fixed and floating charges are not fundamentally different creatures, but that a floating charge is merely a modified form of a fixed charge. Worthington has suggested that the chargee might have the same quality of proprietary interest as is recognized in the context of a fixed charge, but one which is defeasible when the chargor deals with the assets in any of the ways permitted by the charge agreement.[36] On this view a charge classified as floating gives the chargee the same quality of proprietary interest as a chargee with a fixed equitable charge from the inception of the charge, with the same equitable rights to protect those interests, except that the floating interest is defeasible while the fixed one is not. Defeasance will occur whenever and to the extent that a third party acquires an interest in the charged assets through a transaction which falls within the chargor's licence to deal. More recently Nolan has put forward a variation to this view.[37] He suggests that the holder of a floating charge has an equitable interest in the assets within the scope of the charge from the moment when the assets fall within the terms of the charge, but that this interest may be overreached, and if the interest in the asset is overreached it will cease to affect that asset. According to Nolan, overreaching, and not defeasance, is the reason why a company whose assets are subject to a floating charge can deal with them entirely free of the charge prior to crystallization.[38] On this view the chargee's right is not inchoate. It does not 'float' in the sense of failing to affect any particular assets until some future event. The chargee gets a limited immediate proprietary interest in the specific assets covered by the charge at any point in time, but this is subordinated to the ability of the chargor to deal with the assets in the ordinary course of business prior to crystallization, and to overreach those rights. On Nolan's view, too, fixed and floating charges are

Commercial Transactions (1996) 74–7) and her article ('An Unsatisfactory Area of the Law—Fixed and Floating Charges Yet Again' (2004) 1 International Corporate Rescue 175) in which she puts forward the third alternative theoretical view of floating charges, discussed in the text below.

36 S Worthington, 'Floating Charges—An Alternative Theory' [1994] CLJ 81; S Worthington, *Proprietary Interests in Commercial Transactions* (1996) ch 4.

37 R Nolan, 'Property in a Fund' (2004) 120 LQR 108.

38 ibid 129. Nolan argues that defeasance brings an interest to an end and cannot therefore explain why the chargee, whose rights in an asset have been defeated by sale or exchange, then has prima facie equivalent rights to any substitute of that asset. Overreaching, he suggests, can explain this situation. In addition, until defeated a defeasible interest is perfectly valid and capable of taking its full effect, whereas a floating charge prior to crystallization cannot be described in these terms.

broadly the same: 'the floating charge evolved out of the subtle manipulation of the fixed charge'.[39]

While these views, particularly those of Nolan, contain a certain theoretical appeal, they face a major hurdle in that they do not reflect the approach to floating charges which has been adopted by the courts to date. The views put forward by Worthington and Nolan have yet to be considered by the courts. This is true even after the House of Lords' decision in *Spectrum*. Lord Walker makes reference to Worthington's work, with approval,[40] but does not refer to the content of her arguments and does not seek to analyse them in any way. He does not refer to Nolan's views at all. The fact that he adopts Goode's analysis of the chargee holding a proprietary interest in 'a *fund* of circulating capital'[41] strongly suggests that he rejects the view advanced by Worthington and Nolan, but this is implied rather than express. However, the courts *have* previously considered and rejected the idea that a floating charge is a fixed charge combined with a licence from the creditor to the debtor to continue to deal with the assets.[42] Despite attempts by Worthington and Nolan to distinguish the concept of a floating charge as a fixed charge with a licence to deal from their views[43] it is difficult to appreciate any significant difference. In addition, the approach of the courts appears consistent with the view that no proprietary interest in specific assets exists prior to crystallization: 'A floating security is not a specific mortgage of the assets, plus a licence to the mortgagor to dispose of them in the course of his business, but is a floating mortgage applying to every item comprised in the security, but not specifically affecting any item until some act or event occurs or some act on the part of the mortgagee is done which causes it to crystallise into a fixed security.'[44] This approach has received modern confirmation, both by the Court of Appeal in *Re Cosslett (Contractors) Ltd*[45] and, now, by the House of Lords in *Spectrum*.[46]

---

[39] ibid 129. On this point see also R Calnan, 'Floating Charges: A Proposal for Reform' (2004) 9 Butterworths Journal of International Banking and Financial Law 341.

[40] [2005] UKHL 41, [2005] 2 AC 680, para 139. [41] ibid.

[42] *Evans v Rival Granite Quarries Ltd* [1910] 2 KB 979, 999, CA, per Buckley LJ; *Re Benjamin Cope & Sons Ltd* [1914] 1 Ch 800, 806, CA, per Sargant J; *Re Cimex Tissues Ltd* [1995] 1 BCLC 409; *Re Cosslett (Contractors) Ltd* [1998] Ch 495, 509–10, CA, per Millett LJ; *Agnew v IRC* [2001] 2 AC 710, cf *Davey and Co v Williamson* [1898] 2 QB 194, 200, per Lord Russell CJ.

[43] See S Worthington, *Proprietary Interests in Commercial Transactions* (1996) 81.

[44] *Evans v Rival Granite Quarries Ltd* [1910] 2 KB 979, 999, CA, per Buckley LJ. And see, for example, *Illingworth v Houldsworth* [1904] AC 355, HL: 'a floating charge . . . is ambulatory and shifting in its nature, hovering over and so to speak floating with the property which it is intended to affect until some event occurs or some act is done which causes it to settle and fasten on the subject of the charge within its reach and grasp' (358, per Lord Macnaghten).

[45] [1998] Ch 495, CA (510, per Millett LJ): 'The essence of a floating charge is that it is a charge, not on any particular asset, but on a fluctuating body of assets which remain under the management and control of the chargor . . .'.

[46] [2005] UKHL 41, [2005] 2 AC 680, para 139.

The courts' approach can be summarized by saying that on crystallization the charge, which previously floated over all the assets within its scope, attaches to the assets within its scope owned by the chargor at the moment of crystallization. Of course, much depends on what the courts imagine is taking place during this process. On Goode's view the proprietary interest of the chargee in the fund becomes a limited interest in the specific assets in the fund at the time of crystallization. For Nolan, the chargee's proprietary interest in the specific assets in the fund at any given time which had been subordinated to the chargor's ability to deal with the assets becomes an interest in specific assets, free of the chargor's interest.

It is also important to analyse what actually happens at the moment of 'attachment'. Even a fixed charge does not attach to any specific asset until (a) there is a valid charge agreement, (b) the asset is identifiable, (c) the debtor has an interest or rights in the asset, and (d) the debtor owes an obligation to the creditor which the charge secures.[47] Not all of these events necessarily take place at the same time: there may be an agreement, identification and rights in the debtor without value being given. However, once value is given, the charge becomes enforceable (between the parties) and 'relates back' to the time of the agreement.[48] Fixed charges can, of course, cover after-acquired property. However, because of requirement (c), attachment in relation to each asset takes place when that asset is acquired. Again, the enforceable charge in relation to that piece of collateral is said to 'relate back' to the time of the agreement.[49] For the purposes of priority disputes in many, though not all, situations this reasoning also applies to a floating charge. When the charge crystallizes, the attachment can be said to relate back to the date of the creation of the charge as with a fixed charge.[50] Priority disputes are decided on the basis of a *nemo dat* (first in time) rule, with the usual exceptions: priority of legal purchaser without notice, and dispositions which were actually or apparently authorized by the chargee. The decisions on priority between a floating charge and other charges are based on the question of whether the second charge was within the scope of the chargor's authority.[51]

[47] R Goode, *Legal Problems of Credit and Security* (3rd edn, 2003) 2–03.

[48] ibid paras 2–08, 2–11, citing *Rayner v Preston* (1881) 18 Ch D 1, 13, CA, per James LJ (dissenting), *Shaw v Foster* (1872) LR 322, HL; *Lysaght v Edwards* (1876) 2 Ch D 499.

[49] Goode (n 47 above) 2–13; E Ferran, *Company Law and Corporate Finance* (1999) 499; P Ali, *The Law of Secured Finance* (2002) 80; *Re Lind* [1915] 2 Ch 345, CA.

[50] *Bank of NS v Mustang Machinery Ltd* (1980) 35 CBR (NS) 287, Alta QB.

[51] *Re Benjamin Cope & Sons Ltd* [1914] 1 Ch 800, CA; *Re Automatic Bottle Makers Ltd* [1926] Ch 412; *Household Products Co v Federal Business Development Bank* (1981) 124 DLR (3d) 325, Ont SC; *Acmetrack Ltd v Bank Canadian National* (1984) 12 DLR (4th) 428, Ont SC CA. The only case not to follow this reasoning is *Griffith v Yorkshire Bank plc* [1994] 1 WLR 1426 which suggests that priority is determined at the date of crystallization. Similarly, the priority position between a floating charge and a subsequent fixed charge is determined by whether the subsequent charge was within the apparent authority of the chargor: *Wheatley v Silkstone and Haugh Moor*

While purchasers from a chargor will normally take free of the charge because they are purchasing the legal interest without notice of the charge, it is clear that where a disposition is outside the scope of apparent (as well as actual) authority, the purchaser takes subject to the charge.[52] The time of attachment is only of significance in situations where a third party acquires an interest in the charged asset through the operation of the general law, rather than a voluntary disposition by the chargor.[53] It is possible to explain the results on the basis of a wide concept of apparent authority, so that while the chargor is permitted to trade, it must also be permitted to incur the ordinary incidents of trade, which include execution by creditors and set-off by debtors.[54] This explanation is necessary if floating charges are to be described as fixed charges with a licence to deal, but it does not represent the reasoning in a majority of the judgments.

The concepts of attachment and authority are therefore not identical. Attachment fastens the charge to specific, identifiable assets and is a necessary precondition for enforcement of a charge. Authority merely allows someone else to deal with particular assets. Although the concept of immediate attachment coupled with authority to dispose explains much of the law on floating charges, the courts have on many occasions relied on the model of attachment on crystallization. Accordingly, although the concept of a fixed charge with a licence to deal is technically possible, and indeed has been employed in other jurisdictions, it does not accord with the courts' view of a floating charge at the present time. It is Goode's view of the chargee holding a proprietary interest in a fund

Coal Co (1885) 29 Ch D 715; *Cox Moore v Peruvian Corporation Ltd* [1908] 1 Ch 604; *English & Scottish Mercantile Investment Co v Brunton* [1892] 2 QB 700, CA. It is also possible to explain the decisions on contractual liens which bind floating chargees on the basis that the contract was entered into with actual or apparent authority: *George Barker (Transport) Ltd v Eynon* [1974] 1 WLR 462, CA; *Re Diesels & Components Pty Ltd* (1985) 9 ACLR 825, QSC; *Channel Airways Ltd v The Lord Mayor, Aldermen and Citizens of the City of Manchester* [1974] 1 Lloyd's Rep 456.

[52] *Hamilton v Hunter* (1982) 7 ACLR 295, NSWSC, where there was actual notice of the charge. Since the sale is, *ex hypothesi*, outside the ordinary course of business, the purchaser would be expected to search the register, and would therefore not be a purchaser of the legal interest without notice since registration is notice to those expected to search the register.

[53] Creditors who complete execution before attachment gain priority: *Evans v Rival Granite Quarries Ltd* [1910] 2 KB 979, CA. Debtors can set off cross-claims against charged receivables if the cross-claim arises before attachment (and notice to the debtor of attachment): *Biggerstaff v Rowatt's Wharf Ltd* [1896] 2 Ch 93, CA; *Edward Nelson & Co Ltd v Faber & Co* [1903] 2 KB 367; *NW Robbie & Co Ltd v Witney Warehouse Co Ltd* [1963] 1 WLR 1324, CA; *Business Computers Ltd v Anglo-African Leasing Ltd* [1977] 1 WLR 578. Distress for rates can be levied before attachment, but not after *Re ELS Ltd* [1995] Ch 11.

[54] R Nolan, 'Property in a Fund' (2004) 120 LQR 108, 126, and see dicta in *Evans v Rival Granite Quarries Ltd* [1910] 2 KB 979, 987, CA, per Vaughan Williams LJ, also *Robinson v Burnell's Vienna Bakery Company* [1904] 2 KB 624; *Heaton and Dugard Ltd v Cutting Brothers Ltd* [1925] 1 KB 655, 658, cf *Davey & Co v Williamson & Sons Ltd* [1898] 2 QB 194, 200. It is hard to explain *Re ELS Ltd* [1995] Ch 11 on this basis.

(as opposed to the components of the fund from time to time) prior to crystallization which seems closest to the approach of the courts,[55] and indeed, as discussed, this was the approach adopted by Lord Walker in *Spectrum*.[56]

Whether fixed and floating charges are inherently different creatures, or whether floating charges are effectively fixed charges which have been modified by the parties, has important consequences. The first relates to decrystallization. While crystallization[57] involves the extinguishment of the chargor's right to deal with the assets subject to the floating charge so that the floating charge becomes a fixed charge,[58] fastening on all assets in which the company then has or subsequently acquires an interest, decrystallization reinstates the previous security interest of the chargee and allows the chargor once again to deal with the assets.[59]

Crystallization of a floating charge does not lead to the creation of a new charge and hence does not trigger the registration requirements of s 395 of the Companies Act 1985, and there is no danger of the crystallized charge being called into question under s 245 of the Insolvency Act 1986 in the absence of new value. On Goode's analysis this is because the crystallized charge is no more than the original floating charge which has now attached to the assets, ie the floating charge has merely realized its potential by ceasing to float over the assets.[60] On the licence to deal analysis, all that happens on crystallization is that the chargor's licence to deal is revoked. As discussed, this is an issue of authority rather than attachment, and therefore there can be no question of

[55] *Illingworth v Houldsworth* [1904] AC 355, HL and see more recently *Re Cimex Tissues Ltd* [1995] 1 BCLC 409, 420–1, per Stanley Burnton QC who seems to have accepted Goode's views.

[56] [2005] UKHL 41, [2005] 2 AC 680, para 139.

[57] Which may come about as a result of the occurrence of events specified by the parties in the charge agreement ('automatic crystallization') as well as by the appointment of a receiver, the cessation of the business of the company or liquidation.

[58] Once crystallized a chargor can no longer deal with the assets as he would if they were subject to the uncrystallized floating charge. The charge attaches to the assets. This is a fixed charge, despite s 251 of the Insolvency Act 1986, which deems a floating charge to include a 'charge which as created was a floating charge' and which requires the crystallized charge to be treated as a floating charge for the purposes of certain provisions of the Act, ie it is a fixed charge which is treated as a floating charge for some purposes. As a result, therefore, crystallization of a charge before a winding-up or other event attracting the rights of the preferential creditors does not prevent the charge being subordinated to the preferential debts: Insolvency Act 1986, ss 40, 175.

[59] This will only be possible where the chargor has remained in control of the chargor company's business, which would clearly not be the case where the company is in receivership or liquidation.

[60] CH Tan, 'Automatic Crystallization, De-crystallization and Convertibility of Charges' [1998] Company Financial and Insolvency Law Review 41, 49. Goode has argued that the reason why no new charge is created is because the security interest remains unchanged (see 'Charges over Book Debts: A Missed Opportunity' (1994) 110 LQR 592, 604) but he bases his argument in part on the view that security is an indivisible and continuous security moving from original collateral to proceeds, a view which has been doubted by the Privy Council: *Agnew v IRC* [2001] UKPC 28, [2001] 2 AC 710, para 43, per Lord Millett.

any new charge being created at this point—the same charge continues throughout.

The courts have yet to determine whether decrystallization involves the creation of a new charge or not. This is obviously significant. A new floating charge will require registration and will concede priority to existing floating charges.[61] The new floating charge may also be in danger of being invalidated by s 245 of the Insolvency Act 1986 if the company goes into winding up within 12 months of the creation of the floating charge.[62] In addition, the ring-fencing provisions within the Enterprise Act 2002 apply to floating charges created after 15 September 2003, so a new floating charge may be subject to these provisions, whereas an old one might not.[63] Goode has argued that decrystallization does not involve the creation of a new charge, but simply removes the restriction on the chargor's dealing power so that the same charge is refloated.[64] On this analysis the effect of decrystallization is simply that the fixed charge no longer attaches to specific assets but instead detaches in order to allow the charge once again to be characterized as floating: if a floating charge can be converted into a fixed charge, then why not the reverse?[65] This has been doubted by other commentators who suggest that the parties can only restore the rights and interests which existed during the floating phase by creating a new floating charge.[66] Indeed, it is difficult to square Goode's assertion with his own view of the chargee holding a proprietary interest in a fund of assets which then attaches to specific assets on crystallization. Once the charge has attached to specific assets it is difficult to see how that decrystallization can occur without the creation of a new charge.[67] Oddly, Goode's view of decrystallization sits more

[61] *Re Benjamin Cope & Sons Ltd* [1914] 1 Ch 800, CA (which states that priority is determined at the date of creation), cf *Griffith v Yorkshire Bank plc* [1994] 1 WLR 1426 (which suggests that priority is determined at the date of crystallization). On the registration point see A Berg, 'The Cuckoo in the Nest of Corporate Insolvency: Some Aspects of the *Spectrum* Case' [2006] JBL 22, 42.

[62] Twelve months if the charge holder is unconnected, two years if the charge holder is connected to the company: Insolvency Act 1986, s 245.

[63] Insolvency Act 1986, s 176A.

[64] R Goode, 'Charges over Book Debts: A Missed Opportunity' (1994) 110 LQR 592, 604. See also WJ Gough, *Company Charges* (2nd edn, 1996) 407.

[65] For example, LC Chiaw, 'The Crystallization of Floating Charges, Subordination Agreements and Priority Conflicts' [1986] LMCLQ 519, 528; R Goode, *Legal Problems of Credit and Security* (3rd edn, 2003) 150–1.

[66] R Grantham, 'Refloating a Floating Charge' [1997] Company Financial and Insolvency Law Review 53; CH Tan, 'Automatic Crystallization, De-crystallization and Convertibility of Charges' [1998] Company Financial and Insolvency Law Review 41, 49. Post-contractual conduct short of agreement may also have this effect, see S Atherton and R Mokal, 'Charges over Chattels: Issues in the Fixed/Floating Jurisprudence' (2005) 26 Company Lawyer 10, 16–18.

[67] It is possible that the courts would find unappealing the suggestion that a person who holds a fixed charge and then gives a licence to deal still holds the fixed charge, at least so far as the charge is subsequently asserted against a third party such as a purchaser.

comfortably with the view of a floating charge as a fixed charge with a licence to deal. On this view, no 'attachment' occurs at crystallization, instead crystallization means that the chargor's licence to deal with the property has been revoked. Decrystallization merely reinstates the licence to deal which was afforded to the chargor during the original floating phase. On this view the licence can be turned on and off and on again, and although this affects the authority of the chargor to deal with the assets, it does not affect the proprietary interests in the specific assets which fall within the charge at any given time, since these subsist in the chargee throughout. Therefore nothing new is created following decrystallization, the original charge merely continues. No registration is required, no loss of priority occurs, no s 245 vulnerability arises and there is no danger of the ring-fencing provisions applying.

One potential consequence of this line of reasoning is that if the parties create a fixed charge by the charge agreement but at a later date decrystallize that charge without creating a new floating charge, once decrystallization has taken place the lender would be able to obtain all the benefits of a floating charge while not bearing the burden of loss of priority to preferential and unsecured creditors, since it could be argued that the charge is not a floating charge 'as created', within the definition in s 251.[68]

Of course it can be argued that s 251 is aimed at a different situation, namely the crystallization of a floating charge, and that the legislature did not contemplate the possibility of a fixed charge being subsequently converted into a floating charge when this provision was drafted. If they had done so it is possible that the drafting may have been amended to include reference both to a charge which is floating at its inception and one which becomes converted into one subsequently.[69] Nevertheless the fact remains that the present drafting of s 251 does not appear to cover the situation in which a fixed charge is subsequently converted into a floating charge. Of course, we do not mean to suggest that this analysis could be used by parties deliberately to evade the statutory provisions. If the parties provide for a decrystallizing event to occur without the genuine control of the chargee ('automatic' decrystallization) or if the parties contemplate *ex ante* that the chargee will permit decrystallization ('semi-automatic' decrystallization) and that the chargor will then be free to deal with the collateral for the remainder of the life of the security, then at the outset the proper characterization of the single security interest thereby created would be floating and would therefore fall within s 251.

[68] The decrystallization process would, of course, have to be a genuine one. If the parties set out with this structure in mind, it is possible that the courts would re-characterize the original charge as floating on the grounds that the agreement was a sham.

[69] This glitch highlights one of the difficulties of adopting such unstable statutory triggers, which we discuss later in this chapter.

The conceptualization of fixed and floating charges as inherently the same, or different, items of property also has consequences for the process of characterization. If these are entirely distinct categories, then the role of the courts in characterizing a charge as fixed or floating is easier to appreciate. This can be seen in another common characterization scenario, namely the courts' determination of whether an agreement between the parties amounts to a lease or a licence over land.[70] The orthodox view accepts that these are entirely different items of property.[71] A licence is merely a personal contractual arrangement between the parties without any property incidents attached. It creates purely *in personam* rights. By contrast a lease creates *in rem* rights and, additionally, statutory protection for the tenant under the Rent Acts flows from the categorization of the agreement as a lease. According to the House of Lords it is not possible for the parties to turn a tenancy into a licence (or vice versa) merely by saying that is what they intended to do: 'The manufacture of a five-pronged implement for manual digging results in a fork even if the manufacturer, unfamiliar with the English language, insists that he intended to make and has made a spade.'[72] By contrast, if floating charges are merely fixed charges which have been modified by the agreement of the parties, it is less easy to accept that the courts and not the parties should determine the characterization of the charge.

C. The Process of Characterization

Characterization is the process of deciding whether a particular interest created by a contract falls within a particular definition, or deciding whether the contract itself falls within a definition. This definition may be in another contract[73] or in a statute[74] or even part of the common law.[75] In each case, there are two

[70] This was recognized by Lord Walker in *Spectrum*, para 141.

[71] cf *Bruton v London and Quadrant Housing Trust* [2000] 1 AC 406, HL.

[72] *Street v Mountford* [1985] AC 809, 819, HL, per Lord Templeman. cf the earlier approach of the courts, for example *Somma v Hazelhurst* [1978] 1 WLR 1014, CA in which the court accepted the label put on the agreement by the parties, irrespective of the fact that the underlying nature of the agreement pointed to the opposite result.

[73] For example, whether a transaction amounts to 'security' and thereby is in breach of a negative pledge clause.

[74] For example, whether an agreement creates a tenancy within the Rent Acts, whether a charge is a floating charge within the various sections of the Insolvency Act referred to above, whether a transaction creates a charge which is registrable within Companies Act 1985, s 395, whether a contract is a contract of employment so that a party is an employee within Employment Rights Act 1996, s 94 (the right not to be unfairly dismissed).

[75] So that it is necessary to characterize an agreement as a contract of service as opposed to a contract for services if the employer is to be vicariously liable for the torts of the employee (*Cassidy v Minister of Health* [1951] 2 KB 343, CA).

exercises in interpretation: the parties' contract must be interpreted to decide what interest or type of contract is created, but the definition must also be interpreted so that it is known what interest or type of contract is required to fall within the definition. The interpretation of a definition in a contract must be done in accordance with the normal rules of interpretation, that is, the purpose of the exercise is to discover the intentions of the parties, and can therefore vary from contract to contract. However, when the definition is statutory, the courts, while taking into account the intentions of the legislature, must develop a stable definition which can be applied consistently to all cases. It is also desirable (though not always the case)[76] for this stable definition to be used whenever the concept is referred to in a statute. The most straightforward way to achieve this is for the statute to refer to a concept which is already well established in the common law, and as to the definition of which there is substantial agreement.

However, once a concept has been used to trigger certain consequences in a statute, this may have the effect that those drafting agreements attempt to avoid creating such an interest or type of contract in order to avoid the statutory consequences.[77] Thus the courts do not only have to decide whether an interest or type of contract, which by mistake or accident does not fall neatly within a definition, falls within that definition, but they also have to perform the same exercise in relation to interests or types of contract deliberately created to have the same advantages to the parties as those falling within the definition, but which are deliberately designed to fall outside it. It is this factor which often makes the process of characterization by the courts a difficult and controversial one. It also raises the question as to whether parties should be allowed to create whatever interests or types of contract they want, even if this has the effect of defeating the policy aims of the relevant statute. One solution is for the legislature constantly to amend the definition in the statute to include the (new) interests or types of contract.[78] Another solution is for the courts to maintain the boundaries of the stable definition, and, if parties try to create interests or types of contracts which fall just outside those boundaries, to characterize those interests or types of contracts as falling inside the definition. It should, however,

---

[76] For example, the meaning of 'employee' in different contexts: E McKendrick, 'Vicarious Liability and Independent Contractors—A Re-examination' (1990) 53 MLR 770, 782–3.

[77] In relation to fixed and floating charges, it has been particularly easy to attempt to create a fixed charge over as many assets as possible: see remarks of Park J in *Re ASRS Establishment Ltd* [2000] 1 BCLC 727: 'As long as the creditor takes care so to word the debenture that, if it fails to create a fixed charge over an asset of the debtor, it succeeds in creating a floating charge . . . there is nothing to be lost by stating that a charge is to be a fixed charge'. A clumsy attempt by a draftsman to take this belt and braces approach was criticized by Etherton J in *Ashborder BV v Green Gas Power Ltd* [2004] EWHC 1517, [2005] BCC 634, para 189.

[78] This tends to be the approach in the field of tax legislation.

be pointed out that there are also statutory definitions which the courts have to apply which are not susceptible to this problem: these are definitions of things which are created by people other than the parties to the litigation. They can be either tangible things, such as goods,[79] or intangible, such as debts owed by third parties.[80]

If the statutory definition is kept stable, then the courts' exercise in interpretation must be directed at the parties' contract. However, as Lord Millett pointed out in *Agnew v IRC* the process is not merely one of construction of the contract:

> In deciding whether a charge is a fixed charge or a floating charge, the court is engaged in a two-stage process. At the first stage it must construe the instrument of charge and seek to gather the intentions of the parties from the language they have used. But the object at this stage of the process is not to discover whether the parties intended to create a fixed or a floating charge. It is to ascertain the nature of the rights and obligations which the parties intended to grant each other in respect of the charged assets. Once these have been ascertained, the court can then embark on the second stage of the process, which is one of categorisation. This is a matter of law. It does not depend on the intention of the parties. If their intention, properly gathered from the language of the instrument, is to grant the company rights in respect of the charged assets which are inconsistent with the nature of a fixed charge, then the charge cannot be a fixed charge however they may have chosen to describe it.[81]

By carrying out the process of characterization in this way, the courts are able to retain the stable definition of the relevant interest or type of contract, while still allowing the parties the freedom to create whatever rights and obligations between themselves that they wish. The stable definition comprises a particular bundle of rights and obligations, and if the parties have created this bundle the interest or type of contract will fall within the definition, even if the parties call that bundle of rights and obligations by another name. Thus, a charge is a floating charge if the chargor is free to deal with the assets charged, and the chargee does not exercise the degree of control over the assets that is required for a fixed charge. However, the nature of the concepts of the fixed and floating charge are such that full stability of definition is not possible. Since the required amount of control for a fixed charge is a matter of degree, there is inherent uncertainty as to whether the requirement has been satisfied. Although the

[79] For example, whether a conveyance falls within the definition of motor vehicle in the Road Traffic Act 1988, s 185.

[80] For example, whether a debt is a book debt: Companies Act 1985, s 396.

[81] [2001] UKPC 28, [2001] 2 AC 710, para 32. It should be noted that this is a description of what Staughton LJ calls 'the internal route' in *Welsh Development Agency v Export Finance Co Ltd* [1992] BCLC 148, CA. The 'external route' asks whether the document represents the agreement between the parties: if it is not, it is a sham.

House of Lords in the *Spectrum* case has provided some guidance in relation to charges over book debts,[82] uncertainties still remain. The effect of the actual operation of the account is not clear: this is discussed below. It also remains uncertain exactly what amounts to a blocked account (although it is clear that the account in the *Spectrum* case is not one). It is not clear whether a scheme such as that operated in *Re Keenan Bros Ltd*[83] whereby the proceeds were paid into a blocked account, but transferred periodically into a current account from which the chargor could draw, would be effective.[84] It has been suggested that the rigours of *Spectrum* may be mitigated if the proceeds are paid into a partially blocked account, ie an account in which the purposes for which the proceeds may be used are limited[85] or in which a monetary limit is placed on the amount which may be withdrawn from the charge account,[86] but the validity of these methods also remains unclear after the *Spectrum* decision. Further, there remain uncertainties concerning the characterization of charges over income-producing contracts[87] and those which permit the substitution of collateral.[88] Such drafting uncertainties are likely to remain while it is necessary to characterize charges as either fixed or floating.[89]

Three general issues are particularly problematic in relation to the characterization process. The first is the extent to which the nomenclature used by the parties, both in naming the interest or type of contract they are purporting to create, and in naming the various rights and obligations that they are creating, is relevant to the process of characterization. The second is the relevance of other related contracts between the parties, or with others. The third is the relevance of post-contractual conduct.

---

82 Lord Hope, para 54, sets out four ways to create a fixed charge: (1) to prevent all dealings with the book debts, (2) to prevent all dealings with the book debts other than their collection, and to require the proceeds to be paid to the chargee in reduction of the underlying obligation, (3) to prevent all dealings with the debts other than their collection and to require the proceeds to be paid into a blocked account with the chargee bank, (4) to prevent all dealings with the debts other than their collection and to require the proceeds to be paid into a separate account with a third party bank.

83 [1986] BCLC 242, Ire SC.

84 Lord Phillips MR in the Court of Appeal in *Spectrum* says that it is 'beyond dispute' that such a scheme creates a fixed charge, but Lord Walker in the House of Lords says that it 'may not provide a simple solution in every case' ([2005] UKHL 41, [2005] 2 AC 680, para 160). See A Berg, 'The Cuckoo in the Nest of Corporate Insolvency: Some Aspects of the *Spectrum* Case' [2006] JBL 22, 44–46.

85 P Wood, 'Fixed and Floating Charges' [2001] CLJ 472, 473.

86 *ABN Amro Bank NV v Chiyu Banking Corp Ltd* [2000] 3 HKC 381, HK Court of First Instance.

87 R Lowe and S Beale: 'The *Spectrum* Decision: Bad News for Banks' (2005) 20 JIBLR 482, 487, K Baird and P Sidle '*Spectrum Plus*: House of Lords Decision—A Cloud with a Silver Lining?' (2005) 18 Insolvency Intelligence 113, 117.

88 Baird and Sidle (n 87 above) 117.

89 C Hare, 'Charges over Book Debts: The End of an Era' [2005] LMCLQ 440, 445.

1. Nomenclature

One possibility is that the court entirely ignores the nomenclature used by the parties. However, since the contract is to be construed as a whole, this is inconsistent with normal canons of construction. Another possibility is that the court starts with the presumption that the parties intended to create the interest or type of contract that they state, and consider whether there is anything in the contract inconsistent with this intention.[90] This approach has been expressly rejected by the Privy Council and the House of Lords.[91] A more realistic approach is that the nomenclature used provides some evidence as to the parties' intention as to the existence or nature of a right or obligation, especially where the contract is silent on this point.[92] However, where there is other evidence of the parties' intentions (for example, the nature of the assets, the other provisions of the agreement or other related agreements)[93] this should be at least as probative as the parties' labels. When there is a specific provision creating a particular right or obligation, this should be interpreted according to the natural meaning of the words rather than in a way consistent with the label put on the transaction by the parties.[94] Use of these techniques means that the court can characterize a transaction as something other than the way it is described by the parties, without deeming it a sham or finding that the parties were dishonest.[95]

---

[90] This appears to have been the approach of Slade J in *Siebe Gorman & Co Ltd v Barclays Bank Ltd* [1979] 2 Lloyd's Rep 142, of the Court of Appeal in *Re New Bullas Trading Ltd* [1994] 1 BCLC 485, CA. See also, rather bewilderingly, Millett LJ in *Orion Finance Ltd v Crown Financial Management Ltd* [1996] 2 BCLC 78, 84, CA: 'The legal classification of a transaction is not, therefore, approached by the court in vacuo. The question is not what the transaction is but whether it is in truth what it purports to be. Unless the documents taken as a whole compel a different conclusion, the transaction which they embody should be categorised in conformity with the intention which the parties have expressed in them.'

[91] In *Agnew v IRC* [2001] UKPC 28, [2001] 2 AC 710, paras 31 and 32. See also *Smith v Bridgend CBC* [2001] UKHL 58, [2002] 1 AC 336, para 42; *Re Spectrum Plus Ltd* [2005] 2 AC 680, para 119, per Lord Scott and para 141, per Lord Walker.

[92] S Atherton and R Mokal, 'Charges over Chattels: Issues in the Fixed/Floating Jurisprudence' (2005) 26 Company Lawyer 10–18; *Arthur D Little Ltd v Ableco Finance LLC* [2002] EWHC 701, [2003] Ch 217, para 31.

[93] [2005] UKHL 41, [2005] 2 AC 680, para 158, per Lord Walker.

[94] For example, in *Re ASRS Establishment Ltd* [2000] 2 BCLC 631 the court was asked to interpret a clause whereby the company covenanted not 'to sell, part with possession or lease or otherwise dispose of the whole or, except in the ordinary course of (and for the purposes of) carrying on its trading business as now carried on, any other part of the Charged Property'. It was held that sale in the ordinary course of business was permitted, where the only possible source of prohibition was the label of the charge as 'fixed', since this was said to be begging the question. In *Ashborder BV v Green Gas Power Ltd* [2004] EWHC 1517, [2005] BCC 634 Etherton J refused to construe a clause permitting disposals of assets in the ordinary course of business as limited only to assets comprised in the expressly created floating charge, when the only reason for so limiting it was the express creation of a fixed charge over certain assets.

[95] See Part C, Section 3 below.

2. Related contracts

A written contract is not interpreted by merely looking at the words of that contract. The courts can have regard to the 'matrix of facts' against which the contract was entered into.[96] It is now clear from the judgments of the House of Lords in *Spectrum* that the terms of related contracts, such as the contract between the bank lender and the company customer governing the bank account into which the charged debts were to be paid are relevant to the characterization of the charge.[97] Indeed, Lord Walker, while urging lenders to include in their debenture all that is relevant for characterization, acknowledged that in some cases all the documentation[98] and the commercial context would have to be taken into account.[99] While this seems correct as a matter of law, it does throw more doubt on the stability and predictability of the statutory definition, if it depends upon the terms of several different contracts and other commercial considerations. This is particularly true if the parties attempt to set up complex accounting structures to avoid the operation of the House of Lords' ruling in *Spectrum.* Lord Phillips in the Court of Appeal in *Spectrum* said that '[p]riorities in the event of insolvency should not turn upon the technical skill with which the bank accounting arrangements have been set up'.[100]

3. Post-contractual conduct[101]

As a general rule, the conduct of the parties after the contract is made is disregarded when a court is interpreting the contract.[102] However, Lord Millett in *Agnew* said that 'their Lordships would wish to make it clear that it is not enough [to create a fixed charge] to provide in the debenture that the account is a blocked account if it is not operated as one in fact'.[103] To what extent does this

96 *Investors Compensation Scheme Ltd v West Bromwich Building Society* [1998] 1 WLR 896, 912–13, HL.

97 [2005] UKHL 41, [2005] 2 AC 680, paras 56–61, per Lord Hope; paras 116–119, per Lord Scott; paras 153 and 156–161, per Lord Walker.

98 Commonly the debenture creating the charge, the bank's facility letter offering a term loan or an overdraft and the bank's general terms and conditions.

99 [2005] UKHL 41, [2005] 2 AC 680, para 158.

100 [2004] EWCA Civ 670, [2004] Ch 337, para 99.

101 See, generally, S Atherton and R Mokal, 'Charges over Chattels: Issues in the Fixed/Floating Jurisprudence' (2005) 26 Company Lawyer 10 and A Berg, 'The Cuckoo in the Nest of Corporate Insolvency: Some Aspects of the *Spectrum* Case' [2006] JBL 22, 33–44.

102 *James Miller & Partners Ltd v Whitworth Street Estates (Manchester) Ltd* [1970] AC 583, 603, 611, 614, HL; *L Schuler AG v Wickman Machine Tool Sales Ltd* [1974] AC 235, 252, 260, 261, 265–8, 272–3, HL. Despite the general move away from strict rules of interpretation of contracts (*Investors Compensation Scheme Ltd v West Bromwich Building Society* [1998] 1 WLR 896, 912–13, HL), this particular rule is still observed and considered valid: *Dunlop Tyres Ltd v Blows* [2001] EWCA Civ 1032 [2001] IRLR 629, paras 21–22.

103 [2001] UKPC 28, [2001] 2 AC 710, para 48.

represent an exception to the subsequent conduct rule? It has been suggested that his Lordship's dictum related to the characterization of the interest created, rather than the interpretation of the contract.[104] However, in the context of fixed and floating charges, characterization is inextricably bound up with the interpretation of the contract and of the rights and obligations created thereby. A more likely explanation is that Lord Millett was referring to the situation where the contract is a 'sham' or 'pretence'.[105] A sham is where both parties collude to produce a document which does not represent their true intentions, a pretence is where one party has that intention and the other assents through ignorance or force of circumstances.[106] Subsequent conduct is admissible when the court is considering whether an agreement is a sham or pretence.[107] If the parties set out rights and obligations in the charge document which they had no intention of carrying out, or only carrying out sporadically, which intentions were demonstrated by their conduct subsequent to the contract, then this could potentially be a sham.[108] However, it is generally agreed that a sham involves dishonesty, which the court will be slow to find[109] and a transaction that is entered into in a particular way so as to avoid the effects of a statute is not for that reason alone a sham.[110] In the absence of special facts, it is unlikely that a court will make a finding of dishonesty in relation to parties who enter into

[104] G McMeel, 'Prior Negotiations and Subsequent Conduct—The Next Step Forward For Contractual Interpretation' (2003) 119 LQR 272, 292.

[105] Atherton and Mokal (n 101 above); N Briggs, 'Sham Transactions' (2003) 1 Insolvency Lawyer 27.

[106] The distinction between the two has been called into question, Berg (n 101 above) 40 citing *Minwalla v Minwalla* [2005] Family Law 357.

[107] *A G Securities v Vaughan* [1990] 1 AC 417, HL, 466, per Lord Oliver; 475, per Lord Jauncey.

[108] cf cautionary dictum by Diplock LJ in *Garnac Grain Co Inc v HMF Faure & Fairclough Ltd* [1966] 1 QB 650, 683, CA: 'the contemplation or expectation or intention (unless incorporated in the contract) of the parties or either of them as to the way in which it will be performed or left unperformed does not affect their legal rights or obligations under it. To affect these it is necessary to go further and to show that the parties really made some other and different contract between them and agreed that the ostensible contract should not give rise to legally enforceable rights or liabilities'.

[109] *Snook v London and West Riding Investments Ltd* [1967] 2 QB 786, 802, CA, per Diplock LJ; *National Westminster Bank v Jones* [2001] 1 BCLC 98, paras 40, 46. cf *Midland Bank v Wyatt* [1995] 1 FLR 696, 698; cf Lord Templeman, 'Form and Substance', ch 7, 130–4 and B McFarlane and E Simpson, 'Tackling Avoidance' both in J Getzler (ed), *Rationalizing Property, Equity and Trusts: Essays in Honour of Edward Burn* (2003) ch 8, 135–86.

[110] *Belvedere Court Management Ltd v Frogmore Developments Ltd* [1997] QB 858, 876, CA; *Re George Inglefield* [1933] Ch 1, 22, CA, per Lord Hanworth MR: 'There is nothing improper or wrong in obtaining money in this way any more than there is in going to your banker and obtaining money upon documents. There are, no doubt, provisions, such as that in s 79, which require a charge to be registered, but if you enter into a transaction outside these provisions which require registration as a condition of validity, you are unaffected by the law. It is not a question of evasion. A transaction is either within or without the law, and malice is not to be attributed to a person who so carries out a transaction that it remains outside the law.'

debentures based on standard form documents, even if the parties did not give a great deal of thought as to how they were actually going to carry out the precise terms of the agreement in practice. The House of Lords in *Spectrum* did not specifically consider the possibility of a charge document being a sham, although Lord Walker said that Lord Millett's dictum in *Agnew*, that a formal provision for a blocked account is not enough if it is not operated as one in fact, 'may raise difficult questions as to what Staughton LJ . . . referred to as "external" and "internal" routes to the construction of commercial documents'.[111] The result of a transaction being a sham will vary. The transaction as expressed in the agreement will be of no effect, but it may be that the parties will be held to have made a different agreement and created a different interest. This will generally mean that a 'sham' fixed charge will take effect as a floating one.[112]

Another possible analysis is that the subsequent conduct shows that there was no permanent appropriation of the assets and so was no fixed charge.[113] While this has its attractions, as it results in effective re-characterization without the need to allege a sham or pretence and therefore prove dishonesty, it appears to be inconsistent with the doctrine that subsequent conduct is not admissible in construing a contract except to show that it or its terms are a sham or pretence. Either the parties did not intend to appropriate the assets, in which case any terms requiring this are a sham or pretence, or they did, in which case their subsequent conduct is probably a variation or waiver.

Thus the fact that the parties subsequently depart from their agreement does not necessarily mean that they did not intend the agreement to be effective:[114] they may have intended to vary the agreement, or the conduct may operate as a waiver or estoppel.[115] This analysis, however, means that the subsequent conduct is not relevant to the interpretation or characterization of the original agreement, which is therefore characterized according to its terms. Let us consider the position where a fixed chargee allows a chargor to draw money from the 'blocked' bank account into which it has paid the proceeds of the debts. If the permission is expressly given by the chargee each time there is a

[111] [2005] UKHL 41, [2005] 2 AC 680, para 160. Staughton LJ's remarks are to be found in *Welsh Development Agency v Export Finance Co Ltd* [1992] BCLC 148, 186–7, CA. The external route leads to the finding of a sham, the internal route is that described at n 81 above and associated text.

[112] This will, of course, require to be registered, but since a fixed charge over book debts is required to be registered anyway there is unlikely to be a problem.

[113] A Berg, 'The Cuckoo in the Nest of Corporate Insolvency: Some Aspects of the *Spectrum* Case' [2006] JBL 22, 31.

[114] *Hitch v Stone* [2001] EWCA Civ 1224, [2001] STC 214, CA, para 68, per Arden LJ.

[115] S Atherton and R Mokal, 'Charges over Chattels: Issues in the Fixed/Floating Jurisprudence' (2005) 26 Company Lawyer 10, 16.

withdrawal, this is entirely consistent with the charge being fixed, since the chargee is exercising the necessary degree of control. If, as is more likely, permission is given in advance for a number of withdrawals, however, this could be seen as a variation of the agreement to one where the chargor has freedom to use the charged assets, which has the effect of either creating a new floating charge or decrystallizing the existing fixed one.[116] Another possible argument is that the original fixed charge has been released, and the assets fall within the 'catch-all' floating charge in the original debenture. While an agreement providing for this in advance will now be held to be a floating charge,[117] this analysis could still apply to a variation. If there is not the degree of agreement to constitute a variation,[118] but the chargee has represented to the chargor that he will not exercise control, the chargee could become estopped from asserting its right of control,[119] which again has the effect of either creating a new charge or decrystallizing the existing one. Where there is no representation, but mere failure to exert control, this conduct could amount to a waiver. This is not the same as a chargee waiving a breach to prevent crystallization,[120] as here the charge is already, *ex hypothesi*, fixed. The effect of the waiver here is a matter of degree: the waiver of one breach would not be inconsistent with the continuance of a fixed charge, but if there are a number of similar waivers, this could have the effect of creating an estoppel.

If the effect of the subsequent conduct is to create a new floating charge, in terms of distribution to preferential creditors and ring-fencing for unsecured creditors there will be little difference from the conclusion that the original agreement created a floating charge: in both cases the charge was floating 'as created'. However, the creation of a new charge may cause other problems: it may not have been registered[121] and the time of creation may affect priorities.[122] A more worrying conclusion is that the original fixed charge has decrystallized. This would result in the parties being able to obtain the benefits of the chargor's

[116] This is discussed in Part B above.

[117] *Agnew v IRC* [2001] UKPC 28, [2001] 2 AC 710; *Re Spectrum Plus* [2005] UKHL 41, [2005] 2 AC 680.

[118] A variation requires 'analysis in terms of offer, acceptance and certainty of terms': *Flacker Shipping Ltd (The 'Happy Day') v Glencore Grain Ltd* [2002] EWCA Civ 1068, [2002] 2 Lloyd's Rep 487, para 61.

[119] For a detailed description of this process see Atherton and Mokal (n 115 above) 17.

[120] *Campbell v Michael Mount PPB* (1995) 16 ACSR 296, SASC.

[121] R Grantham, 'Refloating a Fixed Charge' [1997] Company Financial and Insolvency Law Review 53, 64–6 takes the view that registration is probably required for a decrystallized charge, even though it merely reinstates the fixed charge that was originally there. Here the nature of the charge has changed, and so the argument for registration is stronger. Registration would not be required if the analysis was that the fixed charge had been released and the assets fell within a floating charge created by the charge agreement, providing that the floating charge was duly registered in the first place, cf Berg (n 113 above) 42.

[122] See cases cited in n 12.

freedom to draw from the proceeds, while the chargee obtains the priority benefits of the charge being fixed 'as created'.[123] If this is the correct conclusion, it demonstrates that there is a serious problem with the stability of the statutory definition.

The process of characterization is necessarily a difficult one, particularly where there are inconsistencies between the labels given by the parties to the transaction or other related contracts or the subsequent conduct of the parties and the rights and obligations created by the transaction. These problems often arise in situations where parties are likely to suffer deleterious statutory consequences if they create a particular type of interest or contract. Parties will naturally try to avoid creating this type of interest or contract, while attempting to achieve the desired commercial consequences of the transaction, and will explore all ways of achieving this. The situation is exacerbated where only one party has an interest in avoiding the statutory consequences. This is the case where a lender wishes to create a fixed charge to avoid losing priority to preferential creditors and the ring-fencing fund, yet the chargor has little interest in avoiding these statutory consequences, but a great deal of interest in the rights and obligations created which affect the charge in the pre-enforcement stage. Two issues arise from this discussion. First, should the parties be able to create whatever interests they wish, or is the court justified in characterizing the transaction in accordance with a court-determined definition of the statutory concept? Secondly, given the difficulties identified, there is a strong argument for using the most stable concepts possible as statutory triggers for priority consequences which adversely affect holders of security interests; maybe even concepts which do not depend upon the contract created by the interested parties.[124] These issues will be addressed below.

D. Justifications for the Process of Characterization

It is undoubtedly the case that the courts possess the power to characterize a charge as fixed or floating, and yet the very fact that the courts possess this power undermines commercial certainty both for the parties to the agreement, for third parties who subsequent deal with the assets underlying the charge, and for other creditors of the company if the company becomes insolvent. The justification for the courts' intervention therefore requires some thought.

As discussed in Part A of this chapter, the courts may need to characterize a

[123] This is discussed above at text to n 68. This is the conclusion drawn in Berg (n 113 above) 42.

[124] See text to nn 79 and 80 above.

charge as fixed or floating for a number of reasons. These may be divided into issues arising pre-insolvency and those arising post-insolvency. In the first category there are, broadly, two reasons why it may be necessary to decide whether a charge is fixed or floating: to determine the rights of the parties *inter se* and to determine the rights of third parties pre-insolvency. Following the insolvency of the company there are a cluster of issues which presently hinge on the determination of whether the charge is fixed or floating: was the charge correctly registered;[125] do the claims of other groups of creditors rank in priority to the claim of the charge holder; can an administrator make use of the assets subject to the charge[126] and is the charge subordinated to the costs and expenses of an administrator; is the charge subject to challenge under s 245 of the Insolvency Act 1986? One other possible question arises: can the charge holder appoint an administrator under the fast track procedure set out in the Insolvency Act following the introduction of the Enterprise Act 2002? The holders of floating charges or other security comprising a significant part of the company's property have the right to petition for an administration order without giving notice in some circumstances.[127] However, this distinction is not felt to be an important one, perhaps because most fixed chargees are also floating chargees and so will have the right to appoint an administrator one way or another, or perhaps because this distinction in no way affects the potential recovery of the chargee, unlike the other four fixed/floating distinctions which arise post-insolvency, or perhaps because this right confers no particular benefit on the appointor, since the administrator owes a duty of care to all creditors unlike the right to appoint an administrative receiver which is valuable because the receiver primarily acts for the appointor.

1. Pre-insolvency

(a) Rights as between the parties inter se

Whether or not the chargor is in breach of contract, for dealings with the secured assets for instance, will depend substantially on whether the assets are secured by way of a fixed or floating charge. Characterization can, therefore, affect the rights of the parties *inter se* as well as the rights of third parties. One possible reason why the courts may decide to set aside the freedom of contract of the parties in order to impose the courts' own decisions as to the proper categorization of the parties' legal relationship is in order to ensure that legal relationships are always

[125] For example, *Smith v Bridgend CBC* [2001] UKHL 58, [2001] 1 AC 336. The major significance of failure to register is felt on insolvency, although there are some consequences which arise outside the insolvency context, for example Companies Act 1985, ss 395(2), 399.

[126] *Re Atlantic Computer Systems plc* [1992] Ch 505, CA.

[127] Insolvency Act 1986, Sch B1.

properly categorized, that a 'five-pronged implement for manual digging'[128] is always categorized as a fork and never as a spade. The quest for the courts is, on this view, to determine the 'true' nature of the agreement between the parties. Of course, whether this is possible at all in relation to charges will depend to a large extent on whether fixed and floating charges are inherently different creatures or whether floating charges are effectively fixed charges which have been modified by the parties.[129] It may be questioned why it is important for the courts to be able to determine the 'true' nature of the parties' relationship if the parties are clear between themselves on the nature of their legal arrangement. This question is particularly relevant in relation to charges where the process of characterization arises following a deliberate attempt by the parties to classify one type of interest as another, rather than through any mistake on their part.[130] The justification in the lease/licence cases is that the courts wish to prevent the parties contracting out of the Rent Acts, the purpose of which is to bestow protection on tenants over and above that bestowed on licensees.[131] It has been suggested that the protective attitude of the court in this context can be justified because of the inequality of bargaining power between the parties.[132] By contrast the protective legislation in place in the context of fixed and floating charges aims to protect third parties rather than the parties themselves. In *Spectrum* Lord Walker refers to the parallel between the courts' role in characterizing leases and licences, and fixed and floating charges and says:

> In each case there is a public interest which overrides unrestrained freedom of contract. On the lease/licence issue, the public interest is in the protection of vulnerable people seeking living accommodation. On the fixed/floating issue, it is ensuring that preferential creditors obtain the measure of protection which Parliament intended them to have.[133]

No protective legislation exists to protect the parties contracting to create a charge, and to the extent that inequality of bargaining power is a concern, this is

[128] *Street v Mountford* [1985] AC 809, 819, HL, per Lord Templeman.

[129] This is discussed in Part B of this chapter.

[130] This is discussed in Part C of this chapter.

[131] Although this was explicitly disclaimed by Lord Templeman in *Street v Mountford* [1985] AC 809, HL, cf Lord Templeman's later statements in *Antoniades v Villiers* [1990] 1 AC 417, 463, HL ('The facts must prevail over the language in order that the parties may not contract out of the Rent Acts').

[132] J Hill, 'Intention and the Creation of Proprietary Rights: Are Leases Different?' (1996) 16 LS 200. In *Street v Mountford* the statement in the agreement between the parties that the occupier was a licensee rather than a tenant was not motivated by a desire to ensure the occupier's interest would not be binding on any subsequent purchaser of the land; it was an attempt to avoid the statutory controls contained in the Rent Acts and designed to protect the occupier.

[133] [2005] UKHL 41, [2005] 2 AC 680, para 141. Lord Walker goes on to state that this public interest is unaffected by the changes in the classes of preferential creditors made by the Enterprise Act 2002, s 251. This is discussed further at Section 2(b) below.

left to protectionist measures that are already in force, implemented either by the legislature[134] or by the common law. Parties to a contract do not have unlimited freedom to agree any terms they choose. In particular, the courts will not enforce contracts involving the infringement of the criminal or civil law or terms which are otherwise contrary to public policy or morals. Penalty clauses are likewise unenforceable to the extent that they provide the claimant with more than the amount of his loss.[135] Further, mortgagees and chargees cannot impose 'clogs' on the right to redeem. Subject to these issues, freedom of contract can be the guiding principle when determining the rights between the parties.[136] The fixed/floating question has no impact on the relations of the parties *inter se*.

(b) Rights vis-à-vis third parties

For third parties, it is relevant whether a charge is fixed or floating because this affects the status and validity of subsequent actions dealing with the charged property. A floating chargor has authority to create any subsequent charge, fixed or floating, ranking in priority to that floating charge, unless it is a floating charge over the same assets as the first charge.[137] The floating chargor also has a freedom to trade prior to crystallization so that dispositions to purchasers in the ordinary course of business will generally be effective.[138]

However, although the fixed/floating distinction is an important one in this context, the real issue of importance is not whether the charge *as created* was fixed or floating, but by reference to the question of whether the charge is fixed or floating at some subsequent point in time, such as when an execution creditor seeks to assert priority over particular assets. However, this latter issue is not generally resolved by reference to characterization, but whether crystallization has occurred. Well-drafted automatic crystallization clauses will ensure that the

[134] For example, Unfair Contract Terms Act 1977.

[135] GH Treitel, *The Law of Contract* (11th edn, 2003) ch 11; H Beale (ed), *Chitty on Contracts* (29th edn, 2004) ch 17.

[136] The courts may need to act to re-characterize a contract which is just internally inconsistent (for example, a mortgage where no right to redeem exists) in order to make sense of the relationship of the parties *inter se* (for example, whether the relationship is one of mortgage or sale).

[137] *Re Benjamin Cope & Sons Ltd* [1914] 1 Ch 800, CA. A second floating charge over part of those assets can rank in priority to the original floating charge if the power to create such a charge is reserved in the earlier charge: *Re Automatic Bottle Makers Ltd* [1926] Ch 412. Goode's view is that in each case it is a question of interpreting the first charge: R Goode, *Legal Problems of Credit and Security* (3rd edn, 2003) para 5–42. A subsequent fixed charge will take priority unless the original clause contains a negative pledge clause of which the subsequent chargee has actual notice: *English & Scottish Mercantile Investment Co Ltd v Brunton* [1892] 2 QB 700, CA. Notice of the negative pledge clause and not just of the charge is needed.

[138] Although the chargor has no freedom to deal with the assets subject to the fixed charge, nevertheless third parties who are bona fide purchasers for value without notice will take free of the chargee's proprietary interest.

claims of subsequent third parties, such as execution creditors, trigger the crystallization of the charge and ensure that vis-à-vis these pre-insolvency third parties the charge will always be fixed.[139] Accordingly the cases in this area tend to focus on the effectiveness of automatic crystallization clauses rather than on the issue of characterization.

It can be seen, therefore, that characterization has little or no role to play in these pre-insolvency issues.

2. Post-insolvency

However, characterization does have an important role to play after insolvency occurs. Four issues are discussed here. The first two, namely whether the charge is void for lack of registration and whether the charge can be set aside under s 245 of the Insolvency Act 1986, are issues going to the vulnerability of the charge. Floating charges, as we shall see, are more vulnerable than fixed charges. The next two issues deal with the question of priority. Various groups, namely preferential creditors, unsecured creditors and administrators, get a certain level of priority over assets subject to a floating charge, but not over assets subject to a fixed charge. These issues will be considered in turn.

(a) Registration

All floating charges need to be registered, whereas not all fixed charges do.[140] A charge which is registrable but unregistered will be void as against a liquidator or administrator and any creditor[141] of the company and the sum secured by the charge will become immediately due and payable.[142] Although the fixed/floating distinction is important in this context, and does involve the courts having to characterize a charge,[143] the importance of this issue is relatively small due to the fact that very few interests are not registrable, and indeed it is likely that

[139] An interesting situation arises when floating charges over all or substantially all of a company's undertaking become fixed but the company remains solvent. Presumably if the chargee allows the company to continue to trade then decrystallization will occur. If it does not, then the company must cease trading.

[140] Companies Act 1985, s 396, for example fixed charges over shares, negotiable instruments. The major significance of failure to register is felt on insolvency, although there are some consequences which arise outside the insolvency context, for example Companies Act 1985, ss 395(2), 399.

[141] ie any secured creditor of the company where the company is not in liquidation or administration.

[142] Companies Act 1985, s 395. This latter effect applies not only on liquidation but also on the grant of a subsequent security by a solvent company: R Goode, *Commercial Law* (3rd edn, 2004) 667.

[143] For example, *Smith v Bridgend CBC* [2001] UKHL 58, [2001] 1 AC 336.

the importance will diminish further if the Law Commission's plans regarding the registration of security interests are introduced.[144]

(b) Claims in priority to the charge holder

Since 1897 legislation has given protection to certain groups in priority to the interests of floating charge holders, but the assets subject to a fixed charge have not been regarded as vulnerable to such claims. Two groups have been given this protection: preferential creditors[145] and, much more recently, unsecured creditors.[146] Prior to the Enterprise Act 2002, preferential creditors comprised two main groups, namely various taxes collected by the debtor on behalf of the Crown, including some PAYE deductions, unpaid VAT, unpaid car tax, unpaid social security contributions, and various other duties, and certain debts related to the insolvent's employees. The first of these categories has now had its preferential status removed,[147] the stated reason being that the removal of tax claim preferences will bring 'major benefits to trade and other unsecured creditors, including small businesses'.[148] As between the unsecured creditors and the Crown's claim to unpaid tax, the former's claim is now regarded as the stronger.[149] The other preferential class, namely the insolvent's employees, or those subrogated to them, is however retained.[150] Although the policy reasoning behind these legislative moves can be questioned[151] it is outside the scope of this chapter to enter this debate. Instead, it is accepted that for more than a century it has been government policy to prioritize the claims of some creditors above those of the floating charge holder, and this looks set to continue in the future.[152] More relevant, for this chapter, is the question of which assets these

---

[144] Law Commission, *Company Security Interests* (Law Com No 296, Cmnd 6654, August 2005).

[145] Insolvency Act 1986, Sch 6. This is not a recent development: see, for example, Preferential Payments in Bankruptcy Amendment Act 1897, s 107.

[146] Insolvency Act 1986, s 176A. [147] Enterprise Act 2002, s 251.

[148] Insolvency Service, *Insolvency—A Second Chance* (Cm 3234, 2001); cf R Mokal, 'Priority as Pathology: The Pari Passu Myth' [2001] CLJ 581, 617.

[149] The criticism of preferential debts is not new, see, for example, R Goode, 'The Death of Insolvency Law' (1980) 1 Company Lawyer 123, 129.

[150] For further discussion of this point and a comparison with the position in Canada, see below, text to n 237.

[151] For example, as regards preferential creditors, see R Goode, 'The Death of Insolvency Law' (1980) 1 Company Lawyer 123, 129; R Mokal, 'Priority as Pathology: The Pari Passu Myth' [2001] CLJ 581; A Keay and P Walton, 'The Preferential Debts Regime in Liquidation Law: In the Public Interest?' (1999) 3 Company Financial and Insolvency Law Review 84.

[152] The Enterprise Act 2002 and the preceding White Paper (n 148 above) abolished one set of preferential creditors, but maintained the other and added unsecured creditors to the list of priority claims via the ring-fencing provisions. There was no suggestion that all priority claims to the floating charge holder should be abolished. We leave open the question of whether prioritization of this kind should occur for discussion by other contributors; see for example J Armour, 'Should We Redistribute in Insolvency?', ch 9 below.

groups should be given priority over. To date the answer has been the assets subject to a floating charge but not the assets subject to a fixed charge. There are two possible policy justifications for this approach.

The first arises from the fact that, unlike a fixed charge, it is possible to give a floating charge over all of the assets of the company. In the parliamentary debates regarding the 1897 legislation a very specific reason for the priority was given. It was stated that floating charges were typically taken over raw materials and wholly or partly manufactured goods, both of which benefited from the efforts of the workforce, so that it would be unfair for their claims not to be given priority when their labours had added value to the floating charge. By contrast mortgages of land and buildings were typically fixed and did not derive added value from the work of the employees.[153] However, a more general argument can also be made. As Lord Millett has commented, one of the consequences of the floating charge is that 'it enable[s] the holder of the charge to withdraw all or most of the assets of an insolvent company from the scope of a liquidation and leave the liquidator with little more than an empty shell and unable to pay preferential creditors'.[154] The same argument can be made in relation to unsecured creditors. It should be noted however that the strength of this justification as a basis for distinguishing between fixed and floating charges can vary over time, and much will depend upon the definition of floating charges. In *Re New Bullas Trading*,[155] for example, the Court of Appeal decided that a debt and its proceeds are separate assets and therefore that the debtor's ability to use the proceeds did not affect the nature of the charge over the debts. On this view it is possible for a company to give a fixed charge over present and future book debts and yet for the company to continue to use the proceeds for the purpose of carrying on its business. Since this makes it possible effectively to take a fixed charge over much of the company's undertaking, these arguments regarding the dangers of charges being so wide as to remove the protection of lower-ranking creditors would apply equally to fixed charges. While the Privy Council in *Agnew*[156] agreed with the premise in *Bullas*, that a debt and its proceeds are separate assets, their Lordships disagreed with the conclusion reached in that case. In *Agnew* it was stated that control of the proceeds is necessary for a fixed charge to exist, a view endorsed by the House of Lords in *Spectrum*. A fixed charge over present and future debts would prevent the use of proceeds by the debtor. Since debtors generally need the proceeds to carry out

153 For discussion, see R Goode, *Principles of Corporate Insolvency Law* (2nd edn, 2005) 208–9.

154 *Agnew v IRC* [2001] UKPC 28, [2001] 2 AC 710, 718.

155 [1994] BCC 36, CA.

156 [2001] UKPC 28, [2001] 2 AC 710.

their business, the circumstances in which a creditor will obtain a charge over the debtor's present and future book debts is likely to be very limited. On this view a distinction between fixed and floating charges based on the potential breadth of the assets covered by the charge remains a valid distinction. The original priority given to preferential creditors was in 1897, when the concept of a floating charge came from that of a (fixed) charge which covered the whole undertaking: as this would paralyse the company, it had to be characterized as a floating charge (including freedom to deal) and so the core concept of a floating charge was one that covered the whole undertaking. Accordingly the preferential creditors needed to be given priority, otherwise they would get very little on insolvency.[157]

The second policy justification is based on the fact that taking a floating charge over all of the assets of a company allows a company to continue to trade in a way which would be impossible if a fixed charge had been taken. The very nature of a floating charge allows a company to continue to trade and incur credit despite the existence of the charge.[158] Ordinary creditors of the company are therefore potentially put at risk for the holder of the charge could step in at any time without warning and obtain priority over them.[159] Unsecured creditors have, until recently, been particularly at risk. Prior to the Enterprise Act 2002 on insolvency both fixed and floating charges ranked ahead of the unsecured creditors, and in the vast majority of insolvencies the unsecured creditors get nothing, the average recovery for unsecured creditors being just 5 per cent.[160] However, blame has fallen on the floating charge in particular for the injustice of this situation. This is in part due to the scope of the floating charge, which effectively scoops all of the assets of the company not covered by the fixed charges, leaving nothing for the unsecured creditors.[161] In addition, however, it has been regarded as a great injustice by various judges that trade creditors could supply goods to a company which a charge holder could then

[157] Mokal argues that the priority given to preferential creditors means that the floating chargee therefore gets very little in theory, although this is generally unproblematic in practice as they are usually covered by fixed charges: R Mokal, *Corporate Insolvency Law* (2005) 190–4.

[158] Of course if unsecured creditors are aware that firms tend to grant floating charges, then it can be questioned whether they are particularly at risk. For discussion, see H Bennett, 'Late Floating Charges' in J Armour and H Bennett (eds), *Vulnerable Transactions in Corporate Insolvency* (2003).

[159] *Evans v Rival Granite Quarries Ltd* [1910] 2 KB 979, CA.

[160] Association of Business Recovery Professional Survey of Business Recovery in the UK, 12th survey (2004). The study carried out by J Franks and O Sussmann suggests even lower levels: *The Cycle of Corporate Distress, Rescue and Dissolution: A Study of Small and Medium Size UK Companies*, Institute of Finance and Accounting (London Business School) Working Paper 306–2000.

[161] Mokal has argued that the main reason for this is not the breadth of the floating charge, but the fact that most of the assets go to pay the fixed chargee (who is usually also the floating chargee) and the preferential creditors: R Mokal, 'Liquidation Expenses and Floating Charges—The Separate Funds Fallacy' [2004] LMCLQ 387, 397–9.

appropriate to the security and realize for its own benefit, leaving the suppliers unpaid.[162]

Until the Enterprise Act 2002, the solution adopted in the United Kingdom in relation to unsecured creditors was not priority but publicity, ie that all floating charges should be registered so that at least the unsecured creditors could discover their existence before providing credit to the company.[163] However, '[s]o far as the ordinary trade creditors were concerned . . . the remedy provided by registration was more theoretical than real'[164] and this was even more clearly the case for involuntary creditors such as tort victims.[165] The Enterprise Act 2002 recognized the need for further protection for unsecured creditors not only by removing the tax claim preference but also by providing that a proportion of the assets subject to the floating charge should be made available for the claims of unsecured creditors.[166] Maintaining the fixed/floating divide is therefore now important to the unsecured creditors in a way it was not prior to the passing of the Enterprise Act: '[f]reedom of contract does not enable the parties to agree to label chalk as cheese, at any rate in such a way as to affect the rights of third parties such as unsecured creditors'.[167]

Therefore one of the justifications for characterization of charges by the courts is to support the redistributive function of the insolvency legislation, initially as regards preferential creditors but increasingly to support the position of the unsecured creditors.[168]

(c) The ability of administrators to dispose of assets

An administrator can dispose of assets subject to a floating charge without the leave of the court.[169] For property subject to a fixed charge leave of the court is

---

162 For example, *Re General South American Co* (1876) 2 ChD 227, 341, per Malins V-C; *Salomon v Salomon & Co Ltd* [1897] AC 22, 53, HL, per Lord MacNaghten; *Re London Pressed Hinge Co Ltd* [1905] 1 Ch 576, 581, 583, per Buckley J.

163 Companies Act 1985, s 396.

164 *Agnew v IRC* [2001] UKPC 28, [2001] 2 AC 710, 718–19, per Lord Millett.

165 For example, LM LoPucki, 'The Unsecured Creditor's Bargain' (1994) 80 Virginia Law Review 1887; V Finch, 'Security, Insolvency and Risk: Who Pays the Price?' (1999) 62 MLR 633; cf R Mokal, 'The Search for Someone to Save: A Defensive Case for the Priority of Secured Credit' (2002) 22 OJLS 687.

166 Insolvency Act 1986, s 176A. For details of the prescribed proportion see Insolvency Act 1986 (Prescribed Part) Order 2003, SI 2003/2097, art 3. The Enterprise Act 2002 also abolishes administrative receivership which was regarded as unfair to the unsecured creditors: White Paper (n 148 above) para 2.2.

167 F Oditah, 'Fixed Charges and the Recycling of Proceeds of Receivables' (2004) 120 LQR 533, 538.

168 This was recognized by Lord Walker in *Spectrum*: [2005] UKHL 41, [2005] 2 AC 680, para 141.

169 Insolvency Act 1986, Sch B1, para 70. This is subject to the chargee's priority being transferred to the proceeds acquired from the disposition of the charged property.

required.[170] This distinction between fixed and floating charges is therefore important. It does involve the court in issues of characterization.[171] The ability of administrators to dispose of floating charge assets in this way was introduced in the Insolvency Act 1986 and was not substantially altered by the Enterprise Act 2002, but its significance was increased by that Act because administration will now be the primary rescue procedure for insolvent companies.[172] The effect of this right is that a creditor will retain a floating charge, for example over the proceeds of book debts, but the administrator can make use of these funds to continue to run the business.[173] The administrator may well trade at a loss in which event the value of the floating charge assets will diminish rapidly. In addition, the expenses incurred by the administrator in carrying out his role also have priority over the floating charge holder's claims.[174]

Administrators are deemed to act as agents of the company in exercising their powers. They are not personally liable on contracts they enter into nor on employment contracts which they adopt. Instead they stand 'in the company's shoes'. Under the Enterprise Act 2002, the administrator must carry out his functions with the objective of (a) resuming the company as a going concern; or (b) achieving a better result for the company's creditors as a whole than would be likely if the company were wound up; or (c) realizing property in order to make a distribution to one or more secured or preferential creditors.[175] However, the administrator may perform his functions to achieve objective (c) only if he thinks that it is not reasonably practicable to achieve either of the first two objectives and he does not unnecessarily harm the interests of creditors or the company as a whole.[176] Subject to that qualification, the administrator must perform his functions in the interests of the company's creditors as a whole.[177] Administration is a collective procedure.

---

[170] Another important distinction is that where property subject to a floating charge is disposed of under these provisions, the holder of the security has the same priority with regard to the proceeds as he would have had in respect of the property itself whereas in the case of fixed charges the proceeds shall first be applied to discharging the sums secured by the fixed charge.

[171] For example, *Re Atlantic Computer Systems plc* [1992] Ch 505, CA.

[172] The House of Lords in *Buchler v Talbot* [2004] UKHL 9, [2004] 2 AC 298 confirmed that a liquidator does not have an equivalent right. Clause 868 of the Company Law Reform Bill (as initially published), which inserts a new s 174A into the Insolvency Act 1986, is intended to reverse this decision so that where necessary assets subject to a floating charge will be available to fund the general expenses of a liquidation.

[173] Insolvency Act 1986, Sch B1, para 70 and a 'floating charge' means a charge which is a floating charge on its creation: Sch B1, para 111.

[174] Insolvency Act 1986, Sch B1, paras 70 and 99.

[175] Enterprise Act 2002, s 248, inserting s 8(1) of the Insolvency Act 1986, which incorporates Sch B1, paras 10–21.

[176] Insolvency Act 1986, Sch B1, para 3(1).

[177] Insolvency Act 1986, Sch B1, para 3(2).

One argument put forward to explain why administrators are entitled to make use of floating charge assets but not fixed charge assets revolves around the question of property. The administrator is entitled to use the property of the company in order to carry out his function of protecting the interests of the company and the general body of creditors. If the floating charge assets are regarded as the property of the company then this would be a good reason for the administrator to be able to access these funds.[178] However, the decision of the House of Lords in *Buchler v Talbot*[179] casts doubt on this analysis. This case involved the question of whether liquidation expenses can be paid out of the assets subject to a floating charge. Their Lordships decided that they could not. To the extent that this case dealt with liquidation expenses rather than any issue arising out of administration, it could be argued that it is not strictly relevant. However, the statements of their Lordships in that case regarding the nature of floating charge assets are of wider application. In *Buchler* their Lordships stated that where property is charged, whether by way of a fixed or a floating charge, it belongs to the charge holder to the extent of the amount secured and it is only the equity of redemption that remains the property of the chargor and falls within the scope of the liquidation. The effect of this decision is to cast doubt on the view that an administrator can make use of floating charge assets because those assets are the assets of the company. An alternative, and preferable, explanation for the administrator's ability to access these funds is that, although the floating charge holder has a proprietary interest in these assets, nevertheless the interests of that person can be subordinated to the interests of others for policy reasons. We have already seen that the interest of the floating charge holder is subordinated to the interests of preferential creditors and, now, to unsecured creditors through the ring-fencing provision, for policy reasons. It is arguable that the ability of an administrator to use floating charge assets to carry on the company's business, and to pay his expenses, is another example of the priority-independent nature[180] of the floating charge. The policy reasons for this further subordination of the floating charge holder's position need to be considered.

Administration was part of the package of measures introduced in 1986 in order to promote the rescue culture encouraged by the proposals of the Cork Committee. The rescue culture has been further promoted by the Enterprise Act 2002. Administration is conceived as a temporary measure which lays the

[178] Some support for this view can be found within the Enterprise Act 2002 which more or less consistently refers to the assets subject to a floating charge as 'property of the company'.

[179] [2004] UKHL 9, [2004] 2 AC 298. For discussion see R Mokal, 'Liquidation Expenses and Floating Charges—The Separate Funds Fallacy' [2004] LMCLQ 387; J Armour and A Walters, 'Funding Liquidation' (2006) 122 LQR 295.

[180] See Mokal (n 179 above) 403–4 who adopts this terminology.

foundations either for the rescue of the company through reorganization or, more commonly, for the more beneficial realization of the company's assets than in liquidation. This occurs either because the company is restored to a condition in which it can be sold off as a going concern or because the assets are dispersed on terms more advantageous than could be obtained by a liquidator. The purpose of administration is to maximize the assets of the company to the benefit of all creditors, not just the secured creditors of the company.[181]

The need for the administrator to make use of the floating charge assets in this process is a practical one. It is the function of the administrator to carry on the business of the company. As described above, companies generally need the proceeds of book debts to carry out their business. This is the reason why the decision of the Privy Council in *Agnew* means that a fixed charge over present and future book debts will be rare. In the same way, when the administrator wishes to carry on the company's business the proceeds of the book debts are likely to be crucial, unless the administrator is prepared to seek out external sources of funding which may be expensive and hard to find. The nature of the floating charge as presently defined[182] means that it is the floating charge assets which will often be needed by the administrator in order to continue the business of the debtor. Once the political decision is taken to promote a rescue culture, a method of providing working capital to enable administrators to continue to trade needs to be found. Although allowing administrators to use floating charge assets is not the only solution, it is the most obvious and convenient one. The floating charge assets are easy for the administrator to access and use, unlike the fixed charge assets. In addition it is these funds which were available to the company pre-insolvency. If the administrator is standing 'in the company's shoes' it does not seem unreasonable to allow the administrator the same access to assets as the company had pre-insolvency. The crystallization of any floating charges on the appointment of the administrator is effectively ignored.[183] The administrator does not have use of the floating charge assets because they are the property of the company. Rather, as in the pre-insolvency situation, the chargee retains property in the (fund of) assets and the administrator merely has the use of those assets in order to run the company. Often, when the company enters administration the book debts will be the *only* funds available for the purposes of financing continuing operations. Allowing administrators to use floating charge assets to pay their expenses is slightly easier

[181] The effect is to promote the interests of the unsecured creditors over the interests of the floating charge holder. This is another reason to regard floating charges as 'priority-independent'.

[182] *Agnew v IRC* [2001] UKPC 28, [2001] 2 AC 710; *Re Spectrum Plus Ltd* [2005] UKHL 41, [2005] 2 AC 680.

[183] Insolvency Act 1986, Sch B1, para 70 and a 'floating charge' means a charge which is a floating charge *on its creation* (Sch B1, para 111).

to justify. The House of Lords in *Buchler v Talbot*[184] distinguished between the property subject to a fixed or floating charge (the receivership assets) and the assets which are beneficially owned by the company (the free assets). Since the liquidator only has the latter at his or her disposal, the costs of the liquidation can only be defrayed out of those assets. Only the receiver's costs can be defrayed out of the charged assets. However, it seems clear from their Lordships' judgment that if there is no receiver and the liquidator has himself been engaged in preserving and/or realizing assets subject to a security then he is entitled to be remunerated and allowed his expenses out of the charged assets for this work. Part of the administrator's job is to preserve and/or realize the floating charge assets, albeit that the administrator will not in the normal course of events pay any dividends to the floating charge holder, and may indeed use these sums in order to carry on the business of the company. Nevertheless this factor can support the view that the administrator is entitled to be remunerated and allowed his expenses out of the floating charge assets, as the Enterprise Act 2002 clearly envisages.

(d) Section 245 of the Insolvency Act 1986

A floating charge created not for new value in the period prior to insolvency is subject to challenge, and may be set aside.[185] No equivalent provision exists for fixed charges, which can only be avoided if they involve a preference.[186] This distinction no doubt reflects once again the two policy justifications for the fixed/floating distinction addressed above, namely the all-embracing nature of a floating charge and the fact that the floating charge enables the company to continue to trade and to incur fresh debt. The Cork Committee gave as the reason for the special statutory treatment of floating charges the fact that it enabled the secured creditor to have his security reinforced by after-acquired property for which the debtor had not paid, at the expense of the unpaid sellers.[187]

However, the reason why s 245 exists in relation to floating charges but not fixed charges requires some thought. Although it is accurate to say that a fixed charge may not be taken over a company's entire undertaking,[188] where the company faces insolvency the obtaining of a fixed charge will, subject to the rules on

[184] [2004] UKHL 9, [2004] 2 AC 298

[185] Insolvency Act 1986, s 245. The period is two years prior to insolvency if the floating charge holder is a person connected to the company, and within 12 months of insolvency for any other person.

[186] Insolvency Act 1986, s 239.

[187] *Insolvency Law and Practice: Report of the Review Committee* (Cmnd 8558, 1982) para 1553.

[188] *Agnew v IRC* [2001] UKPC 28, [2001] 2 AC 710; *Re Spectrum Plus Ltd* [2005] UKHL 41, [2005] 2 AC 680; cf *Re New Bullas Trading Ltd* [1994] BCC 36, CA.

preferences, promote the position of the chargee ahead of most of the other creditors. If the purpose of s 245 is to prevent the conferment of an unfair advantage on an existing creditor at a time when liquidation is imminent, this ought to apply to fixed charges as well. If the suggestion is that the law on preferences offers adequate protection against this possibility, it is difficult to see why a further provision is required for floating charges.

The Cork Committee justified the restriction of s 245 to floating charges on the basis that a creditor with an ongoing business relationship with the company might prefer to take a charge rather than pursuing a demand for immediate payment, thus allowing the company to continue to trade. This is potentially beneficial to other creditors, to the employees, and possibly to the community at large. Any change in the law which enables a security, even for an existing debt, given at arm's length in the ordinary course of business and in response to normal commercial pressures, to be set aside merely because the bankruptcy or liquidation of the debtor occurred within a specified period thereafter, would, according to the Cork Committee, have unfortunate consequences. It would compel creditors to demand immediate payment of the debt rather than seeking a charge, and the failure of the company to result in circumstances in which it might have been averted.[189] However, this reasoning did not, in their view, extend to floating charges:

> The floating charge is an excessive security because, unlike a fixed charge, it extends to future assets not paid for by the company. It is one thing to permit a prudent creditor, fearing for the solvency of his debtor, to insist either upon payment of the debt due to him or a fixed charge upon existing assets of his debtor instead. This is 'priority gaining', but it is tolerable. It is quite another matter to permit a creditor, concerned for the solvency of his debtor, to take security which will allow the debtor to trade and acquire further assets on credit with which to swell the security at the expense of the unpaid vendors.[190]

This suggests that it is acceptable to prioritize floating charges to existing unpaid, unsecured vendors, but not to future unpaid vendors, when the registration system means that the second is actually in a better position than the first to discover the existence of the floating charge in the first place. It could also be argued that the grant of the floating charge permits the company to carry on trading, benefiting future vendors to the extent that they get paid before insolvency and that the accusation of expropriation is unjustified since the risk run by later vendors of losing priority to a floating charge discoverable by them is an acceptable commercial risk.[191] The other difficulty with highlighting the

[189] *Insolvency Law and Practice: Report of the Review Committee* (Cmnd 8558, 1982) para 1494.
[190] ibid para 1553.
[191] H Bennett, 'Late Floating Charges' in J Armour and H Bennett (eds), *Vulnerable Transactions in Corporate Insolvency* (2003) paras 5.5–5.10.

problem of later unpaid vendors in this way is that it does not necessarily justify a distinction between fixed and floating charges. Floating charges may be limited to existing assets, in which case the danger which s 245 seeks to prevent will not arise. Conversely a fixed charge on existing and future assets will presumably lead to the same danger, and yet does not fall within the scope of the section. The distinction between fixed and floating charges drawn in s 245 is therefore difficult to accept.

3. Summary

The justifications for the courts' involvement in characterizing fixed and floating charges arise post-insolvency, not pre-insolvency. At this point the fixed/floating divide is important for a variety of reasons, as discussed above. Two broad trends were identified: that floating charges are more vulnerable than fixed charges at present due to the registration system and the existence of s 245; and that floating charges are subordinated to the interests of preferential creditors, unsecured creditors, and administrators in a way that fixed charges are not. There is a unifying factor, however, namely a policy desire to protect the other creditors of the company. Given that desire two questions may then be asked. First, is the distinction between fixed and floating charges the correct statutory trigger for the various consequences we have considered? Calnan has argued that the distinction between fixed and floating charges should largely be removed.[192] In our view the theoretical divide between fixed and floating charges is unclear and unstable (see Part B above) and the process of categorization actually carried out by the courts is unclear and unsatisfactory (Part C above) and is not a satisfactory statutory trigger. Secondly, what should the statutory triggers for the various consequences be? It should be pointed out that it is not necessarily the case that the same trigger should be used for all four of the consequences we consider. The merits of statutory triggers should be considered taking into account both the policy reasons for the imposition of the particular consequences in question, and also the stability of the concepts proposed as triggers.

E. Possible Alternative Statutory Triggers

In considering possible alternative triggers, it is instructive to consider how other similar legal systems deal with this issue. This Part looks at three common

[192] R Calnan, 'Floating Charges: A Proposal for Reform' (2004) 9 Butterworths Journal of International Banking and Financial Law 341.

law systems, the United States, Canada, and New Zealand,[193] which are close enough to the United Kingdom to provide useful comparisons. It is important to note that the policy aims of each jurisdiction in employing a statutory trigger are not identical, although in general they all involve a balancing of interests between secured creditors, and other creditors which the legislature in that jurisdiction seeks to prefer. Despite these differences, it is nevertheless instructive to examine the different statutory triggers adopted in these jurisdictions and to judge their effectiveness against the background of the particular policy aim which it seeks to further.

The triggers considered in this Part fall into four categories. First, a preference can be given to certain creditors over a particular type of security interest. This really only occurs where preference is given over a floating charge, and occurs in the United Kingdom and in Australia. Secondly, the claims of preferential creditors can have basically the same status as any other security interest, although this can be varied by statute. This is the position of the federal tax lien in the United States and Canada, and was also the case in the early history of the deemed trust in Canada.[194] Thirdly, a claim by a preferential creditor can be given priority over all security interests. This is illustrated by the Crown's 'garnishment' right in Canada, the history of which illustrates the problem of using a potentially complex concept such as 'security interest' as a sole trigger.[195] Finally, a claim by a preferential creditor can be given priority over security interests over particular assets. This can either be drafted as a general priority with exceptions[196] or by defining the assets in question, as in the recent Canadian legislation concerning wage earners, and in the New Zealand legislation.[197]

1. United States

In the United States, claims for unpaid tax only have priority over secured

[193] Australia is the other obvious jurisdiction to examine in this regard. However, in Australia, Crown preference has been abolished although claims by employees still have priority over assets subject to a floating charge, Corporations Act 2001, ss 433 and 561, and also, in a receivership, claims under insurance policies and certain auditor's expenses: s 433. The only statutory trigger used is the fixed/floating charge distinction, and this has generated very little litigation in this context (one exception is *Whitton v ACN 003 266 886 Pty Ltd* (1996) 42 NSWLR 123, NSWSC which followed *Re New Bullas Trading Ltd* [2004] BCC 36, CA). On this basis there seems little to be gained from studying this jurisdiction on this issue.

[194] ie before 1998. This is discussed further at nn 224–230 and associated text below.

[195] This is discussed further at nn 216–223 and associated text below.

[196] See the present position in relation to the deemed trust in Canada, discussed at n 230 and associated text below.

[197] Discussed at nn 231–262 and associated text below. This trigger not only has the advantage of using stable concepts, but also enables a policy balancing the interests of secured and preferential creditors to be implemented.

creditors[198] if a federal tax lien[199] has arisen[200] and has been filed in the relevant registry.[201] Once filed, a tax lien has priority over security interests, except for:

(1) a security interest which, by the time the tax lien was filed, related to property owned by the debtor, related to advances already made and which had been perfected so that it was protected against a subsequent judgment creditor;[202]
(2) a security interest as in (1) above but which relates to advances made before the 46th day after the filing of the tax lien[203] unless the secured party had actual knowledge of the tax lien;
(3) a security interest as in (1) above arising out of a 'commercial financing transactions agreement', a real property construction or improvement financing agreement or an obligatory disbursement agreement but which relates to advances made before the 46th day after the filing of the tax lien and to property acquired within 45 days of the filing of the tax lien.[204]

Since the tax claim becomes a secured claim, and filing is required to gain priority, it is logical that the general priority rule (as is usual under Article 9 of the Uniform Commercial Code) is first to file, rather than being based on any particular characteristic of the security interest itself. However, unlike under the general Article 9 scheme, perfection of the relevant security interest does not give priority in relation to either future advances or after-acquired property. This particular 'trigger' was enacted to replace the previous law, where 'mortgagees' had statutory priority over unfilled tax liens, but only to the extent that the interest was 'choate', which meant that both the property covered and the debt secured had to be identifiable at the time of the filing of the tax lien.[205] It is strict, and, therefore, to meet the criticism that the balance had swung too far in favour of the Revenue, (2) and (3) above were introduced.[206] As a trigger

198 Certain tax claims also have priority in insolvency under United States Code, Title 11 § 507(8), which gives certain classes of creditors priority over the general body of unsecured creditors.

199 A lien in favour of the United States on all property belonging to the debtor: Internal Revenue Code § 6321.

200 This arises at the time a tax assessment is made: Internal Revenue Code § 6322.

201 ibid § 6323(f).

202 ibid § 6323(h)(1). At what point such an interest becomes protected is governed by the Uniform Commercial Code (revised) § 9–317(a), and with some exceptions, relates to time of perfection.

203 Internal Revenue Code § 6323(d).

204 ibid § 6323(c).

205 W Plumb, 'Legislative Revision of the Federal Tax Lien' (1967) 22 Business Lawyer 271. This meant that every time a lender made a further advance or new property which fell within the mortgage was acquired, the lender, to protect himself, had to search to see if any federal tax liens had been registered.

206 The policy aim was to provide a balance between the need for efficient financing, particularly revolving credit, and the need for the State to recover unpaid taxes.

it is complex, requiring much cross-referencing (particularly to Uniform Commercial Code (revised) Article 9),[207] but it is not conceptually difficult, since the chief criterion which determines the priority of the secured party is the 45-day time limit.[208]

2. Canada

Although Revenue Canada gave up most of its priority over creditors in bankruptcy in 1992,[209] some protection was retained for it in specific circumstances. The history of this, and of the recent Canadian attempts to secure priority for unpaid employees in bankruptcy, illustrate the problems that occur in trying to define the circumstances in which an unsecured preferential creditor will obtain priority over secured creditors. A number of cases have occurred in which the courts have favoured secured creditors in their interpretation of the statutes, followed then by a tightening up in favour of the Revenue, either by the legislature or the higher courts.[210] The problems that have been encountered demonstrate the need to use the least complex triggers possible, but also that the attitude of the courts is critical in the preservation of the policy aims furthered by the priority.

(a) Tax

First, the Crown may hold a security interest like any other person,[211] and may have a statutory lien which is registered, in which case priority is determined by first to file.[212] Secondly, the right of the Crown to tax deducted by employers from employees' wages is protected in two ways.[213] The Crown can obtain priority over a secured creditor in relation to sums due to the employer, but subject to the security interest, by serving the debtor with a notice requiring it

207 For example, to determine whether the security interest is protected against a judgment creditor, it is necessary to refer to Uniform Commercial Code (revised) § 9–317(a)(2), which gives such protection where a security interest is perfected before the judgment creditor's interest arises. To determine what is meant by perfection, it is necessary to look at the rules in Uniform Commercial Code (revised) §§ 9-308–9-316.

208 Although the third category referred to above does also refer to certain types of transactions and so potentially could give rise to characterization problems.

209 Bankruptcy and Insolvency Act 1985, s 86 (as amended in 1992). See J Ziegel, 'The Modernization of Canada's Bankruptcy Law in a Comparative Context' (1999) 4 Canadian Bankruptcy Reporter (4th) 151.

210 The process, and the resulting loss of certainty, is described in D Jackson and K Mandzuick, 'Who's on First? Recent Additions to the Motley, Straggling Line of Cases in which Her Majesty Endeavours to Jump the Priority Queue' (2004) 16 Commercial Insolvency Reporter 37.

211 Bankruptcy and Insolvency Act 1985, s 86(2).

212 Bankruptcy and Insolvency Act 1985, s 87(1).

213 This is a very important source of tax for the Revenue, as 85 per cent of income tax collected comes from this source, see *Pembina on the Red Development Corp v Triman Industries Ltd* (1991) 85 DLR (4th) 29, 51, Manitoba CA, per Lyon JA; R Wood and R Reeson, 'The Continuing Saga of the Statutory Deemed Trust: *Royal Bank v Tuxedo Transportation Ltd*' (2000) 15 Banking and Finance Law Review 515.

to pay the sums to the Receiver General ('garnishment').[214] The Crown has also, in relation to the deducted tax, a deemed trust, which has priority over security interests.[215]

Originally, the Crown's right was merely a right to require someone who was obliged to pay the tax debtor to pay the Receiver General instead. Clearly the receivables could not themselves represent the tax deducted, and so the provision was a collection device that would give the Revenue priority over other creditors. The courts consistently held that where the relevant receivables had been assigned, even by way of security, the assignee owned the debts and so the Crown had no claim,[216] thus the only priority obtained was over unsecured creditors. In order that the Revenue could obtain priority over secured creditors, the section was amended in 1987 to provide that the Crown could garnish funds owing to a tax debtor or to a 'secured creditor'. While some Canadian courts held that this was enough to give the Crown priority,[217] others held that, while it enabled the Crown to attach the relevant debts, it did not grant the Crown a property right or priority over the rights of a secured creditor.[218] A further section was added in 1990 providing that the Crown should have a property right in the relevant debts, and priority over the secured creditors. However, the difficulties still continued. The question of whether an absolute assignee of book debts was a 'secured creditor' under the Income Tax Act 1985, where the assignment was held to be by way of security, was decided in favour of the Revenue, but only by a majority of the Supreme Court of Canada,[219] with a strong minority judgment arguing that, although a general assignment of book debts could be a 'security interest' under the Act, the assignee could not be a secured creditor, since it was not a 'person who had a security interest in the property of another' and that clear words were required to expropriate the proprietary rights of third parties.[220]

---

214 Income Tax Act 1985, s 224 (as amended).

215 Most 'deemed trust' provisions are ineffective in bankruptcy (Bankruptcy and Insolvency Act 1985, s 67(2)), but the deemed trust that arises in respect of tax deducted from employees' wages (Income Tax Act 1985, s 227.4) survives (Bankruptcy and Insolvency Act 1985, s 67(3)).

216 *Royal Bank of Canada v R* (1984) 52 CBR (NS) 198, Fed Ct, aff'd (1986) 60 CBR (NS) 125, Fed CA.

217 *Royal Bank of Canada v Saskatchewan Power Corp* [1991] 1 WWR 1, Saskatchewan CA; *Touche Ross Ltd v MNR* (1990) 71 DLR (4th) 648, Nova Scotia court of first instance.

218 *Lloyds Bank of Canada v International Warranty Co* (1989) 68 Alta LR (2d) 356, Alberta CA, *Pembina on the Red Development Corp v Triman Industries Ltd* [1991] 6 WWR 481, 85 DLR (4th) 29, Manitoba CA; *Concorde International Travel Inc v TI Travel Services (BC) Inc* (1990) 72 DLR (4th) 405, British Columbia CA.

219 *Alberta (Treasury Branches) v MNR* [1996] 1 SCR 963, SC.

220 The minority suggested possible alternative formulations, such as that the definition section could have added to the phrase 'property of another person' the words 'or property that but for a security interest in favour of the secured creditor would be the property of another person', or that the definition could merely have read 'a person who has a security interest'.

There has also been a series of cases which deal with whether the interpretation of the definition of 'security interest' in s 224 of the Income Tax Act 1985[221] includes conditional sales, which are included as 'security interests' in the Personal Property Security Acts (PPSAs), which are now in force in most Canadian provinces. In each case it was held that the PPSA definition did not apply in the absence of express words, and that since the definition in s 224 did not expressly include conditional sales, they were not security interests within the meaning of the Act. It is clear that the draftsman of the definition could have made the position clearer by expressly including conditional sales in the definition. However, the first part of the definition almost exactly follows the definition in the PPSAs, which includes conditional sales,[222] and it could therefore be argued that the list is illustrative rather than comprehensive.[223] The result of the line of cases, however, is that at the moment the Revenue's protection is narrower than it could have been, and, perhaps more worryingly, the term 'security interest' has two very different meanings in the Canadian provinces, depending on the context.

The history of the 'deemed trust' is particularly interesting as, at various times, priority over security interests depended on the fixed/floating charge divide. The 'deemed trust' device was introduced to give the Crown a proprietary interest in the tax collected. However, it had priority only in respect of security interests which attached before the deemed trust came into operation, that is, either when the triggering event occurred[224] or when the deductions should have been made.[225] This had the result, under the pre-PPSA law, that the deemed trust had priority over any pre-existing floating charge, which did not attach until crystallization, but not over a fixed charge, which attached at the moment of creation.[226] Thus cases decided under that law had to characterize charges as

[221] Defined in s 224.1.3. as 'any interest in property that secures payment or performance of an obligation and includes an interest created by or arising out of a debenture, mortgage, hypothec, lien, pledge, charge, deemed or actual trust, assignment or encumbrance of any kind whatever, however or whenever arising, created, deemed to arise or otherwise provided for'.

[222] '[S]ecurity interest' means (a) an interest in goods . . . that secures payment or performance of an obligation' (British Columbia PPSA, s 1(1), also found in Ontario PPSA, s 1(1), Saskatchewan PPSA, s 2(1)(qq)).

[223] See J Ziegel, 'Conditional Sales and Superpriority Crown Claims under ITA s 227' (2004) 38 Canadian Bankruptcy Reporter (4th) 161.

[224] This was any liquidation, assignment, receivership, or bankruptcy under the old version of s 227(5).

[225] *Dauphin Plains Credit Union Ltd v Xyloid Industries Ltd* [1980] 1 SCR 1182, 108 DLR (3d) 257, SC.

[226] This distinction is also apparent in the English cases about set-off (*Biggerstaff v Rowatt's Wharf Ltd* [1896] 2 Ch 93, CA; *NW Robbie & Co Ltd v Witney Warehouse Ltd* [1963] 1 WLR 1324, CA) and execution creditors (*Evans v Rival Granite Quarries Ltd* [1910] 2 KB 979, CA; *Re Standard Manufacturing Co* [1891] 1 Ch 627, CA; *Re Opera Ltd* [1891] 3 Ch 260, CA).

fixed or floating, with all the attendant problems.[227] The courts also developed an alternative theory: even if the charge was fixed and had attached, the licence in the charge permitted the debtor to incur liabilities to the Crown ranking in priority to the charge, and so the Crown prevailed. With the enactment of the PPSAs, the floating charge was changed into a fixed charge with licence to deal, which attached when the security agreement is executed by the parties.[228] In *Royal Bank of Canada v Sparrow Electric Corporation*[229] the Supreme Court confirmed this, but the members of the court were divided over the application of the 'licence theory'. The majority held that generally a licence to the debtor to dispose of the assets had only the effect that actual disposals were free from the charge, and did not cover potential disposals. Otherwise the priority rules laid down in the PPSA would be nugatory, since every claim by a subsequent creditor would be within the licence. They also relied on policy considerations: that since the licence theory depended on the exact wording of the charge, the law would become uncertain, and also there could be a deleterious effect on the relevant concepts in the PPSA context. They argued that Parliament could easily close the gap, if it wished, by specifically providing that the deemed trust had priority over any security interest. That was exactly what Parliament did: the Act was amended in 1998 and now provides that the deemed trust has priority over any security interest, with the one exception of real property mortgages.[230]

(b) Unpaid wages

Until very recently, claims by employees for unpaid wages had priority over unsecured creditors under federal law,[231] and also had priority over secured creditors by some provincial laws,[232] although these had often been narrowly interpreted by the courts as not giving priority over prior security interests.[233]

---

227 See *The Queen in right of British Columbia v Federal Business Development Bank* (1987) 43 DLR (4th) 188, Br Col CA, a case about the priority of a lien in relation to sales tax, which discusses the previous authorities. In that case, the majority adopted two alternative analyses: either the charge was floating (and the Crown therefore obtained priority) or the charge was fixed and had attached, yet the licence in the charge permitted the debtor to incur liabilities to the Crown ranking in priority to the charge.

228 Alberta PPSA, s 12. This is also subject to a requirement that value is given and that the debtor has rights in the collateral.

229 [1997] 1 SCR 411, 143 DLR (4th) 385, SC.

230 Income Tax Act 1985, s 227(4.1).

231 Bankruptcy and Insolvency Act 1985, s 136(1)(d).

232 British Columbia Employment Standards Act 1996, s 87, New Brunswick Employment Standards Act 1982, s 38.1, Manitoba Payment of Wages Act 1987, ss 3(4) and 7, Ontario Employment Standards Act 1990, s 15.

233 *Board of Industrial Relations v Avco Financial Services Realty Ltd* [1979] SCR 699, SC.

This latter protection, however, did not apply in bankruptcy.[234] After several failed attempts at reform, the Wage Earner Protection Program Act was given the Royal Assent on 25 November 2005. This amends the Bankruptcy and Insolvency Act 1985 and provides[235] that wage earners' claims up to $2,000 per person are secured on all the current assets as at the date of bankruptcy. The secured claim is expressly given priority over every other claim, right, charge or security over the bankrupt's current assets.[236] The Act also includes a scheme whereby employees can claim compensation for lost earnings out of a central Government-administered fund. The Government is then subrogated to the employee's rights against the employer, including the right to the secured claim.[237]

The interest of this legislation for the purposes of this chapter is in the trigger chosen for determining the priority of the employee's claim over secured creditors. The reluctance of the Canadian courts to hold that an interest created by statute has priority over pre-existing proprietary claims without very clear statutory wording[238] meant that there was considerable concern to achieve a

[234] That priority given to wage earners by security interests or deemed trusts under provincial law did not apply in bankruptcy was confirmed by the Supreme Court of Canada in *Workers' Compensation Board v Husky Oil Operators* [1995] 3 SCR 453, SC. This has the effect that employers can so arrange it that wage earners lose all protection except the 'small and largely futile preference given to wage-earners under section 136(1)(d) of the *Bankruptcy Act*)' and wage earners are in a worse position than if they had not been mentioned in the Bankruptcy and Insolvency Act 1985 (per Esson JA in *Bank of Montreal v Scott Road Enterprises* (1989) 57 DLR (4th) 622, British Columbia CA). Wage earners do have priority in bankruptcy over security interests taken under the Bank Act 1991 (s 427) but banks can circumvent this by taking a security interest under provincial legislation.

[235] Wage Earner Protection Program Act 2005, s 67, amending Bankruptcy and Insolvency Act 1985, s 81.

[236] With some very specific exceptions: (a) the right of an unpaid supplier to repossess goods delivered up to 30 days before bankruptcy (Bankruptcy and Insolvency Act 1985, s 81(1)), with a slightly longer period for agricultural products (s 81(2)) and (b) deemed trusts in favour of the Revenue under Bankruptcy and Insolvency Act 1985, s 67(3) (see n 235 above).

[237] Wage Earner Protection Program Act 2005, s 36. This is similar to the position in the United Kingdom, where employees are reimbursed from the National Insurance Fund, and the Secretary of State is subrogated to the employee's (preferential) rights (see above text to n 150). There is an ongoing debate in the United Kingdom as to whether the Government's subrogated claim should have preferential status: R Mokal, 'Priority as Pathology: The Pari Passu Myth' [2001] CLJ 581. Since the Enterprise Act 2002 abolishes Crown preference in relation to tax claims, it is hard to see why this should not apply where the Crown is subrogated to the employee's claim. Goode has suggested an indemnity fund to which both employers and employees would contribute: R Goode, 'The Death of Insolvency Law' (1980) 1 Company Lawyer 123, 129. Some commentators in Canada also share this view: K Davis and J Ziegel, 'Assessing the Economic Impacts of a New Priority Scheme for Unpaid Wage Earners and Suppliers of Goods and Services' (1998), prepared for the Corporate Law Policy Directorate of Industry Canada (available at <http://strategis.ic.gc.ca/epic/internet/incilp-pdci.nsf/vwapj/unpaid_ws.pdf/$FILE/unpaid_ws.pdf>).

[238] *Board of Industrial Relations v Avco Financial Services Realty Ltd* [1979] SCR 699, SC, see also the dissenting judgment in *Alberta (Treasury Branches) v MNR* [1996] 1 SCR 963, SC (n 219

clear statutory trigger that left no room for contrary interpretation.[239] One option put forward[240] was to give the statutory secured claim priority over all security interests. In case this was considered too harsh on creditors, two possible techniques to ameliorate this harshness were suggested: either the statute could provide for priority over all security interests except those specified[241] or it could provide for priority over security interests relating to particular types of assets. The latter option was preferred by the Senate: the relevant committee recommended a super priority over secured claims to inventory and accounts receivables. This became, in the legislation, priority over secured claims over current assets, defined as 'unrestricted cash, or any other asset that, in the normal course of operations, is expected to be converted into cash or consumed in the production of income within one year or within the normal operating cycle when it is longer than a year'.[242]

3. New Zealand

Although New Zealand has abolished much of the Crown preference,[243] there are still a number of preferential creditors which gain priority both in receivership[244] and in a winding-up.[245] Before the New Zealand PPSA 1999 ('NZPPSA'), which introduced a regime similar to those in Canada and the United States, these creditors had priority over floating charge holders. The NZPPSA abolished the concept of the floating charge, and so an alternative trigger was required. The New Zealand Law Commission recommended a form of words which was designed to 'continue the present regime, in a de facto sense, by creating a right to priority over accounts receivable and inventory of a company'.[246] It was thus

---

above). The need for very clear drafting in this area is also pointed out by Iacobucci J in *Royal Bank of Canada v Sparrow Electric Corporation* [1997] 1 SCR 411, 143 DLR (4th) 385, SC, para 108.

[239] R Cuming, 'Enhanced Enforcement of Wage Claims under Canadian Bankruptcy and Receivership Law' (1998) prepared for the Corporate Law Policy Directorate of Industry Canada, 62 (available at <http://strategis.ic.gc.ca/epic/internet/incilp-pdci.nsf/en/h_cl00202e.html>).

[240] These various options were set out in 'Statutory Priorities in Business Insolvencies' (May 2001) produced by the Corporate Law Policy Directorate of Industry Canada (available at <http://strategis.ic.gc.ca/epic/internet/incilp-pdci.nsf/en/h_cl00198e.html>).

[241] This was the solution preferred by Cuming who favoured an exception for all purchase money security interests: Cuming (n 239 above).

[242] Wage Earner Protection Program Act 2005, s 2(5). One rationale for this limitation was that working capital lenders would be better able to adjust than fixed asset secured lenders, see 'Statutory Priorities in Business Insolvencies' (n 240 above) 12.

[243] B Morgan, 'Should the Sovereign Be Paid First? A Comparative International Analysis of the Priority for Tax Claims in Bankruptcy' (2000) 74 American Bankruptcy Law Journal 461, 482–3.

[244] Receiverships Act 1993, s 30(2), referring to the list of preferential creditors in Companies Act 1993, Sch 7, but also including the expenses of the receivership. Schedule 7 includes mainly claims by employees of the company, certain claims by buyers of goods for money paid on account, and some claims for unpaid taxes.

[245] Companies Act 1993, s 312 and Sch 7.

[246] New Zealand Law Commission Study Paper 2, 1999, ch 2, para 8.

recognized that these forms of assets were those most usually covered by a floating charge, while other assets were usually covered by fixed security. The draft was changed in committee with a view to preserving the status quo[247] to a 'security interest, other than a purchase money security interest, in the company's property that is not prohibited or restricted by the security agreement relating to the security interest from being sold or otherwise disposed of in the ordinary course of the company's business'. Although this was enacted in the 1999 Act, it was amended before the Act came into force, to the original definition,[248] since the 1999 version was thought to be too vague, with priority depending on the exact words of the particular security agreement, and to cover interests which were not previously floating charges, for example, retention of title clauses. It also had the effect of retaining the concept of the floating charge, albeit for a limited purpose.[249] The new definition reads:

> The claims . . . (i) have priority over the claims of any person under a security interest to the extent that the security interest
>
> (A) is over all or any part of the company's accounts receivable and inventory or all or any part of either of them; and
> (B) is not a purchase money security interest; and
> (C) does not arise from the transfer of an account receivable for which new value is provided by the transferee for the acquisition of that account receivable (whether or not the transfer of the account receivable secures payment or performance of an obligation).
>
> (ii) must be paid accordingly out of any accounts receivable or inventory subject to that security interest (or their proceeds).

For the purposes of this clause, the terms 'account receivable', 'inventory', 'new value', 'proceeds', 'purchase money security interest', and 'security interest' have the same meaning as in the NZPPSA. The exceptions in (B) and (C) of a purchase money security interest and a transfer of an account receivable for new value were included in an attempt to preserve the status quo. Under the previous law, preferential creditors did not have priority over retention of title transactions by inventory suppliers and absolute assignments of receivables. These transactions were included in the term 'security interest' by the NZPPSA,[250] and would therefore be caught by the amendment, were it not for the exceptions.

---

247 *Hansard*, 5th October 1999 (speech of Max Bradford).

248 Introduced by Sch 1 to the Personal Property Securities Amendment Act 2001, it takes effect by amending cl 9 of Sch 7 to the Companies Act 1993.

249 We are indebted to discussions with Professor Richard Sutton of the University of Otago in connection with the Personal Property Security Amendment Act 2001. See also M Gedye, 'The Structure of New Zealand's "New" Priority Debts Regime' (2003) 9 New Zealand Business Law Quarterly 220, 226.

250 NZPPSA, s 17. The scheme adopts a functional approach to the classification of transactions, and also includes absolute assignments within the scheme.

Although not all retention of title transactions and absolute assignments would be included in the exceptions, it was the closest approximation.[251]

The definition of 'account receivable' in the NZPPSA is: 'a monetary obligation that is not evidenced by chattel paper, an investment security or by a negotiable instrument, whether or not that obligation has been earned by performance'.[252] It is a sub-category of 'intangible', which is defined by the NZPPSA as 'personal property other than chattel paper, a document of title, goods, an investment security, money or a negotiable instrument'. There has as yet been no case considering the definition of 'account receivable' in New Zealand.[253] Concern has been expressed on two specific counts. First, whether a bank account is an investment security or an account receivable.[254] Secondly, the distinction between an account receivable and chattel paper is said to be vague and uncertain.[255] Although it was a new statutory term in New Zealand, the term 'account' had already been used extensively in Article 9 of the Uniform Commercial Code[256] and in the Canadian PPSAs.[257] The term is defined for the purposes of each of the entire schemes, which include registration of outright transfers of accounts receivable (or accounts): it is not used as a statutory trigger for priority of preferential creditors. The terms 'account' and 'receivable' are well known and were extensively used in the United States and Canada even before they were incorporated into the relevant legislation. In the United States, the term 'accounts' has been widened[258] from 'rights to payments relating to goods and services' to a much wider (and very specific) definition. In Canada, the latter term 'accounts' was used to replace the term 'book debts' in previous legislation: this term had not been defined and had given rise to considerable

[251] Gedye (n 249 above) 227. [252] NZPPSA, s 16.

[253] In *Waller v New Zealand Bloodstock Ltd* [2005] 2 NZLR 549, the High Court of Auckland considered the meaning of 'assignment of a single account receivable' within the meaning of NZPPSA, s 23(1). However, the discussion centred on the meaning of 'assignment' rather than 'account receivable'. This decision was upheld by the New Zealand Court of Appeal in a judgment delivered on 27 October 2005, but there was no further discussion of s 23.

[254] M Gedye, 'Anomalies and Lacunae in the Treatment of Preferential Creditors' (2003) 9 New Zealand Business Law Quarterly 295, 297. It is proposed to narrow the definition of 'security interest' so as to make it clear that a bank account is an account receivable, New Zealand Ministry of Economic Development, 'Business Law Reform Bill 2001: Discussion Document' (2001) 23 (available at <http://www.med.govt.nz/buslt/bus_pol/bus_law/blrb2001/index.html>). A bank will usually be protected by its right of set-off or combination, and so will not lose priority to preferential creditors in practice. However, no such reform was included in the Business Law Reform Bill 2003.

[255] Gedye (n 254 above) 297–9, L Widdup and L Mayne, *Personal Property Securities Act: A Conceptual Approach* (2000) 257–9.

[256] The term is defined in Uniform Commercial Code (revised) § 9–102.

[257] Ontario PPSA, s 1; British Columbia PPSA, s 1; Saskatchewan PPSA, s 2.

[258] In the revision of Article 9 in 1999. This was not merely to achieve drafting clarity, but to widen the scope of the concept so as to capture more transactions.

litigation about its meaning.[259] The defined term 'accounts', however, has given rise to very little discussion in the courts.[260]

The term 'book debts' has been used as a statutory trigger in England and Wales, most notably in relation to the requirement that charges over book debts be registered.[261] There is no definition of book debts in the Companies Act 1985, but it is apparent from discussion in the cases that book debts are such debts as it is the practice to enter in the well-kept books of a company.[262] This link with accountancy practice has led to difficulties as the application of the definition varies according to the prevalent accounting practice at the time and in relation to the particular business.[263] There has also been considerable uncertainty over whether a credit balance at a bank is a book debt[264] and whether negotiable instruments are book debts.[265] However, the concept of receivables is wider than that of book debts, and is not dependent upon accounting practice,[266] and a statutory definition of receivables (or accounts receivable) in the United Kingdom could deal expressly with specific controversies, if desired. For example, negotiable instruments could be expressly excluded, as in the New Zealand definition. It should be noted that the Draft Regulations proposed by the Law Commission in relation to reform of the registration system for companies security interests define receivables as 'monetary obligations, whether or not earned by performance, arising from (a) the supply of goods or services (other than insurance services), (b) the supply of energy, or (c) brokerage fees'.[267] This is a deliberately narrow definition as its only purpose in the Draft Regulations is to define receivables the sale of which is registrable. This registration requirement only applies to the kinds of monetary

---

[259] R Maclaren, *Secured Transactions in Personal Property in Canada* (2005) § 1.02 text to fns 90–91.

[260] There is a brief discussion in *Transamerica Commercial Finance Corporation, Canada v Royal Bank of Canada* (1990) 70 DLR (4th) 627, 84 Sask R 237, Saskatchewan CA, paras 31–34, which concludes that money in a deposit account is not an 'account given for new value' within the terms of s 34(4) of Saskatchewan PPSA. See also *Agent's Equity Inc v Hope (Trustee of)* 30 OR (3d) 557, Ontario Court of Justice, where the definition of account is briefly applied at paras 11–13.

[261] Companies Act 1985, s 396(1)(e).

[262] *Paul & Frank Ltd v Discount Bank (Overseas) Ltd* [1967] Ch 348, 361. See also *Tailby v Official Receiver* (1887) 18 QBD 25, 29, HL; *Shipley v Marshall* (1863) 14 CB NS 566; *Independent Automatic Sales Ltd v Knowles and Foster* [1962] 1 WLR 974.

[263] *Contemporary Cottages (NZ) Ltd v Margin Traders Ltd* [1981] 2 NZLR 114, 121, HC, Auckland. The difficulties in predicting whether debts were book debts are pointed out by the Financial Law Panel in their document *Charges Over Debts* published in July 2001.

[264] *Re Brightlife* [1987] Ch 200; *Re Permanent Houses (Holdings) Ltd* (1988) 5 BCC 151; *Northern Bank v Ross* [1991] BCLC 504, CA (NI); *Re BCCI (No 8)* [1998] AC 214, 227.

[265] F Oditah, *Legal Aspects of Receivables Financing* (1991) 25–7. [266] ibid 19–23.

[267] Draft Company Security Regulations 2006, reg 2(3), available at <http://www.lawcom.gov.uk/docs/Draft_Regulations.pdf>.

obligations commonly sold by companies to factors or discounters.[268] The New Zealand definition is much wider, and more closely accords with the commercial understanding of the term 'receivable'.[269]

The definition of 'inventory' in the NZPPSA is 'goods that are (a) held by a person for sale or lease, or that have been leased by that person as lessor; or (b) to be provided or have been provided under a contract for services; or (c) raw materials or work in progress; or (d) materials used or consumed in business'.[270] The definition is very similar to that of the Canadian PPSAs[271] and the Uniform Commercial Code.[272] It is wider than the colloquial use of the word 'inventory' in that it includes leased goods, goods furnished under a service contract, and raw materials,[273] but the definition appears to have given little problem in practice. There are no cases as yet considering the definition in New Zealand. Those in the United States appear to focus on the distinction between equipment and inventory:[274] it is not always possible to tell merely from the nature of the goods whether they are equipment or inventory as this depends on the use they are put to by the company.[275] For example, a computer may be equipment if used to keep records, but inventory if the company trades in computers.

The New Zealand amendments have attracted some criticism.[276] However, this has been aimed at particular anomalies in the New Zealand legislation. For example, the combination of the purchase money security interest exception, and the NZPPSA requirements for registration of a purchase money security interest could mean that the purchase money security interest loses priority to a general security interest, but retains priority over preferential creditors, which would lead to a circularity issue. Further, the details of the administration of the scheme, particularly by receivers, are unsatisfactory and not clear. Criticism of the basic trigger, that is, priority to the extent that a security interest covers

---

268 Law Commission Explanatory Notes, available at <http://www.lawcom.gov.uk/docs/Explanatory_Notes.pdf>.

269 The Law Commission acknowledges the deliberate narrowness of the definition in the Draft Regulations and contrasts it with 'any form of receivable' a charge over which falls under the registration scheme.

270 NZPPSA, s 16.

271 Ontario PPSA, s 1, British Columbia PPSA, s 1, Saskatchewan PPSA, s 2.

272 Revised § 9-102(a)(48).

273 M Gedye, R Cuming, and R Wood, *Personal Property Securities in New Zealand* (2002) 58.

274 *Morgan County Feeders Inc v James L McCormick* (1992) 836 P 2d 1051, Colorado CA, *First Wisconsin National Bank of Milwaukee v Ford Motor Credit Company*, 94 Wis 2d 622, Wisconsin CA.

275 Gedye, Cuming, and Wood (n 273 above) 69.

276 ibid 21–2; M Gedye, 'The Structure of New Zealand's "New" Priority Debts Regime' (2003) 9 New Zealand Business Law Quarterly 220 and 'Anomalies and Lacunae in the Treatment of Preferential Creditors' (2003) 9 New Zealand Business Law Quarterly 295.

accounts receivable and inventory, is much more limited, and is mainly directed to the difficulty of defining chattel paper.[277]

It should be noted that New Zealand already had a different formulation for the invalidation of charges created in the run-up to insolvency:[278] any such charge was voidable unless it was for new value,[279] or given at a time when the company could pay its due debts, or was in substitution for a charge given before the specified period.

4. Some thoughts on alternative statutory triggers

There are several lessons to be drawn from this. First, no statutory trigger is ever perfect and if parties are determined to argue that their transaction does not fall within it, then courts will have to perform a characterization exercise. Secondly, statutory triggers which are conceptually complex cause more problems. The concepts of a 'secured creditor' and a 'security interest' are not stable ones, as can be seen from the Canadian experience. Similarly, the fixed/floating divide created problems as a trigger in Canada as it has done in this country. However, a conceptually simple trigger, such as the 45-day limit in the United States, may cause practical problems in compliance, albeit few problems for the courts in administering it.

A trigger relating to the type of assets covered by a transaction has a similar simplicity. The point made by the New Zealand Law Commission is a good one:

> It creates a rule, known to all parties when a decision to lend is made, which provides an answer in all cases. The contrary position makes availability of 'accounts receivable' for preferential creditors dependent on the wording of the particular instrument which creates the security interest. The cost involved for other creditors to review those clauses before deciding whether, and if so on what terms, to provide credit is likely to increase the cost of credit.[280]

Moreover, a trigger based on the nature of the asset is less likely to involve interpretation of the charge itself, and thus involve characterizing a transaction to which at least one party has an interest in structuring in a way that will avoid the certain statutory consequences.[281] It is true that in order to determine whether and to what extent a security interest covers accounts receivable or

[277] Which is not a concept used in the United Kingdom.

[278] Companies Act 1993, s 293, which is the equivalent of Insolvency Act 1986, s 245.

[279] This is specifically set out in the section as 'money actually advanced or paid, or the actual price or value of property sold or supplied to the company, or any other valuable consideration given in good faith by the grantee of the charge at the time of, or at any time after, the giving of the charge'.

[280] New Zealand Law Commission Study Paper 2, 1999, ch 2, para 12.

[281] It falls within the definition discussed in text to nn 79 and 80 above.

inventory, the scope of the charge needs to be determined. If these terms are not used in the charge, then it will be necessary to determine, first, what assets the charge covers and, secondly, which if any of those assets fall within the statutory trigger. However, the first exercise will have to be done anyway in order to enforce the charge, and the second exercise does not rely upon the terms of the charge, but upon the nature of the debt. This may depend upon the terms of the debt, but the secured party will not usually be in a position to influence this, or it may depend upon the use to which the company has put the goods covered by the charge, which will depend upon the business of the company and again is unlikely to be influenced by the secured party.

F. Conclusion

The justifications for the courts' involvement in characterizing fixed and floating charges arise post-insolvency, not pre-insolvency. Two broad trends are identified: that floating charges are more vulnerable than fixed charges due to the registration system and the existence of s 245 of the Insolvency Act 1986, and that floating charges are subordinated to the interests of preferred creditors, unsecured creditors and administrators, as discussed in Part D above, in a way that fixed charges are not. We suggest that the distinction between fixed and floating charges is the wrong statutory trigger for the various consequences described in Part D, and that this leads to many of the problems surrounding characterization at the present time.[282]

Alternative triggers need to be found which reflect the purpose of the statutory provision in question. In relation to registration, the policy issue behind registration suggests that all charges need to be registered, and that a distinction between fixed and floating charges here is unhelpful.[283] In relation to s 245, again there does not seem to be a good reason to distinguish between fixed and floating charges. The purpose of this provision seems to be to protect existing creditors of the company, in a period prior to insolvency, against the possibility of the company continuing to trade and acquiring further assets on credit which will swell the security at the expense of the unpaid vendors. What is required, therefore, is a provision which prevents the later creation of any kind of charge after a particular point in time.[284]

[282] On this issue see also R Goode, 'The Case for the Abolition of the Floating Charge', ch 2 above.

[283] The draft Regulations proposed by the Law Commission require registration of all charges except those arising by operation of law, fixed charges over land, and charges over financial collateral.

[284] As in New Zealand (Companies Act 1993, s 293).

In relation to the claims in priority to the charge holder discussed in Part D, namely the preferential creditors and, now, unsecured creditors as a result of the ring-fencing provisions introduced by the Enterprise Act 2002, the relevant issue seems to be to capture charges which cover all the assets of the company, and which allow the company to continue to trade. A preferable trigger in our view would be one that is not based on the nature of the charge, but rather on the nature of the asset, such as that adopted in New Zealand and Canada, ie that preferential creditors should rank ahead of all charges to the extent that they cover inventory and receivables, and that the ring-fencing provisions should likewise bite on these assets. It seems to us that a definition such as this which is based on the assets covered by the charge should (in theory) create fewer characterization problems.

The advantages of this trigger are several. First, it is a more stable trigger than the fixed/floating charge distinction as it does not suffer from the same conceptual uncertainty. In relation to fixed and floating charges, there is widespread disagreement both as to whether they are different or the same concepts, and also about the actual nature of the concept involved. The same cannot be said of the concepts of receivables and inventory. Secondly, the trigger definitions are of things created by persons other than the interested party.[285] It is true that the chargee could take a charge which was drafted so as not to cover receivables and inventory, but then those assets would not be available to fulfil the chargee's claim. If the chargee wished to have recourse to those assets, the charge document would have to cover them, and it would not therefore be possible to draft a charge which gave the chargee what it wanted while avoiding the unwanted statutory consequences. Thirdly, although there could be a concern that such a trigger would widen the pool of assets presently made available to preferential and unsecured creditors, following the House of Lords' decision in *Spectrum* most if not all charges over receivables are likely to be floating charges, and the same is true of charges over inventory, since it will be very difficult to show the necessary degree of chargee control over the proceeds of the inventory. Thus the suggested trigger will cover the same assets that would at present fall under most floating charges. Fourthly, the assets in question are those which it is most appropriate to make available to the preferential and unsecured creditors, since it is the fact that the floating charge covered these assets that was the impetus for the policy of giving priority to those groups in the first place.[286]

The Law Commission suggested that a similar trigger should apply were their

285 See text to nn 79 and 80 above.
286 See nn 153–157 and accompanying text above.

proposals to abolish the distinction between fixed and floating charges to be adopted.[287] The recommendation was for preferential creditors and the unsecured creditors' fund to have 'first claim on (1) any inventory or receivables belonging to the company; and (2) any other asset of the company that, under the charge agreement, the company has the right to dispose of free of the charge'. Presumably what is meant by 'first claim' is priority over any security interest over such assets. Although (2) could be said to be required in order to preserve the status quo exactly, it could lead to difficulties in that it relies on the construction of the charge agreement.[288] Many respondents to earlier consultation papers expressed concern about the insolvency consequences of abolishing the distinction between fixed and floating charges. Reform of insolvency law was outside the Law Commission's terms of reference, and, although it felt that there was a good case for abolishing the distinction and using the substitute trigger, it decided not to recommend this course in its recent report, but instead suggested that the proposed rules be considered again when insolvency law is next reviewed.[289] We suggest, however, that there is a strong case for reform of the statutory trigger, whether or not the distinction between fixed and floating charges is abolished for all other purposes.

As regards the ability of administrators to make use of the assets subject to the floating charge, it seems that once the political decision has been taken to promote this route on insolvency, sufficient assets have to be put into the hands of the administrator in order to allow the administrator to continue to run the company. Often the only assets that are available for the purposes of financing the continued operation of the company through administration will be the inventory and receivables of the company. To promote a rescue culture through the administration procedure these funds need to be maximized to the greatest extent possible. Again, it seems to us that a more stable trigger for these purposes, and one which captures the policy behind these provisions, is one which allows administrators to make use of assets covered by all charges over inventory and receivables. As a result, all inventory and receivables would be available to the administrator to fund the process of administration. The charge holder would, of course, benefit from a successful administration since it would be likely to be paid.

[287] Law Commission, *Company Security Interests* (Law Com No 296, Cm 6654, August 2005) paras 3.165–3.170. For further detail on the Law Commission's proposals, see M Bridge, 'The Law Commission's Proposals for the Reform of Corporate Security Interests', ch 12 below.

[288] This could cause particular problems if the trigger were reformed without abolition of the floating charge. This, however, is not what is envisaged by the Law Commission.

[289] Law Commission, *Company Security Interests* (Law Com No 296, Cm 6654, August 2005) para 3.173.

Although no statutory trigger will ever be perfect, we suggest that reforming the triggers in these ways will solve many of the issues surrounding characterization of charges at the present time, and stem the tide of expensive and time-consuming litigation such as that in *Spectrum.*

5

SPECTRUM—AN END TO THE CONFLICT OR THE SIGNAL FOR A NEW CAMPAIGN?

Nicholas Frome and Kate Gibbons

A. The Impact on Traditional Charge Structures

1. Introduction

This chapter does not seek to re-fight the battle so decisively lost by the financing community in *Re Spectrum Plus Ltd.*[1] All relevant arguments appear to have been marshalled and placed before their Lordships and there is no denying the completeness of a unanimous decision by a seven-strong House of Lords. While many insolvency and finance lawyers may have been disappointed by the result, it could not be said to have come as any great surprise. Rather, the purpose of the chapter is to consider why the *Spectrum* decision and some of its antecedents are likely to remain highly relevant for practitioners at least until the boundaries of the *Spectrum* decision have been clarified. In doing so we also suggest where those boundaries should be.

2. Practical significance of re-characterization risk

The practical significance of the long-running book debts saga is not simply the point referred to by the House of Lords in *Spectrum*, namely, whether or not the claims of preferential creditors rank prior to the claims of the debenture holder pursuant to s 175 of the Insolvency Act 1986 (preferential debts). Nor is it a question of the potential applicability of s 245 of the Insolvency Act 1986 (avoidance of certain floating charges). Even before the Crown surrendered its

[1] [2005] UKHL 41, [2005] 2 AC 680 (hereinafter *Spectrum*).

preferential creditor status,[2] a significant issue to financiers was that of prospective control—control in the direct sense of the timing and manner of realization of charged assets (and of distribution of realization proceeds to creditors) and also in the indirect sense as regards control of any administration process. If the valuable and liquid assets are subject only to a floating charge, they will be available to an administrator to fund an administration.[3] If so, the debtor and any prospective administrator will be empowered to initiate administration proceedings notwithstanding opposition from the debenture holder.[4]

If virtually all valuable assets are subject to fixed charges the debenture holder will in practice be able to dictate whether and on what terms an administration will occur (and may be able to force something close to administrative receivership in all but name). As financiers will only lend to an administration if there are available assets to lend against, if all the valuable assets are charged under fixed charges, the only practical source of finance will be the debenture holder who is then likely to set its own terms for the lending. This point may also impact on the purposes of the administration, for example placing the purpose of rescuing the company as a going concern above the other purposes set out in para 3(1) of Sch B1 to the Insolvency Act 1986 is not usually going to be possible if there is no finance available to fund a rescue-orientated administration.

Financiers should not be criticized for seeking to ensure control of the realization of the charged assets or, because of its potentially negative impact on this issue, on any prospective administration proceedings. Uncertainty of outcome is the bane of financiers and it tends to be an important issue for financing institution credit committees and for rating agencies. Indeed the importance of the issue to rating agencies is touched upon later on in this chapter[5] where we analyse the *Spectrum* decision in the context of Special Purpose Vehicles (SPVs) employed in the securitization and structured finance industries. Ultimately the financing community will always find a way of achieving its control objectives even if the law requires it to use more complex methodologies, for example off balance sheet structures, to do this. Unfortunately, in that event, the additional cost will have to be borne by the borrower community.

Another reality to be borne in mind is the duty of administrators and liquid-

---

[2] A new class of claimant to the proceeds of floating charge assets has in any event been created as under Insolvency Act 1986, s 176A a prescribed proportion of these proceeds currently capped at £600,000 must be made available to unsecured creditors (see Insolvency Act 1986 (Prescribed Part) Order 2003, SI 2003/2097, art 3).

[3] Insolvency Act 1986, Sch B1, para 70(1).

[4] Unless the debenture holder can successfully claim unfair harm to its interests under Insolvency Act 1986, Sch B1, para 74.

[5] See Part A, Section 2 below.

ators. While administrative receivers look to realize charged assets on the best terms reasonably obtainable for the benefit of their appointing charge holder (subject to paying preferential creditors in priority to the extent of floating charge assets) administrators and liquidators owe duties to creditors as a whole.[6] If there are uncertainties in the law as to entitlement to realization proceeds, they are almost bound to explore those uncertainties. This is so regardless of who appointed them (the choice of administrator is, or should be, of illusory benefit only) and they are likely to seek judicial resolution of uncertainties unless a compromise is available which is either accepted by all interested creditors or is clearly to their benefit. It is often difficult for administrators not to be seen to pursue uncertainties and in effect to negotiate the litigation risk (if not pursue litigation directly) for the benefit of creditors generally. This is not improper.

It appears implicit in the waterfall of purposes under para 3(1) of Sch B1 to the Insolvency Act 1986 that there will be reasonable clarity as to the validity and status of charges. If the status of a charge is not clear then an administrator will wish to obtain clarification at the outset, in part to determine the options available to him. If a secured creditor claims to hold fixed charges and simply wants to see assets realized and is not interested in pursuing rescue strategies, the administrator must either comply with the secured creditor's wishes or challenge the security.[7]

For all these reasons it is important for the fixed versus floating issue to be clarified and if it is not it is likely to remain an ongoing source of confusion to the detriment of both financiers and borrowers.

3. How far does the *Spectrum* decision extend?

The *Spectrum* decision is a case dealing with book debts. A key question is, however, whether certain remarks made by Lord Scott and Lord Walker may apply to charges over other classes of assets. The *Spectrum* judgment has also raised questions about the impact upon the categorization of charges of the terms of documents governing the financing (such as loan agreements or servicing agreements) and in particular whether permissions or pre-agreements in relation to the utilization of proceeds of sale or payment waterfalls may negate a fixed charge.

[6] In particular the risk reward equation for an administrator is even more complex and potentially costly than for an administrative receiver or liquidator, as he must balance the competing interests of creditors who wish to see a rescue that may take some time to put together against those who wish to see a sale and some return in the short term.

[7] The administrator may apply under Insolvency Act 1986, Sch B1, para 71 for permission to deal with such assets, but as the cases on its predecessor Insolvency Act 1986, s 15(2) show, this is not straightforward (see, for example, *Re ARV Aviation* [1988] 4 BCC 708).

Probably the most controversial aspect of the *Spectrum* judgment was the statement by Lord Scott that '[i]ndeed, if a security has Romer LJ's third characteristic [ie 'until some further step is taken by or on behalf of those interested in the charge, the company may carry on its business in the ordinary way as far as concerns the particular class of assets . . .' (*Re Yorkshire Woolcombers' Association Ltd* [1903] 2 Ch 284, 295)] I am inclined to think that it qualifies as a floating charge, and cannot be a fixed charge, whatever may be its other characteristics'.[8]

At first sight it might be thought that Lord Scott (with at least the tacit approval of the other six members of the House of Lords) was indicating that the two other characteristics mentioned by Romer LJ in the *Yorkshire Woolcombers* case[9] (namely (1) that it be 'a charge on a class of assets of a company present and future'; and (2) 'that class is one which, in the ordinary course of business of the company, would be changing from time to time') are at best only subsidiary considerations and at worst irrelevant to deciding whether a charge is fixed or floating.

Lord Scott went on to comment upon a situation in which there was an express assignment of an existing debt but under arrangements which included a contractual right for the assignor to be able to use the debt proceeds freely in its business until the assignee intervened. He said that he would view such arrangements as amounting only to a floating charge notwithstanding that vis à vis the third party debtor there had been a legal assignment of the chose in action.

Taking the remarks made by Lord Scott in isolation, it might seem possible to challenge a number of charges in traditional form over specific assets simply because the product of the commercial arrangements between the chargor and the chargee is that the chargor is left free to carry on its business in the ordinary way, as far as concerns the particular class of assets. To state the obvious, that is virtually always the case where the assets do not form part of the circulating capital of the debtor, so it is reasonable to assume that his remarks were intended only to apply when the assets are to be viewed as circulating assets.[10]

4. The equivalence of debts and their proceeds

It is at this stage also relevant to note that although Lord Scott referred to Lord Millett's judgment in the *Brumark* case[11] as to the equivalence between a debt and its proceeds with approval, he did not adopt Lord Millett's language exactly.

[8] [2005] UKHL 41, [2005] 2 AC 680, para 107. [9] [1903] 2 Ch 284, 295, CA.

[10] This also appears to be the assumption behind Lord Walker's observations in *Spectrum* (para 139) (see Section 5 below). On characterization, see further R Goode, 'The Case for the Abolition of the Floating Charge', ch 2; S Worthington, 'Floating Charges: The Use and Abuse of Doctrinal Analysis', ch 3; and L Gullifer and J Payne, 'The Characterization of Fixed and Floating Charges', ch 4 above.

[11] *Re Brumark Investments Ltd sub nom Agnew v Commissioners of Inland Revenue* [2001] UKPC 28, [2001] 2 AC 710 (hereinafter *Brumark*).

In *Brumark* Lord Millett referred to 'a debt or other receivable' saying:

> while a debt and its proceeds are two separate assets, however, the latter are merely the traceable proceeds of the former. A debt is a receivable; *it is merely a right to receive payment from the debtor*. Such a right cannot be enjoyed in specie; its value can be exploited only by exercising the right or assigning it for value to a third party. An assignment or a charge of a receivable which does not carry with it the right to receipt has no value. It is worthless as a security. Any attempt in the present context to separate the ownership of the debts from the ownership of their proceeds (even if conceptually possible) makes no commercial sense.[12]

This was a crucial part of Lord Millett's rationale as to why attempts to distinguish between a debt and its proceeds as regards the nature of the charges over them were fallacious.

Lord Scott referred in his judgment only to 'debts'.[13] Was this difference of language deliberate? We like to think it was and that, with respect, the House of Lords intended that the essence of the *Spectrum* decision apply only to debts.

5. The 'concurrence of the chargee' distinction

Lord Scott in *Spectrum* referred with approval to Buckley LJ's judgment in *Evans v Rival Granite Quarries Ltd*[14] in which he said:

> [A floating security] is not a specific security; the holder cannot affirm that the assets are specifically mortgaged to him. The assets are mortgaged in such a way that *the mortgagor can deal with them without the concurrence of the mortgagee*. A floating security is not a specific mortgage of the assets, plus a licence to the mortgagor to dispose of them in the course of his business, but it is a floating mortgage applying to every item comprised in the security, but not specifically affecting any item until some event occurs or some act on the part of the mortgagee is done which causes it to crystallize into a fixed security.[15]

Lord Scott's analysis appears (a) to reject (as Lord Millett had done) attempts to reconcile inconsistent treatments in charges as regards book debts on the one hand and proceeds on the other (b) to conclude that if the chargor is left free to deal with the proceeds of the charged debts, until the chargee intervenes, so not only is the charge over the proceeds, but also the charge over the debts, merely a floating charge and (c) to conclude that as a result in such a situation there cannot be a specific charge over the debts. Until the chargee intervenes Lord Scott would view the charge (adopting Lord Macnaghten's dicta in *Illingworth v Houldsworth*[16]) as having to be 'ambulatory and shifting in its nature, hovering

[12] *Brumark*, para 46 (emphasis added).
[13] Except in para 110 when he refers to the 'receivable debt'.
[14] [1910] 2 KB 979, CA.
[15] [1910] 2 KB 979, 999 (emphasis added).
[16] [1904] AC 355, HL.

over and so to speak floating with the property which it is intended to affect until some event occurs or some act is done which causes it to settle and fasten on the subject of the charge within its reach and grasp'.

The same logic is adopted by Lord Walker where he says in relation to the distinction between fixed and floating charges: 'Under a fixed charge the assets charged as security are permanently appropriated to the payment of the sum charged, in such a way as to give the chargee a proprietary interest in the assets. So long as the charge remains unredeemed, the assets can be released from the charge only with the active concurrence of the chargee'.[17]

Lord Scott's and Lord Walker's logic (which also fits with Lord Millett's remarks in *Brumark*) is that if the chargee does not control the use of proceeds of debts, it cannot be said to be in control of the debts themselves (as they are to be viewed in the same way for this purpose). If the chargor is left free to deal with the charged assets and, critically, is able to take them out of the ambit of the charge without reference to the chargee, the charge cannot be said to be a specific charge. The chargor's right to move assets into and out of the charge without reference to the chargee determines that the charge must be only a floating charge.

Lord Scott's and Lord Walker's analyses are reconcilable with the sentence in Buckley LJ's judgment in *Evans v Rival Granite Quarries Ltd* that a floating security 'is not a specific mortgage of the assets, plus a licence to the mortgagor to dispose of them in the course of his business . . .'[18] if one focuses upon the fact that when considering book debts and proceeds, the company can, through the operation of the bank account, deal with the charged assets without reference to or need for any consent or release from the chargee. The process through which proceeds are paid into a bank account (even one with the chargee) and then enjoyed or used by payments away from that bank account, never involves or requires a release of the charge.

As we explain in Part B of this chapter, however, there are other examples where a chargor can be constrained in the way it deals with debts and their proceeds without needing express releases from the charge on each occasion. We argue that these situations also demand consideration and a different approach.

Further, this is not the case when considering most other types of property where an express release from the charge is usually required to any disposition or dealing. The *Spectrum* analysis is at its most powerful in a case where the debts are paid to a third party bank and the customer allowed free use of the

[17] *Spectrum*, para 138. [18] [1910] 2 KB 979, 999.

bank account. In Lord Hope's, Lord Scott's and Lord Walker's judgments[19] (sadly rejecting the analysis of the Master of the Rolls in the Court of Appeal[20]) the position is the same in the case of payments to an operating account of the chargor with the chargee itself.

6. Why the *Spectrum* analysis does not apply to other asset classes

In his *Brumark* judgment, Lord Millett observed that: 'Property and its proceeds are clearly different assets'.[21] However, he then went on to explain how, through his equivalence approach, the property in the debt is exchanged for a right in its proceeds and that realizing a debt by assignment and collecting the debt produces the same result, namely its proceeds. Equating an asset with its proceeds should not be confused with equating an asset with income deriving from that asset.

(a) Land

The *Spectrum* decision does not suggest that Lord Millett's analysis in relation to debts is applicable to land or interests in land. Interests in land which carry with them the right to enjoy the land (whether as a lessee or licensee) are to be viewed differently to the income that may be produced by letting property owned by the chargor or by sub-letting property leased to the chargor. Dicta in *Re Atlantic Computer Systems plc*[22] and the Court of Appeal decision in *Re Offshore Ventilation Ltd*[23] confirm this point. An attempt in the *Offshore Ventilation* case to classify rental income as book debts was specifically rejected by the Court of Appeal (which included Lord Nicholls). In the *Offshore Ventilation* case, the Court of Appeal held that as there had been an effective legal mortgage of the company's leasehold interest in the land (and that even though the right to the rental deriving from the sub-leases was a benefit which would pass to the mortgagee upon the mortgagee exercising its rights), allowing the mortgagor to enjoy that income prior to the exercise of those rights did not turn a legal mortgage of the leasehold interest into a floating charge.

(b) Shares

A similar analysis applies to charges over shares. A distinction can be drawn

[19] For example, *Spectrum*, paras 61, 116 and 155.

[20] [2004] EWCA Civ 670, [2004] Ch 337, para 94. The Court of Appeal considered that in cases where the proceeds of the charged debts were actually paid beneficially to the chargee (and thus the proceeds become the chargee's money applying *Foley v Hill* [1848] 2 HL Cas 28, 36–7) this would meet the requirements of a fixed charge.

[21] *Brumark*, para 43. For a full discussion of the relationship between (and problems of analysis related to) a security interest in an asset and its proceeds, see R Goode, *Legal Problems of Credit and Security* (3rd edn, 2003) paras 1–57 *et seq.*

[22] [1992] Ch 505, CA. [23] [1989] 1 WLR 800, CA.

between the bundle of rights associated with ownership of shares and the income that may be enjoyed from them by way of dividends. Most obviously shares carry voting rights (even if only the limited rights to vote on matters which affect the class of shares in question). A recent challenge to a fixed charge over shares was made and rejected in *Arthur D Little (in administration) v Ableco Finance LCC*.[24] The judge held that the chargor company was not left free to withdraw the shares from the security even though they were subject only to an equitable charge (ie they had not been transferred into the name of the chargee). An attempt to characterize the charge as floating on the ground that the chargor was left entitled to receive dividends and enjoy the use of dividend income from its subsidiary for the purposes of its business, was also rejected. The judge having referred to Lord Millett's judgment in the *Brumark* case[25] held that the charge over shares was a fixed charge notwithstanding that the right to receipt of dividends had been expressly referred to in the same charging clause as the shares themselves and that the company was entitled to enjoy the dividend income prior to the bank taking enforcement action. He observed that he did not view the shares as forming part of the fluctuating capital of the company.

(c) *Intellectual property rights*

Intellectual property rights should also (generally speaking) be viewed in a similar way to land or shares. They have a distinct legal identity and carry with them rights in addition to the right to receive income through publishing or other licensing arrangements. Generally, intellectual property rights (like goodwill) accumulate and though subsidiary rights may be granted in the ordinary course of a company's business (for example, through use licences) it is seldom that the underlying intellectual property rights are disposed of in the usual course of business. Even in a case where a company deals in interests in other people's intellectual property rights, the subsidiary intellectual property right usually carries an entitlement beyond the simple receipt of money (for example to copy original works; to use a licensed product; to create derivative products or grant sub-licences). Accordingly Lord Millett's analysis of debts and proceeds (as adopted by Lord Scott) does not appear applicable to intellectual property rights. Generally, the intellectual property rights of a company would not form part of the circulating capital of a company.

(d) *Goods and other chattels*

In *Brumark* Lord Millett confirmed that goods and chattels are to be regarded as separate from their proceeds.[26] Tangible goods can clearly be used and enjoyed

[24] [2002] EWHC 701, [2003] Ch 217.
[25] For example, *Brumark*, paras 13 and 32.
[26] *Brumark*, para 43.

in specie. The thrust of the *Spectrum* and *Brumark* decisions therefore has no particular relevance to charges over chattels or other tangible moveable assets.[27] Given computerization and the ability to identify and track goods and work in progress even through a production process it is now often possible to evidence control with specific releases of goods which form part of the circulating capital of a company from the charge at a time which fits with the business cycle of the chargor. Stock and work in progress typically do form part of the circulating capital of a company. The question is therefore whether the use of release mechanisms which are not compatible with the usual and ordinary course of business of the chargor and fit with the point of sale, means that the courts would still consider the charge only to be a floating charge (and reject the fixed nature of the security). This would appear an extremely uncommercial attitude for the courts to take as they would then be penalizing lenders for sophistication in their control methods.

(e) Receivables

Of greatest difficulty perhaps, are other types of chose in action or, as Lord Millett put it in the *Brumark* case, the general category of 'receivable'.[28] When is a chose in action to be regarded as a mere receivable and when is it appropriate to view a contractual right separately and distinct from a connected right of payment for the purpose of analysing the nature of charges?[29]

The leading case in this area is *Re Atlantic Computer Systems plc* where an attempt was made to attack the 'fixed' nature of a security by way of assignment of the chargor's rights under sub-leases of computers and related equipment which in the ordinary course of *Atlantic*'s business were sub-leased to end users. (Atlantic Computer Systems did not own the equipment but leased it from financiers and then sub-leased it to end users.) The relevant charging clause was contained within an assignment agreement, which expressly referred to the right to receive 'rentals, claims, rights, demands and other moneys or claims for moneys under each of the sub-leases'.

In his judgment in *Atlantic Computer Systems*, Lord Nicholls drew attention to

[27] The two-stage process outlined by Lord Millett in *Brumark* (para 32), namely first to ascertain the nature of the rights and obligations which the parties intended to grant and secondly correctly to categorize the charge as fixed or floating as a question of law, applies no matter what the nature of the asset (see *Arthur D Little Ltd (in administration) v Ableco Finance LLC* [2002] EWHC 701, [2003] Ch 217 (shares); *Smith v Bridgend CBC* [2001] UKHL 58, [2002] 1 AC 336 (plant and machinery)). It is the applicability of some of the broad statements concerning book debts, the nature of this asset type and control thereof that is the critical issue for practitioners in the post-*Spectrum* climate.

[28] *Brumark*, paras 43 and 46.

[29] cf S Worthington, 'Floating Charges: The Use and Abuse of Doctrinal Analysis', ch 3 above and R Stevens, 'Security after the Enterprise Act', ch 7 below.

the fact that the sub-leases which were the subject of the security were already in existence at the time of assignment to the secured creditor and each sub-lease was specifically identified in a deed of assignment. In each case the payments due to the company under the sub-lease stood as security for payments due from the company under the head lease from the financier relating to the same equipment. Again having referred to Romer LJ's three-limb test in the *Yorkshire Woolcombers* case, Nicholls LJ held that the charged assets were not 'future' assets and the fact that sums payable by end users under the sub-leases were paid to the company (and available for its use in the ordinary course of its business) did not prejudice the fixed nature of the charge over the sub-leases.[30] In his view the position was the same with regard to the sub-leases of equipment as it would be in relation to charges over leasehold interests in land, even if the charged interest was very short and the asset was of a wasting character.[31] The essence of the decision was that the rights under the sub-leases, which whilst being connected with the right to receive payment, were not identical with it.[32]

A more controversial decision (at least so it would appear in the view of Lord Millett) was that reached by Vinelott J, in *Re Atlantic Medical Ltd*.[33] The facts in that case were very similar to the facts in *Atlantic Computer Systems*. Once again the business of the charging company was that of an intermediary supplier of equipment owned by financiers and leased to the chargor. The assignment by way of security in the *Atlantic Medical* case applied not only to agreements with end users already in existence but also to 'any other sub-leases, hire purchase agreements or similar agreements from time to time entered into by the [company]'. In the view of Vinelott J, this difference did not amount to a valid ground for distinction with the *Atlantic Computer Systems* decision and he held that the charge was still a fixed charge.

Vinelott J, like Lord Nicholls in the earlier *Atlantic Computer Systems* case, appears to have considered that the sub-leases, the subject of the charges, were more than simply a right to receive income even though that right was an important commercial benefit that arose under the sub-leases. For example, if a sub-tenant ceased to pay, the sub-lessor could then reclaim the goods. Of course, a vendor that sells goods under reservation of title could make a similar argument, but in such a case there would not be the same succession of distinct legal interests in the goods.

[30] *Re Atlantic Computer Systems plc* [1992] Ch 505, 534. [31] ibid.

[32] The reasoning for finding there was no floating charge based upon there being no fluctuating body of assets has been the subject of much criticism. See R Goode, 'Charges over Book Debts: A Missed Opportunity' (1994) 110 LQR 592 and R Goode, *Legal Problems of Credit and Security*, (3rd edn, 2003) para 4–15.

[33] [1993] BCLC 386.

It is suspected that Lord Millett was not persuaded by the *Atlantic Medical* decision and part of practitioners' nervousness about the possible implications of the *Spectrum* decision stems from his, albeit largely obiter, judgment in the case of *Royal Trust Bank plc v National Westminster Bank plc*.[34] In this case, once again, the chargor was in the business of supplying equipment to end users which it had leased from financiers. Royal Trust Bank (RTB) provided the finance to the company and as security for its borrowing the company had executed a deed of assignment of charge under which it assigned to RTB the benefit of the sub-hiring agreements from time to time deposited with RTB. The company was required to observe a cover ratio of the value of the charged agreements to the loan outstanding of 140 per cent. The company was also, if required by RBT, obliged to pay all income received under sub-leases, etc into a nominated account with National Westminster Bank. In practice no such requirement had been imposed and in any event the nominated account in question was a normal operating account of the company with National Westminster Bank (ie it was not set up as a blocked account under the control of RTB).

In his judgment in the *Royal Trust Bank* case Lord Millett remarked: 'I do not see how it is possible to separate *a debt or other receivable* from the proceeds of its realization'.[35] Lord Millett then observed that because the charging document effectively allowed the company to collect proceeds under the charged agreements and (at most) to pay them into an unregulated bank account (and then to make withdrawals from that account as it wished) that the company was free to apply the money it received in respect of deposited agreements in the ordinary course of its business.[36] He also considered that as a result of the 140 per cent cover arrangement the company was able to withhold agreements from the charge and deal with them free from any security interest. The company's ability to apply the proceeds of the charged assets (and in his view therefore the agreements) in the ordinary course of its business was not a matter of acquiescence but of contract. RTB never intervened and the company's contractual right to collect the money for its own benefit was never determined.

Lord Millett clearly regarded the company's right to enjoy the income stream under the sub-leases and the sub-leases themselves as one and the same. It is therefore difficult to reconcile his comments with the decision in *Atlantic Medical*; but for the distinguishing features of present and future agreements and rights of removal, his remarks might seem at odds with the decision in *Atlantic Computer Systems* itself.

It is unlikely that Lord Scott and the House of Lords in *Spectrum* were unaware

34 [1996] 2 BCLC 682, 699.

35 [1996] 2 BCLC 682, 704 (emphasis added).

36 [1996] 2 BCLC 682, 705.

of Lord Millett's remarks in *Royal Trust Bank plc v National Westminster Bank plc*. Hence Lord Scott's references to 'debts' rather than 'receivables' is, perhaps, noteworthy. In *Re ASRS Establishment Ltd (in administrative receivership and liquidation)*,[37] Otton LJ observed that the dicta of Lord Millett in the *Royal Trust Bank* case should be approached with some caution and it is submitted that in *Spectrum* the House of Lords was careful not to venture into the territory of 'other receivable'. Indeed Lord Millett himself in the *Brumark* case, while leaving the door ajar to an extension of his analysis to other types of receivable, excluded from his analysis of the equivalence of debts and proceeds, reference to other receivables.[38]

7. When fixed charges over assets other than debts become floating charges

Even where the charged interests are to be regarded as more than 'merely a right to receive payment',[39] it is clearly possible to transform what are apparently fixed charges into floating charges. This could happen if arrangements between the mortgagor and mortgagee are such as to allow the mortgagor to take assets into and out of the charge as it wishes in the ordinary course of its business. This may be so even though releases or consents are required to remove the asset from the charge if (1) it is pre-agreed that such will be forthcoming; (2) the agreement goes beyond a one-off arrangement; and (3) it would lead the court to view the charged assets as forming (and having been intended by the parties to form) part of the usual circulating capital of a company. Rights of substitution of security are problematic in this regard. The other issue (to be considered below) is that of a partial release back to the chargor of the proceeds of realization or disposal.

8. The dangers of a bundled approach to charging clause drafting

The danger of the court concluding that if some of the assets described in a charging clause are subject only to a floating charge, so all other assets covered by the same clause must also be regarded as subject to a floating charge, was highlighted by the House of Lords' decision in *Smith v Bridgend CBC*.

The case concerned an Institution of Civil Engineers standard form contract which purported to give the employing borough council the right to use and then remove and sell plant belonging to the contractor in the event of the contractor abandoning the contract. Having held that the right was a right in the nature of a charge, the House of Lords considered whether a large coal washing plant was to be regarded as subject to a fixed or a floating charge. In the leading judgment Lord Hoffmann (having determined that the coal washing plant fell within the same charging clause as other small items of plant which

[37] [2000] 2 BCLC 631, CA. [38] *Brumark*, para 43. [39] *Brumark*, para 46.

were likely to come and go during the course of a four-year contract), concluded 'it is in my opinion impossible to construe the latter [the relevant] condition as creating a charge over the washing plant different in nature from that which it created over the other plant and materials brought on site'.[40] The fact that decisions as to whether plant could be removed from the site was delegated to a site agent rather than taken by the chargee was also remarked upon.

Then, in *Re ASRS*, the Court of Appeal considered whether the judge at first instance had been correct in adopting an 'all or nothing' approach to a charging clause (ie he found that as one of the items covered by the clause was subject only to a floating charge so all other items referred to in that clause must also be subject only to a floating charge). In the leading judgment, Robert Walker LJ indicated that he would not accept the 'all or nothing' approach entirely without reservation. He said[41] that while a court would not listen to arguments about the relative permanence or impermanence of a desk, computer, or forklift truck in the same charging clause, it might conceivably listen to an argument that works of art should receive a different treatment from other tangible assets because they were of such a different nature and thus did not fall within the category of circulating assets (within the second characteristic referred to by Romer LJ in the *Yorkshire Woolcombers* case).

It appears that one conclusion to be drawn from these two cases is that if a charging clause charges assets of the same type (for example, tangible goods) the courts are unlikely to distinguish between the nature of the charge which applies to assets within the same clause unless it is persuaded there was a clear intention to this effect (so the 'all or nothing' risk is high). When it comes to clauses which refer to assets which the law regards as of a different type then, it is submitted, the courts are more likely to allow distinctions in their treatment.

The fact that a charging clause dealing with land also refers to income produced from the land does not reduce the charge over the land to the status of the floating charge (see the *Offshore Ventilation* case). The same should be the case with a charge over shares in which the charging clause also refers to the right to receive dividends (see the *Arthur D Little* case). Again, this should be so when considering charges over a chose in action where the underlying agreements which give rise to the right to receive payment can be viewed separately from the debts or income which arise under them (see the *Atlantic Computer Systems* and *Atlantic Medical* cases). Although such distinctions may provide some comfort, a draftsman of a nervous disposition may still prefer to 'unbundle' charging clauses and either refer to income rights connected with other assets in a

40 *Smith v Bridgend CBC* [2001] UKHL 58, [2002] 1 AC 336, para 44.

41 [2000] 2 BCLC 631, 639.

different clause or not at all (on the basis that, as with land, shares, etc, these pass with the main underlying asset and do not need to be referred to).[42]

9. Payment waterfalls and previously agreed release arrangements

(a) General

In *Spectrum* Lord Hope remarked that the contractual right of the company 'to draw out sums equivalent to the amount paid in, is wholly destructive of the argument that there was a fixed charge over the uncollected proceeds'.[43] Lord Scott also considered that because the overdraft facility was there to be drawn on by Spectrum at will[44] so the company was left free as a matter of contract to operate its bank account with the chargee bank within the limits of the overdraft in the ordinary and usual course of its business. These comments signify that both Law Lords concluded that the operating limit applicable to the account into which book debt proceeds were paid did not connote control by the chargor; rather they confirmed a contractual entitlement for the borrower to operate that account freely until an event of default occurred or the limit was reached.[45]

Modern lending agreements often contain a wide range of financial restrictions or ratios. Few of those financial restrictions will be linked directly to associated security (although security cover ratios may be). The existence of such restrictions is likely to provide relatively little assistance to the analysis of the nature of a charge. What of permissions to deal with assets the subject of charges or pre-agreements as to the application of proceeds of realization?

It might be suggested that any agreement which contemplates the borrower being entitled to use part of the proceeds of sale of a charged asset freely for its business purposes renders the charge over the asset in question only a floating charge. This is not, it is submitted, what the *Spectrum* judgments imply. Again, the critical point to note is that *Spectrum* was dealing with a situation in which no consents or releases were required to take the debt proceeds (and therefore the charged assets) out of the ambit of the charge, ie through the operation of a bank account into which the proceeds were paid. When considering other types of asset, this will seldom be the case. The 'concurrence' of the chargee (ie in the form of a release) will have to be obtained. The need for such a release, prima facie, connotes control. Furthermore, an additional distinction may

[42] The general rule is that in the absence of a specific provision in the security document to the contrary dealing with income it will belong to the chargor who is lawfully in possession of a tangible asset such as land or goods. See *Tucker v Farm & General Investment Trust Ltd* [1966] 2 QB 421 and R Goode, *Legal Problems of Credit and Security* (3rd edn, 2003) para 1–61.

[43] *Spectrum*, para 61.

[44] *Spectrum*, para 119.

[45] This point is also implicit in Lord Walker's judgment in *Spectrum*, para 155, when he refers to credit available under an agreed overdraft as being part of a company's circulating capital.

be drawn between cases which involve circulating assets (which is generally the case with debts) and those which involve non-circulating or 'fixed' assets (eg, benefits under insurance contracts, land used to carry on business or plant and machinery used to produce finished goods) which do not fluctuate in the ordinary course of business.

(b) Non-circulating assets

In the case of specific non-circulating assets, an agreement from the lender that a release of security to permit a sale will be forthcoming on certain terms should not detract from the fixed nature of the charge, even if it is agreed that the entire proceeds may be used for working capital purposes by the company. Clearly, if the lender agrees to the release after the charge has been taken there should be no question. In a case where a release of security will be required, it should make no difference to the nature of the charge that the parties have thought about the issue of disposal and agreed a basis for the grant of the release in advance (rather than leaving it to be determined later).

(c) Circulating assets

It is submitted that where the charge relates to specific assets which are to be considered as forming part of the circulating capital of the company, if releases are required to remove the relevant asset from the charge, pre-agreeing the basis for such release (and how proceeds will be shared) should not of itself render a specific charge 'ambulatory or shifting in nature'. However, if the pre-agreement between the parties is such that (as a matter of contract or manifest intention) the releases are a mere formality and granted on the basis that the entire proceeds will be at the free disposal of the company, the position may well be different. In such a case, the courts are likely to view the requirement for releases as illusory and construing the arrangements as a whole, determine that they create only a floating charge. This is hardly a new development in the law.

Even if specific assets form part of the circulating capital of a company a pre-agreement as to how proceeds of sale are to be applied should not detract from the fixed nature of the charge if: (a) a specific release from the charge is required for the asset to be disposed of; and (b) the company is not left free to enjoy the entire benefit of the proceeds as it sees fit.

A pre-agreement between the parties that proceeds from charged assets be applied in a particular manner to discharge stated liabilities in a particular order should constitute adequate control by the lender to support a fixed charge. This should be so even if the charged assets are debts provided the application of the funds in the agreed order is in the hands of a party other than the borrower. If, however, the borrower is left to apply the proceeds of realization of debts in a predetermined manner, the case might be viewed as within the ambit of

Spectrum unless the non-discretionary nature of the waterfall is accepted as adequate control (ie the waterfall would need to be viewed as a restriction on the discretion of the borrower, rather than a sophisticated articulation of the expectation of what usually occurs in the ordinary course of business).

In *Spectrum* Lord Walker when discussing the difference between fixed and floating charges helpfully alludes to the possibility of a 'partial release' in the context of an example involving the development by a developer of a large area of land for a housing estate.[46] He viewed a charge over the land as an example of a purported fixed charge over what was to be regarded as the trading stock (of the developer). He pointed out that it might be short-sighted for the bank chargee not to agree to take only a fraction of the proceeds of sale (ie to allow the developer to continue to fund the development) concluding: 'But under a fixed charge that will be a matter for the chargee to decide for itself'.[47] His concluding remark does not indicate that a partial release would negate a fixed charge. Nor does it imply that pre-agreements to give a partial release of proceeds are fatal to a fixed charge. His remark does, however, leave open the issue of whether in relation to assets that are clearly circulating capital or trading stock, a pre-agreement to allow the borrower full use of all the proceeds of sale in a particular case is compatible with a fixed charge, even if formal releases are required. It is submitted that a distinction should therefore be drawn between, on the one hand, instances when the pre-agreement by the chargee to provide releases to permit disposals of the charged asset is to be regarded as of a 'standing' nature applicable to a class of assets and, on the other, a 'specific' permission which only applies to certain of the assets within the class.

B. *Spectrum* and Securitizations and Other Structured Financings

1. Introduction

One area of the financial markets where clarification of the boundaries of the *Spectrum* decision would be particularly appreciated is structured financing and in particular securitizations. When the *Spectrum* decision is applied to these cases it is difficult to align the historical and policy grounds of the *Spectrum* decision with the sophisticated financing techniques employed and developed in these markets.

For present purposes we take structured financings and securitizations broadly to mean transactions where cash flows are engineered to deliver returns to different classes of investor through the use of companies especially created for

46 *Spectrum*, para 138.

47 ibid.

this purpose and commonly referred to as special purpose vehicles or SPVs. More often than not these transactions will be rated and the quality of a rating is affected by legal uncertainty and the resultant risk which it represents.

There is a prevailing sense amongst securitization practitioners that when the principles set out in *Brumark* and *Spectrum* are applied to the SPVs, the wrong medicine is being applied to the malady, if indeed there is a malady to remedy in the first place.

The reason for this is that the majority of cases on the issue of re-characterization of floating charges (and certainly in relation to the seminal cases, namely *Yorkshire Woolcombers, Brumark* and *Spectrum*) are concerned with what are regarded by the courts as trading companies and the security provided by trading companies in respect of financings afforded to them by their relationship banks.

By way of illustration, the *Yorkshire Woolcombers* case involved the Yorkshire Woolcombers Association Ltd which had an overdraft with the Bradford District Bank Ltd, guaranteed by its directors, which guarantee it had secured through a security trust over its book and other debts. The *Brumark* case involved a debenture granted by Brumark, which was in the construction business, to its bank Westpac Banking Corporation, to secure its indebtedness. The security extended to any of Brumark's book debts which arose in the ordinary course of trading. In *Spectrum*, the company, which was a manufacturer of dyes, paints, pigments, and other chemical products for the paint industry, secured its overdraft facility with NatWest by way of a purportedly fixed charge over all its book and other debts. It is this fact pattern which informs the decisions of the courts on the issue of re-characterization.

The provision by trading companies of security to relationship banks is not the only context in which security is given, albeit that the key decisions on this issue have only concerned this type of arrangement. Applying the statements made in the judgments to structured financings and securitizations proves an uncomfortable fit.

In the rest of this chapter:

(1) we consider the nature of structured financing and in particular securitizations by examining how a typical securitization works;
(2) we draw out some of the distinctions between an SPV employed in a securitization and a trading company raising funds for general purposes;
(3) we argue that the *Brumark* and *Spectrum* principles should not be applied in their narrowest sense to structured financings and securitizations but construed more widely so as to make practical sense in the context of the structured finance and securitization markets; and
(4) we consider whether there are policy grounds which render a wide

interpretation of the *Brumark* and *Spectrum* judgments inappropriate and conclude that there are not.

2. Typical securitization structure

We have briefly defined what is meant by structured financing and securitizations. However, to understand the difficulties which arise when a re-characterization analysis for a trading company and its relationship bank is applied to an SPV a more detailed understanding of the way SPVs operate in this context is required. What follows describes how a paradigm true sale securitization works so that the differences between the securitization and the trading company/overdraft arrangement can be drawn.

The following describes a 'true sale securitization' of unsecured consumer loans. The securitization is designed to permit the originator (namely the company wishing to securitize its unsecured consumer loans) to access funding through a public bond issuance involving senior and junior classes of debt, achieving 'AAA/Aaa' ratings for the highest ranking classes independently of the originator's credit status (since the originator's debt obligations are themselves likely to be unrated or maybe rated to a lesser standard).

(a) The SPV

A special purpose company, in other words the company to which we earlier referred as an SPV, is established to purchase assets, comprising unsecured consumer loans, from a seller known as the originator.

The SPV is a new shelf company with no trading history. It is established solely to purchase the assets and apply their proceeds in a pre-agreed fashion (see below). It is restricted from undertaking any other type of business or transaction other than the securitization. This is achieved by limiting its powers in its memorandum and articles of association and placing tight contractual controls on what it is able to do. The SPV appoints a servicer as its agent to perform its responsibilities concerning debt service. There is no commercial incentive for the SPV to do anything other than enter into and perform its obligations under the securitization. Its directors will typically be independent professional service providers or associated with the originator. Its shareholder will be a charitable trust. The likelihood of it undertaking any other commercial activity, including other trading, is therefore extremely remote, a view which is shared by the rating agencies.

(b) Bond issue

The SPV funds the asset purchase by issuing bonds. The subscription moneys for the bonds are paid by the SPV to the originator in consideration for the purchase of the assets. The bondholders are reliant solely on the proceeds of the assets for payment on their bonds.

(c) Funding parties

The SPV will contract with other counterparties whose role is to provide liquidity or credit enhancement to the transaction to assist in the transaction receiving its desired rating. Typical such roles include a hedge counterparty, to provide hedging, and the provision of additional liquidity in certain other circumstances, for example by an initial subordinated loan provider and an ongoing liquidity facilities provider.

(d) Security

The SPV provides fixed and floating security over all of its assets in favour of a trustee who holds the security on trust for the secured parties who comprise (*inter alios*) the bondholders, the trustee, any receiver, the hedge counterparty, the initial subordinated loan provider and the liquidity facility provider.

(e) Servicer

The SPV's assets are managed by a company known as the servicer, which is normally a subsidiary of the originator, under the terms of a servicing agreement. It will be appointed as agent for the SPV in managing its assets and liabilities until an event of default occurs, when it becomes the trustee's agent, or as agent for the SPV and the trustee jointly until an event of default occurs, when again it becomes the trustee's agent (see Section 6, Using joint agency below for more on this issue). The servicer collects in the proceeds of the assets and is also responsible for ensuring that those proceeds are applied in accordance with the SPV's obligations under the transaction documentation and in particular in accordance with the priority of payments provisions (see (f) below).

(f) SPV's charged account

Proceeds from the assets are first required to be paid into the originator's account, because the sale is not notified to the consumer loan obligors at the inception of the transaction. The originator declares a trust over the account in favour of itself and the SPV in pre-agreed proportions. The issuer's proportion is then paid into the issuer's account.

The issuer's account is secured by way of a fixed charge in favour of the security trustee and is operated by the servicer in accordance with the terms of the servicing agreement.

The way in which amounts credited to the issuer's account from time to time are applied will vary according to whether or not an event of default has occurred. Prior to the occurrence of an event of default the servicer will be charged with making various calculations which will determine whether there are amounts available for application in accordance with the pre-agreed priority of payments.

(g) Priority of payments[48]

The priority of payments provisions typically provide that the following amounts are paid in the following order: all amounts owing by law; all fees owing to date to the secured parties in the transaction (such as the trustee, account bank, liquidity facility provider, etc); payments due under any swaps (interest payments are kept current on all classes of bonds); maintaining certain reserves; amounts owing to any subordinated loan facility provider; accrued servicer fee (which is essentially remaining cash which returns to the originator). It is only after these current transaction costs have been met and any reserves have been made whole (and if there are no available funds from prepayments or repayments on the consumer loans) that funds, up to pre-agreed limits, are available to buy further assets and after a period of reserve are then used to redeem the principal of the issued bonds.

3. Distinguishing between a securitization SPV and a trading company

From the above description the following key differences between a securitization SPV and a trading company can be identified.

(a) Freedom to carry on business

Broadly the cases dealing with the distinction between fixed and floating charges focus on the degree to which the chargor is free to use its assets, in the ordinary course of its business, regardless of the fact that they are secured.

This theme was picked up early on. In the *Yorkshire Woolcombers* case it was clearly expressed by Vaughan Williams LJ, in the Court of Appeal, when he said that when he took the deed in question as a whole he found 'clauses and arrangements which to my mind, are wholly consistent with it having been the intention of both parties here that the association should be allowed to deal with these book debts when they come into existence just as if there had been no mortgage at all, unless and until the mortgagee thought fit to intervene'.[49]

What Vaughan Williams LJ was concerned with was that in that case the chargor

[48] This description is a simplified version of a typical priority of payments provision in so far as it does not distinguish receipts of a 'principal' and 'revenue' nature. To do so would have been to complicate the description since an explanation of the distinction between principal and revenue payments would have been required much of which would have been repetitive without affecting the fundamental point we wish to make which is that no discretion exists in the manner in which payments are applied.

[49] [1903] 2 Ch 284, 292.

was free to behave just as it would have done had it not given security. The chargor is conceived as having a business life which exists separately from its bank financing arrangements and the judges' concerns centre on the fact that business life continues freely notwithstanding that the chargor has granted security over its assets. As we have already discussed,[50] the issue of this freedom was taken up by Lord Scott in *Spectrum* when he summarized Lord Millett's judgment in *Brumark* by saying that 'the critical feature which distinguished a floating charge from a fixed charge lay in the chargor's ability, freely and without the chargee's consent, to control and manage the charged assets and withdraw them from the security'.[51] For an SPV this can never be the case. Without affording security over its assets and making precise arrangements concerning how those assets are regularly to be applied in meeting its debts as they fall due, the SPV would have no business life. There is therefore no sense in which it has a trading life apart from its financing—as discussed above its *raison d'être* is the fulfilment of its obligations under the securitization transaction documents including the security deed which in effect are its agreement to give effect to the priority of payments provisions—and therefore no practical way in which in spite of the provision of security, it can be free to carry on its business unchecked.

Therefore Lord Scott's observation in *Spectrum* that 'it is in the nature of commercial borrowers to want to be able to carry on the business for the purposes of which they are borrowing money with as much freedom from restrictions imposed by their lenders that negotiation can achieve for them'[52] is not applicable to SPVs. SPVs do not require this sort of freedom, indeed they are never intended to be free but instead to be circumscribed in detail. However, nor is it intended that every debit and credit from the charged account be consented to by the chargee, since this would be impractical. Instead pre-agreed controls exist as outlined above which dictate what the SPV can do.

(b) An SPV is not a trading company

Earlier in this chapter[53] we discuss circulating assets and why we consider that a pre-agreed basis for release should not of itself render a fixed charge floating. In the context of SPVs, however, we would go a stage further and argue that the SPV does not have circulating assets in the sense this term is used in the cases in the context of trading companies.

In *Spectrum*, Lord Scott reviewed the nineteenth century commercial concerns which formed the background to legal concerns regarding floating charges and

[50] See pp 108–11 above. [51] *Spectrum*, para 89. [52] ibid.
[53] At Part A, Section 9 above.

spoke of the fact that fixed security operated against the need for companies to have capital to expand. In his judgment he explained that: 'the greater part of most entrepreneurial companies' assets would consist of raw materials, work in progress, stock-in-trade and trade debts. These were circulating assets, replaced in the normal course of business and constantly changing'.[54]

Lord Walker described the position in his judgment as being that 'so long as the company trades in the ordinary way . . . the constituents of the charged fund are in a state of flux (or circulation). Trading stock is sold and becomes represented by book debts; these are collected and paid into the bank; the trader's overdraft facility enables it to draw cheques in favour of its suppliers to pay for new stock; and so the trading cycle continues'.[55]

In our example it can be seen that the securitization SPV does not trade in the manner described above and so does not have circulating assets in the sense that the trading companies considered in *Brumark* and *Spectrum* have. The SPV was created solely to purchase assets, using the subscription moneys from the bonds, which are later repaid from the proceeds of those assets. Typically the SPV will make one such asset purchase. Sometimes, however, early amortization of the debts forming the SPV's assets will give rise to cash flows which may then be recycled to purchase further similar assets from the originator, subject to the existing security and payment applications scheme. However we would argue that this is not akin to the circulating assets, raw materials, work in progress, stock-in-trade, and trade debts of the trading companies which were in the contemplation of the judges in *Brumark* and *Spectrum*. Why? Because the purchase is made from one identified source, the originator. The originator is fully apprised of the position of the SPV and is far removed from the type of vulnerable unsecured trade creditor needing protection with which the cases are concerned. The ability to make these additional purchases is subject to detailed conditions and so is fully controlled, the SPV has no discretion to trade. Clearly then the SPV's existence does not involve a trading cycle of the sort described by Lord Walker.

(c) Trade creditors

The creditors of the SPV are deliberately designed not to be general unsecured trade creditors in need of protection. An SPV's creditors form a limited class, typically the secured beneficiaries under the security trust and referred to above as secured parties. The dangers with which the courts have been concerned and which have been identified repeatedly in the judgments and encapsulated by Lord Walker's observation in *Spectrum* are that 'the widespread use of floating

[54] [2005] UKHL 41, [2005] 2 AC 680, para 95. [55] ibid para 139.

charges over trading stock, book debts and other circulating capital precede a situation in which a company's business might appear to be thriving and prosperous . . . until a sudden and unexpected crystallization of a floating charge revealed that nothing at all was left for the company's unsecured creditors, even if they were preferential creditors'.[56]

4. Applying the *Brumark* and *Spectrum* tests to an SPV

(a) Brumark

The differences between a trading company and an SPV identified above are the reasons why practitioners find the application of the *Brumark/Spectrum* tests to SPV charged accounts a conundrum. This is because on a literal application of those tests, in relation to the operation of charged accounts, it might be suggested that a re-characterization risk exists in relation to the operation of those charged accounts, yet the result makes little sense.

This can be illustrated by applying the approach taken in *Brumark* and *Spectrum* against the fact pattern of the true sale securitization described above. In the days before *Brumark* the tests of Romer LJ in the *Yorkshire Woolcombers* were generally the starting point.

Up until *Brumark* the orthodoxy had been that there had to be 'controls' placed on the company's business and its ability to deal with its assets, with uncertainty surrounding the necessary levels of control. In this context comfort levels generally existed in relation to the restraints imposed by the waterfall and the other contractual restrictions contained in the securitization transaction documents on an SPV's activities. In *Brumark*, Lord Millett made a subtle change to the analysis and the levels of comfort dropped accordingly. Instead of analysing the position by reference to the chargor's ability freely to deal with the assets, as had been typical previously, Lord Millett stressed the position of the charge holder. This is reflected in his judgment when he said that:

> this is the other side of the coin. If the chargor is free to deal with the charged assets and so withdraw them from the ambit of the charge without the consent of the chargee, then the charge is a floating charge. But the test can equally well be expressed from the chargee's point of view. If the charged assets are not under its control so that it can prevent their dissipation without its consent, then the charge cannot be a fixed charge.[57]

This shift of emphasis had two key effects from a securitization perspective.

First it took Lord Millett down a path which ultimately identified only two ways

[56] ibid para 132. [57] *Brumark*, para 23.

of establishing charge holder control (though allowing for other unidentified possibilities). In his judgment he said that:

> to constitute a charge on book debts a fixed charge, it is sufficient to prohibit the company from realising the debts itself, whether by assignment or collection. If the company seeks permission to do so in respect of a particular debt, the charge-holder can refuse permission or grant permission on terms, and can thus direct the application of the proceeds. But it is not necessary to go this far.[58]

Lord Millett went on to say that a blocked account will also work 'since the debts are not available to the company as a source of its cash flow'.

For some the distinction between obtaining a permission for each payment transfer and a blocked account is hard to discern. In any event this left securitizers with a difficulty. Having the security trustee consent to release from an account on every occasion a payment transfer is made is sufficiently time consuming to jeopardize the smooth operation of the bond issuance. Controls were in place over the SPV's activities (as set out above) but these types of control were not specifically approved by Lord Millett. Although Lord Millett had said 'but it is not necessary to go this far', he gave no guidance as to how far was not far enough. In emphasizing that the badge of the fixed charge is the ability of the charge holder to refuse permission to release and that its consent should be sought on each occasion, there was little recognition of other mechanisms for ensuring restrictions on freedom to deal such as the pre-agreed restrictions imposed on SPVs in the true sale securitization outlined above. In this case the SPV is about as controlled as possible, save on the limited basis prescribed by Lord Millett, namely chargor consent on each withdrawal. In particular the SPV cannot 'dissipate' its assets (to use Lord Millett's phrase) notwithstanding that charge holder consent is not required for every release from the account.

(b) Spectrum

In the *Spectrum* case Lord Millett's arguments were developed further. Lord Scott determined that the distinguishing characteristic of a floating charge is that the 'asset subject to the charge is not finally appropriated as a security for the payment of the debt until the occurrence of some future event. In the meantime the chargor is left free to use the charged asset and to remove it from the security'.[59]

Another concept had arrived to beleaguer securitization lawyers: 'Appropriation as a security'. What is meant by this in the context of an SPV in a securitization? We have already referred[60] to Lord Walker's judgment where he commented that a fixed charge exists when 'assets charged . . . are permanently appropriated

[58] *Brumark*, para 48.
[59] *Spectrum*, para 111.
[60] At Part A, Section 5 above.

to the payment of the sum charged, in such a way as to give the chargee a proprietary interest in the assets'. We also referred to his explanation of the phrase, when he went on to say 'so long as the charge remains unredeemed, the assets can be released from the charge only with the active concurrence of the chargee' and further noted that this harks back to Lord Millett's blocked account test for 'control' purposes. We would argue that the restrictions and consents comprising and supplementing the waterfall applications in a securitization should be taken to demonstrate such active concurrence, and that it should not be read in all cases as meaning express consent to each release from an account.

(c) 'Control' should be assessed in the round

The problems associated with trying to apply such an analysis to a securitization structure remain. Lord Walker, as we have seen, supposes that only active concurrence by the charge holder in releases from the charge, will connote a fixed charge. Why? Because as he states, without it, 'it is for the trader and not the bank to decide how to run its business'.[61] Is this so however? The SPV operates by virtue of the servicer under the auspices of the priority of payments and it is questionable whether it is really able to decide how to run its business. The SPV has never been 'free' to run its business, as we discuss above. It is designed to undertake certain activities only, all of which are predetermined and which in particular centre on the performance of the priority of payments provisions. In truth the SPV enjoys no freedoms, nor would the market tolerate its doing so, nor would its directors wish to have any discretions. The focus in *Spectrum* (and indeed *Brumark* and *Yorkshire Woolcombers*) on a charge created by a trading company over its accounts in favour of a relationship bank has resulted in a judgment which, because it has not considered other terms or restrictions placed on a chargor's use of its book debts, does not address the concerns of a significant part of the financial markets. For these reasons it is submitted that if a court were asked to consider, not a trading company, but an SPV in a securitization, it should conclude that the constraints placed on the SPV taken together mean that the charges created by it are of a fixed nature, even if specific chargee consent is not given at the time each payment is made from its bank accounts. In other words that the arrangement is licensed by Lord Millett's category of exceptions to which he alludes when he says, '[b]ut it is not necessary to go this far'.

5. A discussion of policy in this area

The courts have been very concerned to distinguish between fixed and floating

[61] *Spectrum*, para 139.

charges on grounds of policy. This concern is of limited relevance to an SPV in a securitization.

In both *Brumark* and *Spectrum* the historical background to the fixed/floating charge debate was discussed. If this background is examined it is difficult to see how the concerns raised apply in the context of securitizations.

In *Brumark*, Lord Millett states that 'banks did not want to monitor the bank account and be required to give their consent whenever the company made a withdrawal. They wanted the best of both worlds. They wanted to have a fixed charge on the book debts of a company while allowing the company the same freedom to use the proceeds that it would have had if the charge were a floating charge'.[62]

This may be the case with trading companies and their relationship banks, but is not the case with a securitization. In the case of a securitization all parties, such as the originator, the trustee, the bondholders, the hedge counterparty, the liquidity facility provider and indeed the rating agencies who review the transaction documentation for rating purposes, are concerned to ensure that the SPV is not free to apply the proceeds of its debts as it sees fit. Hence the tight contractual constraints on the use to which the proceeds are put, albeit pre-agreed.

Lord Millett in *Brumark* cites two mischiefs which gave rise to the floating charge.[63] One was a concern relating to preferential creditors. This concern remains, but obviously since the Enterprise Act 2002, only in a much diluted form. The other was the concern that ordinary trade creditors were put at risk because the charge holder could step in without warning at any time and obtain priority over them.

This is not really an issue on a securitization, as noted above, because the SPV is limited from incurring general trade debts by virtue of narrow powers in its memorandum and articles of association which permit it to act only for its special purpose, and because of the contractual restrictions which bind it, including the waterfall.

It is possible that parties may seek to fit out a trading company in the clothes of an SPV. The courts would of course be alert to such a possibility. Apart from relying on the common-sense approach of 'spotting a trading company when they see one' we would argue that the courts would look to the critical distinguishing features of the SPV which are (a) the lack of discretion vested in it or

---

62 *Brumark*, para 27.

63 *Brumark*, para 10.

in any party controlling it and (b) the fact that its principal business is nothing more complicated than giving effect to the priority of payments provisions.

Lord Walker elaborated on these concerns in his judgment in *Spectrum*, summarizing that 'the perceived mischief was akin to that underlying the doctrine of reputed ownership in bankruptcy, that creditors should not be misled by appearances'.[64] He was referring to trading companies whose businesses 'appear to be thriving and prosperous, with goods on its shelves and customers at its doors, until a sudden and unexpected crystallization of a floating charge'[65] reveals that nothing at all is left for the company's unsecured creditors. For the reasons reprised above there is really no similar concern for securitizations.

6. Using joint agency

Arguably there is a quick fix available to securitizers even now to enable them to sidestep the impact of *Spectrum*. As discussed earlier, the servicer may be appointed from the outset as the joint agent of the trustee and the issuer. If the servicer is clearly only operating as the trustee's agent in connection with payments from the issuer's bank account, then since the servicer is responsible for transfers from the issuer's account to meet the payments prescribed by the waterfall, it is in effect, as the trustee's agent, consenting to account releases on each occasion on which it authorizes them. Provided that the joint agency with the issuer is not somehow considered to contaminate its authority and the contractual obligation on the servicer to make payments out if tests are met is not regarded as prejudicing the necessary degree of control, this may be enough to demonstrate that the security trustee has the necessary proprietary interest in the charged account.

The difficulty, as with all these arguments, is the lack of a definitive answer to these questions. This uncertainty bedevils the rating agencies and ultimately the securitization market—an increasingly significant part of the UK economy, as the Capital Markets exception to the Enterprise Act 2002[66] acknowledged.

7. Conclusions and the future

The current enthusiasm of lenders to lend without 'gateway' protection[67] shows no sign of abating and given the importance of the issue in terms of 'control' in relation to the availability of charged assets in an administration[68] and the likely

---

64 *Spectrum*, para 132.
65 *Spectrum*, para 133.
66 See Insolvency Act 1986, s 72B.
67 Insolvency Act 1986, ss 72A–72H.
68 See pp 105–7 ff above.

reversal[69] of the *Leyland DAF* decision[70] the distinction between fixed and floating charges is therefore likely to remain commercially significant.

While it may have been disappointing to supporters of fixed charges over debts, the *Spectrum* decision should not be viewed as having either opened a Pandora's box as regards charges over other asset types nor as jeopardizing fixed charges simply because of the existence of pre-agreed arrangements governing proceeds of disposal.

The *Spectrum* judgment, by re-emphasizing the equivalence of debts and their proceeds, has however helpfully clarified the distinction to be drawn between charges over debts (being viewed as mere receivables) and charges over other asset types. Assets which are not debts will be considered as being separate from and therefore susceptible to charging in a different way to their proceeds. A failure to control the use and disposition of proceeds of charged assets which are not debts is not as clearly fatal to the fixed nature of the charge as it is in the case of charges over debts.

The hallmarks of a floating charge identified in the cases which have dealt with re-characterization risk and which focus on a lack of control by the charge holder over utilization of proceeds of disposal (the solution to which is a blocked account) are specific to the trading company/relationship bank situation and do not pertain to securitizations.

The courts have never had to consider re-characterization risk in the context of securitizations, structured financings, and SPVs and so have not taken account of other methods of preventing the SPV from dealing freely with its assets such as the pre-agreed controls, including the waterfall, contractual restrictions, and servicer relationships which apply to securitizations.

Accordingly, the nature and degree of the restrictions placed on operating the SPV's bank accounts in a typical securitization (namely thes waterfall and servicing arrangements) should place the situation beyond the analysis employed in *Brumark* and *Spectrum.*

Regrettably it is likely to take more than commentary on the *Spectrum* decision to bring about the certainty craved for by financial institution lenders and rating agencies alike. Statutory clarification which Lord Phillips refers to as desirable in the postscript to his judgment in the Court of Appeal in *Spectrum*[71] also looks

[69] Under the Company Law Reform Bill, cl 868 (cl 867 as of 25 April 2006)

[70] *Re Leyland DAF Ltd* [2003] BCC 159.

[71] *National Westminster Bank v Spectrum Plus* Ltd [2004] EWCA Civ 670, [2004] Ch 337, para 99.

unlikely except, perhaps, in the context of an abolition of the distinction between fixed and floating charges—something the Company Law Reform Bill, which because it does not take up the Law Commission's proposals in this regard, suggests is a long way off.[72]

[72] As per the Law Commission's proposals; see further M Bridge, 'The Law Commission's Proposals for the Reform of Corporate Security Interests', ch 12 below.

6

A REVIEW OF *BRUMARK* AND *SPECTRUM* IN AN INTERNATIONAL SETTING

Philip R Wood

A. Introduction

This chapter will consider the decisions in *Re Spectrum Plus Ltd*[1] and its forerunner *Brumark*[2] in an international context. Both of these decisions have created considerable controversy.

Brumark decided that, if a company can use the proceeds of its receivables to pay its operating expenses, then the charge on the receivables is a floating charge. This seems, on its face, technical and harmless. The subsequent House of Lords' decision in *Spectrum* in 2005 was a mopping-up operation which merely confirmed this result on special facts. The key decision is *Brumark*. So the issue is whether the ratification of *Brumark* in *Spectrum* is an issue.

What really happened is that the decisions in *Brumark* and *Spectrum* coincided with major legislation which shifted English security interests in a pro-debtor direction and which magnified the impact of the decisions in an unexpected way.

Whether or not the decisions in *Brumark* and *Spectrum* are seriously prejudicial depends upon whether one adopts a wide or narrow interpretation of their ambit. The courts were none too clear about scope. This chapter argues in favour of narrowing their ambit, since this seems more in accordance with common sense, in which case the damage is circumscribed. It will also be argued that the decisions should not be viewed with enthusiasm.

1 [2005] UKHL 41, [2005] 2 AC 680.

2 *Re Brumark Investments Ltd sub nom Agnew v IRC* [2001] UKPC 28, [2001] 2 AC 710.

B. Background to *Brumark*

The background to *Brumark* is as follows. In the nineteenth century England developed a universal corporate charge over all the present and future assets of a company super-generically for all present and future liabilities super-generically. This charge could be documented in three lines with a couple of extra clauses (although lawyers customarily preferred a more eloquent exposition) and it was effective against all creditors on insolvency. All one had to do was to register it at the companies register. It could be enforced immediately and informally by possessory management (receivership) by an accountant as a self-help remedy without court sanction. The receiver could run the company and sell or not sell—if he sold, then again no court sanction was required.

No consumer interests were involved because only companies could do this. No other country matched this cost-free transactional simplicity and efficiency and most still do not.

The arguments in favour of this system were that it enlarged credit, reduced its cost, protected depositors of banks and the investors who bought secured debentures of public companies, helped ensure that unsecured creditors, including employees, got paid out of bank money (because the banks were safer), and did not lead to pervasive market failures or persistent abuse (because responsible banks did not lie coiled to pounce until the position was hopeless, because they had an interest in a rescue and because they had reputations to protect). If the position was hopeless, then there was a seamless change of management and it was not necessary to switch off the power station. The monopoly of universality was seen as a positive advantage since the firm did not have to be sold in bits: so all creditors got more.

Therefore proponents of this approach would maintain that the system was the Holy Grail of financial law in that it supported both debtors and creditors—and their respective creditors. On balance the argument was that market failures were not a major problem, that negative externalities were limited and that efficiency tests were met as closely as one could hope (perfect efficiency with no negative externalities is unlikely, so that a choice has to be made). The free approach was the product of Adam Smith laissez-faire and an entrepreneurial culture—'the railways must be built'.

But back in 1897, before a system of registration of company charges was introduced in 1900 to inform unsecured creditors that they would be trumped on insolvency, Parliament saw it as scandalous that the bank should take all. So they carved out a priority for certain taxes and employee wages as preferentials.[3] But only over assets where the charge seemed the least justifiable. The assets were those which the debtor used in the course of its business and had a free right to use, which in those days was mainly inventory.

The charge over these assets seemed least justifiable because the charge broke three fundamental ideological rules, which, though considered doctrinaire and out of date in the context of modern corporate finance, are essential to an understanding of why security interests in England are so complicated, why *Brumark* added to the complication and why indeed security interests round the world are so difficult to understand.

First the charge broke the publicity rule that other creditors should be warned if the debtor's assets were charged to someone else. Otherwise they would be deceived into giving false credit—the debtor has many possessions but no assets. Since there was no central filing system, the only way a secured creditor could publicize its charge was by getting possession of the collateral, ie a pledge. In the case of claims, the creditor got 'possession' by giving notice to the obligor owing the claim and in the case of land and other title registered assets, like shares, the creditor got himself registered as the holder. In other words, although the concept of reputed ownership was subject to criticism and contraction from the time of Lord Mansfield, the creditor nonetheless had to have 'control and dominion' over the asset.

But possession by the creditor was totally unrealistic. The debtor had to use the inventory and there was no way one could give notice to all the obligors of the bulk receivables. The whole idea of giving the bank all the assets and keeping the business together would be destroyed. So the English alighted on the idea of a public register for company charges—a central filing system—which they installed in 1900. That solved the whole problem of control and dominion. Unsecured creditors could not complain. Germany and the Netherlands by contrast never introduced filing (and still do not have it)—probably because of bank secrecy and because they did not think that unsecured creditors were really interested and indeed would usually assume that that the bank had all the assets anyway. The United States introduced its comprehensive filing system finally in the 1960s.

Secondly, the charge broke the doctrine of specificity. This amazing doctrine originated in the very common-sense and ordinary principle that, in order to

[3] Preferential Payments in Bankruptcy Amendment Act 1897, s 107. For further discussion, see R Goode, 'The Case for the Abolition of the Floating Charge', ch 2; L Gullifer and J Payne, 'The Characterization of Fixed and Floating Charges', ch 4 above; and J Armour, 'Should We Redistribute in Insolvency?', ch 9 below.

transfer an asset, you have to identify the asset. Naturally. You and your creditors have to know what you own.

But the doctrine then got hijacked to serve other ends. First it was considered wrong that the debtor should be compelled by the moneylender to charge all his future assets and means of subsistence. The way to stop this was to insist that the charged assets were specified in detail, therefore they had to be existing, therefore the creditor could not get future assets. As recently as 2000 the United States used specificity to restrict the scope of certain consumer security interests in the revised Article 9 of the Uniform Commercial Code. The use of specificity to restrict secured credit by excluding future assets is standard in more than 60 per cent of the world's jurisdictions: see Part D below.

Next, since the creditor had to get control and dominion to publicize the charge, the creditor had to identify the asset so that he could take possession. So specificity became the bedrock of publicity as well. The result is that specificity became the fundamental underpinning of both the protection of debtors and the protection of unsecured creditors, though irrelevant to corporate finance nowadays.

But the new charge broke the specificity rule too—in fact, completely ignored it: the charge was super-generic, it covered the assets by class and it scooped up all future assets as well, even assets coming to life in the suspect period, even post-commencement assets. Why not? It was good to have all assets in one basket for the Holy Grail reasons just given. Only companies could do this so problems of the useful artisan pledging everything to the lender did not arise. All this was decided by two seminal House of Lords cases in 1859 and 1888.[4]

Thirdly and finally, the new charge broke the enforcement rule that the debtor was entitled to insist that the assets be sold (so that the debt could be paid off), that there be a public auction (to get a fair price), and that the court supervise the whole process (to stop the bank abusing the debtor). On the contrary, under the new charge, the bank could write a short letter to an accountant asking him to step in and this receiver could take over as a complete despot, fire the directors and run the show. No need to bother the court. No sale necessary—better to keep the show on the road. Public auction? Of course not—that's not how you get a good price. This right of receivership—whose distant historical origin lay in the fact that at one time mortgages were created by an absolute transfer by debtor to creditor so that the creditor had the right to possession as owner—was essentially founded on the fact that there was a floater so that all the assets could be managed.

[4] *Holroyd v Marshall* (1862) 10 HLC 151; *Tailby v Official Receiver* (1888) 13 App Cas 523.

It is easy to see therefore why Parliament decided to pick the floating collateral as the assets which should be subordinated to the State and public taxes and to the workers thrown out of a job.

Hence the fateful birth of the fixed and floating charge distinction.

The irony was that the whole control and dominion problem went away three years later when filing was invented. Filing also torpedoed the need for specificity as a publicity doctrine. But by then it was too late. The whole system had got embedded, however irrational, however illogical, however out of date. Lenders went along with it because at least only one class of collateral was subordinated and that class at that time—mainly inventory—was often of low value on insolvency anyway, compared to, say, land and factories.

That therefore is the explanation of why the floater originally had three badges: (1) bulk unidentified non-specific class of assets, (2) future and fluctuating assets, and (3) debtor has right to deal with them in the ordinary course of business (debtor/control and dominion). In the 1980s the badge of the floater was restricted by the courts to only one of these tests, ie the right to deal, thereby widening the scope of the floater and the collateral subordinated to the preferentials. This narrowing (mainly in *Re Brightlife Ltd*[5]) laid the seeds for the sledgehammer of *Brumark*.

The priority of the Crown and the crew were perhaps not in fact a show-stopper or at least people could live with the priority then, even though later receivables became much more important and worth something, compared to inventory.

In any event it was around a century later, from the mid-1980s onwards, that the attack on security interests warmed up via the corporate rescue philosophy. To cut a long story short, the current position is that a charge over floating collateral is—at least as regards black-letter law on the books—weak in England because on administration, enforcement is frozen without formal adequate protection, the administrator can use the assets without formal adequate protection, and, most devastatingly, the collateral is trumped by post-commencement losses and new money.[6] So the secured creditor has no predictability as to the value of the floating collateral and it can get eroded post-commencement.

The theory was that the secured creditor should be frozen to avoid the fragmentation of the business, for example the bank sells the factory. The fragmentation theory was doubtful because, as we shall see, relevant assets would normally be covered by universal charges in favour of house banks or syndicates who have

[5] [1987] 1 BCLC 485.

[6] See especially Insolvency Act 1986, Sch B1, paras 70(1) and 99(3).

every interest in maximizing values by keeping the business together if this was sensible.

The true basis of freezing the secured creditor was to protect unsecured creditors and the diffuse notion that businesses and jobs are better saved that way. Maybe. The countervailing arguments are that businesses were saved by receivership at a high rate and that, since charges are universal in 90 per cent of the relevant cases (at a guess), the bank or the syndicate are effectively in charge and they effectively control new money—which is the last resort finance which keeps the ship afloat and pays the unsecured creditors. So the jury is still out on whether this intrusion on security is in fact productive.

In terms of a wider historical horizon, it is suggested that the weakening of security is a reassertion of the debtor protection which was a feature of the early days of the development of security interests, expressed first in usury laws and then in onerous and unattractive enforcement procedures (court order, public auction, delays, costs). Whether this is a good thing or not is a matter of intense debate.

But to get back to the story. The actual impact of the administration intrusions developed since 1986 is ameliorated by various pragmatic factors, by the protection of financial collateral under the EU Financial Collateral Arrangements Directive (EC) 2002/47[7] and by the presence of gateways in the Enterprise Act 2002 which protect certain mainly wholesale financings by enabling the universally secured creditor to block an administration and thereby to veto the adverse effects of an administration. These gateways include, amongst other cases, a carve-out mainly for bond-financed securitizations over £50 million and for project finance over £50 million with step-in rights[8]—case law interprets project finance widely. The legislature restricted these gateways by insisting on fussy conditions so that the exempted financing is much more complicated than it should be. The legislation reflected the tension between government domestic debtor-protection policies and the needs of the wider financial marketplace.

The effect of the gateways is that a universal secured creditor can block an administration by an ordinary receivership so that the freezes, etc imposed by administration do not apply. But this does not negative the priority of the preferentials which must still be paid in the receivership out of the proceeds of the floating collateral first. The Crown preference has now gone and been replaced by a small £600,000 fund out of the floating collateral.

In both the United States and Germany, adequate protection of secured cred-

[7] [2002] OJ L145/43, 27 June 2002.
[8] The detail is now mainly in Insolvency Act 1986, Sch 2A.

itors is written into the insolvency regime. The German rule is particularly strong—the administrator must compensate for the freeze. There is no express adequate protection in Britain, but there is some degree of protection by virtue of a broad 'unfair prejudice' section, by case law requiring recognition of property rights and also by virtue of pragmatic factors such as administrator risk-aversion. The upshot is that adequate protection is there, but is not easy to evaluate in particular situations and is weakened by express statutory provisions going the other way. A comparison of the US and British regimes is complicated by other factors, for example the treatment of post-commencement interest and post-commencement revenues. On both issues the US regime appears less supportive of security interests.

There are other less important reasons why the floating collateral is poor in England, for example floating charges to support inter-group guarantees have to survive the one-year suspect period.[9] But these cases are minor compared to the subordination of the floater on administration to post-commencement unsecured creditors, not just the Crown and the crew.

The effect was that it was essential from the point of view of banks that the charge over as many assets as possible should be fixed and not floating. Fixed charges get a much better treatment on administration.

C. The Role of Security

The whole point of security is that it should be effective on insolvency. If it is not effective then, it is quite futile. In particular, it is less relevant how wide a security interest can be on creation if it is demoted on insolvency by a corporate reorganization law. Some might argue that the insolvency regime should be flat and that there should be no super-priority creditors at all. Others might argue that it does not matter that the bank position is weakened on the books because the reality is that bank control of new money—which is often essential to keep the business going—means that the banks can control the proceeding.

Arguments in favour of security interests include that it is a basic proposition of a legal system that contract and property rights should be protected, that economic life cannot proceed unless they are, and that banks paid for the assets and that they should therefore be able to reclaim them if unpaid. There are significant arguments that it is economically efficient to protect depositors and to enhance credit by channelling and protecting savings through the banking system. Banks are essential to the credit system. They are intermediaries in

[9] Insolvency Act 1986, s 245.

economic substance and if one strips away the corporate veils, the real creditors in interest are the depositors, ultimately individuals.

As to unsecured creditors, arguments in favour of wide bank security trumping unsecured creditors, mainly suppliers, are that unsecured supply creditors are in practice paid out of stable bank money except those caught at the last moment (of which they usually have ample warning), that unsecured suppliers do not provide medium-term serious credit (30–90 days is the norm), are not intermediaries for depositors' money, do not create major or systemic risks, and cannot supply new money on a default to rescue the debtor (and so are free riders on bank new money), and that suppliers can and do protect themselves by super-super-priority retention of title clauses.

There are other classes of unsecured creditors with pressing claims—notably revenue authorities, employees, pensioners, and tort claimants. Hence the debate about security is fundamentally about priorities between creditors, about who should be on what rung of the ladder and whether there should be a bankruptcy hierarchy or ladder at all. Insolvency is the point at which the choice becomes inescapable.

D. International Survey[10]

The tension between unsecured and secured creditors is evident throughout the world. For example, the Napoleonic group,[11] comprising nearly 30 per cent of the world's jurisdictions (for example, France itself, most of Latin America, large parts of Africa), reduce security interests by a mixture of stratagems—mainly by the ideologies outlined above, namely the doctrine of specificity which requires assets to be specified and so excludes future assets (sometimes easy to circumvent by supplemental lists) and by impracticable publicity rules which require cred-

[10] The brief summaries in this section are mainly based on internal practice notes and transaction memoranda. Published surveys and comments in relation to non-common law security interests are to be found, for example, in M Bridge and R Stevens (eds), *Cross Border Security and Insolvency* (2001); B Constant, *The Law Relating to the Mortgage of Ships* (1920); U Drobnig, 'A Comparative Introduction to Security over Moveables and Intangibles' in J Norton and M Andenas (eds), *Emerging Financial Markets and Secured Transactions* (1998) ch 2, and other papers in that collection; R Hames and GS McBain, *Aircraft Finance: Registration, Security and Enforcement* (1988); G McCormack and F Dahan, 'The EBRD Model Law on Secured Transactions: Comparisons and Convergence' (1999) Company Financial and Insolvency Law Review 65; WE Moojen and MP van Sint Truiden, *Bank Security and Other Credit Enhancement Methods* (1995); PR Wood, *Comparative Law of Security and Guarantees* (1995). See also PR Wood, *Maps of World Financial Law* (5th edn, 2005) for methodology and taxonomy of jurisdictional security interests.

[11] The categorization and identities of the world's jurisdictions referred to in this section of this chapter are set out in Wood, *Maps of World Financial Law* (n 10 above).

itor possession or the equivalent and which, in the traditional jurisdictions, effectively prevent charges over inventory and bulk receivables. So there is more for the unsecureds. Typically, there are also several classes of privileged unsecured creditors.

Some of the advanced Napoleonic group have timid and very narrow enterprise charges, for example France (1909), Belgium (1919), Luxembourg (1937), Spain (1954) and Italy (1994). Unsecured creditors are further protected in this group by onerous enforcement, for example court orders with their attendant delays, and in the advanced group by draconian rescue statutes which subordinate the assets to post-commencement creditors and some pre-commencement creditors as well, for example France (1985), Belgium (1998) and Spain (2004). Various classes of preferentials rank ahead of all security—thus in France employees, administration losses, and new money rank ahead and the court has a large role in overriding creditors on the plan and new money.

In these three EU countries, the highly debtor-protective reorganization statutes are understood to be little used, for example apparently less than 10 per cent in France, perhaps because banks do not like yielding control to the court—which has a much wider say than elsewhere—and perhaps because directors wish to avoid being exposed to personal liability which is easily attracted and which bites when the proceeding starts. So the main participants have less incentive to go into the process—quite apart from the fact that they prefer to do the work-out out of court.

The Napoleonic attitudes may have been influenced by deeper historical objections to usury and sympathy for the individual debtor. The English-based common law jurisdictions escaped that problem because the universal charge could only be created by companies—security interests by individuals in England are amongst the worst in the world although the gap is filled by title finance at the consumer level, for example hire purchase.

In the Roman–Germanic group,[12] broadly comprising somewhat in excess of 20 per cent of the world's jurisdictions, there is much variety but in important members, such as Germany, Japan, and the Netherlands, security over floating assets is widened by case law, publicity by possession is not required for goods and, in half the group, for claims (but is for goods in Austria and Switzerland where charges over inventory are impracticable), and the doctrine of specificity is weaker or disappearing, especially in the Netherlands. Germany has a principle of over-collateralization which however seems generous.

[12] See Wood, *Maps of World Financial Law* (note 10 above).

There are various enterprise charges, for example Finland, Sweden. The Swedish enterprise charge was significantly weakened in 2004. These enterprise charges are wider in transition countries influenced by the EBRD[13] model, for example Poland. Russia started out with a much simplified Uniform Commercial Code (UCC) Article 9, though without a central filing system, then modified it and substantially weakened it on insolvency. China is still considering the matter in the context of its draft bankruptcy statute.

On the whole, as an extremely crude generalization, in both these groups security interests are more restricted than in the English common law group so that the effect is to leave more for unsecured creditors. But there are significant exceptions where the law is broadly protective of security interests, especially Germany and the Netherlands.

E. Sectors of Secured Credit

The argument is complicated by a major change in the use of security interests in advanced economies. There are around seven principal classes.

Large public companies do not normally create security interests—they borrow unsecured from banks and bondholders with negative pledges. The result is that the commanding heights of the economy (and their employees) are outside the debate, except for work-out security for last resort new money (which seems reasonable) and except for special cases, like group acquisitions which are taken private in leveraged deals. Private equity deals are in this class. Target companies involve substantial amounts and are a significant part of the economy. In these cases, there are *Brumark* issues and problems of the type elaborated in this chapter.

One of the biggest sectors is ring-fenced special purpose companies for projects, property, transportation, etc. Enterprise finance is largely through this medium, and, if one were to add securitizations (which are essential for the safety of banks), the sector is huge. In our context, the essential feature of these financings is that bank/bond money pays for substantially all the assets, that employees are few, that the big unsecured contractors, for example construction, fuel, and offtake (ie purchase contracts for the project product, for example electricity), are insiders to the transaction and are not being downtrodden, and that the parties do not need the legislature to tell them how to run a work-out of their project. The upside is that some of these transactions will be within the

[13] European Bank for Reconstruction and Development, see <http://ebrd.org/about/index.htm>.

wholesale gateways in the Enterprise Act 2002 mentioned above or, if not, it could be argued that *Brumark* is irrelevant because only one main syndicate is involved who can control the work-out. Otherwise there are *Brumark* issues.

Another major secured sector is financial markets, where special legislation, mainly EU-inspired, reverses the rescue philosophy and reinstates free contract and property rights in the interests of certainty and safety, notably the Settlement Finality Directive (EC) 1998/26[14] and the Financial Collateral Arrangements Directive 2002. *Brumark* issues are negatived by statute, subject to detailed incursions.

Secured trade letters of credit are trivial in comparison to the other categories. They are extremely short term and involve small amounts.

Apart from consumer credit, a very large class is home loans—more than two-thirds of GDP in the United Kingdom. *Brumark* issues do not arise in relation to non-corporate borrowers.

A large class is small and medium-sized companies (SMEs) who mainly borrow from house banks with universal charges. This is traditional relationship banking. *Brumark* affects this sector.

Sandwiched in between the public companies and the above SMEs are large private companies which may borrow unsecured if they have the necessary credit strength and need for diversified funds. Included in this class is private equity finance involving large amounts of secured debt.

So sometimes *Brumark* bites and sometimes it does not.

It would be useful to have detailed comparative figures of all these seven sectors—they do not seem to have been calibrated according to sector but the data is there, although scattered. The figures would help us get a more nuanced view on the effect of *Brumark* on the economy.

What it seems to boil down to is that the weakening of the universal charge by *Brumark* and rescue legislation mainly impinges on the small and medium-sized sector and also large companies which are privately owned via leveraged buy-outs or private equity transactions. They impinge less on the special purpose vehicle sector, partly because of pragmatic factors, partly because of the Enterprise Act gateways. Listed companies are unaffected because they usually borrow unsecured. Some financial markets are unaffected because of exclusory legislation.

In any event, since there is no free lunch, one of the key issues is whether

[14] [1998] OJ L166/45, 11 June 1998.

redistribution and the welfare state should be expressed through the insolvency system.

F. The *Brumark* Thesis

It was into this noisy arena that the judiciary stepped with *Brumark* in 2001. They were determined to roll back what they saw as the bank erosion of the Crown and crew privilege. They did this by insisting that receivables should be available to the Crown and the crew, not just inventory. Banks had been characterizing charges over receivables as fixed and therefore outside the net of the floater. Once the proceeds were in the bank account and the company could use the proceeds, then it was conceded that the charge over the bank account was floating—not important because on insolvency the account is overdrawn.

The impetus seems to have been that the banks should be stopped from devices seen as evasive. The technical means of achieving this were to hold that, wherever the company could use the proceeds of the receivables to pay operating expenses, which would inevitably be paid into the company's bank account, then the charge on the contract producing the proceeds was a floater.

In other words, the fundamental logic was:

> Asset = its proceeds.
> Therefore right to use the proceeds = right to deal with the asset
> Therefore charge on *asset* = floater.

G. The Effect of *Brumark*

The problem with this is that potentially every asset would now be floating collateral. Just about all assets, except unlet land, produce income—that is what they are for. Long-term charterparties, specific purchase contracts for project products (electricity, metals, etc), long-term supply contracts, construction contracts, they all produce revenues. Leases of land produce revenues. Licences of intellectual property produce revenues. Investments produce revenues.

In addition, all companies, whether in the small sector or project companies or anywhere else, need to use their revenues to pay their operating expenses. Thus in the case of special finance raised by Special Purpose Vehicles, such as project finance companies, there is usually a cascade or waterfall clause in the financing documents which provides that revenues from the project go first to pay operating expenses, then debt service, then reserves, and the rest to dividends or subordinated shareholder loans. It is impracticable from the point of view of companies, and also counter-productive, that revenues should be used solely for debt service. This would be the equivalent of building societies insisting that homeowners use all their earnings to pay off the mortgage.

So the worst case conclusion is that the charge over all assets is a floater and therefore poor unless the secured creditor could get itself through one of the Enterprise Act gateways or into financial collateral protection under the Financial Collateral Arrangements Directive 2002, as mentioned above. The effect of a combination of a judicial decision plus government intervention would be in a single year to shift English security interests from a stable and predictable property right towards something ephemeral and insecure. That would be an extraordinary thing to do.

But is the above gloomy analysis correct? It is considered that it is not.

The better view is that the *Brumark* principle only applies to receivables from commercial sale contracts, not from other property, for example investments, land or intellectual property.[15] It should apply only if the proceeds are bullet payments which extinguish the contract. Therefore it should not apply to medium-term contracts, payable by instalments, for example charterparties, hire contracts, fund or project purchase contracts, or secured home loans. If the bank has a complete discretion as to whether to allow drawings from the bank account, then most agree that the block is enough to prevent the charge from being a floater—the problem with this is that directors could not properly in most cases agree to freeze their revenues. Whether it does not apply even to this rigorous class of one-shot contract receivables if a substantial amount of the proceeds are applied to debt service, for example 10–15 per cent per annum, is open.

It seems necessary to narrow the case because it is considered that the courts did not intend to turn the law upside down in one go or intend to make all revenue-producing assets subject to the preferentials. It is considered that they did not intend, for example, to abolish fixed charters over charterparties in ship financings or over long-term purchase contracts in projects. The problem is that the courts were at pains to padlock the exits, that there are contrary judicial statements, and that the courts themselves did not expressly limit the case. So the above conclusion is a matter of inference.

The real objections to having to employ these arguments are that they seem over-refined, involve a rerun of old notions drawn from the formative period

15 See N Frome and K Gibbons, '*Spectrum*: An End to the Conflict or the Signal for a New Campaign?', ch 5 above.

of security interests about specificity, control and dominion, and publicity (we already have publicity by filing), and are unpredictable. They might seem somewhat metaphysical to those engaged in international finance globally, notably international lenders to whom legal advisers have to explain the situation. The fog and smoke might lead financiers to think there is a larger problem than there really is: perception is crucial to the goodwill of a legal system.

The court could have avoided the adverse consequences by holding that the contract from which the receivable sprang was a separate asset and, if blocked, would not be floating collateral—the solution of the Court of Appeal in *Re New Bullas Trading Ltd*,[16] now overruled by *Spectrum*. The reality is that the contracts from which receivables spring are usually significant contracts and distinct assets in their own right which are not just their proceeds. One cannot say that a construction contract is just a receivable. Even a simple sales contract is more than just money and has continuing obligations, for example warranties. Economists do not classify sale contracts as near money. So the central technical thesis of *Brumark* that a commercial contract is just its proceeds seems hard to justify.

At bottom, there is the policy issue of whether the Crown and the crew did deserve to have the scope of their priority widened by enlarging the scope of the floater collateral. As to the Crown, their preference was legislated out in 2002 and replaced by a small fund out of the floater. As to the crew, one recalls the resounding declaration of a US court in an old 1898 maritime lien case that the seaman's claims for his wages are 'secured liens, and so long as a plank of the ship remains, the sailor is entitled, against all other persons, to the proceeds as security for his wages'.[17] Views now differ on the degree of employee exposure, the degree to which they are in practice paid until the last moment out of bank last resort new money, their role as insiders (including management), whether the floating inventory is a sufficient buffer and whether their protection should come from direct taxation of the citizen producing unemployment benefit and redundancy pay or by indirect taxation of the banks and depositors via insolvency law.

It is notable that both the United States and Germany—the world's largest and third largest economies—have substantially universal charges and neither trump these by employees. Nor does the Netherlands, which also has a substantially universal charge. In transition countries, the Crown/crew preference is discouraged. German security interests rank ahead of taxes.

[16] [1994] BCC 36, CA.
[17] *The John E Stevens* 170 US 113, 118, 18 S Ct 544 (1898), per Justice Grey.

In the United States the notorious 1925 Supreme Court case of *Benedict v Ratner*[18] held that if the creditor did not have control and dominion over the assets, it had no charge at all, because there was no publicity to unsecured creditors. At that time there was no UCC filing system in the United States. The decision seriously weakened lending to manufacturing companies in the United States until it was all swept away by Article 9 of the UCC. Until then the United States had endless hair-splitting decisions as to what blocking or control was enough.

Brumark has resurrected the discarded *Benedict v Ratner* philosophy plus the complex distinctions it engendered at a time when we have had a publicity system for more than a century so that the control and dominion rule seems no longer relevant.

When *Brumark* was decided, its wider implications in terms of the weakening of the floating charge by Parliament in the Enterprise Act 2002 were not envisaged. But when *Spectrum* was decided in 2005, the larger consequences of *Brumark* precipitated by the weakening of floating charges by Parliament had been in the public domain for several years. It was hoped that *Spectrum* would give guidance on how the problems outlined above were to be dealt with and what the scope of the case was. This guidance was not forthcoming; instead the court reaffirmed and strengthened the *Brumark* thesis.

H. Conclusions

Some conclusions may be drawn.

Security interests are a significant means of risk reduction in modern societies. It is not considered that market failures and negative externalities justify their abandonment. They are in the same super-priority group as insolvency set-off and the trust (immunization of assets from private creditors of the trustee and including some restitutionary claims) in terms of risk protection on insolvency. Their use pervades the whole legal system, not just financial markets. The combination and strength of the three together is the most distinctive feature of the common law group in financial law—nearly half the world's jurisdictions. Once the decision is taken to support them, they should be supported with robust decisiveness and eroded only where the erosion is clearly justified.

A mix of judicial decision and legislative measures have combined to cast a

[18] 268 US 354, 45 S Ct 566, 69 Ed 991 (1925).

cloud over the clean and efficient system of security interests in England. One of the main objects was to protect unsecured creditors, including employees. The legislative policy may have been influenced by a desire to protect the small sector. It is questionable whether this sector is better off and whether the benefits, if any, outweigh the adverse impact on the legal system as a whole.

The fixed/floater distinction has a distorting effect on security interests, an argument sensibly advanced in another chapter in this book.[19] The treatment of the preferentials and of universal charges on administration should be reformed in a way which does not perpetuate this out-of-date distinction. It is suggested that *Brumark* should have reduced the importance of the divide instead of strengthening it.

About 25 per cent of the world's 300 or so legal systems regard English law as persuasive. This covers 30 per cent of the world's population, including the largest financial centre in China and one of the largest in the world (Hong Kong), including a pivotal country in Asia (Singapore), including the world's largest democracy (India) and Africa's most populous country (Nigeria). Controversial and inward-looking decisions like *Brumark* and *Spectrum* weaken the unity of the group.

Together with New York law, English law has a dominant position in international finance. The international financial community needs a legal system with which it is familiar, which it can trust, which is predictable in key areas, which is stable, and which has regard to its international responsibilities.

An essential aim of law in this area is simplicity, especially in a global world. Complication creates risk. One of the results of the floater decisions and the rescue philosophy is that England now has a system of security interests having at least seven tiers. They range from the free contract and insolvency-proof regime inaugurated under the Settlement Finality Directive 1998, through financial collateral protection, through the three-runged Enterprise Act ladder, through the small company regime under the Insolvency Act 2000, and finally down to the extremely restrictive regime for individuals. England does not need seven tiers. There are 319 jurisdictions in the world: $319 \times 7 = 2{,}233$.

Another essential aim of the law is to reduce transaction costs. Lip service is everywhere paid to this proposition, but few actually estimate the costs, especially the hidden costs. So let us hazard an example. If 10,000 lawyers

[19] See further Gullifer and Payne, ch 4 above.

worldwide in the English-based group each document 1,000 secured transactions over 10 years at an average extra cost flowing from the law's complexity of $1,000 per transaction (to include their training costs), the total avoidable cost would be:

$10,000,000,000.

7

SECURITY AFTER THE ENTERPRISE ACT

Robert Stevens

A. Introduction

After the developments of the last three years, secured lenders may be forgiven for feeling that they have been subject to a 'double whammy' from Parliament and the courts. One of the consequences of the Enterprise Act 2002 was that floating charges within its scope became less attractive forms of security. For the lender who wishes to take security, the pressing question is what alternatives to the floating charge are available in order to avoid some of the consequences of the Act? The decision of the House of Lords in *Re Spectrum Plus Ltd*[1] has placed serious limits on the ability of secured lenders to use fixed security either as an alternative to, or in conjunction with the floating charge.

This chapter will seek to address three questions. Why were the reforms of the Enterprise Act 2002 of insolvency law thought necessary? Have the goals which the reformers set themselves been achieved? What options after *Spectrum* are left open to a secured lender seeking to avoid the effects of the Enterprise Act?

B. Reform

The extraordinarily brief White Paper *Insolvency—A Second Chance*[2] set out a number of arguments as to why corporate insolvency law as found after the Insolvency Act 1986 was defective. The arguments for reform are reproduced at the end of this chapter.

---

1 [2005] UKHL 41, [2005] 2 AC 680 (hereinafter *Spectrum*).

2 'Insolvency Service' (Cm 5234, 2001), available at <http://www.insolvency.gov.uk/cwp/cm5234.pdf>. An extract is included in the Appendix to this chapter.

The most important mechanism for the enforcement of debt that a floating charge holder possessed was the appointment of an administrative receiver. The Government initially proposed the abolition of administrative receivership, and envisaged the secured creditor, like an unsecured creditor, going to court to obtain the appointment of an administrator. It was thought that this would become the secured creditor's 'remedy of choice'.

Unsurprisingly, secured creditors were rather less than favourable towards this method of reform and strongly petitioned for methods of enforcement which would not involve the time and expense of going to court. The Government responded with a change in its proposals, which was called an 'update':

> For administration to be as widely effective as possible, it needs to be easy to access for companies and their creditors. While respondents to the consultation generally supported plans to promote collective insolvency procedures and the majority agreed with the need to streamline administration, many felt that a court-based procedure could not achieve the necessary speed and flexibility that are seen as strengths of administrative receivership. In addition, there was a view that a substantial increase in the number of administration orders would create pressure on, and possibly delay in, the courts.[3]

The conclusion of the process was a compromise between the Government's original proposals and the banking community's objections. On 7 November 2002 the Enterprise Act was passed. The collection of disparate and unrelated measures included means that it is something of a mess. The relevant corporate insolvency provisions came into force on 15 September 2003.

The goals that the White Paper sought to further may be summarized as:

(1) promotion of rescue;
(2) preventing precipitate behaviour by lenders in putting the company into an insolvency proceeding;
(3) making the office holder more accountable to all those with an interest in the proceeding;
(4) increasing the transparency of the conduct of the insolvency proceeding;
(5) making the insolvency proceeding more collective;
(6) improving the congruence of English law with the model of insolvency law found in international insolvency regimes.

Were these goals achieved by the legislation as enacted?

[3] An Update on the Corporate Insolvency Proposals, 14 January 2002, available at <http://www.insolvency.gov.uk/articref1.htm>.

C. Rescue

When we seek to pursue a goal of rescue, what are we seeking to achieve? In the context of personal bankruptcy, society clearly has an interest in bankrupt individuals being rehabilitated. We want people to be able to start again with a clean slate. By contrast society has no interest in the rehabilitation of companies as such.[4] Ensuring that businesses prosper, generating wealth and employment, is clearly important, but the same is not true of the legal construct which owns the business. A business as a going concern may be more valuable than its constituent parts. One reason for this, but not the only one, is that commercially valuable goodwill will be lost if the business's assets are split up. Putting to one side wider social goals, creditors as a group may have an interest in the business being sold as a going concern if this will lead to higher realizations than sale on a piecemeal basis. It cannot be concluded from the failure of a company that the business which it owns is also a failure which is similarly deserving of being put out of its misery. However, no one could think that rescuing the corporate shell per se was a goal worth pursuing.

The real choice is between focusing on rescuing the business alone or on rescuing the business within the company. Administrative receivership was and, of course, still is where available well suited to the former goal. It is possible, as the Cork Committee contemplated, that an administrative receiver appointed over a business could prove much more competent at running the business than the displaced management and thereby enable the company to be returned to solvency. However, this is an unlikely scenario. Far more likely is where the underlying business owned by the company is profit-making but unable to generate sufficient funds to finance the company's indebtedness. If an administrative receiver is appointed over the 'whole or (substantially the whole) of a company's property'[5] he has the ability to sell off the business as a going concern. To achieve this goal, the Insolvency Act 1986 enables the administrative receiver to apply to court to have assets subject to prior or equal security rights disposed of as if they were not subject to the security. This power facilitates the sale of the business as a going concern.[6]

In order to rescue a balance sheet insolvent *company*, other than by fortuitously trading out of difficulty, the approach will be to reorganize the company's capital structure through an arrangement. There are three groups who have an interest in the business being rescued within the company. First, the management of the company will not necessarily be given any role in the management

[4] Cork Committee, *Insolvency Law and Practice* (Cmnd 8558, 1982) para 193.

[5] Insolvency Act 1986, s 29(2).

[6] Insolvency Act 1986, s 43.

of the business once it is sold. They may prefer the company itself to survive in order to enhance their prospects of maintaining their, possibly lucrative, positions. Secondly, where the company is insolvent, the shareholders will get nothing from the sale of the business as a going concern and the subsequent winding up of the company. If the company can be reorganized in such a way as to be viable, it may be that they preserve some stake, albeit a much diminished one, following a reorganization. It may be objected that once a company is insolvent the true owners are the creditors. It is they who stand to lose out through any further deterioration in the company's balance sheet position. However, an 'emotional commitment to the entrepreneurial ethic'[7] might lead us to have some reluctance to leave the previous owners with nothing. Of course, in many smaller businesses the management and shareholders are one and the same, with a consequent combination of incentives to prefer this form of rescue. Thirdly, and probably most importantly, the Government has an interest in the insolvency figures. Most lay observers do not appreciate that the winding up of a company does not necessarily mean the loss of the business which it owned. If businesses can be rescued within companies, fewer companies will go into winding up and the figures will look better.

The partial abolition of administrative receivership and the attempts to widen the use of administration as an insolvency proceeding reflects a decision to go for the rescue of businesses within companies, rather than of businesses per se. There are possible advantages and disadvantages to this approach. The major potential advantage is that it increases the likelihood of the management and shareholders being prepared to instigate or cooperate with administration. The largest number of insolvency proceedings are creditors' voluntary liquidations, commenced by the company itself, which in practice means initiated by the management.[8] In corporate insolvency, suicide is far more common than murder. The management is in the best position to monitor a company's health. Giving the management and shareholders an incentive to act at an early stage to help save the business as a going concern and minimize loss to creditors makes sense.

One risk is that by giving the management and shareholders the prospect of getting something out of administration, the procedure will be abused. In England, this possibility is reduced by the fact that administration is not a 'debtor in possession' procedure. The label 'debtor in possession' is misleading. In all corporate insolvency proceedings the debtor, the company, is left with title to its estate, unlike personal bankruptcy where legal title is vested in the trustee

[7] J Westbrook, 'A Comparison of Bankruptcy Reorganisation in the US with Administration Procedure in the UK' [1990] Insolvency Law and Practice 86, 88.
[8] DTI Statistics and Analysis Directorate, *Insolvency*, Statistics Release, 6 May 2005.

in bankruptcy. The change which occurs in both liquidation and administration is that the management of the company is displaced. Procedures such as Chapter 11 in the United States, and in their much more limited scope company voluntary arrangements outside of administration in England, are more accurately described as 'management in possession' procedures as such displacement does not take place. The displacement of management minimizes the risk of abuse as management and shareholders cannot be certain that the office holder will act in the manner they desire. There is, however, a consequent increase in the costs of the procedure.

It has also been suggested[9] that there may be no market for the business as a going concern, and so rescue by reorganization will, in many cases, be preferable. However, if there genuinely is no market for the business it does not seem correct to compel a minority creditor who has been outvoted in any reorganization to take illiquid shares in the company in lieu of any payment.

Where the administrator attempts rescue under the Enterprise Act 2002 it is 'the company as a going concern' which he is to rescue. As will be seen, however, the Enterprise Act may encourage certain forms of behaviour by secured lenders which will lead to the rescue of fewer businesses.

D. Precipitate Behaviour by Lender

A holder of a valid debenture may, subject to certain conditions,[10] appoint a receiver where the power so to do has become exercisable under the debenture's terms. One of the most common grounds for appointment is the non-compliance with a demand for payment. The courts have interpreted the power to appoint on this ground broadly. So, it suffices that the demand is for 'all moneys due' without stipulating an amount,[11] and the borrower is only entitled to such time as is reasonable to implement the mechanics of payment but is not entitled to the time to organize refinancing.[12] Where the debenture gives more than one ground for appointment, for example balance sheet insolvency may be stipulated, it does not matter that the wrong ground was given at the time of appointment.

The debenture holder's power over the borrower is, as the White Paper stresses,[13]

[9] R Mokal, *Corporate Insolvency Law* (2004) 210–12.

[10] See R Goode, *Principles of Corporate Insolvency* (3rd edn, 2005) 266–7.

[11] *Bank of Baroda v Panessar* [1987] Ch 335.

[12] *Cripps (Pharmaceuticals) Ltd v Wickenden* [1973] 2 All ER 606; *Bank of Baroda v Panessar* [1987] Ch 335.

[13] Insolvency Service, *Insolvency—A Second Chance* (Cm 5234, 2001) para 2.3.

potentially destructive one. The mere fact of a company's entering into an insolvency proceeding will cause a destruction in value, with many trading partners not being willing to trade except on a short-term no-credit basis. Although no evidence for the 'widespread concern' that secured lenders were abusing their position in a way which destroyed value for other creditors was presented, the possibility is apparent. The initial proposal that administrative receivership should be abolished and that the only entry route into administration would, as previously, be through a court order, would have done much to control the possibility of such abuse. Does the legislation as enacted do so?

The holder of a qualifying floating charge may appoint an administrator out of court where the charge is enforceable.[14] The generous rules on appointment following a demand for payment of an administrative receiver continue to apply. The only additional restriction is that the debenture holder must file a notice of appointment and certain additional documents with the court. Special provision has been made to enable this to be done outside of court hours.[15] Precipitate behaviour would appear, therefore, to be just as strong a possibility under the new regime as under the old. Indeed as, on any view, administration is an insolvency proceeding, unlike administrative receivership which is 'essentially a debt enforcement mechanism',[16] it could be said that its commencement sends a more serious signal to the outside world. The potential for harm is therefore greater.

It may be that because administration is simply less attractive than administrative receivership that such precipitate behaviour will happen less frequently. For example, the requirement that the administrator's proposals be approved by a creditors' meeting will act as a brake on irrational lender behaviour. In *Re Transbus International*[17] the possibility of so-called 'pre-packaged' administrations was recognized, where the business could be sold without seeking prior creditor approval, the proposals settled in advance of the commencement of administration. This route is possible where the administrator can do so in accordance with his duties, in particular his duty to obtain a true market price. However, it would be exceptionally difficult for a lender to organize such a pre-packaged procedure without the cooperation of the borrower.

[14] Insolvency Act 1986, Sch B1, para 16.
[15] Insolvency Rules 1986, SI 1986/1925, r 2.19(1), (3).
[16] Goode (n 10 above) 248.
[17] [2004] EWHC 932, [2004] 1 WLR 2654, ChD.

E. Making the Office Holder More Accountable

The duty owed by an administrative receiver to the company has been thought to be of a very limited kind. The decision of the Privy Council in *Downsview Nominees Ltd v First City Corp Ltd*[18] conceives of the duty of a receiver to a subsequent encumbrancer as being merely a duty of good faith, and not a duty of care. Even though the statements of Lord Templeman were obiter as the receiver was found to be in bad faith, and that the case concerned a receiver's duty to a subsequent encumbrancer and not an administrative receiver's duty to the company, and that much of the reasoning is unpersuasive, and that as a decision of the Privy Council it is not binding in England in any event, nonetheless it has been taken by some to be authoritative.

It had earlier been established that whilst a receiver owed a duty to take care to obtain a proper price when selling an asset of the company,[19] he owed no duty in relation to the timing of sale.[20] It is clearly correct that a receiver should not be held liable for misjudging a market movement, especially in a business which he may have no familiarity with. However, if the secured asset is ice cream or fruit it would seem to go too far to say no duty is owed in relation to the timing of sale.

The decision of the Court of Appeal in *Medforth v Blake*[21] establishes that if an administrative receiver decides to trade he must act with due care in doing so. However, as it is thought that there is no duty owed in relation to the decision whether to trade or not, there is a perverse incentive placed upon the administrative receiver not to trade and thereby escape possible liability.

The limited duties of the administrative receiver are most seriously defective where the debenture holder is over secured. If the debenture holder can obtain payment from the disposal of an asset which may be essential for the business's ability to continue to trade, there is little incentive not to sell without regard to the interests of other creditors. The response of other common law jurisdictions has been the logical one of reforming the duties owed by receivers.[22]

If the White Paper's initial suggestion as to the entry routes into administration had been adopted it would potentially have led to a dramatic change to the way

---

18 [1993] AC 295, PC.

19 *Cuckmere Brick Co Ltd* v *Mutual Finance Ltd* [1971] Ch 949; *Silven Properties v Royal Bank of Scotland* [2003] EWCA Civ 1409, [2004] 1 WLR 997.

20 *China and South Sea Bank Ltd v Tan Soon Gin* [1990] AC 536.

21 [2000] Ch 86, CA.

22 New Zealand Receiverships Act 1993, s 18; Australian Corporate Law Reform Act 1992, s 232(4); Canadian Bankruptcy and Insolvency Act 1992, s 247.

in which insolvency practitioners behave in practice. However, as enacted the ability of a qualifying floating charge holder to appoint an administrator, of his choice, out of court and to replace an administrator appointed by another route with his own choice,[23] will mean that behaviour will change little. Insolvency practitioners must eat. Banks are repeat players who will employ those whom they trust. If an insolvency practitioner wishes to continue to eat he will not behave in a way which is contrary to the interests of those who will choose whether he works again.

In the light of this financial reality, it was essential that the duties of an administrator were clearly spelled out and the method of their enforcement made obvious and given teeth. Unfortunately the former are 'Delphic'[24] and the latter are 'not a model of clarity' with remedial consequences which are 'obscure'.[25]

Paragraphs 3 and 4 of Sch B1 to the Insolvency Act 1986 now provide as follows:

> *Purpose of administration*
>
> **3.** (1) The administrator of a company must perform his functions with the objective of—
> (a) rescuing the company as a going concern, or
> (b) achieving a better result for the company's creditors as a whole than would be likely if the company were wound up (without first being in administration), or
> (c) realising property in order to make a distribution to one or more secured or preferential creditors.
>
> (2) Subject to sub-paragraph (4), the administrator of a company must perform his functions in the interests of the company's creditors as a whole.
>
> (3) The administrator must perform his functions with the objective specified in sub-paragraph (1)(a) unless he thinks either—
> (a) that it is not reasonably practicable to achieve that objective, or
> (b) that the objective specified in sub-paragraph (1)(b) would achieve a better result for the company's creditors as a whole.
>
> (4) The administrator may perform his functions with the objective specified in sub-paragraph (1)(c) only if—
> (a) he thinks that it is not reasonably practicable to achieve either of the objectives specified in sub-paragraph (1)(a) and (b), and
> (b) he does not unnecessarily harm the interests of the creditors of the company as a whole.
>
> **4.** The administrator of a company must perform his functions as quickly and efficiently as is reasonably practicable.

[23] Insolvency Act 1986, Sch B1, paras 12, 25–26, 36.

[24] J Armour and R Mokal, 'Reforming the Governance of Corporate Rescue: The Enterprise Act 2002' [2004] LMCLQ 28, 49.

[25] ibid 55.

The importance to be attached to the aspiration in para 3(2) that 'the administrator of a company must perform his functions in the interests of the company's creditors as a whole' is difficult to ascertain. On one view it is a mere exhortation. An analogy could be drawn with s 1(1) of the National Health Service Act 1977: 'It is the Secretary of State's duty to continue the promotion . . . of a comprehensive health service . . .'. This duty is essentially non-actionable and certainly would not sound in damages if breached.

There is more substance in the hierarchy of purposes contained in para 3(1). While the order in which they are presented would lead us to conclude that 'rescuing the company as a going concern' is the 'top-ranking priority'[26] the qualification in para 3(3)(b) would indicate that where the administrator thinks that doing something else would achieve a better result for the company's creditors as a whole, this is what he should do. Realizing property in order to make a distribution to secured or preferential creditors clearly ranks lowest. The degree to which these paragraphs will ever be actionable is undermined by the use of the subjective 'thinks' which gives great deference to the personal judgment of the administrator, which merely needs to be rational and not reasonable.[27]

Probably of more practical significance is that the established common law duties owed to the company by an administrator will continue to apply. In *Re Charnley Davies Ltd (No 2)*[28] Millett J accepted, albeit without contrary argument, that an administrator, unlike an administrative receiver is under a duty to take care in relation to the timing of sale of property. It can also be assumed that unlike an administrative receiver, the administrator must take care in deciding whether to continue to trade. This change in the duties owed by most office holders which results from the partial abolition of administrative receivership is to be welcomed, and is probably the most important change to corporate insolvency law made by the Enterprise Act 2002.

Enforcement of the administrator's duties is now governed by paras 74 and 75 of Sch B1 to the Insolvency Act 1986. Paragraph 74(1) gives standing to a creditor who can show 'unfair harm' and reflects no significant change on the old regime. Paragraph 74(2) gives standing to apply to the court claiming that the administrator is not performing his functions as quickly or as efficiently as is reasonably practicable. More importantly, para 75 introduces a new summary remedy for misfeasance by the administrator that is capable of being commenced by a creditor without the need to commence liquidation proceedings.

Whether the Enterprise Act 2002 will result in a genuine change in the

[26] R Goode, *Principles of Corporate Insolvency Law* (3rd edn, 2005) 335.
[27] *Unidare v Cohen* [2005] EWHC 1410 (Ch) para 71.
[28] [1990] BCLC 760.

behaviour of lenders will only become apparent where market conditions are such that lenders are under great commercial pressure to maximize realizations at all costs. Put another way, we will only discover whether it works during a recession.

F. Increasing Transparency

Once he has gathered sufficient information, the administrator must set out his proposals for achieving the purpose of administration and send a copy to the registrar of companies and every creditor and member of whose address he is aware. The time limit for this process has been shortened to eight weeks, subject to extension. An initial creditors meeting within 10 weeks of commencement of the proceeding, at which the proposals are presented, must then be held. No meeting need be called if the administrator thinks that the company has sufficient property to enable each creditor to be paid in full, insufficient to make a distribution to unsecured creditors or that neither of the two primary objectives of administration can be achieved. At the meeting, the creditors can either approve the proposals without modification or with modifications to which the administrator consents.[29]

There is no doubt that this scheme leads to transparency and may assist in ensuring that the administrator's duties are carried out with due care. However, there is no such thing as a free lunch. The preparation of such documentation and the running of meetings can be time-consuming and incurs expense.

G. Improving Collectivity

There is no doubt that administration is more 'collective' than administrative receivership. In addition the abolition of Crown preference and the creation of a 'prescribed part' also furthers this goal.

In 1986 the scope of Crown preference was restricted to collected taxes, following recommendations of the Cork Committee. In many cases, the next in order of priority after preferential creditors is the holder of a floating charge. The restriction in 1986 on Crown preference consequently operated as a windfall for banks. Determined not to repeat this outcome, the reforms created a 'carve-out' of assets from the scope of the floating charge for the benefit of

[29] Insolvency Act 1986, Sch B1, para 53.

unsecured creditors generally, as the quid pro quo for the forfeiture of Crown preference.[30]

Cork had originally recommended the creation of a 10 per cent fund carved out from the floating charge for the benefit of unsecured creditors. In the new edition of *Principles of Corporate Insolvency Law*, Professor Goode states that the origin of this recommendation was a conversation over two pints of beer he had at St Pancras Station with a member of the committee.[31] Whilst amusing, this story also highlights the essential arbitrariness of the 10 per cent figure. Why 10? Why not 5? 2? 50?

The Prescribed Part Order does not apply a simple percentage figure but has a more complex method of calculation intended to replicate broadly the amount given up by the Crown as a preference. Whilst this may make political sense, in policy terms it is just as arbitrary as Cork's original suggestion. In 20 years time, will it look like a satisfactory justification for the complex percentages in the Prescribed Part Order that at some point in the distant past there was something called Crown preference? This is reform based upon historical accident and compromise rather than principle.

It may also be noted that the carve-out for the prescribed part does not apply to charges created before 15 September 2003. In relation to such cases the abolition of Crown preference will accrue, in the first instance, to floating charge holders. Again, Christmas has come early for the banks.

H. Improving the Congruence with International Insolvency Regimes

The EC Regulation on Insolvency Proceedings, which confers automatic recognition throughout member states on collective insolvency proceedings, does not include administrative receivership as such a procedure.[32] Administration whether by court order or out of court is recognized.

However, it should not be concluded that the partial abolition of administrative receivership has brought English law more into line with international norms. Administrative receivership is less, not more, anomalous than the new administration regime. Administrative receivership is a debt enforcement procedure and resembles that found in many other countries. There is no other legal system

[30] Enterprise Act 2002, s 252(2); Insolvency Act 1986 (Prescribed Part) Order 2003, SI 2003/2097.
[31] Goode, (n 26 above) 166.
[32] Regulation (EC) 1346/2000 [2000] OJ L160/1, 29 May 2000, Annex A.

anywhere in the world of which I am aware, and certainly none in either the common law world or the rest of Europe, which permits the opening of an insolvency proceeding by a security holder out of court. The English law of administration is peculiar. It is doubtful whether any other legal system will be tempted to follow its path-breaking lead. The reason English law has adopted this approach is because of the history of the original proposals and the resistance to them by the banking community. Again, reform by historical accident not principle.

I. Have the Reformers' Goals Been Achieved?

If we accept that the duties of an administrative receiver to the company over the assets of which he has been appointed are inadequate, failing as they do to take into account the interests of other interested parties, the partial abolition of administrative receivership is to be welcomed. The duties of the administrator, at common law at least, may help to maximize recoveries for all creditors in certain cases.

However, if this is to be the justification for the reforms, the Enterprise Act 2002 was a particularly heavy sledgehammer to crack a rather small nut. The approach of other common law jurisdictions was simply to reform the duties owed by receivers. Further there will continue to be a very large number of administrative receiverships as the prohibition on appointment does not apply to charges created before 15 September 2003. Even for floating charges created after this date there are a number of carve-outs from the prohibition,[33] in particular in relation to capital market arrangements, public private partnerships and project finance situations. If we accept the premise that the duties of administrative receivers are inadequate they remain inadequate in these areas. The duties of Law of Property Act receivers are similarly unaffected by the Enterprise Act. The sledgehammer has only given the kernel of the problem a glancing blow.

The radical changes enacted in the Enterprise Act 2002 are lengthy and complex. In place of one regime (administrative receivership) we now have three: companies with charges created before 15 September 2003, those with charges created afterwards and those carved out of the abolition. Costly litigation seems inevitable. The Financial Collateral Arrangements (No 2) Regulations 2003, SI 2003/3226 disapply the Enterprise Act restrictions to the taking of security within its scope. We no longer have joined-up law.

[33] Insolvency Act 1986, Sch B1, paras 70 and 71.

J. How Can the Enterprise Act Be Evaded after *Spectrum*?

The abolition of the ability of qualifying floating charge holders to appoint administrative receivers has no impact upon the ability of fixed charge holders to appoint receivers. Similarly the carve-out from the floating charge in the Prescribed Part Order has no effect upon the priority of fixed charge holders. Assets which are merely subject to a floating charge are available for the funding of an administration.[34] These developments increase the attractiveness of taking fixed security.

The decision of the Privy Council in *Brumark*[35] and that of the House of Lords in *Spectrum* have cut back the availability of such security. However, their effect should not be exaggerated, although it is possible to rely upon some loose remarks of Lord Scott[36] and Lord Walker[37] in order to do so.

With some assets the correct metaphor to employ is that of the tree and its fruits. Many assets are income-generating. Land, goods, intellectual property, and shares may all generate income but a fixed charge can be taken over these assets without the necessity of taking a charge over the proceeds. The income generated by the assets is separate from the assets themselves. As income falls in, the scope of assets caught by the charge remains constant and under the control of the debenture holder. The tree is separate from the fruits. It is therefore possible to take a fixed security over the tree alone, whilst taking a floating security, or no security at all, over the fruit. In principle the same should apply even though the tree is a depreciating asset. It is possible to take fixed security over coastal land on the East coast of England, even though it is falling into the sea over time. Similarly, it should be possible to take a fixed security interest over a leasehold interest, even though that interest is gradually disappearing over time. It should not be necessary to also take a fixed security over the proceeds (if any) of such a lease which are a separate asset.

Debts are quite different. Here a better metaphor is the caterpillar which becomes a butterfly. The payment of a debt creates proceeds. However, the debt and the proceeds do not exist separately, they are different forms of the same asset. A fixed charge over debts must also include a fixed charge over the proceeds. The proceeds generated by the payment of debts are not separate from the debts themselves. As proceeds fall in, the scope of assets caught by the charge changes. If the security holder either does not require debts which are paid to be replaced or does not assert a fixed security over the proceeds, no control is

34 Insolvency Act 1986, Sch B1, para 70.

35 *Re Brumark Investments Ltd sub nom Agnew v IRC* [2001] UKPC 28, [2001] 2 AC 710.

36 [2005] UKHL 41, [2005] 2 AC 680, para 107.

37 ibid paras 138 and 139.

being exercised over the scope of the assets which are at any given time within the ambit of the charge. This is so even where the proceeds are paid into an (unblocked) account of the chargor with the chargee itself. A charge over debts but not over proceeds is consequently a floating charge. *Spectrum* and the earlier decision in *Brumark* are relevant to charges over book debts, and should not be seen as significant for the ability to take security over capital assets which generate a (separate) income.

Other than taking fixed security what other techniques are available to a lender who wishes to lend but not be subject to the controls of the Enterprise Act? A qualifying floating charge holder may not appoint an administrative receiver. A qualifying floating charge is one which either alone or in combination with other security held by the chargee relates to the whole or substantially the whole of the company's property.[38] One option is therefore to take a charge which is not a qualifying floating charge, but one which only covers a portion of the company's assets. The holder of such a charge may enforce by appointing a receiver, not an administrative receiver. More complex arrangements of the same technique can be envisaged where the lending is carried out by a number of subsidiaries, each of which has security over a portion of the company's property but none of which individually have security over the whole or substantially the whole.

These carve-out techniques will not give the lender the priority over preferential creditors or the prescribed part which a fixed charge would afford. Further, such floating charge holders would not have the ability to commence or block administration and, once administration is commenced, they would have no control over the identity of the administrator. Further an administrator may dispose of assets subject to a floating charge without going to court, whilst for fixed security a court order is required.[39] Taking deliberately limited floating charges does not therefore seem a sensible commercial course.

A preferable technique is to make use of the fact that s 72A of the Insolvency Act 1986 only prohibits the appointment of an administrative receiver. Other methods of enforcement are still available. For example, where the charge is under seal and the charge has crystallized the chargee has a statutory power of sale.[40] Alternatively, an administrative receiver is a receiver appointed over the whole or substantially the whole of the company's property. A charge holder is at liberty to appoint a Law of Property Act 1925 receiver,[41] provided that such a receiver is not within the definition of an administrative receiver. A receiver can

---

[38] Insolvency Act 1986, s 29(2).
[39] Insolvency Act 1986, Sch B1, para 70(1) and (3).
[40] Law of Property Act 1925, ss 101(1), 205(1)(xvi).
[41] Law of Property Act 1925, ss 101(1)(iii) and 109.

therefore be appointed over part of the assets of the company. Again, no priority advantages arise from this and the charge holder does not have power to block the subsequent appointment of an administrator, but the charge holder retains the option of putting the company into administration and has control over the identity of any administrator.

The disadvantage, as a matter of policy, with the encouragement the Enterprise Act 2002 gives to the adoption of both of these techniques is that they militate against the survival of the business. Encouraging the selling off of the company's assets in a piecemeal fashion by encouraging either partial security or partial enforcement does not make sense. The very thing we want to rescue is destroyed.

The same policy criticism can be made of the Law Commission's proposals for the registration of security.[42] These will also have the consequence of the creation of partial security. At present, a seller of goods is able to retain title to the goods he supplies until the fulfilment of the condition for title transfer, usually payment. However, if he seeks to 'retain' title to the proceeds of sale of the goods or of an asset into which the goods have been mixed he will be faced with the difficulty that such a claim is an assertion of a proprietary right in a different asset to that supplied. The interest the seller is asserting is a security interest: 'That is mine to the extent I remain unpaid'. Such a security interest, which is either a charge on book debts or a floating charge, is registrable and void against the liquidator upon the buyer's winding-up.[43] For most suppliers it is not currently worth the time and expense of registering such charges because of the small sums owed. If, however, registration becomes achievable at the click of a mouse, this disincentive is removed. It can be expected that there will be a large increase in the numbers of partial security interests to secure small sums if the Law Commission's proposals are brought into effect. The prospects of businesses being carved up piecemeal will be consequently greater.

K. Conclusion

The perceived 'double whammy' to secured lending probably amounts to no more than a couple of taps. The Enterprise Act 2002 whilst potentially important will probably only make a difference to the behaviour of office holders in the marginal case. Anyone lending money on the basis that the decision of the

[42] Law Commission, *Company Security Interests* (Law Com No 296, Cm 6654, August 2005).
[43] *E Pfeiffer Weinkellerei-Weinenkauf GmbH & Co v Arbuthnot Factors Ltd* [1988] 1 WLR 150.

Court of Appeal in *Re New Bullas*,[44] disapproved in *Spectrum*, was correctly decided frankly needs to get out more. The criticisms of Professors Goode[45] and Worthington,[46] whilst not unopposed,[47] were persuasive. The surprise in *Spectrum* was not the decision of the House of Lords but that of the Court of Appeal which they overturned.

One available defensive measure in order to escape the effects of the Enterprise Act is, of course, not to lend. However, it must be doubtful whether it is a viable option for commercial lenders to leave money under the bed in this way. A more plausible reaction is a change in the terms and patterns of lending. Marginal fee increases to reflect greater risks and a reluctance to lend to certain kinds of borrower may be expected, although this will be dependent upon market conditions and will consequently be difficult to assess. The lack of any marked market reaction to either the Enterprise Act or *Brumark* and *Spectrum* indicates that their impact will not be dramatic.

[44] [1991] 1 BCLC 485, CA.

[45] R Goode, 'Charges over Book Debts: A Missed Opportunity' (1994) 110 LQR 592.

[46] S Worthington, 'Fixed Charges Over Book Debts and Other Receivables' (1997) 113 LQR 562.

[47] For example, A Berg, 'Charges over Book Debts: A Reply' [1995] JBL 433.

Appendix

The Insolvency Service, *Insolvency—A Second Chance* (Cm 5234, 2001), ch 2, paras 2.1–2.6

Introduction

2.1 For the last twenty-five years or so, the focus of insolvency law reform in the United Kingdom has increasingly been on the promotion of a rescue culture, a trend which started with the work of the Cork Committee, chaired by Sir Kenneth Cork. The Cork Report recommended encouraging the continuation and disposal of a debtor's business as a going concern wherever possible. The Government responded by introducing new mechanisms to facilitate these objectives—Administration and Company Voluntary Arrangement (CVA) procedures—in the Insolvency Act 1986. However the take-up of those procedures since 1986, whilst on an increasing trend, has been seen by many as disappointingly low. There was also widespread concern that the large number of administrative receivership appointments in the early 1990s may have represented precipitate behaviour on the part of lenders, causing companies to fail unnecessarily. More recently the Government initiated a review of company rescue and business reconstruction mechanisms as described in Annex B [*not reproduced*].

The Position of Unsecured Creditors

2.2 Throughout this period there has also been widespread concern as to the extent to which administrative receivership as a procedure provides adequate incentives to maximise economic value. There has, equally importantly, been concern about whether it provides an acceptable level of transparency and accountability to the range of stakeholders with an interest in a company's affairs, particularly creditors. For secured lenders, administrative receivership is an important mechanism, not least given that it is one over the inception of which they have complete control. Since 1986, a person acting as an administrative receiver of a company has had to be an authorised insolvency practitioner. There is little doubt that the existence of professional obligations on insolvency practitioners has had a beneficial effect on the way in which they discharge their duties. But the fact remains that, notwithstanding recent case law, an administrative receiver's principal obligation is towards his appointor. At law, they remain substantially unaccountable to any other creditor for the way in which a company's assets are dealt with. There is no equivalent of the duty owed by an administrator in an administration procedure to act in the interests of the creditors as a whole.

2.3 The maximisation of recoveries and the minimisation of costs are areas where the lack of a wider and more general accountability, and with it the absence of properly aligned incentives, can impact very substantially on the interests of unsecured creditors in an administrative receivership. For example, an administrative receiver is entitled to solely consider the interests of his or her appointor when determining the timing of a sale of a business. Where an offer is made which is sufficient to satisfy the secured creditor's claim and the administrative receiver's costs, there would appear to be little incentive for the receiver to delay the sale with a view to obtaining a better offer which might provide some return for unsecured creditors. Furthermore, it should be borne in mind that unsecured creditors have no right to challenge the level of costs in a receivership, even though they have an identifiable financial interest where there are sufficient funds to pay the secured creditor in full. The Insolvency Act 1986 (Sections 46, 48 and 49) did introduce requirements on administrative receivers to notify and report to creditors and provides for the possibility of a committee of creditors being established. But, in practice, very few such committees are appointed. Finally, it seems clear that the increasing importance of the international dimension in insolvency is likely to highlight the poor fit between international law, based on collective procedures, and administrative receivership. Taking all these factors into account, we do not believe that the present framework for administrative receivership provides an adequate basis for accountability or properly aligned incentives in relation to the bulk of cases giving rise to administrative receivership.

The Way Forward

2.4 In deciding how best to take forward the modernisation of insolvency law in this area, the Government has had regard to the methodology adopted by the review group which focused extensively on the relative merits, cost and benefits of administrative receivership and administration. By way of recapitulation, we now set out at Annex C [*not reproduced*] a comparative analysis of the two procedures. (The results of an empirical study undertaken by Professor Julian Franks and Dr Oren Sussman of the London Business School were published with the Review Group's report in November 2000.)

2.5 The Government's view is that, on the grounds of both equity and efficiency, the time has come to make changes which will tip the balance firmly in favour of collective insolvency proceedings—proceedings in which all creditors participate, under which a duty is owed to all creditors and in which all creditors may look to an office holder for an account of his dealings with a company's assets. It follows that we believe that administrative receivership should cease to be a major insolvency procedure. We therefore propose to restrict the right to appoint an administrative receiver to the holders of floating charges granted in connection with transactions in the capital markets . . .

2.6 In taking this step we recognise that in order to ensure the position of secured creditors within collective procedures there will need to be substantial reform to the process of administration so as to make it more effective and accessible. Whilst our aim is to guarantee unsecured creditors a greater say in the process and its outcome, secured creditors should not feel at any risk from our proposals. We see no reason why, given the changes we propose to make to the administration procedure . . ., their interests should not be protected equally well by an administrator as by an administrative receiver. Indeed we are confident that, over time, secured creditors will come to see administration as their remedy of choice for maximising value.

8

THE DEBENTURE HOLDER'S LIABILITY IN UNJUST ENRICHMENT AFTER *SPECTRUM*

*Look Chan Ho**

The declaratory theory of judicial decision has it that, when the judges state what the law is, their decisions have a retrospective effect.[1] The retrospective effect of the House of Lords ruling in *Re Spectrum Plus Ltd*[2] means that many charges previously characterized as fixed on the basis of *Siebe Gorman & Co Ltd v Barclays Bank Ltd*[3] were in fact floating. Payments made in reliance on this characterization were payments made in reliance on a mistake of law.[4] Charge holders who received such payments stand the risk of having to disgorge their receipt now.

This chapter considers the possibility of recovering the payments made to charge holders on the basis of unjust enrichment.

A. Unjust Enrichment Claims against the Chargees

The typical setting in which a claim against the debenture holder for mistaken payment is as follows.[5] The debenture holder, having a global security over the

* I am most grateful to Joshua Getzler, Riz Mokal, Jennifer Payne, and Iain Pester for their kind and helpful comments. All views expressed and any mistakes made are of course my sole responsibility.

1 *Kleinwort Benson v Lincoln City Council* [1999] 2 AC 349, HL.

2 [2005] UKHL 41, [2005] 2 AC 680 (hereinafter *Spectrum*).

3 [1979] 2 Lloyd's Rep 142.

4 *Kleinwort Benson v Lincoln City Council* [1999] 2 AC 349, HL. For a debate on what should count as a mistake of law, see P Birks, 'Mistakes of Law' (2000) 53 CLP 205; D Sheehan, 'What Is a Mistake?' (2000) 20 LS 538.

5 The relevant payments to the debenture holders were most likely made before the Privy Council decision in *Agnew v IRC* [2001] UKPC 28, [2001] 2 AC 710, thus before the abolition of administrative receivership by the Enterprise Act 2002.

company's assets, appointed an administrative receiver to collect and realize the secured assets. Shortly afterwards, the company went into liquidation. Then the administrative receiver paid the proceeds of realizations to the debenture holder (on the basis that most of the proceeds derived from fixed charge assets in light of *Siebe Gorman*) and any surplus to the liquidator.[6] The liquidator found himself with insufficient assets to discharge the preferential debts of the company.[7]

The liquidator now seeks restitution from the debenture holder under the law of unjust enrichment. For the sake of exposition, an unjust enrichment claim entails answering the following four questions:[8]

(1) Has the defendant benefited or been enriched?
(2) Was the enrichment at the expense of the claimant?
(3) Was the enrichment unjust?
(4) Are there any defences?

There can be no doubt that the debenture holder has benefited from the receiver's payment. Whether the other elements of an unjust enrichment claim exist in the fact-pattern outlined above will be considered at some length below.

1. Mistake of law

We now know after *Spectrum* that most of the proceeds of realizations received by the debenture holder derived from floating charge assets which should have been paid to the liquidator to discharge the preferential debts. Could the liquidator compel the debenture holder to disgorge his receipt on grounds of mistake of law as stated in *Kleinwort Benson v Lincoln City Council*? No, says *Re BHT (UK)*.[9]

The facts in *BHT* were materially the same as the fact-pattern outlined above, except that the debenture holder's claim remained unsatisfied and the administrative receiver handed nothing to the liquidator. The court dismissed the liquidator's unjust enrichment claim against the debenture holder. The court reasoned thus.

First, as a matter of the general law, once a floating charge crystallized, the charged assets became the debenture holder's property. As a result, the deben-

[6] In other words, but for this reliance on *Siebe Gorman*, some of the proceeds of realizations would not have been paid to the debenture holder. cf *Nurdin & Peacock v DB Ramsden & Co* [1999] 1 WLR 1249.

[7] Which would have a priority over a floating chargee's claim with respect to the floating charge assets: Insolvency Act 1986, s 175(2)(b).

[8] *Banque Financière de la Cité SA v Parc (Battersea) Ltd* [1999] 1 AC 221, 227, HL.

[9] [2004] EWHC 201, [2004] 1 BCLC 568, ChD.

ture holder had not been enriched at the expense of the company: 'In the circumstances of this case, the company would never have been entitled to receive any part of the book debt realizations.'[10]

Secondly, since anything recovered from the debenture holder would be used to discharge the preferential debts, the company had suffered no loss. There was no difference between a breach of contract claim and an unjust enrichment claim. Accordingly, the debenture holder had not been enriched at the expense of the company.

Thirdly, seemingly supporting the previous two reasons, the court noted that the preferential creditors were able to pursue whatever claims they might have against the debenture holder.

Each of these reasons is unconvincing and will be evaluated in turn below.

(a) Floating charge assets as the debenture holder's property

As a matter of general law, it is incorrect to say that assets subject to a crystallized floating charge become the debenture holder's property.[11] As Lord Hoffmann pointed out, a 'charge is a security interest created without any transfer of title or possession to the beneficiary'.[12] It follows, as the Court of Appeal noted in *Department for Environment, Food and Rural Affairs v Feakins,*[13] that 'the granting of . . . charges did not deplete [the chargor]'s assets . . . Thus the [charged property] remained [the chargor]'s to dispose of for its full open market value (albeit that the net proceeds of any sale would be largely if not wholly swallowed up in payment of the secured debts)'. The recent decision in *Ultraframe (UK) Ltd v Fielding*[14] also reaffirms that, both in law and in accounting terms, secured assets are beneficially owned by the chargor or mortgagor, as the case may be.

It has been said that the crystallization of a floating charge effects an equitable assignment in favour of the secured creditor,[15] and hence the charged property 'became in equity the property of the [secured creditor]'.[16] However, any such assignment would at most amount to an equitable mortgage. A mortgage would

---

10 *Re BHT (UK)* [2004] EWHC 201, [2004] 1 BCLC 568, ChD, para 24.

11 An authority to the contrary is *Buchler v Talbot* [2004] UKHL 9, [2004] 2 AC 298. The weaknesses of this decision have been demonstrated elsewhere. See RJ Mokal, 'Liquidation Expenses and Floating Charges—The Separate Funds Fallacy' [2004] LMCLQ 387; LC Ho, 'Reversing *Buchler v Talbot*—The Doctrinal Dimension of Liquidation Expenses Priority' (2006) 21 JIBFL 104.

12 *Re BCCI (No 8)* [1998] AC 214, 226, HL.

13 [2005] EWCA Civ 1513, para 72.

14 [2005] EWHC 1638, [2006] FSR 17, ChD, paras 1401–1405.

15 *Business Computers v Anglo-African Leasing* [1977] 1 WLR 578.

16 G Moss QC, 'The Red End of the Spectrum: Liquidators are the Wrong Claimants' (2004) 17 Insolvency Intelligence 143.

not make the mortgagee the beneficial owner of the mortgaged assets. For a mortgagor is in equity the beneficial owner of the mortgaged assets, and the mortgagee is a mere incumbrancer.[17] 'The estate, rights and powers of a mortgagee . . . are only vested in a mortgagee to protect his position as a mortgagee and to enable him to obtain repayment. Subject to this, the property belongs in equity to the mortgagor.'[18]

The crystallization of a floating charge therefore does not alchemize the charged assets into the chargee's property.

As a matter of insolvency law, any suggestion that assets subject to a crystallized floating charge are the debenture holder's property is inconsistent with the unambiguous language of the Insolvency Act 1986, which refers to assets subject to a crystallized floating charge created by a company in winding up (or indeed in administration, provisional liquidation, or receivership) as 'property of [the] company'.[19] It also overlooks the provisions of Article 5(1) of Council Regulation (EC) 1346/2000 on Insolvency Proceedings, whose wording was finalized after much input from the UK delegation, that assets subject to security interests are assets 'belonging to the debtor'.

In fact, successive primary and secondary insolvency legislations have proceeded on the basis of the decision in *Re Barleycorn Enterprises*[20] that floating charge assets are assets of the chargor company.[21] This is also a judicially recognized fact.[22]

While *Barleycorn* was overruled by *Buchler v Talbot*, the Government is in the process of reversing the latter by legislation.[23] Furthermore, as demonstrated by the Financial Markets and Insolvency (Settlement Finality) (Amendment) Regulations 2006, SI 2006/50, Parliament does not seem to recognize the validity of *Buchler v Talbot* at all.[24]

---

[17] *Ultraframe (UK) Ltd v Fielding* [2005] EWHC 1638, [2006] FSR 17, ChD, paras 1401–1405.

[18] *Quennell v Maltby* [1979] 1 WLR 318, 324, CA.

[19] See, for example, Insolvency Act 1986, s 176A(1). The same goes for the property of a company in administration; see Insolvency Act 1986, Sch B1, paras 14, 35, 36, 37, 70, 96, 97, etc.

[20] [1970] Ch 465, CA.

[21] See, for example, the successive versions of reg 14(6) of the Financial Markets and Insolvency (Settlement Finality) Regulations 1999, SI 1999/2979; see LC Ho, 'Reversing *Buchler v Talbot*—The Doctrinal Dimension of Liquidation Expenses Priority' (2006) 21 JIBFL 104.

[22] *Re MC Bacon Ltd (No 2)* [1990] BCLC 607, 610, per Millett J. As a general rule, Parliament is taken by the courts to have legislated against the background of the common law, which forms a necessary part of the exercise of construing a statute; see *Wisley v John Fulton (Plumbers) Ltd* [2000] 1 WLR 820, 823–4, HL.

[23] See cl 907 of the Company Law Reform Bill (as of 24 May 2006).

[24] For a fuller explanation of these issues, see Ho (n 21 above).

Some have argued that the commencement of winding up makes all the difference such that a distinct debenture holder's fund arises upon a winding up. The commencement of winding up creates two funds, namely (1) 'the company's free (unencumbered) assets as at the date of winding up together with its equity of redemption in relation to any charged assets' and (2) the charged assets.[25] This argument is misconceived on any number of levels.[26] First, it disregards the unambiguous language of the Insolvency Act 1986 and other insolvency legislations mentioned above. Secondly, it overlooks the simple distinction between a charge and a mortgage. Since a charge is a security interest created without any transfer of title or possession to the chargee, the chargor does not have the right to a re-transfer. Since he has conveyed nothing, there is simply nothing to re-transfer. It is also because the chargor has conveyed nothing and hence requires no right to any re-transfer that he retains no equity of redemption. The chargor does not need any equity of redemption.[27] Thirdly, even assuming the argument is limited to a mortgage, it misunderstands the true nature of an equity of redemption.[28] To say that a mortgagor has an equity of redemption only means that 'the [mortgaged] property belongs in equity to the mortgagor'.[29] It does not mean that the equity of redemption is an independent corpus separable from the mortgaged property. There is no distinction in equity between the equity of redemption and the mortgaged property. To say that winding up creates two funds, namely the mortgagor's equity of redemption and the mortgagee's mortgaged property, is to engage in conceptual impossibility and to separate the inseparable.

At this juncture, the 'two funds' theorists[30] might object by pointing to the following statement in Cotton LJ's judgment in *Re Pyle Works*:[31]

> [I]f the legal estate, so to speak, is outstanding in a mortgagee, then the only portion of that property which the liquidator can look upon as a fund in the winding-up for payment of the debts of the creditors will be the equity of

[25] A Walters and J Armour, 'The Proceeds of Office-holder Actions under the Insolvency Act: Charged Assets or Free Estate?' [2006] LMCLQ 27, 36–7.

[26] For a fuller discussion, see Ho (n 21 above).

[27] Performance of the secured obligation simply extinguishes the albatross on the *chargor's* property, that is the charge (*G & C Kreglinger v New Patagonia Meat and Cold Storage Co Ltd* [1914] AC 25, 52, HL).

[28] For an authoritative exposition of the nature of an equity of redemption, see *G & C Kreglinger v New Patagonia Meat and Cold Storage Co Ltd* [1914] AC 25, 48, HL. See also *Ultraframe (UK) Ltd v Fielding* [2005] EWHC 1638, [2006] FSR 17, ChD, paras 1401–1405.

[29] *Quennell v Maltby* [1979] 1 WLR 318, 324, CA.

[30] For example, J Armour and A Walters, 'Funding Liquidation: A Functional View' (2006) 122 LQR 295, 308.

[31] (1890) 44 ChD 534, 577–8, CA.

> redemption, or, in other words, that portion of the property remaining after the satisfaction of all the obligations which the directors have properly thrown upon this part of the property of the company . . . [P]roperty which is in mortgage is not . . . 'assets' of the company in the sense in which that is to be done, namely, free assets, assets which can be dealt with by the company in payment of their debts without regard to those who have a mortgage on this portion of the property of the company.

However, this passage does not support the 'two funds' theory at all and in fact is fully consistent with the orthodox understanding of the equity of redemption discussed above. Although the existence of an equity of redemption means that the mortgagor is the owner in equity of the mortgaged property, the mortgagor's liquidator must respect the mortgagee's proprietary right to priority in payment out of the mortgaged property. In other words, the liquidator can look to the equity of redemption (ie the mortgaged property) to repay the unsecured creditors only after the mortgagee has been repaid in full.[32] That is why Cotton LJ referred to the mortgaged property as '*the property of the company*', and correctly noted that it does not represent the company's 'free assets'. Mortgaged assets are not free assets precisely because they are encumbered.

Another argument the 'two funds' theorists might run is as follows. The effect of the commencement of winding up is that the company's assets become subject to a statutory trust for unsecured creditors only. Thus, since secured creditors and their security fall outside the statutory trust,[33] two funds are created. However, as the majority of the High Court of Australia in *Commissioner of Taxation v Linter Textiles Australia* aptly pointed out, the reference to a statutory trust is:

> at best analogical or metaphorical, as an attempted description of the operation of the statutory regime of winding up . . . The use of trust language in this context invites error. There is no trust in any sense that equity would recognise. To describe the manner in which the company holds its assets for the purpose of discharging its liabilities in accordance with the statutory scheme as bearing the indicia of an equitable trust is erroneous.[34]

Even Kirby J acknowledged in his dissenting judgment that the reference to trust property in the English authorities such as *Ayerst v C & K (Construc-*

[32] Subject to any statutory priority of liquidation expenses and preferential claims over the collateral holder's claims with respect to the proceeds of the collateral. Note, however, that there was no such statutory priority when *Re Pyle Works* was decided.

[33] *Re Oasis Merchandising Services* [1998] Ch 170, 181, CA.

[34] [2005] HCA 20, paras 32 and 128.

tion)[35] 'was not, as such, an attempt to import all of the features of the law of trusts into defined statutory relationships following a company liquidation'.[36] Therefore, even leaving aside whether the reference to a statutory trust is a useful analogy to describe the winding-up regime, it offers no support for the argument that the winding up confers a distinct fund on the debenture holder.

Put another way, while the initiation of a winding up leaves unaltered and does not diminish the proprietary interests in the company's assets of others (such as chargees),[37] the creation of a statutory trust equally does not expand the property rights held by any party in the company's assets. The initiation of a winding up does not *expand* the rights of such parties, for example, by transferring to chargees beneficial ownership of charged property which they did not have before. Chargees are no more beneficial owners of any of the company's assets (including assets subject to a floating charge) than are any of the company's other creditors.

So there simply is no warrant for the *non sequitur* that the creation of a floating charge, its crystallization or the initiation of a winding up gives rise to something like 'the debenture-holder's property'. It is something of a mystery exactly where this property would come from.

Therefore, it simply is wrong to say, as the court in *BHT* did, that the chargor company would never have been entitled to receive any part of the book debt realizations subject to a floating charge. It follows that, contrary to *BHT*, the mere creation or crystallization of the floating charge is by no means sufficient to establish that the debenture holder had not been enriched at the expense of the company.

(b) No loss to the company

The argument that the company suffered no loss because any recovery would go straight to the preferential creditors is hopeless. As pointed out by Birks, '[t]his case is not even properly one in which the claimant suffered no loss, merely one in which it was likely that if it recovered it would be swiftly disenriched'.[38]

---

35 [1976] AC 167, HL. See also *Re Oriental Inland Steam Company, ex p Scinde Railway Company* (1874) LR 9 Ch App 557; *Wight v Eckhardt Marine* [2003] UKPC 37, [2004] 1 AC 147, para 22; *Buchler v Talbot* [2004] UKHL 9, [2004] 2 AC 298, para 28.

36 *Commissioner of Taxation v Linter Textiles Australia* [2005] HCA 20, para 243.

37 *Buchler v Talbot* [2004] UKHL 9, [2004] 2 AC 298, para 28.

38 P Birks, *Unjust Enrichment* (2nd edn, 2005) 80.

Moreover, the court merely equated the law of unjust enrichment to the law of wrongs which requires a loss. However, the English law of unjust enrichment appears not to have adopted such a narrow view.[39]

(c) Preferential creditors having an alternative remedy against the debenture holder

The court's additional comment that the preferential creditors were able to pursue their own remedy against the debenture holder only, if anything, tends to support the liquidator's claim against the debenture holder. All creditors' interest (including the preferential creditors' interest) is mediated through the company and enforced on their behalf by the company. If the preferential creditors could pursue their own claim because their debtor's assets have been wrongly paid away, it would seem odd that their debtor's liquidator could not recover those assets, granted that the liquidator would be in effect pursuing the same preferential creditors' interest.[40]

It is therefore submitted that, on the fact-pattern outline above, there exists a prima facie case for recovery for mistake of law by the liquidator, and *BHT*'s reasoning ought not to be followed.

2. Receipt-based liability

Since a chargor owns the floating charge[41] assets legally and beneficially, it should also own the proceeds of realizations in the same manner. To the extent that the chargor retained legal title to the proceeds of realizations in the receiver's hands, the chargor's liquidator would appear to have a straightforward unjust enrichment claim against the debenture holder pursuant to *Lipkin Gorman v Karpnale*.[42] In *Lipkin Gorman* a solicitor stole money from his firm's client account (thus legally vested in the firm) and gambled it away at a casino. The House of Lords held that the casino was under an obligation arising from unjust enrichment to repay the amount received to the law firm. Here the receiver wrongly (ie without the necessary statutory authority) paid away moneys legally vested in the company. It follows that the recipient of the moneys, namely the debenture holder, should be under an

[39] ibid 78–82.

[40] cf *Sharma v Yardley* [2005] EWHC 3076, [2006] 1 BCLC 440, ChD.

[41] 'The floating charge is the only kind of floating security encountered in practice, but there seems no theoretical objection to a floating mortgage, by which the mortgagee acquires ownership of the fund by way of security and, upon crystallization, ownership of the individual components of the fund. The mortgage would, of course, take effect in equity only, there being no present transfer of ownership of identified assets': R Goode, *Legal Problems of Credit and Security* (2nd edn, 2003) para 1–10.

[42] [1991] 2 AC 548, HL.

obligation arising from unjust enrichment to repay the amount received to the liquidator.

In addition, even if one agrees with the proposition that the winding-up regime suspends the company's beneficial interest in its assets by way of a statutory trust, such 'trust' only relates to the company's unencumbered assets. Accordingly, the liquidator would seem to be able to argue that the receiver wrongly paid away proceeds of realizations beneficially owned by the company, and the recipient, namely the debenture holder, should be under an obligation arising from unjust enrichment to repay the amount received to the liquidator.[43]

This receipt-based liability is generally known as knowing receipt and has been explained thus:

> To make a recipient liable as constructive trustee on the basis of knowing receipt, the recipient's state of knowledge must be such as to make it unconscionable for the recipient to retain the benefit of the receipt . . . That knowledge may be acquired at the time of receipt, or later.[44]
>
> Although a claim in knowing receipt is receipt-based, it is not dependent on the recipient having retained the trust property.[45]

It has been held that although a company is the legal and beneficial owner of its own assets, there is no difficulty in classifying property belonging to a company as trust property for the purpose of knowing receipt, where the company's property has been alienated by its directors in breach of their fiduciary duty.[46] It follows that the company's legal and beneficial ownership of the floating charge realizations is no barrier to the liquidator's knowing receipt claim, where the receiver paid away the realization proceeds in breach of his statutory duty.

There is little doubt that the debenture holder became aware, at the latest by *Spectrum*, that his appointee receiver had wrongly paid away moneys which should have been paid to the liquidator. This arguably renders it unconscionable for the debenture holder to retain the benefit of the payment.[47]

---

[43] The liquidator's recovery would then be subject to a statutory trust for the benefit of the unsecured creditors, if the authorities on statutory trust are to be believed.

[44] *Nabb Brothers v Lloyds Bank International (Guernsey)* [2005] EWHC 405 (Ch), para 71. See also *Bank of Credit and Commerce International (Overseas) v Akindele* [2001] Ch 437, CA; *Agip (Africa) v Jackson* [1990] Ch 265, 291.

[45] *Ultraframe (UK) Ltd v Fielding* [2005] EWHC 1638, [2006] FSR 17, ChD, para 1486.

[46] ibid para 1487.

[47] An objection might be raised here that, by the time the debenture holder became aware of the receiver's improper payment, the debenture holder no longer retained the payment or its traceable proceeds. See D Hayton, *Underhill and Hayton: Law Relating to Trusts and Trustees* (16th edn, 2003) 975; J Mowbray, L Tucker, N Le Poidevin, and E Simpson, *Lewin on Trusts* (17th edn, 2000) para 42–51.

What is more, there are now many influential judicial and academic statements to the effect that the receipt-based liability ought to be strict, thus independent of the recipient's state of knowledge, consistent with the House of Lords' decision in *Lipkin Gorman.*

> Liability for 'knowing receipt' is receipt-based. It does not depend on fault. The cause of action is restitutionary . . . There is no basis for requiring actual knowledge of the breach of trust, let alone dishonesty, as a condition of liability. Constructive notice is sufficient, and may not even be necessary. There is powerful academic support for the proposition that the liability of the recipient is the same as in other cases of restitution, that is to say strict but subject to a change of position defence.[48]

On this approach, the debenture holder's prima facie liability to repay the liquidator would seem to follow as night follows day.

Nevertheless, it would be difficult for the preferential creditors to maintain this type of unjust enrichment claim because it is hard to establish that the debenture holder had been enriched at the expense of the preferential creditors. As noted above, the authorities suggest that the unencumbered assets of a company in liquidation are held in a statutory trust with the company's beneficial interest being in suspense. '[N]either the creditors nor anyone else have a proprietary beneficial interest in the [liquidation trust] fund.'[49] The creditors have only a right to have the assets administered by the liquidator in accordance with the provisions of the Insolvency Act 1986.[50] In other words, as the preferential creditors never owned any property in the liquidation fund, they would not be able to say that the moneys paid by the receiver to the debenture holder

[48] *Twinsectra v Yardley* [2002] UKHL 12, [2002] 2 AC 164, para 105, per Lord Millett. Albeit being a dictum, it gives powerful support to the strict liability approach. See also *Ultraframe (UK) Ltd v Fielding* [2005] EWHC 1638, [2006] FSR 17, ChD, para 1485; *Say-Dee v Farah Constructions* [2005] NSWCA 309, para 232; *Dubai Aluminium v Salaam* [2002] UKHL 48, [2003] 2 AC 366, paras 87 and 111; *Kuwait Airways Corpn v Iraqi Airways (Nos 4 and 5)* [2002] UKHL 19, [2002] 2 AC 883, para 79; *Grupo Torras v Al-Sabah* [2001] Lloyd's Rep PN 117, para 122, CA; P Birks, *Unjust Enrichment* (2nd edn, 2005) 156–7; Lord Walker, 'Dishonesty and Unconscionable Conduct in Commercial Life—Some Reflections on Accessory Liability and Knowing Receipt' (2005) 27 Sydney Law Review 187; D Hayton and C Mitchell, *Hayton and Marshall: Commentary and Cases on the Law of Trusts and Equitable Remedies* (12th edn, 2005) 770–1; D Hayton, *Underhill and Hayton: Law Relating to Trusts and Trustees* (16th edn, 2003) 975–6; P Birks, 'Receipt' in P Birks and A Pretto (eds), *Breach of Trust* (2002) ch 7; Lord Nicholls, 'Knowing Receipt: The Need for a New Landmark' in W Cornish, R Nolan, J O'Sullivan, and G Virgo (eds), *Restitution Past, Present and Future* (1998) ch 15.

[49] *Buchler v Talbot* [2004] UKHL 9, [2004] 2 AC 298, para 28.

[50] *J Sainsbury v O'Connor (Inspector of Taxes)* [1991] 1 WLR 963, 972, CA; *Re Calgary and Edmonton Land* [1975] 1 WLR 355, 359.

represented the traceable proceeds of their property.[51] Accordingly, a receipt-based claim would seem hard to sustain.[52]

3. *Re Diplock*

The preferential creditors might attempt to assert a personal claim against the debenture holder, relying on case law such as *Re Diplock*[53] to the effect that where personal representatives have paid money from the deceased's estate to a person not entitled to it, the next-of-kin or legatees entitled under the will, or any creditor of the estate, can recover the money from the recipient, subject to such defence as bona fide purchase.[54] *Butler v Broadhead*[55] suggests that a *Re Diplock* claim may be available to creditors of a company where the liquidator distributes assets under mistake. Similarly the preferential creditors might maintain a *Re Diplock* claim against the debenture holder on the basis that the receiver distributed assets under mistake or without proper authority or both. However, a *Re Diplock* claim is subject to a number of limitations, in particular the following. First, the preferential creditors must show that they have exhausted their remedies against the persons primarily responsible (namely, the receiver and probably the debenture holder)[56] and their claim is limited to the amount which they cannot recover in the primary action.[57] It would seem to follow that, since the preferential creditors' primary remedy against the receiver

[51] It is true that in *Ministry of Health v Simpson* [1951] AC 251, HL, the testator's next of kin maintained successful *proprietary* claims against the beneficiaries to whom the testator's residual estate had been misdirected. However, this is one of 'those cases . . . in which a creditor or a pecuniary or residuary legatee has been allowed to follow and recover assets which have been improperly abstracted from an estate. The basis of such proceedings is that they are taken on behalf of the estate and, if they are successful, they can only result in the lost property being restored to the estate for use in the due course of administration. Thus, while they assert the beneficiary's right of remedy, they assert the estate's right of property, not the property right of creditor or legatee; indeed, the usual situation in which such an action has to be launched is that in which the executor himself, the proper guardian of the estate, is in default, and thus his rights have to be put in motion by some other person on behalf of the estate': *Comr of Stamp Duties v Livingston* [1965] AC 694, 713–14, PC. See also G Jones (ed), *Goff and Jones on Restitution* (6th edn, 2002) para 30–002, fn 9.

[52] cf G Virgo, *The Principles of the Law of Restitution* (1999) 667.

[53] [1948] Ch 465, CA; [1951] AC 251, HL (*sub nom Ministry of Health v Simpson*).

[54] The theoretical basis for this line of cases remains unsettled. See, for example, P Birks, *Unjust Enrichment* (2nd edn, 2005) 157; A Burrows, *The Law of Restitution* (2nd edn, 2002) 203–6; G Virgo, *The Principles of the Law of Restitution* (1999) 667–8; L Smith, 'Unjust Enrichment, Property, and the Structure of Trusts' (2000) 116 LQR 412.

[55] [1975] Ch 97.

[56] The preferential creditors' primary remedy against the receiver (and the debenture holder) would be a claim for breach of statutory duty: *IRC v Goldblatt* [1972] Ch 498.

[57] See, for example, *Re J Leslie Engineers* [1976] 1 WLR 292, 299; *Butler v Broadhead* [1975] Ch 97. Note that this limitation has been academically criticized, see for example P Birks, *Unjust Enrichment* (2nd edn, 2005) 76–7; cf L Smith, 'Unjust Enrichment, Property, and the Structure of Trusts' (2000) 116 LQR 412.

or debenture holder would be for compensatory damages, the quantum of their *Re Diplock* claim would be limited to the same compensatory amount.

Secondly, 'it seems that no claim will lie if when the payment was made to the defendant the assets were sufficient to pay all claims in full but a deficiency has subsequently arisen'.[58] While it remains unclear whether this limitation applies to a claim by a creditor,[59] this limitation probably would not matter as we are dealing with insolvent companies.

Finally, even a liquidator may be able to avail himself of a *Re Diplock* claim against the debenture holder. In *Re J Leslie Engineers*,[60] a liquidator, relying on an analogy with *Re Diplock*, sought to recover the company's property wrongfully procured by its controlling directors and paid to the defendant after the commencement of winding up. Although the claim failed on other grounds, the court did not dispute the analogy with *Re Diplock*. However, a liquidator would probably not rely on *Re Diplock* now, given the availability of the strict receipt-based liability discussed above.

B. Defences to Unjust Enrichment Claims

We now turn to the defences to an unjust enrichment claim the debenture holder might rely upon. While all the usual defences to an unjust enrichment claim are in theory available, the more likely defences are as follows.

First, in so far as the liquidator's claim is based on mistake of law, the debenture holder might argue that the receiver was not mistaken because he was aware of the instability of *Siebe Gorman*, but he made the payment regardless. In other words, the receiver took the risk of being wrong.[61] The debenture holder would point to the remarks in *Spectrum* that *Siebe Gorman* was only a first instance decision which could not have been regarded as definitively settling the law in this field and, like any other first instance decision, it was always open to correction if the country's highest appellate court was persuaded that there was something wrong with it.[62] However, these objective factors alone would not be sufficient to show that the receiver made the payment on risk. It is not enough to say that those who rely upon a first instance decision must be taken to have

[58] P Pettit, *Equity and the Law of Trusts* (10th edn, 2006) 565.

[59] Compare J Sunnucks, *Williams, Mortimer and Sunnucks on Executors, Administrators and Probate* (18th edn, 2000) 1098 with R Kerridge, *Parry & Clark: The Law of Succession* (11th edn, 2002) 623.

[60] [1976] 1 WLR 292.

[61] *Kleinwort Benson v Lincoln City Council* [1999] 2 AC 349, 363, 401, 410, HL.

[62] [2005] UKHL 41, [2005] 2 AC 680, paras 43 and 64.

been aware of its potential reversal by a higher court. The receiver's subjective state of mind has to be proved, which may involve difficult evidential questions.[63] 'There is room for a spectrum of states of mind between genuine belief in validity, founding a claim based on mistake, and a clear acceptance of the risk that they are not.'[64] Furthermore, the receiver's negligence would not hinder an unjust enrichment claim.[65]

In any case, the fact that the receiver made the payment on risk would help demonstrate that the receiver made a statutorily unwarranted payment. This in turn would help establish the receipt-based claims and claims based on *Re Diplock*.

Secondly, the debenture holder might rely on a time bar, generally six years after the action accrued. An unjust enrichment claim for mistake falls within s 32(1)(c) of the Limitation Act 1980 so that time would start to run from when the claimant discovered, or could with reasonable diligence have discovered, the mistake. Berg suggested that, because of the Court of Appeal decision in *Spectrum*, time did not start to run until the House of Lords ruling on 30 June 2005.[66] This is most unlikely, considering the following chronology of events. First, *Agnew* cast significant doubt on *Siebe Gorman*, when Lord Millett pronounced that the necessary chargee control to establish a fixed charge '*was thought* to obtain in *Siebe Gorman* and did obtain in *Re Keenan*'.[67] Then *Agnew* received its House of Lords' endorsement in *Smith (Administrator of Cosslett (Contractors)) v Bridgend CBC*.[68] Next came the first instance decision in *Spectrum* which removed any doubt that *Siebe Gorman* was unreliable. Even the Court of Appeal in *Spectrum* had 'little doubt' that *Agnew* would be followed by the House of Lords.[69] Therefore, it is submitted that time should have run, at the latest, after the first instance decision in *Spectrum* on 15 January 2004, if not immediately after the *Agnew* decision on 5 June 2001.

With regard to the receipt-based claims and claims based on *Re Diplock*, time is

[63] Ideally the debenture holder would want to prove that, before payment, the receiver had obtained legal advice to the effect that *Siebe Gorman* was dubious. However, the debenture holder's burden of proof would seem easier to discharge if the payment were made after *Agnew* ([2001] UKPC 28, [2001] 2 AC 710) which, at the very least, must have triggered considerable doubt about the validity of *Siebe Gorman*.

[64] *Kleinwort Benson v Lincoln City Council* [1999] 2 AC 349, 401, HL.

[65] *Kelly v Solari* (1841) 9 M & W 54, [1835–42] All ER Rep 320; *Dextra Bank & Trust v Bank of Jamaica* [2001] UKPC 50, [2002] 1 All ER (Comm) 193.

[66] A Berg, 'The Cuckoo in the Nest of Corporate Insolvency: Some Aspects of the *Spectrum* Case' [2006] JBL 22, 48.

[67] [2001] UKPC 28, [2001] 2 AC 710, para 38 (emphasis added).

[68] [2001] UKHL 58, [2002] 1 AC 336, para 41.

[69] [2004] EWCA Civ 670, [2004] Ch 337, para 58.

likely to run from when payment was made to the debenture holder because the action would have accrued from the time of payment.[70]

Thirdly, the debenture holder might argue that the payment was made for good consideration. It has been said that '[the company's] balance sheet position was unaffected by the use of the monies to repay the debt due from the [c]ompany to the [debenture holder]'.[71] But this assumes that the company's debt to the debenture holder had been validly discharged by the receiver's payment.[72] 'In order for the payee to have given good consideration it is necessary that the payment operate in discharge of the debt and for that to occur the payment must have been made and received with the necessary authority.'[73]

Here the receiver's payment would not discharge the company's debt to the debenture holder because the receiver had no authority to make the payment under the Insolvency Act 1986. Moreover, such payment would run counter to the legislative policy of protecting preferential creditors, an important policy consideration underlying the *Spectrum* decision.[74] There is thus a strong policy argument that the receiver only managed to make a void payment to the debenture holder and did not discharge the company's debt.[75]

Fourthly, the debenture holder might plead change of position by arguing that it had spent the money received from the receiver in its ordinary lending business. It might also have released any personal guarantee given by the company's director. However, these matters are unlikely to establish the change of position defence. As has been repeatedly held, the essential question is whether a person's position has so changed as to make it inequitable in all the circumstances to require him to make restitution.[76]

> [A]ny change of position relied on must have some causal connection with the mistaken payment, so that, for example, mere unconnected misfortune, such as failing to pursue an alternative debtor . . . would not suffice as a defence. It must also be shown that it would cause real hardship to the [recipient] now to be called

[70] G Jones (ed), *Goff and Jones on Restitution* (6th edn, 2002) paras 43–002 and 43–018. cf W Swadling, 'Limitation' in P Birks and A Pretto (eds), *Breach of Trust* (2002) 319, 341–2.

[71] G Moss QC, 'The Red End of the Spectrum: Liquidators are the Wrong Claimants' (2004) 17 Insolvency Intelligence 143.

[72] A claim to recover mistaken payment would be defeated if the payment is made to discharge, and does discharge, a debt owed to the payee. *Barclay's Bank v WJ Simms, Son & Cooke (Southern)* [1980] 1 QB 677, 695. See also *Lloyds Bank v Independent Insurance* [2000] QB 110.

[73] *Standard Bank London v Canara Bank* [2002] EWHC 1574 (Comm), para 99. See also G Virgo, *The Principles of the Law of Restitution* (1999) 172 (footnote omitted): 'Whether the . . . payment will have discharged a debt depends on whether the payment is authorised by the debtor'.

[74] [2005] UKHL 41, [2005] 2 AC 680, paras 43, 98, 111, 127 and 141.

[75] cf Berg (n 66 above) 50–1.

[76] See for example *Vaught v Tel Sell UK* [2005] EWHC 2404 and the authorities cited therein.

upon to repay, so that, for example, paying off a debt which was otherwise nonetheless due to be paid can be no hardship in this context.[77]

Other conceivable defences such as estoppel, laches, *res judicata* and settlement of dispute are not discussed here as they probably do not raise any *Spectrum*-specific issues.[78]

C. Conclusion

The retrospective effect of *Spectrum* means that many payments made by the receivers to their appointor debenture holders on the basis of *Siebe Gorman* were improper. The discussion above shows that the chargors' liquidators may now compel the debenture holders to disgorge their receipt on the basis of unjust enrichment. The specific heads of claim span the common law–equity divide, including mistake of law and the receipt-based liability.

Critics would of course point to the common law origin of unjust enrichment claims and the equitable provenance of knowing receipt claims, as if that were reason enough for the court to refuse to take account of common law jurisprudence when developing the equitable principles. Any such critics would do well at least to take to heart the following advice:

> The growing specialisation of sectors of the legal profession, particularly the Bar, is constricting and in some instances fragmenting the sources of law which are deployed in argument. Planning cases on issues of natural justice, for example, are repeatedly argued by reference only to other planning cases, when more often than not a body of wider and more useful principle exists. The argument on abuse of process at the bar of the House in *Autologic Holdings* appears to have been based entirely on other tax cases. The law of restitution is at risk of going down a similar path of self-referential jurisprudence, with consequences, among others, of the kind addressed in the earlier part of this judgment. Such habits can retard and even reverse the growth of the law as a consistent body of principle. Professor Burrows' warning about this—'We do this at common law but that in equity' [2002] OJLS 22—deserves to be heeded.[79]

In addition, the 'two funds' theorists would argue that payments made by the receivers to the debenture holders could not be 'at the expense' of the chargors because all charged assets (and their realization proceeds) already belonged to the debenture holders. The discussion above shows that this argument must be

[77] *Fea v Roberts*, unreported, 9 September 2005, para 77.

[78] For a general treatment of the restitutionary defences, see G Jones (ed), *Goff and Jones on Restitution* (6th edn, 2002) chs 39–44.

[79] *NEC Semi-Conductors v Revenue and Customs Commissioners* [2006] EWCA Civ 25, [2006] STC 606, para 101.

regarded as illusory. For neither the creation nor the crystallization of a floating charge transfers beneficial ownership of the charged assets to the chargee. Nor does the creation of a so-called statutory trust upon winding up effect any such beneficial transfer. The winding up simply leaves unaltered the creditors' rights, be they *in rem* or *in personam*; it does not either create new substantive rights in the creditors or destroy the old ones.[80]

'[W]hile winding-up does not *diminish* a chargee's pre-existing proprietary rights', Walters and Armour observe, 'it is difficult to see why it should be a forum for *enhancing* chargee rights . . .'[81]

This is indubitably true, hence bad news for the 'two funds' theory and *BHT*.

[80] *Wight v Eckhardt Marine* [2003] UKPC 37, [2004] 1 AC 147.

[81] A Walters and J Armour, 'The Proceeds of Office-holder Actions under the Insolvency Act: Charged Assets or Free Estate?' [2006] LMCLQ 27, 43 (original emphasis, footnote omitted).

9

SHOULD WE REDISTRIBUTE IN INSOLVENCY?

*John Armour**

A. Introduction

The House of Lords' decision in *Re Spectrum Plus*[1] concerned the appropriate characterization of a security over book debts as a fixed or floating charge. The question matters primarily because a floating charge is subordinated by statute to various other claims in the insolvency of the debtor, whereas a fixed charge is not. This chapter uses the example of the floating charge to argue that such statutory redistribution between claimants in corporate insolvency is generally undesirable.

Floating charges are created by voluntary transactions between lenders and borrowers. If the legislature subjects particular types of voluntary transaction to statutory 'taxation' (as through the prospect of redistribution in insolvency), then sophisticated parties may be expected to structure their affairs differently so as to avoid the ambit of the legislation. In the case of insolvency, such 'avoidance action' has resulted in relatively little funds reaching the intended beneficiaries of the statutory redistribution. What is worse, the law's redistributive policy has engendered significant costs. Indeed, the juridical history of the floating charge is largely a product of litigation driven by such avoidance action. The *Spectrum* decision is only the most recent (and unlikely to be the final) chapter in a long series of such cases, which have, over the years, consumed many thousands of hours and pounds.

---

* I am grateful to the editors and to Vanessa Finch, Riz Mokal, Richard Nolan, and Adrian Walters for their helpful comments on earlier versions. I also thank participants in the *Spectrum* symposium held in Oxford in September 2005 for discussion following my presentation. The usual disclaimers apply.

[1] [2005] UKHL 41, [2005] 2 AC 680.

In addition to the *direct* costs engendered by transaction planning and litigation, such statutory redistribution may also give rise to *opportunity* costs. These arise where parties choose not to use a transaction structure which would otherwise be useful, solely so as to avoid the statutory 'taxation'. This chapter argues that there are opportunity costs associated with the current scheme, which render the floating charge very unattractive to lenders.

A floating charge over circulating assets can facilitate so-called 'relationship' lending by a concentrated creditor—that is, lending on the basis of the debtor's business prospects, as opposed to collateral values. Such a lender is best able to make informed decisions about the company's future in times of financial distress. Making it impossible for such a lender to take worthwhile security over circulating assets without exercising specific control will mean that companies find it cheaper to finance receivables from asset-based lenders, who are better placed to exercise such control. This chapter argues that the statutory scheme, when coupled with the hardened judicial line confirmed in *Spectrum*, will lead to further fragmentation in small businesses' borrowing. There is little reason for thinking that this will be a positive step.

The rest of this chapter is structured as follows. Part B looks at how redistribution is effected in English corporate insolvency law, and its historical relationship with the development of the floating charge. Part C turns to the impact of the scheme on corporate financing practice, and Part D argues that redistribution cannot be justified by reference to the benefits it brings to its recipients. Part E concludes.

At the outset it should be made clear that this chapter does not question whether the House of Lords' decision in *Spectrum* is consistent with existing legal principle. In contrast, the point in issue is whether the statutory policy of treating floating charges differently from fixed, which is given teeth through the characterization rules articulated in cases such as *Spectrum*, is desirable.[2]

B. Redistribution and the History of the Floating Charge

1. How does English corporate insolvency law redistribute?

'Redistribution' is taken in this chapter to mean the transfer of wealth from one party to another. English corporate insolvency law requires redistributive payments to be made out of floating charge assets in a variety of different ways. The three most important of these may be summarized as follows. First, the

[2] A question posed in RJ Calnan, 'Floating Charges: A Proposal for Reform' (2004) 9 Butterworths Journal of International Banking and Financial Law 341.

claims of *preferential creditors* are statutorily elevated above those of other unsecured creditors and those of the holder of a floating charge.[3] Secondly, the Enterprise Act 2002 has introduced a requirement that a '*prescribed part*' of assets subject to a floating charge must be set aside for payment to unsecured creditors.[4] Thirdly, until recently, the *expenses of liquidation* were also thought to be payable out of floating charge assets,[5] even though the procedure exists for the benefit of unsecured creditors alone. Although this instance of redistribution was recently brought to an end by the House of Lords,[6] the Government intends to restore it shortly.[7]

A crucial (but frequently overlooked) point is that imposing *ex post* obligations on parties to certain sorts of transaction gives those parties powerful incentives to adjust their affairs *ex ante* so as to fall outside the scope of the 'tax'. For these reasons, it is commonly thought that attempts to use the law governing voluntary transactions to effect distributive justice are unlikely to be successful.[8] The history of the relationship between the floating charge and the redistributive provisions of insolvency law provides a salutary example.

2. The early history of the floating charge

The advent of incorporation by registration in the mid-nineteenth century meant that shareholders, shielded by limited liability, were able to carry on business with reduced risk consequent on corporate failure.[9] Unlike modern listed companies in the United Kingdom, with share ownership dispersed amongst many investors, voting control in Victorian companies was almost always in the hands of the board of directors.[10] This, coupled with the lack of reliable information about the finances and prospects of such businesses meant

[3] Insolvency Act 1986, ss 40, 175, 386 and Sch 6, Sch B1, para 99(5). Following the Enterprise Act 2002, preferential debts no longer include claims by the Crown in right of unpaid taxes, and so now consist largely of employee claims.

[4] Insolvency Act 1986, s 176A. [5] *Re Barleycorn Enterprises Ltd* [1970] Ch 465.

[6] *Buchler v Talbot* [2004] UKHL 9, [2004] 2 AC 298.

[7] Company Law Reform Bill, cl 867 (as of 25 April 2006).

[8] AT Kronman, 'Contract Law and Distributive Justice' (1980) 89 Yale Law Journal 472. cf D Kennedy, 'Distributive and Paternalist Motives in Contract and Tort Law, with Special Reference to Compulsory Terms and Unequal Bargaining Power' (1982) 41 Maryland Law Review 563.

[9] Incorporation by registration was first made generally available by the Joint Stock Companies Act 1844. Limited liability was made available to shareholders in such companies shortly afterwards: Limited Liability Act 1855. These statutes were later consolidated into the Joint Stock Companies Act 1856, which also laid the foundations of modern corporate insolvency law. See generally LCB Gower, *Principles of Modern Company Law* (5th edn, 1992) 37–47.

[10] See J Franks, C Mayer, and S Rossi, 'Ownership: Evolution and Regulation', Working Paper, London Business School/Saïd Business School, March 2005, 42–3 (detailing decline of family ownership since 1900 in sample of UK listed firms).

that investment in 'outside' equity was often a hazardous affair unless the investor had some pre-existing knowledge of, or geographic proximity to, the business opportunity in question.[11] For these reasons, debentures were widely considered to be a safer investment. The protection of debenture holders' interests was therefore crucial to the facilitation of investment.

Whilst company law—through the doctrines of *ultra vires* and capital maintenance—did impose rules which can usefully be understood in terms of the interests of outside investors (and creditors in particular), the actual level of protection they gave was strictly limited.[12] The continuing need for debenture-holder protection was met in part through the use of ever-broader security interests.[13] An innovation that seems to have occurred, for limited companies incorporated by registration, at some point during the mid-1860s was the grant to debenture holders of a charge over the 'entire undertaking' of the company (or words to that effect).[14] It seems likely that such charges were inspired by provisions commonly included in the private Acts of Parliament that were used to incorporate railway companies.[15] These provisions, which had their source in the Companies Clauses Consolidation Act 1845, permitted such companies to grant mortgages over their 'undertakings'.[16]

There appears, at the outset, to have been considerable uncertainty as to the efficacy of, and if so, the appropriate form of words for, such 'entire undertaking' charges granted by registered companies. Early examples of such charges contained clauses expressly stipulating that the company should be free to deal with the charged assets until some future event—such as default on the debt secured, winding up, or cessation of the business.[17] It was commonly thought that in the absence of such a clause, an implied term would prevent the chargor from disposing of the charged assets without the chargee's consent.[18] A clause

[11] JB Baskin and PJ Miranti Jr, *A History of Corporate Finance* (1997) 146–51.

[12] See BR Cheffins, *Company Law: Theory, Structure and Operation* (1997) 526–37.

[13] Baskin and Miranti (n 11 above) 147–8.

[14] On the development of the floating charge, see GF Curtis, 'The Theory of the Floating Charge' (1941) 4 University of Toronto Law Journal 131; RR Pennington, 'The Genesis of the Floating Charge' (1960) 23 MLR 630; R Gregory and P Walton, 'Fixed and Floating Charges—A Revelation' [2001] LMCLQ 123; R Nolan, 'Property in a Fund' (2004) 120 LQR 108, 120–3.

[15] Gregory and Walton (n 14 above) 137.

[16] Companies Clauses Consolidation Act 1845, s 38. This Act contained a set of default provisions for special Acts of Parliament incorporating enterprises.

[17] Nolan (n 14 above) 120–4 (citing contemporary practitioner works and precedents). Some examples can be found amongst reported cases: see, for example, *Re General South American Co* (1876) 2 Ch D 337, 338 (debentures issued in 1874); *Re Horne and Hellard* (1885) 29 Ch D 736, 739 (debentures issued in 1874).

[18] See for example *Re Marine Mansions Co* (1867) LR 4 Eq 605, 609. The idea that such a term would be implied was based on thinking at the time in relation to general mortgages of personalty by individuals. Gregory and Walton (n 14 above, 130–5, 144–6) argue that, rather than reflecting a timeless certainty, it can be traced to a single heretical decision (*Graham v Chapman* (1852) 12 CB 85).

expressly granting a power to deal avoided immediate paralysation of the company's business, and, at the same time, deterred a court from concluding that the parties 'could not have intended' to create a charge over the company's *assets* at all, as opposed to the income therefrom.[19] The courts became more familiar—and comfortable—with this combination, such that the existence of such a power could readily be implied from the grant of a security over 'all the property' of the company.[20] Over time, the term 'floating charge' came to be used as shorthand for a type of security which comprised this package of rights and powers.[21]

Closely related was the development of contractual receivership. Traditionally, a receiver was appointed on a petition to the Court of Chancery to oversee the income arising from mortgaged property. However, it became common for parties to stipulate in a debenture that the chargee should, on default by the chargor, be entitled to appoint a receiver out of court, who would then be deemed to be the agent of the company.[22] In an important development, the Court of Appeal held, in *Re Henry Pound*,[23] that a debenture holder was entitled to exercise a contractual power to appoint a receiver, notwithstanding that the company had already gone into winding up. Thus the holder of a floating charge was assured of being able to control its enforcement, and the important legal preconditions for its utility had been established.[24]

Evidence on the commercial use of the floating charge can be obtained from prospectus advertisements in *The Times* for issues of debentures.[25] The first such advertisement was placed by the Royal Exchange Shipping Company Ltd on 4 May 1880, announcing an issue of debentures secured by a 'floating charge on the whole of the ships, undertakings, and effects of the Company'.[26] The terminology must still have seemed novel amongst the investment community, for

[19] As in *Gardner v London, Chatham & Dover Railway Co* (1867) LR 2 Ch App 201, the leading decision on the interpretation of charges created in the form prescribed by the Companies Clauses Consolidation Act 1845. This case created what an editorial in *The Times* two months later described as 'panic' in the investment community: *The Times*, 23 March 1867, 9.

[20] *Re Florence Land Co* (1878) 10 Ch D 530; *Re Colonial Trusts* (1879) 15 Ch D 465.

[21] Nolan (n 14 above) 123–4.

[22] *Gaskell v Gosling* [1896] 1 QB 669, 692–5.

[23] (1889) 42 Ch D 402.

[24] Two other significant steps were: (1) Jessel MR's ruling, in *Re Crumlin Viaduct Works Co* (1879) 11 Ch D 755, that the bankruptcy doctrine of 'reputed ownership'—which would have rendered such a charge vulnerable—did not apply in company liquidations; and (2) the Court of Appeal's decision, in *Re Standard Manufacturing Co Ltd* [1891] 1 Ch 627, that company charges were not registrable under the Bills of Sale Act 1878, the requirements of which would have made floating security impossible.

[25] These were located using *The Times Digital Archive*, which permits full-text searches of all content from 1785–1985.

[26] Classified Advertising, *The Times*, 4 March 1880, 13.

it provoked a letter from a reader enquiring what was meant by the term 'floating charge'. *The Times* thought the question sufficiently important to solicit and publish a response from the company's lawyers, Messrs Ashurst, Morris, Crisp & Co, which explained:[27]

> [S]uch a charge is now very familiar to commercial lawyers, and has been upheld by the Courts, including the Court of Appeal, on several occasions.
> The effect of it, as well settled by these decisions, is that all the property of the company, both present and future, is liable for payment of the debenture-holders . . .

Railway companies, which as we have seen did not utilize 'true' floating charges,[28] accounted for a large portion of the capital raised by British enterprises until the end of the nineteenth century.[29] This was perhaps one of the reasons why it appears to have taken 15 more years for the floating charge to achieve ubiquity. With the exception of two issues advertised in 1882, no further 'floating charge' debentures were advertised in *The Times* until 1887, when there were six. The years that followed saw companies other than the railways starting to raise capital in much larger amounts than before.[30] Much of this was debt finance, and the numbers of advertisements in *The Times* for 'floating charge' debentures soared,[31] suggesting these securities had become commonplace.

The position of debenture holders was thereby protected. What, though, of unsecured creditors? The attitude of the nineteenth century judiciary appears at first to have been sanguine: it was the unsecured creditor's responsibility to inquire whether or not security had been granted. As Malins V-C put the matter in an early floating charge case, *Re General South America Co*, decided in 1876:[32]

> [A] person dealing with a company knows also its powers of borrowing, and that the company has power to pledge every part of the property of the company. . . . Now if the creditors had been told that every particle of the property of this company was pledged to secure £72,000, could they have complained? And were they not told all this by the fact of its being a limited company? Were they not bound to make all these inquiries?

[27] Money-Market and City Intelligence, *The Times*, 10 March 1880, 6.

[28] They relied on the Companies Clauses Consolidation Act power to grant mortgages of their 'undertaking': see nn 15–16 above.

[29] See RS Grossman, 'New Indices of British Equity Prices, 1870–1913' (2002) 62 Journal of Economic History 121, 129–31; A Fishlow, 'Lessons from the Past: Capital Markets During the 19th Century and the Interwar Period' (1985) 39 Industrial Organization 383, 392.

[30] Grossman (n 29 above) (in 1870, 76 per cent of traded equities on British stock markets, by market capitalization, were railway company shares; this fell to 50 per cent by 1893 and 25 per cent by 1901); see also JB DeLong and RS Grossman, 'The British Stock Market and British Economic Growth 1870–1914', Working Paper, UC Berkeley Department of Economics, 1996, 12 (Table 1); J Getzler, 'The Role of Security over Future and Circulating Capital: Evidence from the British Economy *circa* 1850–1920', ch 10 below.

[31] See Figure 1 below, text to n 43.

[32] (1876) 2 Ch D 337, 341–3.

3. Legislative rebalancing

Leaving financial creditors to their own vigilance was one thing, but what of those classes of creditor—in particular, employees—that had been deemed worthy of preferential status in liquidation, on the basis that their ability to protect themselves *ex ante* was limited? The decision in *Richards v Overseer of Kidderminster*,[33] in which it was held that preferential creditors' claims did not extend to assets that were subject to security, provoked a swift statutory response.[34] The Preferential Payments in Bankruptcy Amendment Act 1897 introduced, for the first time, redistribution from floating charge assets, by making them expressly subject to preferential debts.[35]

In the parliamentary debates on the 1897 Act, there was discussion as to whether the priority so granted should not extend to fixed as well as floating security.[36] There was, however, concern that subordinating fixed security would be a step too far.[37] Ultimately the argument that permitted a distinction to be drawn between fixed and floating security was based on a labour theory of value: workmen should be permitted to have a prior claim for unpaid wages against stock-in-trade, which would fall within the floating charge, because their labour had contributed to its production.[38]

Meanwhile, in what was perhaps a sign of changing judicial attitudes, Lord Macnaghten called, in *Salomon's Case*, for more general redistribution in favour of unsecured creditors:[39]

> For such a catastrophe as has occurred in this case some would blame the law that allows the creation of a floating charge. But a floating charge is too convenient a form of security to be lightly abolished. I have long thought, and I believe some of your Lordships also think, that the ordinary trade creditors of a trading company ought to have a preferential claim on the assets in liquidation in respect of debts incurred within a certain limited time before the winding-up. But that is not the law at present. Everybody knows that when there is a winding-up debenture-holders generally step in and sweep off everything; and a great scandal it is.

His suggestion was not taken up by the legislature of the time, although the debenture taken by Aaron Salomon over the assets of his own company laid bare

---

[33] [1896] 2 Ch 212.

[34] See A Keay and P Walton, 'The Preferential Debts Regime in Liquidation Law: In the Public Interest?' [1999] Company Financial and Insolvency Law Review 84, 90.

[35] Preferential Payments in Bankruptcy Amendment Act 1897, s 2.

[36] See, for example, *Hansard, Parliamentary Debates* (4th Series) 60 Vict, vol XLVI (10 February 1897) 86 col 2, 87 col 1 (Sir Robert Findlay, Solicitor General).

[37] ibid 83 col 1 (Mr Alfred Hopkinson MP).

[38] ibid 73 col 1 (Mr George Kemp MP).

[39] *Salomon v Salomon & Co* [1897] AC 22, 53.

the weaknesses of the contemporary notice system,[40] and seems likely to have formed the impetus for the introduction in the Companies Act 1900 of a public registration requirement for floating (and other) charges granted by a company.[41] Moreover, a few years later, the Companies Act 1907 introduced a provision whereby a floating charge granted within a 'twilight period' shortly prior to the commencement of winding-up proceedings, otherwise than for new money, might be set aside by a liquidator.[42]

It is worth pausing here to reflect on the thinking that underpinned both the 1897 Act and Lord Macnaghten's call for redistribution in favour of unsecured creditors. Both appear to proceed from the assumption that insolvency is a common misfortune that must be borne by the creditors. If this is the case, then it naturally seems unfair that one party—the debenture holder—should be able to take everything. A call for a fairer balance seems quite appealing. It seems reasonable that workmen should have a right to be paid out of assets to which they have contributed value, but equally it might be tipping the balance too far in the opposite direction were *all* security to be so subject.

The problem with such thinking is that it neglects the fact that subjecting voluntary transactions to redistributive liabilities gives parties to those transactions a powerful incentive to structure their affairs differently.[43] Figure 1 provides some suggestive evidence.[44] It shows (the lower line) the number of pages in *The Times* on which advertisements appeared for debentures secured by 'floating charges' during the period 1880–1910. This gives a proxy for the frequency for which floating charges were used. To be sure, not all issues of securities would be advertised in *The Times*. However, by also measuring the number of pages on which advertisements for 'debentures' appear (with floating charges or otherwise), it is possible to give an indication of the *relative* frequency with which floating charges were used in debt finance. This is also reported (divided by 10 so as to render the scales comparable) in Figure 1.

During the period 1887–97, advertisements for floating charges grew relative to advertisements for all debentures. This growth is particularly dramatic in 1897, in which year the floating charge measure reaches more than one-tenth of the measure for all debentures. This growth trend is then reversed, such that

[40] Companies were required to keep a register of charges at their place of business (Companies Act 1862, s 43), but only existing (as opposed to potential) creditors or members were entitled to look at the register: *Wright v Horton* (1887) 12 App Cas 371, 376.

[41] Companies Act 1900, s 14. See Editorial, *The Times*, 19 February 1900, 11.

[42] Companies Act 1907, s 13. See generally HN Bennett, 'Late Floating Charges' in J Armour and HN Bennett (eds), *Vulnerable Transactions in Corporate Insolvency* (2003) 183, 183–4.

[43] See DG Baird, 'Bankruptcy's Uncontested Axioms' (1998) 108 Yale Law Journal 573, 589–92.

[44] Text to n 30 above.

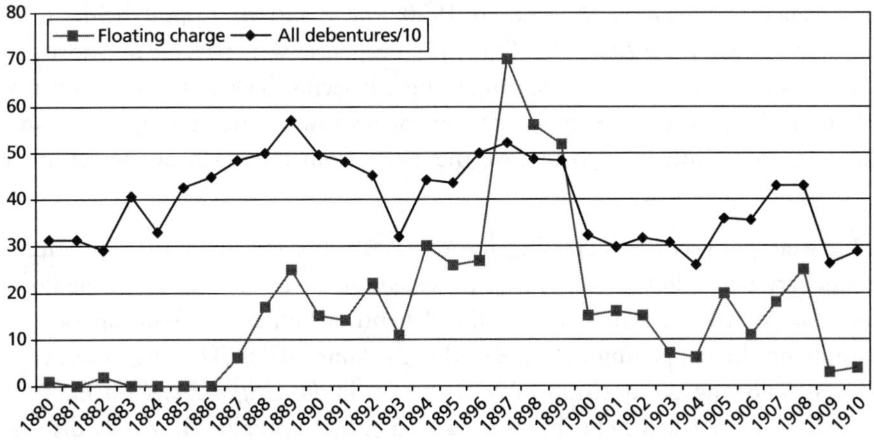

Figure 1 Advertisements for debenture prospectuses in *The Times*, 1880–1910
Source: The Times Digital Archive

the measure for floating charges fell off very quickly relative to that for all debentures after 1897, then tracked the overall measure fairly closely for the remainder of the period until 1910. The growth until 1897 is consistent with a pattern of increasing uptake of the floating charge following both its established legal efficacy and the increasing demand for finance by 'non-railway' companies in the 1890s. After 1897, the capitalization of these companies did not stop growing.[45] This implies that the most likely explanation for the sudden decline in the floating charge's relative popularity thereafter was that the 1897 Act made it less attractive to investors who wanted a secure protection against risk.

4. Secured creditors respond

During the first half of the twentieth century, public companies' relations with investors were transformed by, amongst other things, improvements in the quality of information available to investors.[46] As a result, it became unnecessary to offer security to persuade lenders to advance funds to listed companies. Secured debentures now came to be seen as the transaction structure of choice for banks lending to private companies,[47] reflecting the relative lack of information available about such borrowers.

Over the years, the range of taxes which attracted preferential status in corporate

[45] See R Michie, *The London Stock Exchange: A History* (1999) 88–9; Grossman (n 29 above) 128; DeLong and Grossman (n 30 above) 12 (Table 1).

[46] See Franks, Mayer, and Rossi (n 10 above); Baskin and Miranti (n 11 above) 183–6.

[47] See M Collins and M Baker, 'English Bank Business Loans, 1920–1968: Transaction Bank Characteristics and Small Firm Discrimination' (2005) 12 Financial History Review 135, 146, 165–7.

insolvency was increased.[48] And in 1970, the Court of Appeal held, in *Re Barleycorn Enterprises Ltd*,[49] that liquidation expenses were payable in priority to the claims of the holder of a floating charge. It seems likely that the cumulative effect of these developments was to spur banks towards developing new transactional forms intended to remove the assets from the reach of the statutory provisions.

One example was the increasing use of so-called 'semi-automatic' and 'automatic' crystallization clauses. These provided for the crystallization of the floating charge either on demand by the debenture holder (semi-automatic), or simply on the happening of a specified event (automatic). They had been conceived following the decision 30 years earlier in *Re Griffin Hotel Co Ltd*,[50] in which Bennett J had held that once a charge had crystallized, it ceased to be 'floating' for the purposes of the legislative scheme. The idea was for the debenture holder to use such a clause to crystallize the charge before liquidation commenced, and thereby avoid being subject to statutory redistribution. The efficacy of such clauses was finally recognized by the courts in the mid-1980s.[51] However, this was a Pyrrhic victory for banks, because the legislature closed the loophole in 1985 by providing that a 'floating charge' should henceforth mean, 'a charge which, as created, was a floating charge'.[52] What now matters is the character of the charge at the time of creation, rather than at the commencement of liquidation.

The second, and more far-reaching, innovation was that banks sought to create 'fixed' charges over circulating assets. This development appeared to receive judicial sanction in *Siebe Gorman Ltd v Barclays Bank*,[53] when Slade J declared that a debenture creating a 'fixed charge' validly took effect as such over the chargor company's book debts. However, in *Re Brightlife Ltd*,[54] Hoffmann J signalled a more restrictive judicial approach to the application of the statutory regime. His Lordship considered that the labels given by parties to their transaction should not be determinative. Rather, whether a charge was fixed or floating should be determined by reference to the characteristics of the security that the parties had created. Crucial, in the case of book debts, was the question of who had control over the proceeds of payment from debtors.[55] A requirement that the proceeds be paid into an account from which the chargor was permitted

[48] Keay and Walton (n 34 above) 89; 'Legal Snags for the Liquidator', *The Times*, 23 November 1974, 20; 'The Rich Rewards of Insolvency', *The Times*, 5 October 1984, 22.

[49] [1970] Ch 465, CA.

[50] [1941] Ch 129. It was followed in *Re Christonette International Ltd* [1982] 1 WLR 1245.

[51] *Re Woodroffes (Musical Instruments) Ltd* [1986] Ch 366, 374 (a concession); *Re Brightlife Ltd* [1987] Ch 200, 214–15.

[52] Insolvency Act 1986, s 251. This change was introduced by Insolvency Act 1985, s 108(3).

[53] [1979] 1 Lloyd's Rep 142.

[54] [1987] Ch 200.

[55] ibid 209.

to withdraw funds in the ordinary course without the consent of the chargee would not suffice as 'control'. There followed further attempts to avoid statutory redistribution through the drawing of an artificial distinction between debts and their proceeds, some of which found favour for a while with the judiciary,[56] but the basic approach articulated in *Brightlife* was subsequently affirmed by the Privy Council in *Agnew v IRC*.[57]

However, the position was thought by many to be different as regards charges over receivables granted to clearing banks. In *Brightlife*, Hoffmann J had carefully distinguished *Siebe Gorman* on the basis that the account in question was with the company's bank, and contained an implied term that the bank should be able to prevent the company from making withdrawals from the account if it was overdrawn.[58] This distinction was not judicially challenged until *Spectrum*. It meant that for a clearing bank lending on an overdraft basis, it was possible to take security over book debts that did not become subject to statutory redistribution.

That commercial lenders took advantage of this possibility is strongly suggested by empirical evidence from a new study of bank recoveries in France, Germany, and the United Kingdom. Davydenko and Franks report, amongst other things, on the extent to which different classes of asset were taken by banks as collateral for loans during the period 1996–2003.[59] They find that between three and four times as much money was lent by banks on the security of receivables than on stock-in-trade.[60] Stock-in-trade is of course another of the classical categories of circulating asset, but one in relation to which it was not thought that a *Siebe Gorman*-style fixed charge would be feasible.

In addition to structuring transactions *ex ante* so as to avoid security being characterized as a 'floating charge', it appears that banks also took steps *ex post*—that is, once the debtor had become financially distressed—to minimize the amount of redistributive exposure that they faced. Most small businesses that go into receivership have first spent some time in the hands of their bank's 'intensive care' unit, which will have tried to orchestrate a rescue, if possible.[61]

[56] The story of *Re New Bullas Trading Ltd* [1994] 1 BCLC 485 is too well known to be repeated here. See generally, *Agnew v IRC* [2001] UKPC 28, [2001] 2 AC 710, paras 29–35; S Worthington, 'Fixed Charges over Book Debts and Other Receivables' (1997) 113 LQR 562.

[57] [2001] UKPC 28, [2001] 2 AC 710 on appeal from the New Zealand Court of Appeal, *sub nom Re Brumark Investments Ltd* [2000] 1 BCLC 353.

[58] [1987] Ch 200, 210.

[59] SA Davydenko and JR Franks, 'Do Bankruptcy Codes Matter? A Study of Defaults in France, Germany and the UK', ECGI Finance Working Paper No 89/2005.

[60] ibid 41 (Table VII).

[61] See J Armour and S Frisby, 'Rethinking Receivership' (2001) 21 OJLS 73, 91–5; V Finch, *Corporate Insolvency Law: Perspectives and Principles* (2002) 211–18.

One suggestive finding from Franks and Sussman's empirical study of bank rescues was that, for those debtors that the intensive care unit was unable to save, banks tended to reduce their exposure over time, with the result that the companies instead incurred greater amounts of trade credit.[62] It seems therefore that banks have considerable opportunity to minimize their floating charge exposure during this period. Findings from the same study regarding receiverships are also suggestive of avoidance action by banks: it seems to have been common for receivers to allocate a disproportionate amount of their expenses to floating charge assets rather than fixed charge assets. In effect, this meant that the expenses were paid by the preferential creditors rather than the bank.[63]

Through a combination of these tactics, it appears that banks were remarkably successful in minimizing their exposure to statutory redistribution. Thus data from the Association of Business Recovery Professionals suggests that during the late 1990s, preferential creditors received full payment in less than 30 per cent of insolvencies, and in between 23 per cent and 40 per cent of cases, received nothing at all.[64] This impression of low recoveries is reinforced by data reported by Franks and Sussman, which suggests that the median recovery for preferential creditors in receiverships orchestrated by one of three banks studied was only 1 per cent of the debtor company's assets.[65]

These findings are, in a sense, unsurprising: they reflect the more general point that if one type of commercial transaction is subjected to a redistributive liability, commercial parties will take steps so as to structure their affairs differently. This receives more general confirmation from Davydenko and Franks' international study of bank recoveries, which reports that both the overall amount, and the types, of collateral taken by banks varies significantly by country, according to the extent to which it is subject to liabilities to preferential creditors.[66] Similarly, studies of venture capital contracting practices in different

[62] J Franks and O Sussmann, 'Financial Distress and Bank Restructuring of Small to Medium Size UK Companies' (2005) 9 Review of Finance 65, 85–6; J Franks and O Sussman, 'The Economics of English Insolvency: Some Recent Developments', ch 11 below.

[63] Franks and Sussmann, 'Financial Distress and Bank Restructuring of Small to Medium Size UK Companies' (n 62 above) 93 (sample of 35 receiverships: in all but two cases, the receiver's allocation of costs to the floating charge was more than pro rata to the value of the floating charge assets).

[64] Society of Practitioners of Insolvency, *8th Survey of Company Insolvency* (1999) 17 (Figure 32) (1997–8: 42 per cent received nothing, 27 per cent received full payment); Association of Business Recovery Professionals ('R3'), *9th Survey of Business Recovery in the UK* (2000) 18 (Chart 16) (1998–9: 23 per cent received nothing, 27 per cent received full payment).

[65] Franks and Sussman, 'Financial Distress and Bank Restructuring of Small to Medium Size UK Companies' (n 62 above) 83.

[66] Davydenko and Franks, n 59 above, 12, 16–17 and Tables V, VII and VIII.

countries suggest that national taxation may affect the way in which transactions are structured and indeed the level of funds invested.[67]

5. The legislature strikes back

The past few years have seen a dramatic series of legislative and judicial developments affecting floating charges. The Enterprise Act 2002, which came into force on 15 September 2003, made three major changes. First, it abolished the Crown's preferential status, leaving only employee claims as preferential creditors. Secondly, it introduced a requirement that a 'prescribed part' of floating charge assets, initially set at 20 per cent,[68] must be set aside for unsecured creditors. This idea had a long history. It was first suggested by Lord Macnaghten as long ago as 1896,[69] and later formed one of the more controversial recommendations made by the Cork Committee.[70] Its introduction in the Enterprise Act 2002 was intended to serve as a quid pro quo for the abolition of Crown preference: the Government wanted to ensure that the recoveries given up by the Crown would go, not to the banks, but to unsecured creditors.[71]

The Enterprise Act's third change was to abolish the institution of receivership, long understood as being the fall-back mechanism by which a floating charge holder might exit from a distressed business, in favour of a new 'streamlined' administration procedure.[72] Whilst the holder of a qualifying floating charge has a right to appoint an administrator of his choosing out of court,[73] his

---

[67] See RJ Gilson and DM Schizer, 'Understanding Venture Capital Structure: A Tax Explanation for Convertible Preferred Stock' (2003) 116 Harvard Law Review 874; J Armour and DJ Cumming, 'The Legislative Road to Silicon Valley' (2006) 58 Oxford Economic Papers.

[68] Insolvency Act 1986, s 176A; Insolvency Act (Prescribed Part) Order 2003, SI 2003/2097. The precise amount is 50 per cent of the first £10,000 of 'net property' (that is, assets otherwise available to satisfy a floating charge holder, net of preferential claims), then 20 per cent of the rest, up to a global maximum payment of £600,000. This maximum would be achieved for net property worth a total of just under £3 million.

[69] See n 39 above and text thereto.

[70] *Insolvency Law and Practice: Report of the Review Committee* (Cmnd 8558, 1982) paras 1538–1549 ('Cork Report').

[71] Insolvency Service, *Insolvency—A Second Chance* (Cm 5234, 2001) 12. The quid pro quo is not, however, immediate. Owing to concerns about the application of the Human Rights Act 1998, the operation of the 'prescribed part' and the abolition of receivership are purely prospective: that is, they apply only to floating charges created after 15 September 2003. The abolition of Crown preference, however, applies in respect of all floating charges. Thus lenders with security taken before the commencement date stand to receive a windfall.

[72] Insolvency Act 1986, s 72A. Administrative receivership will, however, remain open to creditors with floating charges created prior to 15 September 2003. Even for subsequent charges, there are a number of 'carve-outs' from the prohibition, relating to amongst other things to capital market arrangements, public–private partnerships and project finance structures: Insolvency Act 1986, ss 72B–72H. See generally J Armour and RJ Mokal, 'Reforming the Governance of Corporate Rescue: The Enterprise Act 2002' [2005] LMCLQ 28.

[73] Insolvency Act 1986, Sch B1, para 14.

enthusiasm to do so will be tempered by the fact that the office holder will be under a statutory duty to all creditors, and that the costs of their efforts are payable out of floating charge assets.[74]

Shortly afterwards, in *Buchler v Talbot*,[75] the House of Lords overruled the Court of Appeal's 1970 decision in *Re Barleycorn Enterprises*,[76] holding that the insolvency legislation did not mandate liquidation expenses to be paid out of floating charge assets after all. This was a positive development from banks' point of view. However, the Government has indicated its intention to reverse this decision by legislation, so it seems likely that in due course the former position will be restored.[77]

Finally, in 2005, the House of Lords' decision in *Spectrum* has confirmed the correctness of the view, widely held since the *Agnew* decision, that *Siebe Gorman* could no longer stand. The judicial approach to the application of the statute has hardened over time, in a way that may be summarized as a move from *description* to *prescription*. The legal connotations of the term 'floating charge' have correspondingly shifted from referring to a particular body of commercial transactions to a presupposition that a single reified concept can be applied to all cases involving security over which the debtor has control. The effect is to make it much more difficult, if not impossible, for banks to take security over receivables without micro-managing the debtor company's dealings in those assets.

6. How will the market respond?

It seems unlikely that banks will respond to *Spectrum* by taking floating, rather than fixed, charges to secure receivables financing. It is of course true that the recent statutory developments have not been unequivocally bad for floating charge holders. The abolition of Crown preference and the decision in *Buchler*, for example, have both ameliorated the debenture holder's position. However, these benefits are obscured by countervailing steps in the opposite direction. The Crown preference moneys are to be 'rerouted' to unsecured creditors.[78] And receivership, a procedure that was undoubtedly of great benefit to floating charge holders, is being replaced by the new administration procedure, which

[74] Insolvency Act 1986, Sch B1, paras 3, 4, 70, 99.

[75] [2004] UKHL 9, [2004] 2 AC 298.

[76] [1970] Ch 465, CA, see text to n 49 above.

[77] Company Law Reform Bill, cl 868 (cl 867 as of 25 April 2006).

[78] Whilst the prescribed part is taken from *part of* the secured creditor's recoveries, as opposed to coming *in advance of* them (as the Crown preference formerly did), it is clearly anticipated that the impact on banks of the change will be neutral. The amount of the prescribed part will be adjusted, if necessary, to ensure this: see Insolvency Service, 'Enterprise Act Evaluation: Planning Paper' (2005) 10–11.

is funded from floating charge assets. Moreover, the respite from liquidation expenses is due to end. The floating charge is therefore unlikely to become any more attractive to banks. Whilst they may wish to structure their lending so as to include a 'lightweight' floating charge over corporate assets, so as to be able to appoint an administrator,[79] banks will be unlikely to wish to lend significant sums against the security of a floating charge.

It also seems unlikely that banks will respond by assuming day-to-day control over their customers' spending so as to ensure that a charge over receivables would be characterized as 'fixed' after *Spectrum*. The exercise of such control would be likely to be uneconomic for banks,[80] whose overdraft lending operations are not organized on this basis. Moreover, if such control requires the making of regular and repeated decisions about the wisdom of the debtor's spending, then lenders may be concerned about the possibility of attracting liability as shadow directors.[81]

These considerations might seem to imply that *Spectrum* will make it more difficult to raise finance against receivables. If banks will not wish to lend against floating charges, or to exercise day-to-day control, and can no longer take fixed security over receivables, will this not mean that they are less willing to lend against receivables at all? Posing the question in this way, however, omits the possibility of financing receivables by other means. From the point of view of a small company seeking finance, the most likely outcome would be to forego that proportion of its overdraft finance that it might formerly have raised on the security of a fixed charge over book debts, and instead to enter into an asset-based finance arrangement in relation to receivables.

Such an arrangement could take the form either of invoice discounting or factoring. Invoice discounting involves the company agreeing to assign receivables to a financier by way of outright sale, and is therefore not subject to statutory redistribution. The 'price' paid by the financier is the face value of the receivable, minus a finance charge. This is paid in two stages: an upfront payment on assignment, of some proportion of the face value of the debt, and the remainder when the receivable is collected. The company collects as agent for the financier, and pays the proceeds into a trust account, from which it may

[79] See Insolvency Act 1986, Sch B1, para 14; *Re Croftbell Ltd* [1990] BCLC 844.

[80] The reasons for this are explored in more detail in Part C, Section 3 below.

[81] Insolvency Act 1986, s 251. The fact that a lender is exercising control in order to protect its interests as such is not sufficient, without more, to constitute it as a shadow director (*Ultraframe (UK) Ltd v Fielding* [2005] EWHC 1638, [2006] FSR 17, ChD, para 1267); the question will depend on whether the cumulative pattern of conduct (ibid para 1609) is such that the lender has become the 'locus of effective [corporate] decision making': *Secretary of State for Trade and Industry v Deverell* [2001] Ch 340, at 354.

then draw the remainder of the 'price' owing. The financier will make ongoing decisions about withdrawals by the company from this account, which will be based on assessments of the value of the receivables transferred. Such a financier, specializing in lending against receivables, may be expected to have a comparative advantage in performing such assessments over banks lending on an overdraft basis, which specialize in making general assessments about debtors' business prospects. Moreover, by specifically linking withdrawals to the ultimate value realized from the receivables which have been 'sold', this transaction avoids any real risk of constituting the financier a shadow director.

Invoice discounting is functionally very similar to a loan of the amount of the upfront payment secured by a charge over the receivables.[82] It is therefore a close substitute for lending on the security of receivables.[83] As it is not subject to statutory redistribution, we might expect that, after *Spectrum*, companies would use more invoice discounting. This prediction receives preliminary support from data on invoice discounting for the past few years. Figure 2 reports the value of domestic UK invoice discounting finance and factoring during the period 1999–2005. It shows that invoice discounting has grown dramatically over the period since the *Brumark* decision was handed down by the New Zealand Court of Appeal in 1999.

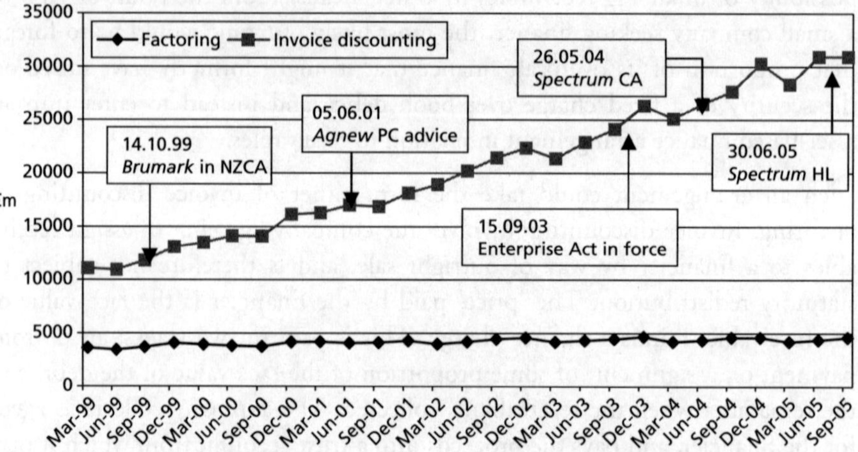

Figure 2 UK domestic factoring and invoice discounting 1999–2005

Source: Factors & Discounters Association

[82] The line is very fine indeed where the 'sale' is effected on a recourse basis: see *Re George Inglefield Ltd* [1933] Ch 1, 12, 22–3, 24–6, 27–8.

[83] SH Mian and CW Smith, 'Accounts Receivable Management Policy: Theory and Evidence' (1992) 47 Journal of Finance 169, 171 (Table I).

On the other hand, factoring has not grown at all over the same period. Factoring is another form of receivables funding arrangement offered by specialist financiers. It differs from invoice discounting in that the factor, for a fee, takes control over the company's credit assessment and debt collection functions, whereas under an invoice discounting arrangement, the company usually continues to collect its receivables as agent for the financier.[84] Invoice discounting is therefore a much closer substitute for secured lending against receivables, because the debtor retains control of its sales ledger in both cases, neither arrangement being disclosed to customers. Whilst this is simply 'raw' data, which does not control for any other variables that might be affecting the levels of factoring and in invoice discounting, it is at the very least suggestive of the prediction made above. We might expect general macroeconomic trends to affect both factoring and invoice discounting. Yet the levels of factoring have remained virtually constant over the period under consideration, whereas invoice discounting has grown sharply. This is consistent with the view that the increase in invoice discounting is driven by substitution from secured lending, as opposed to macroeconomic conditions. The implication is that since banks first began seriously to question the efficacy of the *Siebe Gorman* debenture—around the time that the *Brumark* decision was decided—they have been reducing their exposure against charges over receivables, and that borrowers have consequently been turning to invoice discounting instead.

Of course, a shift towards invoice discounting does not imply that banks will cease their involvement in receivables financing. Indeed, all the main clearing banks have asset finance divisions which offer invoice discounting products. Moreover, it seems a reasonably safe prediction that some banks will simply seek to structure as 'sales' what in reality may better be characterized as *loans* against the security of receivables,[85] and that these will in due course be challenged as being in substance (floating) charges. In this event, *Spectrum* would not be the final chapter in litigation concerning the floating charge.

This section has emphasized the interrelationship between statutory redistribution and the juridical evolution of the floating charge. Sophisticated lenders have repeatedly altered their behaviour so as to reduce their exposure to statutory

[84] On the use of this terminology, see the website of the Factors & Discounters Association: <http://www.factors.org.uk/public/faq.asp>.

[85] The line of least resistance for an overdraft lender wishing to convert its arrangement to 'invoice discounting' would be to use documentation providing for a global assignment of receivables, as opposed to more onerous individualized approval of receivables. This would, however, run a real risk of being characterized as a charge: see *Motor Trade Finance Ltd v HE Motors Ltd* (HL, unreported, discussed in *Re George Inglefield* [1933] Ch 1, 20–1); *Re Kent and Sussex Sawmills Ltd* [1947] 1 Ch 177, 179–80; *Orion Finance Ltd v Crown Financial Management Ltd* [1996] 2 BCLC 78, 84–5.

redistribution. This has not only resulted in relatively little actually reaching preferential creditors by way of recoveries, but has also generated substantial transaction and litigation costs. Our provisional assessment, therefore, might be that the statutory scheme is an expensive, and not particularly effective, way of protecting the interests of its 'beneficiaries'.[86]

C. The Impact of Redistribution on Corporate Finance

In this Part, we address the question whether the tendency of the statutory scheme to deter lenders from using floating charges entails any opportunity cost. That is, does it make any difference to corporate affairs whether or not a floating charge tends to be used to finance receivables? Indeed, might it be that the floating charge is in some way pathological, such that we should think it *beneficial* that its use is restricted? These questions require us to consider why security is taken, and the particular circumstances in which we might expect a *floating* charge to be used in the absence of statutory 'taxation'.

1. How is secured credit used?

The grant of a security interest confers upon the lender two sets of entitlements, which relate respectively to *priority* of payment and to *control* of the collateral. The control rights are what economists call 'state contingent'—in this case, their extent depends on whether the debtor continues to meet its obligations under the loan. Provided the debtor is not in default, the secured creditor's control is of a purely negative variety, consisting of the ability to veto sales of the collateral. If the debtor is in default, then the secured creditor has a positive right (subject to any procedural restrictions imposed by insolvency law)[87] to control the liquidation of the collateral.

Granting security is therefore costly for a debtor. The creditor's veto rights will restrict the debtor's control over its business, and the creditor's priority will make it more difficult for the debtor to obtain finance in future. On the other hand, security is thought to be able to assist creditors in lowering 'financial agency costs'; that is, the costs of conflicts of interest between shareholders and creditors.[88] For example, if the business is financially distressed, shareholders—

[86] See, similarly, A Keay and P Walton 'The Preferential Debts Regime in Liquidation Law: In the Public Interest?' [1999] Company Financial and Insolvency Law Review 84, 103–5.

[87] Such as the moratorium on the enforcement of security imposed in administration proceedings: Insolvency Act 1986, Sch B1, para 43.

[88] MC Jensen and WH Meckling, 'Theory of the Firm: Managerial Behaviour, Agency Costs and Ownership Structure' (1976) 3 Journal of Financial Economics 305, 333–43. The term 'financial agency costs' is taken from GG Triantis, 'A Free-Cash-Flow Theory of Secured Debt and Creditor Priorities' (1994) 80 Virginia Law Review 2155, 2158.

or managers acting on their behalf—may have incentives to pursue highly risky strategies that actually have a negative net present value, simply because they stand to benefit from the upside in the unlikely event that the strategy is successful. By restricting the ability of a debtor to alienate collateral, security enables the creditor to prevent the debtor from selling assets of stable value to fund more risky business ventures.[89]

Security also restricts the debtor's ability to borrow to fund such ventures. By granting existing lenders priority to the firm's assets, security forces new lenders to look primarily to the value generated by the ventures they fund, and thereby to scrutinize more carefully the purposes for which the debtor is borrowing.[90] The grant of security is thus a bond by the debtor not to engage in wealth-reducing transactions.[91] Such a bond is valuable to the debtor, because by 'tying its hands' to prevent itself entering such transactions *ex post*, it increases its borrowing capacity *ex ante*.[92]

Thus modern finance theory views security as closely related in function to loan covenants and contractual priority arrangements, which also impose restrictions on the debtor's freedom of action that may be justified as bonds against wealth-reducing transactions.[93] In each case, we would expect these arrangements to be agreed to only where the benefits to the debtor outweigh the costs—hence riskier firms, which we might expect to be more prone to financial agency costs, would be more likely to use loan covenants and security.

In this context, the utility of secured credit is a function of its advantages over and above contractual covenants.[94] The key to the difference lies in the

[89] CW Smith and JB Warner, 'Bankruptcy, Secured Debt, and Optimal Capital Structure: Comment' (1979) 34 Journal of Finance 247.

[90] A Schwartz, 'A Theory of Loan Priorities' (1989) 18 Journal of Legal Studies 209; O Hart, *Firms, Contracts and Financial Structure* (1995) 126–51. Were the existing lender not granted priority, the new lender would be able to poach, as its cushion against default, part of the 'cushion' of assets which protected the earlier lender against the risk of default. The competitive interest rate required for the second loan would therefore be commensurately lower. In effect, the firm would have been able to secure finance at less than the competitive rate by expropriating the earlier creditor: Schwartz, above in this note 228–34.

[91] GG Triantis, 'Secured Debt Under Conditions of Imperfect Information' (1992) 21 Journal of Legal Studies 225.

[92] The impact on debt capacity could be interpreted either as an interest rate reduction from the secured creditor, or, in a market characterized by credit rationing owing to adverse selection problems (J Stiglitz and A Weiss, 'Credit Rationing in Markets with Imperfect Information' (1981) 71 American Economic Review 393), an increase in the amount of credit offered.

[93] CW Smith and JB Warner, 'On Financial Contracting: An Analysis of Bond Covenants' (1979) 7 Journal of Financial Economics 117; MJ Barclay and CW Smith, 'The Priority Structure of Corporate Liabilities' (1995) 50 Journal of Finance 899; GG Triantis, 'Financial Slack Policy and the Laws of Secured Transactions' (2000) 29 Journal of Legal Studies 35.

[94] A Schwartz, 'Priority Contracts and Priority in Bankruptcy' (1997) 82 Cornell Law Review 1396.

consequences if the debtor ultimately defaults. As security creates proprietary rights, it is 'self-enforcing', whereas loan covenants are not. Security also has another difference from loan covenants: it allocates control (subject to restrictions imposed by insolvency law) over the enforcement process.[95] This permits creditors to allocate control over enforcement to those best-placed to maximize the value realized, and to deter other creditors from engaging in a wasteful 'race to collect' when the debtor is in financial difficulty.[96] We would therefore expect security to be used by those firms which are riskiest, or about which creditors have least information. Risky firms are more likely to default, and hence more likely to go into insolvency proceedings. In keeping with these predictions, empirical studies from both the United Kingdom and other jurisdictions establish that security tends to be used principally in relation to smaller, younger, and riskier firms.[97]

The ability of corporate debtors to grant security has the potential to yield social benefits extending beyond the parties to the security agreement (that is, 'positive externalities').[98] *Ex ante*, by facilitating bonding and monitoring activity, security lowers the probability that the debtor will engage in wealth-reducing transactions, and helps to reduce the probability of default. This increases the value of all creditors' claims. *Ex post*, by facilitating efficient enforcement, it can increase the overall 'size of the pie' for distribution. As we shall see, the way in which these benefits may be generated depends in part upon the identity and lending strategy of the creditor and the scope of the collateral. In the discussion that follows, attention will be restricted to the context of small and medium-sized firms, since, as we have seen, these are the principal users of secured credit.

(a) Asset-based lending: 'focal' monitoring and/or enforcement

Consider first a security interest in a single asset, or a particular class of assets. This would be a natural complement for a creditor following an asset-based lending strategy. Such a lender relies not upon its predictions about the debtor firm's creditworthiness, but on the ability of specific asset classes to cover repayment.[99] In the modern business lending environment, such 'asset-based

[95] RE Scott, 'The Truth About Secured Lending' (1997) 82 Cornell Law Review 1436.

[96] RC Picker, 'Security Interests, Misbehaviour, and Common Pools' (1992) 59 University of Chicago Law Review 645.

[97] AN Berger and GF Udell, 'Collateral, Loan Quality, and Bank Risk' (1990) 25 Journal of Monetary Economics 21; SS Chen, GHH Yeo, and KW Ho, 'Further Evidence on the Determinants of Secured Versus Unsecured Loans' (1998) 25 Journal of Business Finance and Accounting 371; MA Lasfer, 'Debt Structure, Agency Costs and Firm's Size: An Empirical Investigation', Working Paper, Cass Business School, 2000.

[98] See Triantis (n 91 above); S Schwarcz, 'The Easy Case for the Priority of Secured Claims in Bankruptcy' (1997) 47 Duke Law Journal 425; R Mokal, 'The Search for Someone to Save: A Defensive Case for the Priority of Secured Credit' (2002) 22 OJLS 687.

[99] See AN Berger and GF Udell, 'Small Business and Debt Finance' in ZJ Acs and DB Audretsch (eds), *Handbook of Entrepreneurship Research: An Interdisciplinary Survey and Introduction* (2005).

finance' encompasses hire-purchase or leasing agreements and factoring arrangements, which together account for a share of the external finance sought by UK SMEs second only to banks.[100] It also includes trade credit granted on title retention terms. In practice each of these tends to utilize transactional structures that, strictly speaking, involve the financier having outright ownership of the asset, as opposed merely to a security interest.[101] In function, however, these are equivalent to security.[102]

Consider the effect of granting a security interest over a single asset or class of asset to a financier who has specialist knowledge about the asset class in question, and/or the market(s) in which it is sold. The lender's expertise would enable her to exercise her control rights effectively, and thereby facilitate the monitoring of the debtor's use of the collateral and—should default occur—enforcement against it. Moreover, the *priority* associated with the security interest can sharpen the lender's incentive to do so. As the lender's priority will be limited to the proceeds of sale of these assets, this will focus her attention on the fate of that asset, as opposed to that of the debtor company's business generally.[103] Thus a security interest in a particular asset is most usefully granted to a creditor with specialist knowledge regarding the asset class in question. It not only allocates control rights to the party best placed to exercise them, but also gives the lender a powerful incentive to care about how they are exercised.

The use of title retention clauses in conjunction with a grant of trade credit provides an intuitive example.[104] A trade creditor who supplies a particular type of input, being in the business of selling that product, is probably best-placed amongst the debtor's creditors to liquidate unused quantities of that input on

[100] See A Cosh and A Hughes, 'Profitability, Finance and Acquisition Activity' in A Cosh and A Hughes (eds), *Enterprise Challenged: Policy and Performance in the British SME Sector 1999–2002* (2003) 72, 80 (external finance sought by sample of 1,712 UK SMEs during 2000–2: hire-purchase/leasing accounted for 24.8 per cent, factoring for 6.1 per cent, banks for 52.3 per cent); S Fraser, 'Finance for Small and Medium-Sized Enterprises: A Report on the 2004 UK Survey of SME Finances', Working Paper, Centre for Small and Medium-Sized Enterprises, Warwick Business School, 2004, 61 (external finance sought by sample of 1,443 SMEs during 2004: 72.0 per cent of firms seeking bank finance, 40.9 per cent of firms seeking leasing, hire purchase or factoring).

[101] See MG Bridge, 'Form, Substance and Innovation in Personal Property Security Law' [1992] JBL 1.

[102] One of the reasons such arrangements are employed is to avoid difficulties that might be encountered with negative pledges granted to banks, were 'traditional' security to be taken by asset financiers.

[103] S Levmore, 'Monitors and Freeriders in Commercial and Corporate Settings' (1982) 92 Yale Law Journal 49; SD Longhofer and JAC Santos, 'The Paradox of Priority' (2003) 32 Financial Management 69.

[104] Strictly speaking, of course, title retention involves a retention of outright ownership, rather than a grant of an interest by way of security: see, for example, *Armour v Thyssen* [1991] 2 AC 339, 352–4, HL.

the debtor's insolvency. On this view, the original supplier's comparative advantage makes it efficient for them to control enforcement against goods they have supplied, provided that in removing these inputs they do not destroy operating synergies with other assets belonging to the debtor.[105] It also provides a justification for the judicial limitation of such a creditor's priority to the original goods: there is no reason to suppose that the title retention creditor would have any comparative advantage in realizing these.[106]

(b) Relationship lending: general monitoring and/or enforcement

In contrast to asset financiers, the approach generally adopted by banks—which provide the majority of the external finance to SMEs in the United Kingdom[107]—is to advance funds on the basis of the debtor's general business prospects. A bank's credit decision could either be made using publicly available financial information, or could involve the creditor developing a relationship with the debtor where 'soft' information may be gathered on an ongoing basis to assist in making decisions about further advances in the future—so-called 'relationship' lending.[108]

A lender advancing credit on business-based criteria may be expected to invest in specialist knowledge about business generally, or—in the case of relationship lending—the debtor's business in particular. Granting a general security interest to such a lender can assist in controlling financial agency costs.[109] Where the debtor is relatively high risk—as is the case with small businesses—then a relatively tight control is called for.[110] Giving veto rights to a range of creditors will lead to coordination costs in their decision-making. In contrast, concentrating the decision rights in the hands of a single, well-informed, creditor (which for simplicity we will call a 'bank') may be the most efficient way of managing the problem.[111] Financial econo-

[105] The circumstances under which the moratorium in administration proceedings will not be lifted approximate to the situations in which such synergies exist. See, for example, *Re Atlantic Computer Systems plc* [1990] BCC 859, 880–2.

[106] This provides a rationalization of the courts' approach to the characterization of extended retention of title clauses, which, in England and Wales at least, have universally been held to create charges rather than outright beneficial ownership. In practical terms this limits the trade creditor's priority to the original goods.

[107] See n 100 above.

[108] See Berger and Udell, 'Small Business and Debt Finance' (n 99 above).

[109] RE Scott, 'A Relational Theory of Secured Financing' (1986) 86 Columbia Law Review 901, 926–9, J Armour and S Frisby, 'Rethinking Receivership' (2001) 21 OJLS 73, 79–86.

[110] See M Carey, M Post, and SA Sharpe, 'Does Corporate Lending by Banks and Finance Companies Differ? Evidence on Specialization in Private Debt Contracting' (1998) 53 Journal of Finance 845, 847.

[111] MA Petersen and RJ Rajan, 'The Benefits of Lending Relationships: Evidence from Small Business Data' (1994) 49 Journal of Finance 3.

mists speak of the bank acting as a 'delegated' monitor on behalf of the other creditors.[112]

It might be thought that the priority associated with such a general security would weaken the bank's incentive to invest in gathering information about, and monitoring, the debtor's business.[113] The intuition is that if the bank is a senior claimant, it will not be sufficiently concerned with monitoring the debtor. This intuition is based on two assumptions: (1) that more creditor control is always better than less; and (2) that a junior creditor always has the strongest incentives to monitor. However, neither turns out to be reliable.

Creditor control has significant costs as well as benefits. These costs are the inverse of the costs of shareholder control. Just as the shareholders have an incentive to prefer excess risk, creditors have an incentive to prefer too *little* risk.[114] And just as shareholders' incentives are misaligned from maximizing the firm's value when it is financially distressed, creditors' incentives are misaligned from value maximization when it is solvent. It follows that the more financially distressed the debtor's position, the greater will be the benefits of creditor control, and the lower the costs. Thus it makes sense to give a concentrated creditor an incentive to intervene which will become progressively greater with the severity of the firm's financial distress.

However, a junior creditor's incentive (and ability) to exert control does not increase in linear fashion with the financial difficulties of the firm as a whole. Rather, a junior creditor's incentive to intervene begins early, when its claim is 'close to the money'. This may result in too much creditor 'discipline' for the firm.[115] Moreover, if the firm's financial position deteriorates seriously, a junior creditor will find its incentive and ability to intervene will decline, at the very point when it is potentially most valuable. Its incentive will be dulled by the fact that the marginal benefit of its efforts will now go to creditors ranked above it.[116] Its ability to influence the debtor by threatening insolvency proceedings will weaken. The threat will cease to be credible as the creditor's likelihood of

[112] See, for example DW Diamond, 'Financial Intermediation and Delegated Monitoring' (1984) 51 Review of Economic Studies 393.

[113] TH Jackson and AT Kronman, 'Secured Financing and Priorities Among Creditors', (1979) 88 Yale Law Journal 1143, 1149–61; E Fama, 'Contract Costs and Financing Decisions' (1990) 63 Journal of Business S71, S84; V Finch, *Corporate Insolvency Law: Perspectives and Principles* (2002) 258.

[114] MC Jensen and WH Meckling, 'Theory of the Firm: Managerial Behaviour, Agency Costs and Ownership Structure' (1976) 3 Journal of Financial Economics 305.

[115] DW Diamond, 'Seniority and Maturity of Debt Contracts' (1993) 33 Journal of Financial Economics 341.

[116] C Park, 'Monitoring and the Structure of Debt Contracts' (2000) 55 Journal of Finance 2157; SD Longhofer and JAC Santos, 'The Importance of Bank Seniority for Relationship Lending' (2000) 9 Journal of Financial Intermediation 57.

repayment in insolvency diminishes.[117] Thus making bank debt senior gives the concentrated creditor an incentive to intervene when it matters most, and the ability to exert meaningful control.

That banks, with senior priority status, do in fact exercise this control when the debtor is financially distressed, in a way that is beneficial for other creditors, is apparent from empirical studies of banks' orchestration of informal rescues.[118] Franks and Sussman found that the average firm in their sample of financially distressed borrowers spent seven and a half months with banks' Business Support Units (BSUs, or colloquially, 'intensive care'), and that (depending on the bank) about somewhere between half to three-quarters of these firms emerged from the BSU without going into formal insolvency proceedings.[119]

It is also worth reflecting on the consequences of the implicit alternative to giving seniority to a concentrated lender such as a bank. Making the bank junior would mean that a variety of other creditors, each with smaller claims, would be senior to it. If they were called upon to effect an informal rescue, it would be relatively costly for them to coordinate. They are more likely to seek to enforce, in order to protect their positions.[120] At best, this will frustrate informal rescues; at worst, it will bring about the break-up of the debtor. Franks and Sussman emphasize the passivity of junior creditors with small claims during the orchestration of an informal rescue by a concentrated senior creditor. This is because, being junior, they stand to gain nothing by seeking to enforce against the firm's assets.[121]

2. Is secured credit harmful?

It is argued by some that a social loss may result from the use of secured credit in the presence of 'non-adjusting' creditors: that is, creditors whose decision to extend credit does not fully reflect the increased risk (to them) associated with

[117] Park (n 116 above); R Elsas and JP Krahnen, 'Collateral, Relationship Lending and Financial Distress: An Empirical Study on Financial Contracting', Working Paper, Department of Finance, Goethe-Universität Frankfurt, 2002.

[118] Armour and Frisby (n 109 above) 91–5; J Franks and O Sussman, 'Financial Distress and Bank Restructuring of Small to Medium-Size UK Companies' (2005) 9 Review of Finance 65, 84–93. See also, in an historical context, M Baker and M Collins, 'English Commercial Banks and Business Client Distress, 1946–63' (2003) 7 European Review of Economic History 365.

[119] Franks and Sussman (n 118 above) 76–7.

[120] See D Webb, 'An Economic Evaluation of Insolvency Processes in the UK: Does the 1986 Insolvency Act Satisfy the Creditors' Bargain?' (1991) 43 Oxford Economic Papers 139, 143–6 (model resulting in 'asset-grabbing' where more than one creditor has senior status).

[121] Franks and Sussman (n 118 above) 88–91.

the fact that the debtor has granted security.[122] The intuition is that, all other things being equal, a loan made on a secured rather than an unsecured basis will carry with it a lower rate of interest, reflecting the reduction in risk that the lender will bear. Moreover, all other things again being equal, an unsecured creditor is worse off if his debtor has granted security to another creditor. Thus unless unsecured creditors 'adjust' to reflect the increased risk it brings for them, a grant of security may result in a transfer of wealth—in an expected-value sense—from unsecured debtors to the borrower. By borrowing on a secured basis, the debtor obtains a lower interest rate; by failing to adjust, the 'cost' is borne by unsecured creditors.

This claim does not necessarily imply that the benefits of security discussed in the previous section do not exist. Yet at the very least it implies that, even if such benefits exist, the possibility of such wealth transfers will lead debtors to take 'too much' security.[123] The costs of granting such 'unnecessary' security will be wasted. Moreover, non-adjusting creditors who thereby end up bearing the additional risk may be poorly diversified and so least well-placed to bear it.[124] Nevertheless, whilst the current state of the empirical evidence does not permit us to answer the question unequivocally, it does seem more likely than not that the benefits associated with security outweigh its costs.

As we have seen, security tends to be granted by firms which are at relatively greater risk of default.[125] This seems consistent with the predictions of both theories that explain security by reference to its function in reducing agency costs and by reference to its potential for transferring wealth from non-adjusting creditors. The benefits of policing a debtor so as to reduce its likelihood of default will clearly increase with the debtor's riskiness. At the same time, the expected value of the 'insolvency share' of unsecured creditors, which the critics of security argue it permits to be 'sold' to secured creditors, also increases with the probability of the debtor's default. The pattern of security, in and of itself, could be explained by reference to either, or a combination of both, effects.

It has been suggested by some that the 'wealth transfer' theory may be rejected on the basis that there is little for debtors to gain from 'selling' the insolvency

[122] JH Scott Jr, 'Bankruptcy, Secured Debt and Optimal Capital Structure' (1977) 32 Journal of Finance 1; L LoPucki, 'The Unsecured Creditor's Bargain' (1994) 80 Virginia Law Review 1887; LA Bebchuk and JM Fried, 'The Uneasy Case for the Priority of Secured Claims in Bankruptcy' (1996) 105 Yale Law Journal 857; V Finch, 'Security, Insolvency and Risk: Who Pays the Price?' (1999) 62 MLR 633. The terminology 'non-adjusting' is taken from Bebchuk and Fried above, 885–6.

[123] Bebchuk and Fried (n 122 above) 895–903.

[124] Finch (n 122 above) 645.

[125] n 97 above and text thereto.

share of unsecured creditors to secured creditors.[126] On the one hand, it appears that the use of security over corporate assets is correlated with the taking of personal security from company directors, in the form of personal guarantees of corporate indebtedness.[127] To the extent that a grant of corporate security precipitates a grant of personal security by owner-managers, the latter incur a cost by granting corporate security.

Correlatively, it has been argued that a grant of security does not necessarily result in any reduction in interest rates for borrowers. Debtors may therefore have little to gain by 'selling' the insolvency share of non-adjusting creditors to secured creditors.[128] For example, Davydenko and Franks' recent study of bank recoveries finds no statistically significant relationship between loan interest margins and the presence of security;[129] a finding which is robust for results relating to the United Kingdom, France, and Germany. However, this might simply be because the authors have not controlled completely for the fact that security tends to be most valuable to lenders in relation to higher-risk borrowers, and that therefore a firm borrowing on a secured basis tends in any event to be charged a higher interest rate.[130]

A third objection to the claim that security is harmful is that it seems unlikely that there are significant numbers of 'non-adjusting' creditors. Those claiming that security is used to transfer wealth typically assume that trade creditors' adjustment is only partial, on the basis that they face relatively high information and transaction costs relative to the amount at stake.[131] Yet we have seen that security tends to be ubiquitous amongst smaller, younger firms.[132] A priori, it

[126] R Mokal, 'The Search for Someone to Save: A Defensive Case for the Priority of Secured Credit' (2002) 22 OJLS 687, 713–17.

[127] See Franks and Sussmann (n 118 above) 80. Moreover, in Franks and Sussman's dataset, taking personal security was positively correlated with risk of insolvency: ibid 90.

[128] Mokal (n 126 above) 713.

[129] SA Davydenko and JR Franks, 'Do Bankruptcy Codes Matter? A Study of Defaults in France, Germany and the UK', ECGI Finance Working Paper No 89/2005, 46 (Table XII) (presence of security is, if anything, positively correlated with loan interest margins).

[130] See JR Booth and LC Booth, 'Loan Collateral Decisions and Corporate Borrowing Costs', Working Paper Arizona State University, 1996 (finding that secured credit is offered at a reduced interest rate compared to unsecured credit, controlling for the simultaneity of the decision to take security and the observed riskiness of the borrower).

[131] Tort victims are also often said to constitute a class of 'non-adjusting' creditor. However, their interests are well protected in the United Kingdom through systems of mandatory insurance for the most empirically significant categories of tort claim, coupled with the Third Parties (Rights Against Insurers) Act 1930, which transfers to the injured party an insolvent company's claim against the insurer. Moreover, the author conducted interviews with approximately 20 insolvency practitioners during 1999–2000 (see J Armour and S Frisby, 'Rethinking Receivership' (2001) 21 OJLS 73, 102), amongst other things asking participants whether they had ever had to deal with significant tort liabilities in relation to a case they had conducted. No participant was able to identify a case where this had occurred.

[132] See sources cited at n 97 above.

would be surprising if trade creditors could not use these borrower characteristics as readily observable proxies for whether or not security had been granted. Moreover, the assumption that trade creditors only adjust to a limited extent does not seem consistent with empirical data. Whilst trade creditors do tend to offer the same *terms* to all 'borrowers' (that is, customers who purchase on credit),[133] the non-adjustment idea is contradicted by evidence that trade creditors tend to adjust the *amount* of trade credit granted in accordance with the debtor's creditworthiness and the scope for misbehaviour by the debtor.[134] Thus, whilst it is possible that some grants of security may be harmful to non-adjusting creditors, it seems likely that the beneficial aspects of security are empirically more significant.

3. Is the floating charge different from other types of security interest?

As we have seen, the floating charge is singled out by English corporate insolvency law for special treatment. It is therefore appropriate to ask whether there are functional differences between this and other forms of security. The case for special treatment of floating charges turns on two points. First, it is argued that floating charges are likely to be of limited use in controlling debtor misbehaviour, and therefore give rise to less benefits than other forms of security.[135] The debtor's ability to deal with the collateral in the ordinary course of business (OCB) weakens the creditor's ability to control asset substitution. Moreover, the fact that a floating charge is subordinated to subsequent fixed charges clearly restricts its usefulness as a means of 'locking in' priorities.[136] Secondly, it is thought that the way in which the floating charge is typically general in its scope, and extends to after-acquired property, renders it particularly likely, as

---

[133] Trade credit is typically offered on very similar terms within an industry: CK Ng, JK Smith, and RL Smith, 'Evidence on the Determinants of Trade Credit Terms in Interfirm Trade' (1999) 54 Journal of Finance 1109, 1120–1.

[134] See, for example, MA Petersen and RJ Rajan, 'Trade Credit: Theories and Evidence' (1997) 10 Review of Financial Studies 661, 678–9 (borrowers with observably higher credit quality obtain more trade credit); M Burkart, T Ellingsen, and M Giannetti, 'What You Sell is What You Lend? Explaining Trade Credit Contracts', ECGI Finance Working Paper 071/2005, November 2004 (more trade credit is granted where a buyer is less able to divert inputs supplied to another use).

[135] R Mokal, 'The Floating Charge: An Elegy' in S Worthington (ed), *Commercial Law and Commercial Practice* (2003) 479. The floating charge formerly gave its holder powerful rights to control the debtor, through the use or threat of receivership (Armour and Frisby, n 109 above, 79–91). Mokal claims that this was the *only* useful function served by the floating charge, and that, after the abolition of receivership by the Enterprise Act 2002, this form of security has outlived its usefulness. In contrast, this chapter argues that the floating charge still facilitates concentrated creditor control even without receivership, and that the statutory scheme of redistribution, by deterring creditors from making as much use of this form of security as they might otherwise, creates opportunity costs.

[136] *Wheatley v Silkstone & Haigh Moor Coal Co* (1885) 29 Ch D 715, 724; *English and Scottish Mercantile Investment Co v Brunton* [1892] 2 QB 700, 711.

compared with other types of security, to permit the holder to 'poach' the insolvency value of assets that the company has acquired with finance provided by subsequent lenders.[137] To be sure, provided they are notified of the existence of the charge, subsequent lenders are able to protect themselves by adjusting the terms of their contracts, but clearly not all of them do so. Thus emerges the case against the floating charge: on this analysis, it has few benefits and high costs.

However, both of these features need to be placed in context. The floating charge was, as we have seen, originally developed as a means of taking security over circulating assets. The way such assets are used in business is such that the costs of the control rights associated with a fixed security (in terms of impeding useful business activity) would, for many lenders, outweigh the benefits (in terms of avoiding harmful actions).[138] As we shall see, the costs of exercising such control rights would only be manageable for a lender following an asset-based lending strategy, who has invested in specialist knowledge of this asset class. The issue is therefore whether, *for this type of asset*, the floating charge may be a useful form of security if taken by a relationship lender.

(a) *Circulating assets: asset-based lending*

Consider first an asset financier specializing in circulating assets—such as receivables.[139] Such a financier—an invoice discounter, for example—will take either a security interest over, or ownership of, specified receivables, in return for which they will advance funds to the borrower company. The better the quality of the receivables, the greater the proportion of their face value which the financier will be willing to advance.[140] The financier will therefore need to engage in monitoring the quality of receivables, and will likely bring specialist knowledge to bear in making this assessment.[141] He will also wish to control what the borrower does with the proceeds of payment from receivable debtors—for example requiring the proceeds to be paid into a trust account, from which it would only be permitted to withdraw funds in excess of the amount advanced

[137] Finch (n 122 above) 659. See also Lord Macnaghten's observations, text to n 39 above.

[138] See text to nn 92–94 above.

[139] See generally, SH Mian and CW Smith, 'Accounts Receivable Management Policy: Theory and Evidence' (1992) 47 Journal of Finance 169.

[140] From the financier's point of view, 'quality' here means the probability that payment will be made by the receivable debtor.

[141] This monitoring might occur in the context of an arrangement whereby the debtor must request approval of finance against individual receivables, or batches of receivables. Alternatively, there might be a single general agreement to fund the borrower's sale ledger, in which case the financier's specialist knowledge will have been used at the outset in scrutinizing the quality of the borrower's sales book, and will continue to be used in ongoing monitoring of the quality of the debts.

in respect of outstanding receivables. Because of the way such a financier is making continuous assessments of its exposure based on the quality of the receivables, and requiring payments into a trust account to control its exposure, such a financing arrangement could practicably be structured either on the basis of sale of the receivables, or through a fixed charge.

(b) Circulating assets: relationship lending

Now consider the case of a lender advancing funds on the basis of the debtor's business prospects. As has been discussed, a relationship lender would wish, in order to maximize its influence, to take security over as much of the debtor's assets as possible.[142] In relation to circulating assets, however, and lacking specialist knowledge, it would not be economic for such a lender to take fixed security, because of the need for frequent turnover of the assets.

Yet if the lender instead takes floating security, this nevertheless improves its ability to prevent the debtor from acting contrary to its interests.[143] Recall that the nature of the monitoring performed by such a lender is different to an asset-based lender: a relationship lender's expertise lies in its ability to assess the debtor's business. What is useful is a veto over decisions that will change the debtor's line of business. Thus the usefulness of a floating security over receivables to such a lender lies not in the details of specific book debts, but in the lender's ability to control their use (along with all the debtor's other assets) in extraordinary circumstances.[144]

Such a lender would of course structure its debenture security as fixed charges over specific assets coupled with a residual floating charge.[145] Yet, because the debtor will not typically be alienating its fixed assets in the ordinary course of business, the circumstances under which the lender will be called upon to exercise its veto rights will actually be similar in relation to each type of collateral—that is, transactions outside the ordinary course of business. In

---

142 Text to n 109 above. 143 cf Mokal (n 135 above) 505–6.

144 To be sure, a basic floating charge would permit a debtor to use the charged assets 'in the ordinary course of business', words which have been interpreted to include unusual transactions designed to save the business from failure (see *Ashborder BV v Green Gas Power Ltd* [2004] EWHC 1517; [2005] 1 BCLC 623, ChD, paras 192–227). However, additional restrictions—for example on sale or assignment of book debts—can of course be drafted into the security agreement, as can provisions for automatic crystallization on specified conduct (see *Fire Nymph Products Ltd v Heating Centre Pty Ltd* (1992) 7 ACSR 365). The most powerful control, however, comes from the lender's threat—where the finance is coupled with an overdraft—to terminate, on demand, the company's power to deal.

145 This combination is preferred to a general ('entire undertaking') floating charge by itself, because the latter would not offer the relationship lender sufficient protection from the possibility of having its priority subsequently downgraded by the subsequent grant of fixed charges over specific assets to other lenders.

addition, when coupled with the power to deny the debtor the ability to continue to use the circulating assets, this could act as a powerful threat to deter misbehaviour generally. Moreover, a floating charge will lock in the lender's priority to circulating assets, provided it is not possible to grant a fixed charge over such assets.[146]

Moreover, such a security is no more likely to be harmful to unsecured creditors than any other. The apparent generality of its scope is illusory—it will in reality only cover circulating assets, because fixed charges will be taken over the rest. To be sure, it captures after-acquired property, but this is only in return for other assets being permitted to leave the security. It is because of this that unsecured creditors can get paid by the debtor in the ordinary course of business without infringing the security.

Thus a floating charge would be most likely to be used by a relationship lender as part of a package of general security. However, the statutory 'taxation' imposed on floating charges means that they are rendered less attractive to lenders. After *Spectrum*, no longer able to avoid this by characterizing their security as 'fixed', banks will find it difficult to couple a relationship lending approach with effective security over book debts. The likely effect, as suggested by Figure 2,[147] will not be for small businesses to start borrowing on an unsecured basis from their banks. Rather, they are likely to find it cheaper to substitute asset-based finance over receivables, structured on the basis of an outright sale rather than security.[148]

4. Asset-based versus relationship lending?

Sections 1 and 2 of this Part have argued, respectively, that security is capable of leading to benefits in relation to both asset-based and relationship lending, and that these benefits outweigh the costs of the institution. However, Section 3 above implies that statutory redistribution from the floating charge, coupled with the decision in *Spectrum*, will engender a shift towards asset-based finance in relation to receivables.

The most significant difference between these two types of strategy concerns

[146] A second floating charge over the same assets will rank behind the earlier one: *Re Benjamin Cope & Sons Ltd* [1914] 1 Ch 800, 806–7; *Re Automatic Bottlemakers Ltd* [1926] Ch 412, 423.

[147] Text to n 85 above.

[148] This is not to say that relationship lenders such as banks will not take floating charges. On the contrary, it is likely to continue to be worthwhile for them to take a 'lightweight' charge in order to be able to control the appointment of an administrator. Rather, the prediction is that they will not *lend significant sums on the security of such charges*, because of liability to fund statutory redistribution. Their unwillingness to do so, coupled with their inability to take fixed security over book debts, will lead to companies turning to invoice discounting instead.

decisions regarding a debtor in financial distress. Asset-based lenders are numerous, and they focus on specific collateral. Thus they have comparative advantage at liquidating that collateral, but have difficulty in coordinating to make decisions about the business as a whole. Relationship lenders, on the other hand, have comparative advantage in organizing rescue operations and making difficult decisions concerning the fate of a troubled firm as a whole.

A typical small firm might use a mixture of relationship and asset-based finance.[149] All other things being equal, we would expect to see asset-based finance being used in relation to assets that are not complementary to the business as a whole: that is, they could be repossessed by the financier without inflicting harm on the business. In a period of financial distress, however, it would be the relationship lender to which the debtor would turn for extra funds. Once asset-based lenders become aware that the debtor is having financial difficulties, then their collective behaviour may be hard to control.[150] There is a likelihood that at least one or two might seek to liquidate their collateral. This may precipitate corporate insolvency proceedings. To be sure, administration proceedings would impose a moratorium on such actions, but the very fact of having entered formal insolvency proceedings will be extremely destructive to the debtor's goodwill and greatly reduce its chances of being successfully rescued.[151] Thus the debtor will be likely to seek additional finance from a relationship lender, which can be used to pay debts falling due to asset-based financiers in the interim. That way, distress does not become public knowledge.

The foregoing has three salient implications for our inquiry. First, pushing small firms towards asset-based finance in relation to receivables is likely to increase the level of payments that a bank funding a 'work-out' must cover, in order to ensure that the company maintains current payments to all its creditors. Secondly, the reduction in a firm's exposure to its bank which this shift implies is likely to make the bank less willing to invest in the first place in gathering information about the debtor's business and prospects. Thirdly, receivables are likely to be highly complementary to a firm's business, and so the introduction of an asset-based lender may make rescue operations rather more difficult for

[149] As between the two, it seems appropriate that asset-based financiers should take priority (as they generally do): in focusing their attention on particular assets, it is more fundamental to their lending strategy than is general priority for relationship lenders: see RC Picker, 'Perfection Hierarchies and Nontemporal Priority Rules' (1999) 74 Chicago–Kent Law Review 1157.

[150] See J Armour and S Frisby, 'Rethinking Receivership' (2001) 21 OJLS 73, 79–86; J Franks and O Sussman, 'Financial Distress and Bank Restructuring of Small to Medium-Size UK Companies' (2005) 9 Review of Finance 65, 88–91.

[151] See G Meeks and JG Meeks, 'Self-Fulfilling Prophesies of Failure: The Endogenous Balance Sheets of Distressed Firms', Judge Business School Working Paper, 2004.

this reason. The implication is that increasing fragmentation and a shift towards asset-based lending may make it more difficult for work-outs to succeed.[152]

D. The Impact of Redistribution on Recipients

We have seen that statutory redistribution from the floating charge has yielded direct costs in terms of avoidance action, and may distort borrowing patterns in a way that will generate further costs. However, in order to complete our assessment of redistribution in insolvency, we need now to consider the case for *making* payments to the various beneficiaries. If there are sufficiently large benefits for these groups, this may lead us to conclude that the costs of the scheme are worth bearing. Alternatively, if the benefits are not sufficiently large, but nevertheless positive, we may wish to consider ways of effecting payments to these groups which involve less distortion of lending practice.

1. Employees

Perhaps the strongest prima facie claim may be made in relation to employees. Statutory priority for employee claims forces the company (and through it, the other creditors) to insure them to a certain extent against the risk of failure. This may generate benefits where employees are risk-averse,[153] and particularly where they are asked to make investments in firm-specific human capital (which will be a risky investment).[154] The argument is that employees may be unwilling to make risky investments of this sort unless they are insured against the possibility of firm failure. Their elevation in insolvency increases their chance of repayment should the firm fail, thereby lowering the risk involved in such an investment.

A moment's reflection shows that the extent to which these theoretically plausible benefits are captured by the statutory regime is negligible. Employees obtain priority for unpaid wage claims only up to a maximum of £800 per person.[155] This sum, which has not been increased since 1976,[156] cannot sensibly be

[152] It is well known that for larger firms, more heterogeneous capital structures are associated with a lower probability of successful work-outs: see, for example, S Chatterjee, US Dillon, and GG Ramirez, 'Resolutions of Financial Distress: Debt Restructurings via Chapter 11, Prepackaged Bankruptcies, and Workouts' (1996) 25 Financial Management 5, 12–13.

[153] TH Jackson and RE Scott, 'On the Nature of Bankruptcy: An Essay on Bankruptcy Sharing and the Creditors' Bargain' (1989) 75 Virginia Law Review 155.

[154] J Armour and S Deakin, 'Insolvency and Employment Protection: The Mixed Effects of the Acquired Rights Directive' (2003) 22 International Review of Law and Economics 443, 444–6.

[155] Insolvency Proceedings (Monetary Limits) Order 1986, SI 1986/1996, art 4.

[156] A Keay and P Walton, 'The Preferential Debts Regime in Liquidation Law: In the Public Interest?' [1999] Company Financial and Insolvency Law Review 84, 91.

claimed to operate as any sort of insurance. However, employees also have entitlements under the Employment Rights Act 1996 to payments out of the National Insurance Fund in respect of unpaid wages where their employer has entered insolvency proceedings.[157] More than twice as much may be claimed under this Act, and the payments are usually made far more quickly than by a liquidator.[158] The National Insurance Fund is then subrogated to employees' preferential claims in their employers' insolvency where they have been paid under the 1996 Act.[159]

The existence (and effectiveness) of the employees' claims against the National Insurance Fund shows that, in order for employees to receive the insurance-related benefits which are claimed to be provided by their preferential status, it is not necessary to engage in redistribution between the claimants in insolvency. Rather, employees can (and, in fact, largely do) get the same benefits by means of direct payments from the State. Moreover, by a scheme structured in that fashion, the need for distorting effects on lending patterns would be avoided. If the benefits to employees of such insurance are real, then a case may be made for increasing the level of payments made by the State.

2. The Crown

The inclusion of Crown claims for tax amongst those preferentially entitled was said to be justified on the basis that the Crown is an 'involuntary' creditor, which cannot adjust the terms on which 'credit' for unpaid tax is extended.[160] This, however, is not really true, as the Crown has control over the resources dedicated to the enforcement of unpaid taxes, and can thereby very much affect the 'terms' debtors can expect to experience.[161] Moreover, it seems that Crown preference created unanticipated costs in corporate rescue proceedings. The Inland Revenue was reported to take an unduly negative approach to reorganization proposals.[162] The Revenue would stand in most cases to be paid in full in liquidation, ahead of the holder of a floating charge, whereas in a CVA they would need to wait before receiving payment. They therefore lacked any incentive to agree. Bearing these points in mind, the abolition of Crown preference by the Enterprise Act 2002 seems clearly to be welcomed.

---

[157] Part XII (ss 182–190).

[158] The amount is £290 per week, up to a maximum of eight weeks: that is, £2,320 per employee: Employment Rights Act 1996, s 186(1)(a), as amended by Employment Rights (Increase of Limits) Order 2005, SI 2005/3352, art 3.

[159] Employment Rights Act 1996, s 189.

[160] Cork Report, *Insolvency Law and Practice: Report of the Review Committee* (Cmnd 8598, 1982) para 1412.

[161] ibid para 1413.

[162] D Milman and F Chittenden, *Corporate Rescue: CVAs and the Challenge of Small Companies*, ACCA Research Report No 44 (1995); Keay and Walton (n 156 above) 96.

3. Liquidation expenses

It is commonly thought to be necessary to pay liquidation expenses ahead of unsecured creditors' claims in order to induce liquidators to undertake their work. Yet it is also desirable to ensure that they are not given incentives to incur more expenditure than is justified by the value of the assets at stake. If liquidation expenses take precedence only over unsecured claims, then the unsecured creditors have both the incentive and the ability to control the liquidator's expenses. They appoint (and remove) the liquidator, and it is their money at stake.

Yet if liquidation expenses take priority over the claims of secured creditors, this creates an incentive for more to be spent than is justified by reference to the recoveries flowing to the unsecured creditors. The unsecured creditors will not be with expenses paid from funds which would not otherwise be available to them. Permitting liquidation expenses to be paid for out of secured assets therefore tends to encourage excessive expenditure.[163]

A particularly egregious form of overspending arises from attempts by the liquidator to increase the value available to the unsecured creditors, by challenging the validity of security. Paying liquidation expenses out of floating charge assets actually permits the liquidator to use the *chargee's* funds to challenge his own security.[164] Following a change to the Insolvency Rules in December 2002, the costs of such litigation brought by a liquidator would clearly be classified as 'expenses of the liquidation'.[165] A chargee faced with such a challenge would of course respond by spending money on defending its status. On neither side would the expenditure increase the size of the asset pool available for the creditors as a whole; in contrast, it would simply *deplete* the creditors' total recoveries.

It might be argued that a social benefit is derived from requiring liquidation expenses to be paid out of floating charge assets.[166] Liquidators frequently investigate fraudulent conduct by company directors, and if floating charge assets are not available to them, they may not be able to do so. Such a concern certainly appears to have motivated the Court of Appeal in *Re Barleycorn*

[163] See A Bris, A Schwartz, and I Welch, 'Who Should Pay for Bankruptcy Costs?', Yale Law School Center for Law, Economics, and Public Policy Research Paper No 277 (2004) 1–8; A Schwartz, 'A Normative Theory of Business Bankruptcy' (2005) 91 Virginia Law Review 1199, 1235–8.

[164] A desire on the part of the judiciary to avoid this outcome under the previous version of the rules lead to considerable complexity in the law: see *Re MC Bacon Ltd (No 2)* [1991] Ch 127; J Armour and AJ Walters, 'Funding Liquidation: A Functional Perspective' (2006) 122 LQR 295.

[165] Insolvency (Amendment) (No 2) Rules 2002, SI 2002/2712, modifying Insolvency Rules 1986, SI 1986/1925, r 4.218(1)(a).

[166] RJ Mokal, 'Liquidation Expenses and Floating Charges—The Separate Funds Fallacy' [2004] LMCLQ 387, 401–3.

Enterprises.[167] However, this investigatory function is imposed on all office holders—including administrators, who act for both debenture holders and unsecured creditors.[168] It is not clear why, in liquidation, it should be imposed on a party who does not stand to benefit from the proceedings. More generally, such a benefit would equally well be obtained if the cost of such 'public' aspects of insolvency proceedings were funded by the state.

4. Unsecured creditors generally

Some of those who emphasize the potentially harmful or inefficient aspects of security argue that a 'carve-out' from secured credit—that is, a certain proportion of secured creditors' recoveries should be set aside for general unsecured creditors—would ameliorate these problems.[169] On first blush, the 'prescribed part' of floating charge assets set aside for unsecured creditors might look like the implementation of such a policy. However, if that is its purpose, it is likely to be inefficacious, even if we assume for the moment that security *is* harmful to unsecured creditors. This is because, as we have seen, the impact of statutory redistribution under English law is not to encourage debtors to take less security, but rather—because the redistribution is only from the floating charge—to encourage them to take different *kinds* of security. Indeed, once this adjustment has been made by sophisticated creditors, unsecured creditors may well be collectively *worse* off as a result of the redistributive scheme: on the one hand, they will receive only a trivially small increase in their expected payout on insolvency through the prescribed part;[170] on the other hand, if fragmented capital structures make it more difficult for banks to orchestrate work-outs of financially distressed companies, this may increase the probability of default. Bearing in mind these costs, it seems difficult to justify the 'prescribed part' regime introduced by the Enterprise Act 2002.

This does, however, raise a related question. Might it be desirable to extend the policy behind the prescribed part so that it applies to all security, as opposed simply to floating charges? Such a measure would suffer from two practical problems. First, such a move would not prevent avoidance activity entirely. Rather, it would simply shift the locus away from the divide between fixed and

[167] [1970] Ch 465, 475–6. [168] See Armour and Walters (n 164 above) 311–15.

[169] LA Bebchuk and JM Fried, 'The Uneasy Case for the Priority of Secured Claims in Bankruptcy' (1996) 105 Yale Law Journal 857, 904–12; V Finch, 'Security, Insolvency and Risk: Who Pays the Price?' (1999) 62 MLR 633, 664–5.

[170] See, for example, Association of Business Recovery Professionals, *11th Survey of Company Insolvency* (2003) 11 (estimate based on data for 2001–2 that Enterprise Act 2002 reforms would yield an extra 2 per cent in the pound for unsecured creditors on average: however, this appears to be based principally on abolition of Crown preference); RJ Mokal, 'Priority as Pathology: The *Pari Passu* Myth' [2001] CLJ 581, 616–19 (arguing that unsecured creditors' recoveries under the prescribed part are likely not to justify the *ex post* expenses of collecting them).

floating charges, and towards the question whether a transaction was security or a 'true sale'. Secondly, unless the funds 'carved out' are targeted specifically at non-adjusting creditors, such a measure gives adjusting unsecured creditors an opportunity to free-ride at secured creditors' expense.

E. Conclusions

This chapter has considered the scope, effects, and merits of redistribution from the floating charge in English corporate insolvency law. The statutory policy is effected through the preferential debts regime, the 'prescribed part', and (if, as seems likely, *Buchler v Talbot* is legislatively overruled) the liquidation expenses regime. In relation to this policy, this chapter has made three principal points.

First, it has examined the way in which the history of the floating charge has been closely intertwined with that of statutory redistribution in corporate insolvency. Against this context, it is clear that it was the statutory regime which provided the pressure for the constant litigation that has gradually hardened the juridical concept of the floating charge. The history of this litigation is that of sophisticated creditors seeking to adjust their affairs so as to fall outside the ambit of the statutory scheme. It appears that in so doing, they were remarkably successful, given the relatively low returns to preferential creditors. The House of Lords' decision in *Spectrum* has closed one of the most significant routes by which banks were able to avoid the legislative scheme: the 'fixed charge' over book debts. In the wake of this ruling, it seems likely that companies will now find asset-based receivables finance to be more attractively priced than overdraft lending on the security of a floating charge over receivables.

Secondly, it has been argued that the *ex ante* effect of the statutory scheme on corporate finance is to make the floating charge relatively unattractive as a means of securing lending. The effect of this, which we may expect to be intensified by *Spectrum*, is to engender increased fragmentation in corporate borrowing. For an asset-based lender, with specialist knowledge about a particular asset class, a floating charge is unnecessary: the lender has the necessary expertise to be able to exercise control sufficient for a fixed charge (or outright sale). On the other hand a creditor following a relational approach to lending will gather specialist knowledge about the debtor's business, as opposed to particular assets. It is this type of lender (typically a bank) for whom a floating charge may be the most useful means of taking security over circulating assets. If this cannot be done as cheaply as asset-based finance, because of the statutory 'tax' on floating charges, then small businesses will increasingly turn to invoice discounters and fragment further their borrowing. This may lead to difficulties in times of financial distress, when a single concentrated lender would be able to make the best-informed and most effective decisions regarding the firm's future.

Thirdly, it has been suggested that the *costs* created by the redistributive scheme (namely, the direct costs of avoidance action, and the opportunity costs of induced changes in corporate finance) are not counterbalanced by any significant *benefits* created by redistributive payments being received by the relevant groups. The case for redistribution in favour of unsecured creditors on the grounds of their 'non-adjustment' is unpersuasive, and even if it is accepted, it appears the position of unsecured creditors may well be worsened by the redistributive scheme. Both the payment of liquidation expenses and the former payment of Crown preference out of floating charge assets gave the recipients incentives to engage in wasteful rent-seeking activity: that is, no social benefit at all resulted from these measures. Employees are the only current recipient group for whom redistribution may create some benefit. However, their more successful cover by payments from the National Insurance Fund suggests that direct payments from the State can be used to achieve the benefits of providing employees with insurance, without the distortive effects and costs of redistribution.

In sum, the scheme of statutory redistribution in English corporate insolvency can hardly be called a success. This chapter's analysis consequently provides support for recent calls for the abolition of the distinction between fixed and floating security[171]—and with it, the redistributive scheme.

[171] RJ Calnan, 'Floating Charges: A Proposal for Reform' (2004) 9 Butterworths Journal of International Banking and Financial Law 341.

10

THE ROLE OF SECURITY OVER FUTURE AND CIRCULATING CAPITAL: EVIDENCE FROM THE BRITISH ECONOMY *CIRCA* 1850–1920

*Joshua Getzler**

> A system of credit which has slowly grown up as years went on, which has suited itself to the course of business, which has forced itself on the habits of men, will not be altered because theorists disapprove of it, or because books are written against it.
>
> Walter Bagehot, *Lombard Street, A Description of the Money Market* (1873) 160

A. Freedom of Contract and the Supply of Debenture Finance

Freedom of contract suggests that credit secured against corporate assets is created because it is in the interests of the parties to do so. We can presume that if secured credit arrangements did not bring benefits, then parties would pursue alternative methods of raising finance. Corporations favour secured credit as a means to access a wider pool of impersonal creditors, thus making it possible to enlarge their investment base and operating capital; and lenders prefer secured claims because the expected return on loan capital can be calculated to a nicety, execution is simplified and all or most entrepreneurial risk is left with the borrower. Indeed lenders in impersonal credit markets might choose not to

* I thank James Edelman, Louise Gullifer, Michael Macnair, Jennifer Payne, Lionel Smith, Robert Stevens, and Oren Sussman for much helpful discussion; and I owe a special debt to John Armour for his excellent advice and criticism. Errors that persist are my responsibility alone.

supply any capital without security; thus collateral may be important primarily for ensuring the supply rather than reducing the price of loan capital.[1]

If such freedom of contract reasoning is correct, then it follows that English law has rightly pursued a policy since the 1860s of inventing legal facilities to satisfy the desire for credit secured against future and circulating assets such as receivables and book debts, as well as fixed assets. For most commentators, the economic functionality of security over floating collateral is seen as the key to its emergence in the late nineteenth century; law follows market need.[2]

Modern debates over characterization of floating and fixed charges and powers and priorities on insolvency may be framed within the freedom of contract model. Parties may have contributed to the value of an enterprise, but in some cases will not be able to bargain *ex ante* or *ex post* to enhance their payment claims against those lenders able to take security. Their exposure to the risk of debtors' insolvency is therefore not amenable to control by contractual arrangements; freedom of contract does not benefit them as 'non-adjusting' creditors.[3] Examples include employees who contribute their labour to enterprise wealth, the State which provides infrastructure in return for taxes, and perhaps smaller creditors who are prevented by transaction costs or bargaining disabilities from exacting security. Tort victims owed compensation are yet another case. The advantages of security granted to some lenders are therefore imposed as externalities or unbargained costs to those who are not privy to credit deals, and the argument goes that these externalities should be reduced by promoting certain unsecured creditors' claims in an insolvency distribution to take ahead of the secured lenders.

The older policy of the law was to look askance at all non-possessory security and require that notice to other creditors be signalled by some level of receipt or possessory control of security by the lender. Judges from the 1860s who wished to facilitate non-possessory security over productive assets in the hands of the borrower removed a series of doctrinal barriers and allowed security to be given over generic future and circulating assets. One crucial

[1] For an overview of economic theories, see BE Adler, 'Secured Credit Contracts' in P Newman (ed), *The New Palgrave Dictionary of Economics and the Law* (1998) vol III, 405–10.

[2] For historical analysis of the floating charge, seeing its root in the needs of entrepreneurs, see GF Curtis, 'The Theory of the Floating Charge' (1941) 4 University of Toronto Law Journal 131, 132–4; RR Pennington, 'The Genesis of the Floating Charge' (1960) 23 MLR 630, 630–4; R Gregory and P Walton, 'Fixed and Floating Charges—A Revelation' [2001] LMCLQ 123, 125–6, 135–9ff; R Nolan, 'Property in a Fund' (2004) 120 LQR 108, 118–30; J Armour, 'The Chequered History of the Floating Charge' (2004) 13 Griffith Law Review 27, 27–32; and J Armour, 'Should We Redistribute in Insolvency?', ch 9 above.

[3] See L Bebchuk and J Fried, 'The Uneasy Case for the Priority of Secured Claims in Bankruptcy' (1996) 105 Yale Law Journal 857, especially 864–5.

step taken in the late 1870s was to eliminate from company insolvency law the long-established reputed ownership doctrine, by means of a creative reading of the effect of the Judicature Acts.[4] The late nineteenth-century legislature was uneasy about the reduction of notice to third party and non-adjusting creditors and took countermeasures, restoring notice protections through bills of sale and company law statutes, and carving out exemptions to floating charge priority for preferential creditors (employees and the State) who were perceived to have directly contributed to circulating capital.

It may be that in the twenty-first century the fixed/floating charge distinction provides a poor basis for discriminating between situations when preferential creditors should be promoted and when not; the use of that distinction is widely perceived to be a hangover from past legislative compromises. But across this entire debate over characterization and redistribution, the basic efficiency and validity of secured credit is not put into issue—only how far the private arrangement of priorities should be regulated in favour of the non-adjusting creditors, and what should be the appropriate legal triggers for redistribution, if any is to occur.[5]

It is no exaggeration to say that the freedom of contract assumptions outlined above inform nearly all academic accounts of the rise of the charge over floating assets and the function of such credit instruments in the modern corporate economy.[6] This same economic model is also the implicit—and sometimes

[4] See especially Gregory and Walton (n 2 above). The key cases in the elimination of the reputed ownership doctrine were *Re Stockton Iron Furnace Company* (1879) 10 Ch D 335, and especially *Re Crumlin Viaduct Works Company* (1879) 11 Ch D 755, both decisions of Jessel MR in the Court of Appeal that amounted to abrupt judicial legislation. The disquiet of some Chancery judges at Jessel MR's uprooting of reputed ownership surfaced in later cases but was put down in *Gorringe v Irwell India Rubber and Gutta Percha Works* (1885) 34 Ch D 128, CA. The legislature at the same time pushed in the other direction, with the Bills of Sale Act 1878–82, ss 5 and 17 in effect prohibiting individuals and partnerships from using floating charges and so subjected non-corporate traders to the continued restraint of reputed ownership rules. Jessel MR's favouring of specifically corporate debentures against reputed ownership policies may have provided the fillip for the late nineteenth-century rush to incorporation, exemplified in *Salomon v A Salomon & Co Ltd* [1897] AC 22, HL.

[5] See S Worthington, 'Floating Charges: The Use and Abuse of Doctrinal Analysis', ch 3 above, L Gullifer and J Payne, 'The Characterization of Fixed and Floating Charges', ch 4 above, and J Armour, 'Should We Redistribute in Insolvency?', ch 9 above.

[6] See references in n 2 above. Some writers accept the need for charges over future and circulating assets, but doubt the optimality of the specific floating charge institution itself. For example, Roy Goode in the important essay 'The Exodus of the Floating Charge' in D Feldman and F Meisel (eds), *Corporate and Commercial Law: Modern Developments* (1996) 193 argues that alternative credit instruments (such as those created by Article 9 of the Uniform Commercial Code in the United States) can supply more of the needs of entrepreneurs more successfully. Goode called for the abolition of the floating charge, even if 'English law can take pride in having fashioned through the ingenuity of its equity judges an instrument of great power and even greater

explicit—theory of judges and lawyers in practice. A clear judicial statement of the economic model may be found in the House of Lords' decision in *Re Spectrum Plus Ltd*,[7] in the speech of Lord Scott:

> By the middle of the 19th century industrial and commercial expansion in this country had led to an increasing need by companies for more capital. Subscription for share capital could not meet this need and loan capital had to be raised. But the lenders required security for their loans. Traditional security, in the form of legal or equitable charges on the borrowers' fixed assets, whether land or goods, could not meet the need. The greater part of most entrepreneurial companies' assets would consist of raw materials, work in progress, stock-in-trade and trade debts. These were circulating assets, replaced in the normal course of business and constantly changing. Assets of this character were not amenable to being the subject of traditional forms of security.[8]

There are perhaps three important claims in this passage: the scarcity of equity investment after initial economic modernization; the preponderance of circulating capital such as inventory and receivables within enterprises; and the need to improve security for large-scale loans by making circulating capital available to lenders as collateral.

The goal of this chapter is to examine more closely these judicially noticed historical claims concerning the economic need for effective legal security over future and circulating collateral.[9] My argument is that the importance of such

mystery' (at 203, and see also R Goode, *Legal Problems of Credit and Security* (3rd edn, 2003) 111–53, especially 152–3; R Goode, 'The Case for the Abolition of the Floating Charge', ch 2 above). Gregory and Walton (n 2 above) 123–6, 146–9, suggest that the personalty mortgage permitting partial enforcement would have been a superior institution to the floating charge. RJ Mokal, 'The Floating Charge—An Elegy' in S Worthington (ed), *Commercial Law and Commercial Practice* (2003) 479 argues that the floating charge brings with it unjustified control and priority rights, problems exacerbated by the reforms to insolvency administration under the Enterprise Act 2002. Despite hostility to the floating charge amongst academic lawyers it remains popular with practitioners, and abolition has not been pursued by the Law Commission in its latest reform proposals (*Company Security Interests*, Law Com No 296, Cm 6654, August 2005); and see M Bridge, 'The Law Commission's Proposals for the Reform of Security Interests', ch 12 below.

[7] [2005] UKHL 41, [2005] 2 AC 680, para 95 (hereinafter *Spectrum*).

[8] Lord Scott's statement appears to be a paraphrase of Pennington, 'Genesis' (n 2 above) 631. Pennington's great article, now nearly 50 years old, has been a dominant presence in all debates over the floating charge since its publication. Gregory and Walton (n 2 above) offer a revisionist challenge to the received 'Genesis' story, emphasizing the lead role of bankruptcy statutes and the haphazard responses of the courts.

[9] Circulating capital has to be distinguished from future property that stays within the assets of an enterprise once it has been received; if future property such as receivables is placed in a blocked account with control rights split between chargor and chargee, then it still can be regarded as a form of fixed or non-circulating collateral. *Spectrum* and *Re Brumark Investments Ltd sub nom Agnew v IRC* [2001] UKPC 28, [2001] 2 AC 710 (hereinafter *Brumark*) set limits on how much control the chargor could have over the economic value contained within a so-called blocked account before the collateral would have to be characterized as floating: see S Worthington, 'Floating Charges: The Use and Abuse of Doctrinal Analysis', ch 3 above, and L Gullifer and J Payne, 'The Characterization of Fixed and Floating Charges', ch 4 above.

secured lending may have been considerably overestimated by lawyers. The history of the late Victorian corporate and financial sectors significantly undermines the thesis that security over receivables and other circulating assets was essential for the health of the economy. Rather it was essential for the profitability of credit banking, and it may be that the law, by meeting the banks' sectoral needs through provision of the floating charge as a security device, may have damaged the longer-term prospects of the economy. Lawyers and economists have assumed the efficacy of security over receivables for smoothing of trade and consumption cycles. My concern is rather with the efficacy of such security for longer-term production cycles, especially industrial production with high fixed costs. The lesson is that what market actors seek is not necessarily optimal for the market overall.

Lord Millett's speech in *Brumark* provides an important lead in this inquiry. In the midst of his detailed review of the doctrinal history of the floating charge Lord Millett commented:

> Such a form of security is particularly attractive to banks, and it rapidly acquired an importance in English commercial life which the Insolvency Law Review Committee (1982 Cmnd. 8558 at para. 1525) later considered should not be underestimated.[10]

This was not simply a restatement of the historical orthodoxy. Lord Millett noted the especial attraction of the floating charge for banks, and we will pursue this insight into the data of the late Victorian corporate economy. So my concern is with the economic history, and analysis of the jurisprudential history of the floating charge will have to wait for another occasion.

B. Why Secured Lending?

At a simple analytical level, improving security for one class of lender or investor to an enterprise must immediately weaken security for rival lenders or investors by depleting the available asset pool to satisfy claims (or misleading as to the size of the available assets)—though all parties may ultimately benefit if the secured credit injection improves the overall health of the enterprise.[11] Nonetheless on a static analysis, a cheapened cost of credit or enlarged supply of credit from the

[10] [2001] UKPC 28, [2001] 2 AC 710, para 8, and see Lord Millett, 'Company Charges', Foreword to this volume.

[11] For an argument along these lines, see RJ Mokal, 'The Search for Someone to Save: A Defensive Case for the Priority of Secured Credit' (2002) 22 OJLS 687. The controversial *Quistclose* trust illustrates one form of secured credit injection: see M Bridge, 'The *Quistclose* Trust in a World of Secured Transactions' (1992) 12 OJLS 333; E McKendrick, 'Commerce' in WS Swadling (ed), *The Quistclose Trust: Critical Essays* (2004) 145.

favoured class of creditor should, with proper notice to the other creditors, lead to those creditors raising the cost of credit or reducing credit supply in response. The borrower therefore cannot improve his overall position by segregating his capital into classes and giving different orders of claim to different creditors (or equity holders, for that matter, who may themselves have a spectrum of rights from preferential fixed interest shares without votes to full control and entitlement to returns on total capital).[12] Nineteenth-century judges may have intuited such economic considerations. Malins V-C in the seminal 1876 case of *Re General South America Co*,[13] defended the fairness of the floating charge against the claims of unsecured creditors by arguing that such creditors must be taken to have known of the possibility of pledges over corporate assets being issued, and they could have made inquiries at the time they extended credit without security. The implicit notice argument, strengthened by the requirement of registration of company charges to prevent loss of priority since 1900,[14] is indeed one of the dominant justifications for the recognition of the justice of charges, be they fixed or floating. But this assertion of the fairness of these devices through implicit notice only tips the inquiry back to the economic problem of how borrowers in well-informed markets can possibly improve their overall position by differential security in the first place.[15]

One explanation for the efficacy of secured debt is that the short-term operating capital necessary to bridge liquidity gaps over the span of the production cycle of a firm can only be procured by offering more liquid and more highly secured collateral to, for example, a lending bank. This is a different type of capital injection to the long-term debenture, whether secured against fixed or circulating assets, which helps form the fixed capital of an undertaking and which can attain its own form of liquidity through secondary market trading. In other

[12] This is a re-working of the Modigliani–Miller theorem of corporate finance to the narrower problem of rival issues of corporate debt: cf F Modigliani and M Miller, 'The Cost of Capital, Corporation Finance and the Theory of Investment' (1958) 48 American Economic Review 261; A Schwartz, 'A Theory of Loan Priorities' (1989) 18 Journal of Legal Studies 209.

[13] [1876] 2 Ch D 337, 341–3.

[14] Companies Act 1900, s 14; WR Cornish and G de N Clark, *Law and Society in England 1750–1950* (1989) 261–2. Registration was introduced partly in response to a clamour from typically 'non-adjusting' creditors that the floating charge be abolished, especially in the wake of *Salomon v A Salomon & Co Ltd* [1897] AC 22, HL. This was no new hostility; in the 1880s the Associated Chambers of Commerce made annual resolutions along the lines 'That the Joint Stock Companies Acts require amendment to make it illegal to defraud their ordinary creditors for the benefit of debenture holders as they may now do by mortgaging their future property and book debts': (1881) 3 Journal of the Institute of Bankers 247, quoted in JB Jefferys, *Business Organisation in Great Britain 1856–1914* (PhD dissertation, University of London, 1938, published 1977) 256.

[15] The implicit notice theory of priorities can be seen to shade into the theory that insolvency administration itself is the product of an implied creditor contract: see RJ Mokal, 'The Authentic Consent Model: Contractarianism, Creditors' Bargain, and Corporate Liquidation' (2001) 21 Legal Studies 400.

words we must take account of dynamic capital flows within companies over different time horizons in order to understand the need for different forms of corporate finance, and here historical data can provide an important testing ground.

An alternative defence of floating charges, which is much in favour today, focuses not on the need for different types of capital in founding and running corporate enterprises, but rather the need for effective monitoring by creditors of the quality of management, especially of distressed and dying enterprises, whether in relation to the entire undertaking or to specific assets of the company. The argument runs that senior creditors, especially where they wield a contractual power to appoint receivers,[16] can concentrate information about an enterprise and monitor its management of assets effectively on behalf of all other stakeholders. Such monitoring can prevent opportunistic managerial behaviour such as distribution of capital, excessive risk-taking including trading on brink of insolvency, or undue delays in initiating liquidation—negative behaviours that may tempt directors and shareholders protected by limited liability and indemnity in the declining stages of their enterprise. Yet the reverse may as well be true, that senior creditors can use their powers to appoint receivers or to precipitate liquidation in an opportunistic manner, in order to protect their collateral at the expense of overall enterprise value or with bland disregard for other stakeholders. In the late nineteenth century it was established that the contractual receiver was appointed as an agent of the company and not of the creditors, thus shielding the creditors from suit for running down the assets of the company and also putting up a wall between the debts of the company and the assets of the chargees. Receivers appointed by banks or other lenders under charging instruments were not directly concerned with the interests of unsecured stakeholders in companies; in any case the agency owed to the company was non-fiduciary and the primary legal duty was to realize the bondholders' security.[17] We cannot broach the history of corporate receivership

[16] Contractual receivership is displaced by the new administration procedure of the Enterprise Act 2002, Pt 10, esp s 250: see J Armour, 'Should We Redistribute in Insolvency?', ch 9 above; RJ Mokal, 'The Floating Charge—An Elegy' in S Worthington (ed), *Commercial Law and Commercial Practice* (2003) 479; V Finch, 'Control and Co-ordination in Corporate Rescue' (2005) 25 Legal Studies 374; for the pre-2002 regime see Sir Gavin Lightman and G Moss QC, with R Snowden, *The Law of Receivers and Administrators of Companies* (3rd edn, 2000) 1–173.

[17] The non-fiduciary quality of the receiver's agency is set out in WW Kerr, *A Treatise on the Law and Practice as to Receivers Appointed by the High Court Of Justice* (3rd edn, 1891) 179–84, 198–200; and see RP Meagher, JD Heydon, and MJ Leeming, *Meagher, Gummow and Lehane's Equity: Doctrines and Remedies* (4th edn, 2002) 926–51 for the remarkably complex equitable rules allocating rights and duties to receivers and receiver-managers. A defence of the wide powers of administrative receivership against State regulation is given in J Armour and S Frisby, 'Rethinking Receivership' (2001) 21 OJLS 73. The non-fiduciary character of credit relations is a general feature of English law, as with the merely contractual nature of the core banker–customer

and liquidation here; instead we shall focus on the upstream question of whether capital needs drove the development of new forms of company charges.

C. Did Scarcity of Share Capital Require Debenture Lending to Companies?

1. The beginnings of corporate capital

Lord Scott's most prominent historical claim in *Spectrum* was that equity capital was inadequate and new debt instruments had to be found to meet the corporate sector's capital needs in the latter part of the nineteenth century. In the earlier period of industrial and commercial expansion from 1760 to 1850 the opposite was true: equity was issued only when loan finance ran out. New enterprises preferred retained profits as a source of capital, and when this was inadequate to kickstart or expand a business, entrepreneurs turned to local sources of credit.

Sources of loan capital in the eighteenth and earlier nineteenth centuries included funds raised in family, religious and business circles, moneys pooled by local attorneys, goldsmiths, or other professionals, and later in the century, liquid assets pooled in regional banks. Such 'relationship lending' commonly involved no security beyond the informal trust and information extant in face-to-face dealings by actors in local markets. Often the personal assets of managers, whether as partners of firms or directors of companies, would be made available as a backing of the loan, whether under joint and joint-several liability regimes or through special covenants.[18] In this world of personal, local finance, issue of new equity was resisted as this might mean sharing control and profits with incoming partners who were strangers to the inside group of investors and entrepreneurs.[19]

relationship established in the great case of *Foley v Hill* [1848] 2 HL Cas 28, 9 ER 1002, HL; though there are overlays of confidentiality and in some circumstances fiduciary duties can be superadded. See further R Cranston, *Principles of Banking Law* (2nd edn, 2002) 129–33, 159–65, 167–81; EP Ellinger, E Lomnicka, and R Hooley, *Ellinger's Modern Banking Law* (4th edn, 2006) 121–35, 165–9.

[18] See J Getzler and M Macnair, 'The Firm as an Entity before the Companies Acts' in P Brand, K Costello, and WN Osborough (eds), *Adventures of the Law* (2005) 267, 278–85.

[19] It is a common claim that with imperfect information in early capital markets, improved security had to be provided to tempt outsiders to invest in enterprise at all: see for example, J Armour, 'The Chequered History of the Floating Charge' [2004] Griffith Law Review 27, 27–28. But in many cases outside equity was not wanted; or only wanted if concomitant control rights could be excluded, as with preference shares.

There were institutional constraints on the supply side as well. Publicly traded common stock before the 1840s was regarded with suspicion in the wake of speculative manias; the 1720 South Sea Bubble had burnt itself into the consciousness of the nation, and 100 years later confidence in stock markets could still be shaken; in the crash of 1827, for example, some three-quarters of all recent company flotations foundered. In 1835 at the start of the railway age it was claimed that local finance mediated by public stock exchanges accounted for only 5 per cent of total capital invested in railways north of Manchester.[20] Joint stock capitalism was hampered because it was difficult to separate ownership from control and allow any form of monitoring of non-owning managers within early firms; and some conservative judges frowned on private law attempts to allow freely tradable shares with constantly shifting investor-owners moving in and out of relations with a company. Lawyers were nonetheless adept at creating the necessary legal vehicles for larger enterprises using partnerships and trusts, deed of settlement companies, and corporations constituted by charters and special statutes, but these techniques could be costly and accounting and governance and auditing structures were weak.

Two factors external to the law transformed local and national security markets to make possible more extensive equity investment in joint stock corporations. The large liquid markets for government issue in the eighteenth century provided a model for private equity shares to be floated and traded impersonally,[21] though outside certain narrow sectors such as transport the joint stock company never won an easy dominance against other forms of business and investment.[22] Then the railway boom of the 1840s provided a spur to joint stock enterprise, and equity capital reached new levels of magnitude and liquidity.[23] Legislation was then used to overcome early nineteenth century judicial hostility to joint stock enterprise, with company acts being passed to

[20] 'Circular to Bankers' (1835), cited in JB Baskin and PJ Miranti Jr, *A History of Corporate Finance* (1997) 136.

[21] L Neal, *The Rise of Financial Capitalism: International Capital Markets in the Age of Reason* (1990); L Neal, 'The Finance of Business during the Industrial Revolution' in R Floud and D McCloskey (eds), *The Economic History of Britain Since 1700, Volume 1: 1700–1860* (1994) 151, 171–81; S Quinn, 'Money, Finance and Capital Markets' in R Floud and P Johnson (eds), *The Cambridge Economic History of Modern Britain, Volume I, Industrialisation, 1700–1860* (2004) 147, 167–73.

[22] R Harris, in *Industrializing English Law: Entrepreneurship and Business Organization 1720–1844* (2000) 85–198, shows how path dependence and legal inhibitions could prevent adoption of joint stock corporate form even where investors and managers desired it, as in the insurance sector.

[23] RW Kostal, *Law and English Railway Capitalism 1825–1875* (1994) 11–52; RC Michie, *The London Stock Exchange, A History* (1999) 52–69; MC Reed, 'Railways and the Growth of the Capital Market' in RC Michie (ed), *The Development of London as a Financial Centre, Volume 1: 1700–1850* (2000) 266.

permit general incorporation, separate legal personality, and free joint stock investment in 1844, and then in 1855–8, allowing limited liability to all companies that wanted it,[24] so encouraging raising of capital by security issues. Trading in the stock of utilities, trading, commercial and financial enterprises took off, though it was still a much smaller market than that for government issue until at least the 1860s. Alongside new sources of equity, lawyers and enterprises developed new forms of credit, including debentures with or without collateral in manufacturing and commerce, and, particularly in the railway industry and other utilities, preference shares that supplied a fixed income, a right to some distribution of further profits, but with no control rights as with common stock and no right to seek liquidation for non-payment of interest or to recover secured capital.[25]

2. Corporate capital after 1862

The later nineteenth century witnessed an explosion in share capital as a source of corporate finance and a corresponding diminution in the importance of debt. Table 1 gives statistics derived from the Companies Register setting out rough figures of the accumulation of equity capital within the corporate sector from the time of the modernizing Companies Act of 1862 into the interwar period. Figures 1 and 2 give the same data in pictorial form.

This data shows a crescendo of capital formation in the form of share equity investments from 1862 until the First World War, with 20–25 per cent accretions to aggregate corporate share capital every five years in this period. There are significant dips before 1870 and again before 1880, balanced by significant accelerations before 1875 and after 1880; one would expect such movements as simple reflections of the business cycle.

Close to one-half of equity capital had qualities of long-term loan finance, being preference shares that gave fixed interest and some profit-sharing, but without voting rights and also without security or liquidation powers to enforce payment. To the reported sums of equity capital may be added long-term fixed interest debentures issued by companies to augment their fixed capital base, and which were traded like securities. Such loan instruments, pioneered in the

[24] Cornish and Clark (n 14 above) 246–59. Insurance was an important exception, attaining access to limited liability only in 1862; hitherto insurance entrepreneurs had to construct limited liability by network contracts, see RR Pennington, 'The Genesis of the Floating Charge' (1960) 23 MLR 630, 640–2; Harris (n 22 above) 100–9; B Supple, *The Royal Exchange Assurance: A History of British Insurance, 1720–1920* (1970) 56–61, 118–20; CA Cooke, *Corporation, Trust and Company: An Essay in Legal History* (1950) 163–8.

[25] Harris (n 22 above) 127; J Reeder, 'Corporate Loan Financing in the Seventeenth and Eighteenth Centuries' (1973) 2 Anglo-American Law Review 487; G Heberton Evans, *British Corporation Finance 1775–1850—A Study of Preference Shares* (1936) 107–34.

Table 1. Capital formation through joint stock equity investment in registered companies, England 1862–1920

	New nominal share capital Annual	New nominal share capital Five-yearly totals	Running total paid-up share capital Five-yearly totals
		£ millions at contemporary prices	
1862	51.1		
1863	137.9		
1864	232.5		
1865	198.7	620.3	NA
1866	68.9		
1867	29.0		
1868	34.1		
1869	138.9		
1870	37.4	308.3	NA
1871	66.0		
1872	122.8		
1873	144.4		
1874	104.0		
1875	76.7	513.8	NA
1876	41.8		
1877	53.0		
1878	60.0		
1879	69.6		
1880	160.6	385.0	NA
1881	190.4		
1882	220.3		
1883	144.1		
1884	125.3		
1885	111.4	791.5	39,816
1886	138.4		
1887	160.8		
1888	340.0		
1889	229.5		
1890	222.3	1091.0	52,183
1891	126.4		
1892	95.7		
1893	84.7		
1894	108.9		
1895	216.3	632.0	75,113
1896	285.3		
1897	269.4		
1898	247.7		
1899	229.6		
1900	206.8	1238.8	121,002
1901	137.5		
1902	147.6		
1903	115.7		
1904	83.9		
1905	108.7	593.3	159,853
1906	125.2		
1907	125.2		
1908	96.9		
1909	132.1		

Continued overleaf

	New nominal share capital	New nominal share capital	Running total paid-up share capital
	Annual	Five-yearly totals	Five-yearly totals
		£ millions at contemporary prices	
1910	205.1	684.6	183,307
1911	150.6		
1912	165.0		
1913	146.8		
1914	104.3		
1915	49.2	616.0	210,396
1916	46.5		
1917	62.1		
1918	119.0		
1919	384.1		
1920	559.3	1171.0	272,232

Sources: Report by the Board of Trade on the matters within the Companies Acts (1924), Annex No VI—*Statement of the Total Number and Nominal Capital of . . . Companies . . . registered under the Companies Acts, 1862 to . . . 1920*, 12; Report by the Board of Trade on the matters within the Companies Acts (1928), Annex No V—*Statement of the Total Number and Paid-Up Capital of all Companies having a Share Capital . . . on the Register*, 11.

railway era and then copied by other sectors, were favoured by cautious private and institutional investors who sought higher returns than consols. They were favoured by directors as they gave companies stable interest rates and accorded management a relatively unrestricted power to raise capital for expansion, especially in the cheap money era of the later nineteenth century. Fixed interest debenture funding without profit-sharing, whether secured against fixed assets, floating assets or unsecured, may be estimated to add another 20 per cent to the equity capital of private concerns in 1885, rising to just below 30 per cent in 1915.[26] In the result, the orthodox pre-war company flotation used roughly equal parts of ordinary and preference shares and debenture stock. Issue of the three forms was typically simultaneous, but since much equity capital was raised in nominal form, debenture finance could make up a greater weight of the paid capital. Debenture capital was increasingly raised institutionally by banks and insurance companies who favoured the perceived security of capital and income, and also by new investment trusts who retailed debenture products to the public, and especially to trustee investors.[27] Demand for debentures in fact eased off from the 1890s as prices rose and share profits became more attractive. At any rate the annual and five-yearly fluctuations of capital formation using equity and debentures cannot obviously be mapped onto judicial concerns about weak capital supplies for corporate enterprise across the period when floating charges

[26] JB Jefferys, *Business Organisation in Great Britain 1856–1914* (PhD dissertation, University of London, 1938, published 1977) 266–9.

[27] KF Sin, *The Legal Nature of the Unit Trust* (1997) 19–27.

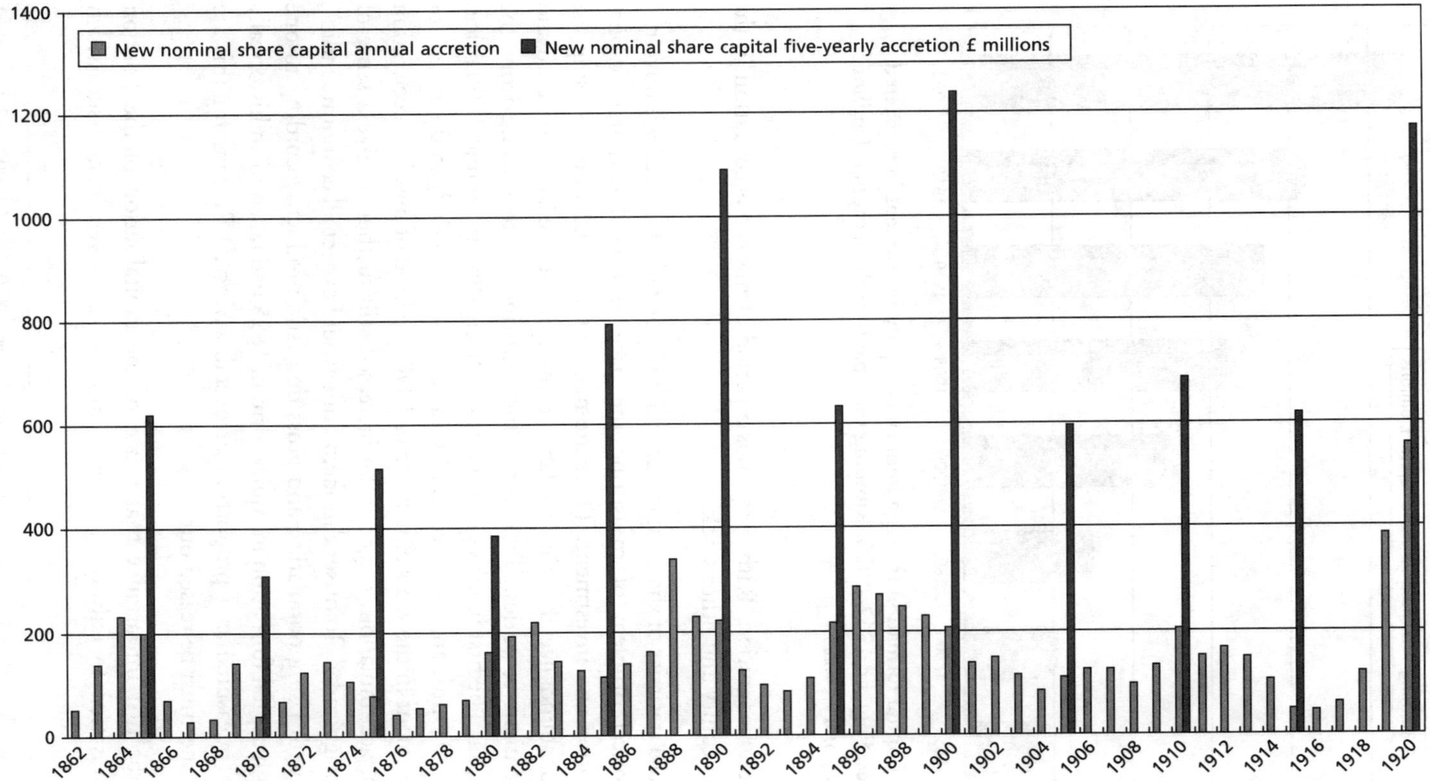

Figure 1 Capital formation through joint stock equity investment in registered companies, England 1862–1920. Annual and five-yearly accretions to nominal capital, £ millions at contemporary prices

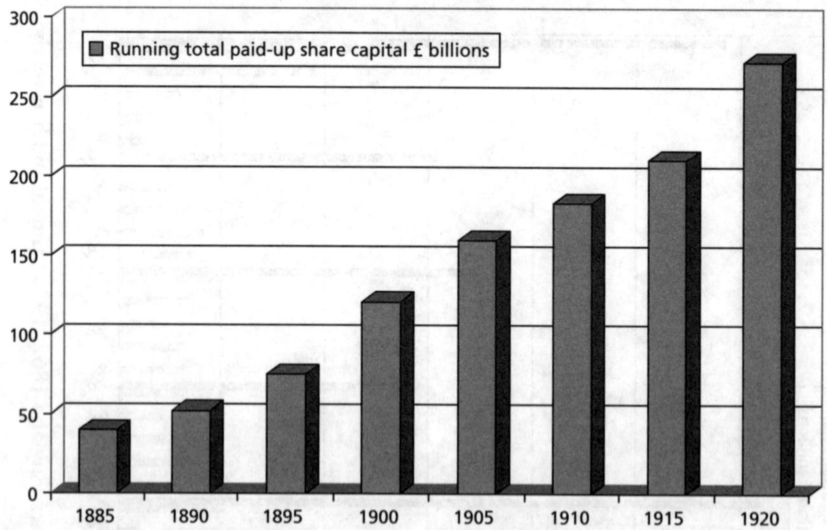

Figure 2 Capital formation through joint stock equity investment in registered companies, England 1862–1920. Running total paid-up share capital, £ billions at contemporary prices

were given recognition. Rather this was a period of marked acceleration in the growth of equity and other stock.

The official statistics of share capital growth provide only a limited window into the historical problem of measuring the pace of overall corporate capital accumulation and investment. There are many other variables in assessing the scarcity or abundance of capital available to enterprise in the late nineteenth and early twentieth centuries. Two important adjustments are missing from the Table 1 data. The first involves relative prices: from 1862 to around 1890 prices decline by a third, and then recover by the end of the period, so the extent of new investment in the years either side of 1890, a period of massive acceleration of capital accumulation, ought to be increased still further to give a sense of relative magnitudes. To offset this factor, one would expect all economic indicia to grow with rising population and gross domestic product; according to one calculation capital formation in equity form in 1895 had fallen to an historically low point measured as a proportion of overall savings.[28] Reasons for this are complex and must be teased out.

It is of the first importance that much of the capitalization of the London market was tied to railways, and even more so to government issue which

[28] RS Grossman, 'New Indices of British Equity Prices, 1870–1913' (2002) 62 Journal of Economic History 121, 126–8. I am grateful to John Armour for this point.

embraced other utilities. In 1873, of the London capital market's total of £2.27 billion, well over half was government issue, split between British (38 per cent) and foreign (21 per cent) debt; fully 32 per cent was in railways, split equally between domestic and foreign systems; 5 per cent was bank capital, 1 per cent was in utilities, and just 1 per cent was in industry and commerce. These aggregate figures for capital traded in London do not capture the extensive networks of local credit outside London that helped form the capital stock of industrial enterprise outside gilts and utilities. But even with a large weight of local investment in local industry, one may conclude that in 1873 non-utility and non-governmental enterprise placed a very small demand for capital on the overall financial system. It is notable that the share of government debt in the London market fell steadily until the First World War, reducing from 70 per cent of market capitalization in 1853 to 9 per cent in 1913, as set out in Table 2. These figures are consistent with an improved tax base reducing the need for bond issues in public finance (indeed national debt was being rapidly amortized in this period), and as a concomitant it indicates a deepening private capital market.

The marked shift in allocation from public to private investment indicates a heightened supply for private enterprise, a 'crowding in' which further cheapened the cost of private domestic capital. Indeed low nominal and real interest rates (often negative) are a feature of the period, and finance capitalists impatient for quick profits therefore sought fresh arenas for growth outside the domestic economy. This is one explanation for the considerable capital export from the London markets to the formal empire and especially to the Americas and the Dominions after 1865. It has been estimated that new issues in the London securities markets rose from £34 billion in 1865 to £192 billion in 1914 in adjusted real values; of that some £3 billion was exported, with £1.2

Table 2. Growth and structure of the London Stock Exchange, 1853–1920

	Total nominal value £ millions	UK Government share per cent
1853	1,215	70.2
1863	1,683	53.6
1873	2,270	37.6
1883	5,677	24.0
1893	6,561	16.5
1903	8,834	13.4
1913	11,263	9.0
1920	16,626	32.6

From: N Ferguson, *The Cash Nexus: Money and Power in the Modern World 1700–2000* (2001) 136; *source*: RC Michie, *The London Stock Exchange, A History* (1999) 88ff, 175, 184, 320, 322, 360ff, 419, 421, 440, 473, 521ff, 589ff.

billion going to the British Empire.[29] National accounts show a shift in the proportion of net capital outflow to GDP rising from 0.4 in 1856 to 0.8 in 1873, to peak at 1.8 in 1913 (representing one-third of non-land UK capital and half of all new gross domestic savings) and then rapidly to decline.[30] It is hotly debated what these significant capital exports revealed. On one view, weak demand pull at home, whether on the production or consumption side, could not attract that new capital available from the maturing industrial and financial economy, especially when quicker profits were available in governmental and utility investment abroad. The result was underinvestment in human and fixed capital at home, which cut growth rates in the longer term. The alternative view is that retained business profits, debt, and equity could provide all necessary capital to fund the home market; all extant domestic demand was met. Hence the significant spill-over from domestic accumulation to foreign investment; investors simply moved to higher rates of return overseas when the domestic market became saturated. There was no point in building a second English railway system when a first system could be built in Australia or America for a better return.[31]

Such debates tend to focus relentlessly on the role of the City and the Bank of England that regulated City finance. We must recall that until close to the end of the nineteenth century much business and industrial investment was local and personal; London securities markets that brokered government and overseas

---

[29] LE Davis and RA Huttenback, *Mammon and the Pursuit of Empire: The Political Economy of British Imperialism, 1860–1912* (1986) 30–72.

[30] RCO Matthews, CH Feinstein, and JC Odling-Smee, *British Economic Growth 1856–1973* (1982) 128 (Table 5.2); NFR Crafts, *British Economic Growth During the Industrial Revolution* (1985) 63. The debate on the scale and effects of British capital export has extended from the time of JA Hobson and the early twentieth century Marxist theorists of imperialism to today; for recent calculations, see DCM Platt, 'British Portfolio Investment Overseas before 1870: Some Doubts' (1980) 33 Economic History Review 2nd ser 1; PJ Cain and AG Hopkins, 'The Political Economy of British Expansion Overseas, 1750–1914' (1980) 33 Economic History Review 2nd ser 463; S Pollard, 'Capital Exports, 1870–1914: Harmful or Beneficial?' (1985) 38 Economic History Review 2nd ser 489; M Edelstein, *Overseas Investment in the Age of High Imperialism: The United Kingdom, 1850–1914* (1982); M Edelstein, 'Foreign Investment, Accumulation and Empire, 1860–1914' in R Floud and P Johnson (eds), *The Cambridge Economic History of Modern Britain, Volume II, Economic Maturity, 1860–1939* (2004) 190; Davis and Huttenback (n 29 above); I Stone, *The Global Export of Capital from Great Britain, 1865–1914: A Statistical Survey* (1999).

[31] N Ferguson, *The Cash Nexus: Money and Power in the Modern World, 1700–2000* (2000) 297–302. Ferguson cites Edelstein and Pollard for support concerning the benefits of capital export; but Edelstein (*Overseas Investment* (n 30 above) 194–5, 232) and Pollard ('Capital Exports' (n 30 above) 512–14) were careful to avoid claiming that overseas investment and profit-taking strengthened the domestic economy in the longer term. For the controversy as to whether entrepreneurs neglected investment opportunities at home, see DN McCloskey, 'Did Victorian Britain Fail?' (1970) 23 Economic History Review 2nd ser 450; NFR Crafts, 'Victorian Britain Did Fail' (1979) 32 Economic History Review 2nd ser 533; DN McCloskey, 'No It Did Not: A Reply to Crafts' (1979) 32 Economic History Review 2nd ser 538.

stocks did not comprise or control the entire capital supply.[32] Britain's development as an industrial power from the eighteenth century to the twentieth occurred largely outside the corporate joint-stock sector in the *mittelstand* of partnership firms, family enterprises, and sole traders, forming clusters of industry and entrepreneurship drawing on local sources of credit and mutually supporting a division of labour encouraging innovation. The Company Acts of 1844–62 did not lead to a significant shift of business into corporate form. As late as 1880 joint-stock enterprise was a weak presence outside transport and utilities, and corporatization of the economy only really took place between 1880 and 1914, with a further concentration of enterprises in the interwar period.[33]

Let us take a closer look at forms of finance outside that traded in the City. The bulk of commercial, industrial, and agricultural investment before the 1860s, and hence well before extensive corporatization had taken place, was arranged by country banks, attorneys, and networks of bill discounters—'relational investment' on a small scale based on personal connections and information.[34] A shift towards use of bank capital in trade and industry from the 1870s can be observed as a more centralized banking sector emerged providing impersonal credit pools, replacing personal credit relations in local stock markets and business networks.[35] It is crucially important to determine the nature of this new type of bank lending. Studies of loan relationships between banks and the English industrial corporate sector between 1860 and 1914 suggest that typical loans were made to well-established companies with regular turnovers, in the form of six-month overdraft facilities, with the loan relationship typically rolled over once to last one year.[36] The average bank loan to business in 1890 hovered

---

[32] C Muldrew, *The Economy of Obligation: The Culture of Credit and Social Relations in Early Modern England* (1998); LS Pressnell, *Country Banking in the Industrial Revolution* (1956) 75–125, 322–43; Quinn (n 21 above) 157–67; PL Cottrell, *Industrial Finance 1830–1914: The Finance and Organization of English Manufacturing Industry* (1979, reprinted 1993) 248–73; PL Cottrell, 'Domestic Finance 1860–1914' in R Floud and P Johnson (eds), *The Cambridge Economic History of Modern Britain, Volume II, Economic Maturity, 1860–1939* (2004) 253.

[33] J de Vries, 'The Industrial Revolution and the Industrious Revolution' (1994) 54 Journal of Economic History 249; S Pollard, *The Genesis of Modern Management: A Study of the Industrial Revolution in Great Britain* (1965); F Crouzet (ed), *Capital Formation in the Industrial Revolution* (1972); Jefferys (n 26 above) 54–154; Cottrell, *Industrial Finance* (n 32 above) 162–93; Cottrell, 'Domestic Finance' (n 32 above) 261–70; Matthews, Feinstein, and Odling-Smee (n 30 above) 359–61; L Hannah, *The Rise of the Corporate Economy* (2nd edn, 1983) 8–26; AD Chandler, *Scale and Scope: The Dynamics of Industrial Capitalism* (1990) 235–392.

[34] A representative portrait of this world, that went into many printings, is found in G Rae, *The Country Banker: His Clients, Cares, and Work, From an Experience of Forty Years* (1885). See also Pressnell, *Country Banking* (n 32 above).

[35] WA Thomas, *The Provincial Stock Exchange* (1973); PL Cottrell, 'The Domestic Commercial Banks and the City of London, 1870–1939' in RC Michie (ed), *The Development of London as a Financial Centre, Volume 2: 1850–1914* (2000) 106.

[36] See, for example, F Lavington, *The English Capital Market* (1921) 143–5.

around the mean of £10,824 and the median of £2,000. Loans of this scale and duration were not used to finance capital expansion or to promote entrepreneurial risk-taking on any extent of time. Rather this was bridging finance, typically for acquisition of raw materials and inventory, with the invoices of expected profit being used to secure and then pay off bank overdrafts, and with banks shuffling the trade profits of one set of clients into overdraft for another set.[37]

The residual personal nature of much of this local bank finance is shown by the finding that for some decades after the 1860s, perhaps half of such bank overdrafts and loans were not secured, or were secured only by personal covenant of the directors in closely held corporations, a practice descended from the giving of personal credit to partners. But towards the end of the century pressure grew on bank managers, increasingly line managers of amalgamated banking groups with London headquarters, to lend against collateral. These short-term bank injections of liquidity could at the margin free up enterprises' retained cash profits to be directed into longer-term investments, though banks might monitor to prevent too much illiquidity in firm assets. But banks were committed to avoiding any long-term illiquid investments in firms with bank money, so much so that the avoidance of committed loans became a banker's dogma. A striking feature of the English industrial finance system that emerged was that bank loans, like preference shares and long maturity bonds, did not give rise to managerial credit relationships as in German and French industry. Rather, banks and other creditors remained at arm's length from their investment targets, eschewing seats on boards or close accounting and reporting praxis. The collapse of two provincial banks that had attempted to fund industrial expansion in 1878 only strengthened the instinct that banks should not share enterprise risk with industrial clients.[38] British banks instead sought profits in amalgamations and cartelization of services, or in intermediated investment in London securities, rather than pursuing active investment policies involving entrepreneurial asset allocation. We do not find the development of large investment banks that supplied

[37] RP Higonnet, 'Bank Deposits in the United Kingdom, 1870–1914' (1957) 71 Quarterly Journal of Economics 329; Neal, 'Finance of Business' (n 21 above) 153–62, 168–70; Cottrell, 'Domestic Finance' (n 32 above) 270–9; FH Capie and M Collins, 'Banks, Industry and Finance, 1880–1914' (1999) 38 Business History 26; FH Capie and M Collins, 'Bank/Industry Relations, 1870–1990' in RC Michie (ed), *The Development of London as a Financial Centre, Volume 2: 1850–1914* (2000) 178, 182–8; MH Best and J Humphries, 'The City and Industrial Decline' in B Elbaum and W Lazonick (eds), *The Decline of the British Economy* (1986) 223, 226–9.

[38] See M Collins, 'The Banking Crisis of 1878' (1989) 42 Economic History Review 2nd ser 504.

long-term capital, especially to industry with heavy fixed costs as was common practice in the German economy.[39] To sum up, the English banks did not pursue a significant role as 'gatekeepers' of the economy. They did not serve as arbitrageurs of capital through superior access to information.[40] Rather they acted as cash grocers.

Debate continues as to whether the unique structure of the British banking sector—its commitment to liquidity, its lack of commitment to industry save for short-term, small-scale credit relations, its centralization and divorce from the regions—was responsible for British industry's failures in investment and technology that led it to fall behind its rivals before the Great War. Adverse comparisons are sometimes drawn with the system of bank investment, monitoring, and supervision in German industry, but the relevance of this rival model may be doubted. There is evidence that the German universal banks with their concentrated holdings and seats on company boards simply substituted for an underdeveloped share market in providing capital to heavy industry; further that the banks neglected the *mittelstand* or small to medium enterprises, even though barriers to entry stopped such firms raising share finance; and finally that banks were ineffective monitors of management.[41] The active defence of the British corporate finance system before the Great War is that retained profits and developed stock markets provided all the capital that was desired. The causes of inadequate investment therefore must be sought elsewhere, for example in the cultures of management and labour—not in the praxis of

---

[39] The debate was enlivened by A Gerschenkron's famous 1952 essay on 'Economic Backwardness in Historical Perspective', where he stated:

> The difference between banks of the crédit-mobilier type and commercial banks in the advanced industrial country of the time (England) was absolute. Between the English bank essentially designed to serve as a source of short-term capital and a bank designed to finance the long-term needs of the economy there was a complete gulf. The German banks, which may be taken as a paragon of the type of universal bank, successfully combined the basic idea of the crédit mobilier with the short-term activities of commercial banks.

(in A Gerschenkron, *Economic Backwardness in Historical Perspective. A Book of Essays* (1962) 13).

See further M Collins, 'English Bank Development within a European Context, 1870–1939' (1998) 51 Economic History Review 2nd ser 1; DM Ross, 'Commercial Banking in a Market-Oriented Financial System: Britain between the Wars' (1996) 49 Economic History Review 2nd ser 314; J Edwards and K Fischer, *Banks, Finance and Investment in Germany* (1994). For French bank participation in industry, see E Paulet, *The Role of Banks in Monitoring Firms: The Case of the Crédit Mobilier* (1999).

[40] cf JA Schumpeter, *The Theory of Economic Development* (1911), postulating a direct link between the quality of financial institutions and economic development.

[41] Ross (n 39 above); Edwards and Fischer (n 39 above); RH Tilley, 'German Banking 1850–1914: Development Assistance for the Strong' (1986) 15 Journal of European Economic History 113.

bankers.[42] A further defence is that the isolation of banking from industry helped Britain avoid the banking crises of the interwar period that afflicted Europe and the United States. It is fair to say that the jury is still out on this controversy.

3. Prominence of circulating capital

Lord Scott in *Spectrum* suggested that circulating capital took on more importance than fixed capital at the time the floating charge developed.[43] Assessing such a claim requires sensitivity to different periods. Early industrialization based on textiles employed slight fixed capital, with a greater proportion of investment in inventory.[44] American evidence reinforces this claim.[45] It was the rise of heavy industry such as metallurgy in the later nineteenth century that led to heavier fixed investments.[46]

For the later period from 1870, encompassing the creation of the floating charge, aggregate formation of fixed, inventory, and exported capital is captured in the data in Tables 3–6 below, which gives some sense of relativities.

These aggregate figures do not permit much discrimination in assessing the balance of fixed and circulating capital in English enterprise, but they do not suggest a major tilt towards circulating capital as the economy developed, but rather the opposite. The figures for non-land fixed capital in manufacturing show a flattened increase in the 1880s but otherwise between a 25 per cent and

[42] The case for the prosecution against the British banking and financial sector is stated in WP Kennedy, *Industrial Structure, Capital Markets and the Origins of British Economic Decline* (1987) and Crafts, 'Victorian Britain Did Fail' (n 31 above) focusing on the opportunity costs of foregone domestic investment; and Best and Humphries, 'The City and Industrial Decline' (n 37 above), seeing entrepreneurial failures and weak demand for investment as caused by the commercial slant of the banks; see also M Dintenfass, *The Decline of Industrial Britain 1870–1980* (1992) 40–9; W Hutton, *The State We're In* (1995) 132–68. Defence of the financial sector's role as meeting all extant demand is given in WA Thomas, *The Finance of British Industry, 1918–1976* (1978) 53–82; Cottrell, *Industrial Finance* (n 32 above) 194–247; FH Capie and M Collins, *Have the Banks Failed British Industry? An Historical Survey* (1992) 20–43; M Collins, *Money and Banking in the UK: A History* (1988) 92–122. The cultural debate over industrial failure is pursued in MJ Wiener, *English Culture and the Decline of the Industrial Spirit, 1850–1980* (1981); MJ Daunton, ' "Gentlemanly Capitalism" and British Industry 1820–1914' (1989) 122 Past and Present 119 and WD Rubinstein, 'Debate—"Gentlemanly Capitalism" and British Industry 1820–1914' (1989) 132 Past and Present 150; Y Cassis, *City Bankers, 1890–1914* (1994) 139–81.

[43] See text accompanying n 8 above.

[44] See essays in F Crouzet (ed), *Capital Formation in the Industrial Revolution* (1972), especially S Pollard, 'Fixed Capital in the Industrial Revolution in Britain', 145–61, originally published (1964) 24 Journal of Economic History 299.

[45] KL Sokoloff, 'Investment in Fixed and Working Capital During Early Industrialization: Evidence From U.S. Manufacturing Firms' (1984) 44 Journal of Economic History 545.

[46] Matthews, Feinstein and Odling-Smee (n 30 above) 222–35, 381–95; S Pollard, 'Entrepreneurship, 1870–1914' in R Floud and D McCloskey (eds), *The Economic History of Britain Since 1700, Volume 2: 1860–1939* (1994) 62.

Table 3. Growth and structure of UK circulating capital, stocks, and inventory, 1850–1920

	Total farm stocks	Non-farm stocks £ millions at 1988 prices	Total stocks
1850	266	169	435
1860	352	254	606
1870	363	356	719
1880	362	435	797
1890	289	469	758
1900	279	621	900
1910	328	729	1,057
1920	930	2,054	2,984

Source: CH Feinstein, 'Stocks and Work in Progress, Overseas Assets, and Land' in CH Feinstein and S Pollard (eds), *Studies in Capital Formation in the United Kingdom 1750–1920* (1988) 394.

Table 4. Gross reproducible (non-land) assets, 1856–1913

	Gross domestic fixed assets	Inventories	Net overseas assets	Total
		£ billions at 1938 prices		
1856	4.22	0.6	0.5	5.4
1873	5.92	0.7	1.5	8.2
1913	12.86	1.3	7.3	21.5

Source: RCO Matthews, CH Feinstein, and JC Odling-Smee, *British Economic Growth 1856–1973* (1982) 129 (Table 5.3). Land is omitted from the estimates; land values are augmented by investment, but aggregate historical values cannot be calculated with any accuracy: ibid 121.

Table 5. Growth of UK manufacturing fixed capital, gross and net stocks, 1850–1920: machinery and equipment

	Gross fixed capital formation per annum	End-period gross stock	End-period net stock
		£ millions at 1900 prices	
1850		142	88.3
1851–1860	8.36	210.9	126.6
1861–1870	10.91	291.1	167.1
1871–1880	15.18	401.3	216.2
1881–1890	13.61	438.9	217.6
1891–1900	23.86	526.6	298.1
1901–1910	37.63	751.1	451.9
1911–1920	44.98	1061.4	592.0

Source: CH Feinstein, 'Manufacturing' in CH Feinstein and S Pollard (eds), *Studies in Capital Formation in the United Kingdom 1750–1920* (1988) 300.

Table 6. Growth of UK manufacturing fixed capital, gross and net stocks, 1850–1920: total fixed assets

	Gross fixed capital formation per annum	End-period gross stock	End-period net stock
		£ millions at 1900 prices	
1850		252.4	165.7
1851–1860	12.60	360.4	228.7
1861–1870	14.75	471.7	285.2
1871–1880	21.07	632.9	365.0
1881–1890	17.95	704.0	376.3
1891–1900	29.94	839.3	478.7
1901–1910	47.51	1140.0	679.8
1911–1920	66.63	1622.0	952.6

Source: CH Feinstein, 'Manufacturing' in CH Feinstein and S Pollard (eds), *Studies in Capital Formation in the United Kingdom 1750–1920* (1988) 300.

30 per cent growth rate per decade across the 1850–1920 time period. The ratio of domestic fixed to circulating capital is 8.45 in 1873 and 9.89 in 1913; the ratio moves even more strongly towards fixed capital in this period if overseas capital formation is included.

To summarize the data presented so far: after 1870 there was an explosion in equity shares and also in total fixed capital; there was no proportionate increase in circulating capital and possibly a declining ratio; there was a vast supply of domestic credit, leading to sizeable capital exports; and at the same time there was quite limited availability of loan capital, typically in the form of short-term bank overdraft facilities. All of this casts doubt on the view that the floating charge over the circulating assets of enterprise was a crucial element of corporate expansion from the 1870s onwards.

4. Liquidity preferences of banks

In light of these historical arguments Lord Scott's claim in *Spectrum* might perhaps be adapted to yield the following claim: that there was a large amount of available capital for investment in enterprise both within and outside equity markets from the 1870s; and some of those funds took the form of loan capital that lenders such as banks (who can be seen as agents for both bank shareholders and depositors) *preferred* to invest in short-term overdraft facilities and debentures of limited size rather than in equity or long-term bonds. A favouring of floating security by the banks represented an entrenched liquidity preference.

Floating charges, especially over receivables such as book debts, were readily realized as cash assets unlike fixed assets that required liquidation, and without the price volatility of liquid equity assets.[47] We have seen that the median loan from bank to business before 1900 was around £2,000 for six months, to be repaid from profit and rolled over, and manuals of banking practice expressly recommended that there be no deeper involvement in the capital structure or management of enterprise.[48] There may have been good reason for such liquidity preferences. At all times in the late nineteenth century bank investments had to compete with the availability of stable earnings from purchase of government issue; discount rates could affect the expected return on 3 per cent consols but the nominal government rate still set a benchmark. In pursuing a competitive return banks needed to maintain liquidity since the bill payment, discount, and clearing systems were maintained by cash to deposit ratios often running as low as 10 per cent. Central reserve banking by a responsible public authority was not yet in place, and runs by depositors could easily put a bank to the wall if it could not access cash quickly in a crisis. Local banks had lower reserve to lending ratios than London banks, and it was the local banks that financed home industry.[49]

The banks' short-term liquidity preferences dictated by their high leveraging within a relatively unregulated and uninsured financial system may be the key explanation of why the English legal system in the 1870s helped lenders develop the facility of security instruments attaching readily available circulating corporate capital such as book debts or receivables. Credit rationing to business and the invention of new forms of security such as the floating charge expressed a policy of ensuring easy and rapid realization of security, rather than representing an assessment of the expected return from corporate debt. Curiously the liquidity preference of the banks may not have been dictated by raw economic function as time passed on; inland bill of exchange financing declined and bank deposits rapidly grew at the end of the century as the banking and financial system matured and as capital accumulated in the late Victorian economy, almost eliminating leveraging by most banks in the 1890s. So lenders' liquidity preferences from the turn of the century may have been dictated by the internal culture of banks as formed in prior decades, more than by contemporary

[47] Though evidence of difficulties in realization of book debts are adduced by J Armour and S Frisby 'Rethinking Receivership' (2001) 21 OJLS 73, 94–5.

[48] SE Thomas, *British Banks and the Finance of Industry* (1931) 112–37, citing James William Gilbart's classic treatise *The History and Principles of Banking* (1834, 2nd edn, 1866) as having stated the norms of lending practice for the nineteenth century. See also HT Easton, *History and Principles of Banks and Banking* (1904) 93–123. Bank control of stock in American corporations tells a different story: see AA Berle, *Studies in the Law of Corporation Finance* (1928) 41–63.

[49] CAE Goodhart, *The Business of Banking, 1891–1914* (1972) 167–91; Capie and Collins, 'Banks, Industry and Finance' (n 37 above); Capie and Collins, 'Bank/Industry Relations' (n 37 above) 182–8; Cottrell, 'Domestic Commercial Banks' (n 35 above); Cottrell, 'Domestic Finance' (n 32 above) 270–9.

economic conditions. A particularly strong form of path dependence had set in to determine bank–industry relations.

5. Summary

Arguments from historical evidence can only be approximations, suggestive of possible causalities. Nonetheless the history of banking and corporate finance does suggest that our current understanding of the economic need for the rise of company charges, and in particular of charges over receivables, is ripe for review. Capital supplies in the late Victorian period were not running short due to limitations in the size of banking pools or equity markets. Nor was security over circulating capital including receivables the only plausible method to secure working capital for enterprise. An alternative thesis is that banks at one particular stage in their development from the mid-nineteenth century had certain liquidity preferences involving short time horizons, and this led to pressure for certain types of realizable security that met those preferences. Finance was only made available to enterprise if credit suppliers' preferences for short-term liquidity could be met. Whether the law should have adapted its institutions to satisfy and entrench the banks' preferences raises another set of questions.[50]

D. Was American Prohibition Efficient?

It is striking that American credit markets had to do without floating liens from 1925 until the advent of registration under Article 9 of the Uniform Commercial Code,[51] on the basis that the debtor who controlled and disposed of receivables could not be said to have constituted *any* kind of charge over them—*Spectrum Plus*-plus, if you like. There is controversy to this day as to whether Justice Brandeis' denial of floating charges over receivables in *Benedict v Ratner*[52] adversely affected capital supply in the corporate economy. The pressure for short-term finance may have been reduced by American corporations' heavy reliance on long-term bonds for finance, with significant issues around 1900, and then huge growth after the First World War.[53] In any case the decision excluding floating charges arguably may have enhanced rather than degraded

[50] There was of course pressure from other credit suppliers, not just banks, for recognition of floating security; a range of publicly traded debentures were secured against entire undertakings, not just against fixed assets (see J Armour, 'Should We Redistribute in Insolvency?', ch 9 above). But much of this debenture market was colonized by banks and other institutional investors.

[51] Article 9 of the Uniform Commercial Code was drafted by 1950, and the Uniform Commercial Code itself was first promulgated in 1951, but only widely adopted in revised form in 1962. See G Gilmore, *Security Interests in Personal Property* (1965) vol I, 288–94.

[52] 268 US 353 (1925), Sup Ct US.

[53] See WB Hickman, *The Volume of Corporate Bond Financing Since 1900* (1953) 44.

disciplined lending and strengthened the management and monitoring of debtor companies in the United States, by requiring notice to assignees of changes in the collateral and giving chargees a strong legal incentive to police the debtor businesses lest priority be postponed.[54] In this chapter I have offered a similar argument in reverse: that the benefits of the floating charge in English corporate finance have been overplayed, and that the inimical effects of such charges, contributing to and symptomatic of a weak system of industrial finance with severely constrained time horizons, have consistently been underestimated. This may further suggest that those who predict harm to the United Kingdom's credit system and economy as a result of the downgrading of bank security over receivables as decided in *Spectrum* may simply be wrong. At the very least they cannot assume that they have history on their side.

[54] Gilmore analyses the impact of the *Benedict* rule in detail in his study of accounts receivable financing in *Security Interests* (n 51 above) 250–86. He notes that steep transaction costs may have offset some of the advantages of the rule forcing parties to use what in effect were fixed charges over itemized receivables with licences to deal. Devices developed in the wake of *Benedict* included channelling inventory receipts through assignees' accounts, using revolving credit, and old-fashioned factoring arrangements—all devices that find an echo in English receivables financing today. At the peak of the *Benedict* regime in the mid-1950s some $10 billion was loaned under such arrangements. See further EJ Janger, 'Brandeis, Progressivism, and Commercial Law: Rethinking *Benedict* v. *Ratner*' (1998) 37 Brandeis Law Journal 63; GR Warner, 'The Anti-Bankruptcy Act: Revised Article 9 and Bankruptcy' (2001) 9 American Bankruptcy Institute Law Review 3. Louis Brandeis, the author of *Benedict* in 1925, had earlier signalled his reservations about the power of banks and corporate managers to extract monopoly rents in *Other People's Money and How the Bankers Use It* (1914, RM Abrams (ed), 1971). For a recent study of Brandeis's business ideology, see RA Posner, 'Brandeis and Holmes, Business and Economics, Then and Now' (2005) (1) Review of Law and Economics § 1.

11

THE ECONOMICS OF ENGLISH INSOLVENCY: SOME RECENT DEVELOPMENTS

Julian Franks and Oren Sussman

A. Introduction

Since debt is the workhorse of even the most sophisticated financial system[1] and since insolvency procedure is the threat-point of the debt contract—upon which debt enforcement ultimately depends—insolvency procedures are among the most important institutions of capitalism. According to one measure—the amount of power or 'protection' allocated to the creditor—the institution varies significantly across countries: England scores highest at 4, France scores 0 and the United States scores a mere 1.[2] And yet, these economies have one thing in common: in all—and in most other countries—there is a widespread perception that the system is flawed and requires major reform.

Recently a committee in France recommended that radical reforms should be implemented towards a US-style Chapter 11. The United States itself has recently passed important bankruptcy legislation restricting the rights of bankrupt companies in Chapter 11, and strengthening creditors' rights. In the United Kingdom, a report by a DTI/Treasury Working Group on Company Rescue Mechanisms (of which the first author was a member) was followed by

[1] Even large, US listed companies fund most of their 'big projects' by debt; see C Mayer and O Sussman, 'The Financing of Investment: Is It Internal?', Working Paper, Saïd School of Business, Oxford, 2005.

[2] R La Porta, F Lopes-de-Silanes, A Shleifer, and R Vishny, 'Law and Finance' (1998) 106 Journal of Political Economy 1113–55.

the Enterprise Act 2002.[3] In this chapter we try to understand the source of the dissatisfaction with insolvency and bankruptcy law; we also examine the empirical evidence to see whether it supports the notion that English insolvency is flawed and under-performing.

It is important to understand that England's high score on creditor protection reflects a fundamental property: that although not entirely free to contract, relative to other countries the default clauses in private contracts have a much greater impact on the resolution of distress. Historically, the main involvement of the courts has been to enforce whatever arrangements were privately negotiated. Over the years, these contracts have been standardized into a few popular and widely used instruments (for example, fixed and floating charges). Although a series of statutes and court decisions have limited the parties' ability to contract, relative to the United States it is the case that private debt contracts have shaped English insolvency procedures. In the United States, the law has evolved out of landmark nineteenth century railroad reorganizations,[4] which formed the basis of insolvency law, allowing judges to review creditors' liquidation rights, leave the debtor in possession, postpone repayment, and enable the company to raise new senior finance thereby diluting the rights of existing creditors. These Chapter 11 provisions give the distressed company both a breathing space and fresh funds that increases its rescue prospects, to the benefit of its stakeholders and (presumably) society at large. To put it simplistically, in England insolvency law was made by debtors and creditors while in the United States it was made by judges and legislators. English insolvency law is an instrument of the market while United States law is an instrument of public policy.

In some respects, the recent decision of the House of Lords in the case of *Re Spectrum Plus Ltd*[5] is a response to a market-based 'financial innovation': securing book debt by a fixed charge. The economic rationale of the innovation was to limit the Crown's preferential rights on the liquidation value. Since these rights can be likened to a tax, the innovation may be analysed as a tax arbitrage. Though in our view the decision is of limited practical relevance—as the tax that created the arbitrage opportunity was largely abolished by the Enterprise Act 2002, the case still raises some crucial issues with respect to English insolvency procedures.

[3] The report is included in a White Paper, *Insolvency—A Second Chance* (Cm 5234, 2001), available at <http://www.insolvency.gov.uk/cwp/cm5234.pdf>.

[4] For a comparative history of England and the United States, see J Franks and O Sussman, 'Financial Innovations and Corporate Bankruptcy' (2005) 14 Journal of Financial Intermediation 283–317.

[5] [2005] UKHL 41, [2005] 2 AC 680.

This chapter is structured as follows: Part B summarizes the criticism of the English insolvency system and examines some evidence regarding the efficiency of the English system, Parts C and D analyse the Enterprise Act and the *Spectrum* decision, respectively. Part E concludes.

B. Criticism of the English Insolvency System

The critique of the English system, prior to the Enterprise Act, comes from two directions. On the one hand, there was a feeling that creditors are simply too powerful. Since the floating charge gives the creditor effective control rights in default, strictly enforced by the courts, and since the floating charge is typically held by a bank, the balance of power it is argued is weighted too much towards the secured creditor. This is regarded as unfair, but may also be inefficient. Webb argues that, 'certain kinds of financial structure [like the United Kingdom's] create an incentive for creditors to prematurely and inefficiently liquidate companies. . . . The problem stems from the feature of this system, which allows the creditors to act in individual self-interest. They have the right to recover the value of their claim without considering what happens to the overall pool of assets upon which they draw'.[6] Hart also believes that the concentration of liquidation rights in the hands of the main bank, while preventing one market failure, ie a creditors' run, creates another, inefficient liquidations: [the bank] 'may decide against keeping a good company going because it does not see the upside potential. Moreover, even when the bank does decide to sell a company as a going concern, it may not have an incentive to push for a high sale price, given the ceiling on its returns. As a result, there may be little left over for junior claimants'.[7]

On the other hand, it was also felt that the English system had slipped into institutional stagnation. A strategy paper by the UK Government stated 'that the laws on insolvency and bankruptcy have their origins in the nineteenth century, and some of the principles underlying them are now out of date'.[8] In a keynote speech to the Cambridge law faculty, Patricia Hewitt, a government minister, spoke more generally of English corporate law which—

> was largely created in the nineteenth century. But what was a source of competitive advantage to us then, is now a source of competitive disadvantage. The law has got out of date and became encrusted with all sorts of amendments and case law. . . .

[6] D Webb, 'An Economic Evaluation of Insolvency Procedures in the United Kingdom: Does the 1986 Insolvency Act Satisfy the Creditors' Bargain?' (1991) 43 Oxford Economic Papers 139, 144.

[7] O Hart, *Firms, Contracts and Financial Structure*, Clarendon Lectures (1995) 168.

[8] HM Treasury and Department of Trade and Industry, *Enterprise and Productivity: The Government's Strategy for the Next Parliament* (June 2001) 15, available at <http://www.hm-treasury.gov.uk/media/B3D/87/Ent-Prodchall.pdf>.

> [We now] need to reflect the huge change we have seen in our economy since Victorian times. . . . Back then, Rowland Hill had just introduced the Penny Post. Now we've got emails, the Internet, text messaging, faxing, computerised book-keeping and so on.[9]

The two views augment and reinforce each other. To the extent that the terms of the contract are freely negotiated by the parties, the creditor's powers in distress are allocated to it by a voluntary contract. It follows from the Coase theorem that these powers maximize the joint surplus across a set of feasible institutional arrangements. The relative bargaining power of the parties may affect the distribution of that value, but not the entire sum. Suppose, for example, that the dominant position of the bank in distress discourages effort by the owners, leads to excessive liquidations and thereby destroys value, then it is in the best interests of the bank to relax its own control over distress (contracting away some of its rights as a creditor), encourage the owners to be more proactive in rescuing the company and share the extra value with them. That this is not done was blamed on institutional stagnation and the lack of innovation in the English system. Somehow, it was argued that the English system had fossilized and was locked into the wrong institutional arrangements, from which only statute could rescue it. We have shown elsewhere that this argument has at least some theoretical validity.[10]

We summarize this critique in three principal arguments. First, the distressed company is at the mercy of the secured creditors, who are interested primarily in preserving the value of their collateral with little regard to the company, its rescue prospects and going concern value. Thus, secured lenders are provided with an incentive to be lazy, and put little effort or money into the rescue of the company. Their primary focus is to monitor the liquidation value of their collateral and foreclose when it roughly equals the value of the loan.

Secondly, not only do these procedures encourage the creditors to behave selfishly, it provides them with incentives to act against their own interests. As soon as they detect distress they rush for the exit simultaneously. In some cases, this is not even motivated by the state of the company, but rather by the concern of each creditor that another creditor will grab the assets before him.[11] Since the run is not necessarily caused by insolvency, it follows that a viable firm may be liquidated. This notion of a coordination failure can be

[9] Transcript available on demand from the authors.

[10] J Franks and O Sussman, 'Financial Innovations and Corporate Bankruptcy' (2005) 14 Journal of Financial Intermediation 283.

[11] As we have argued elsewhere, for this argument to work, creditors *need not* be ordered by seniority; for a counterfactual, see J Franks and O Sussman, 'Financial Distress and Bank Restructuring of Small to Medium Size UK Companies' (2005) 9 Review of Finance 65.

extended to other aspects of distress; hence, litigation may be interpreted as a costly battle between the creditors—each trying to increase his own share of the liquidation value—rather than any substantial decision process about the viability of the firm. As a result, the secured creditors liquidate the company before it reaches the insolvency point, when it still has enough value to pay not only the creditors but also their lawyers. This issue is of some importance, since there is some evidence that legal costs are relatively high for smaller companies.

Thirdly, UK procedures are simply 'unfair' to junior (usually unsecured) creditors, who have few control rights in bankruptcy and therefore have little influence on how the company is reorganized. As a result, they recover little of the debts owed to them. For these creditors UK bankruptcy procedures do not represent a level playing field.

To what extent are these concerns supported by the evidence? To answer this question, we have collected data on 542 small to medium-sized distressed private companies,[12] which during 1997–8 (before the Enterprise Act 2002) were placed by the banks in one of their Business Support Units (BSUs), a head-office unit for managing distressed companies. The placement of a company in a BSU is an internal administrative procedure with no legal implications; it does reflect, however, a perception of financial distress by a company's credit officer. Around one-third of these companies went—eventually—into formal insolvency proceedings. Most of the rest were rescued and were returned to their local bank branch. A certain number have repaid their loans and moved on to another bank.

The companies' average size, as measured by sales turnover, was around £3 million. In almost every case, the bank was the prime lender to the distressed company, supplying around 40 per cent of all lending (our definition of lending includes trade credit). Virtually all of the banks' loans were secured by either a fixed or a floating charge or—often—both. Owing to their senior position, the banks recover on average around 75 per cent (median of 94 per cent) of the face value of their debt. Other creditors, such as trade creditors, recover very little, about 3 per cent, unless their loans are secured against specific collateral. Many would consider this low recovery rate to be evidence of an uneven playing field. We analyse the evidence in response to the points above.

[12] The data was collected from three clearing banks; we have taken measures in order to make the sample comparable between the banks; for more detail, see Franks and Sussman (n 11 above).

1. Is there evidence of 'lazy banking'?

The evidence is mixed. On the one hand, banks do not automatically liquidate distressed firms. The BSU's primary stated objective is to achieve rescue where possible. This does not necessarily reflect good citizenship but rather the painful experience of the recession of the early 1990s. With hindsight, it is widely recognized that during that period many viable companies in temporary difficulties were liquidated; with proper rescheduling of the loans, there is a perception that some could have survived. The uncoordinated liquidations depressed the prices of real estate and other capital goods, resulting in unnecessary losses to banks, other creditors and owners. The creation of the BSUs brought much needed expertise into the rescue process. Moreover, dealing with distress at the level of head-office (rather than branches) has allowed the BSUs to take some account of the macroeconomic effects of their own liquidation policies.[13]

At the same time, recovery rates are close to if typically *smaller* than 100 per cent. This implies that the banks indeed time bankruptcy close to the point at which the value of the collateral starts falling below the value of the loan; although the banks give the distressed company some time to repay, this period of grace is tightly rationed. If there is some dispensation for the distressed company, there is little for the unsecured creditors whose recovery rates are typically close to zero.[14]

The evidence suggests that while the banks are willing to put some effort into the rescue process, they are less willing to advance further funds to the distressed company. Moreover, the study found only one case of debt forgiveness by the bank, in spite of a strong theoretical prediction of such an outcome in cases where future cash flows fall short of the loan value but still exceed the liquidation value of the firm. Banks very rarely expand credit during the distress period.[15] Interestingly, while bank lending falls, the trade creditors expand their own lending. We find that on average, for every pound that lending by banks retrieves, there is an expansion of £0.5 in trade credit. It is not clear whether this pattern emerges because the trade creditors are less informed than the banks or because—having a greater stake in the distressed company—they are willing to bear more risk in an attempt to rescue it. Consistent with the second explanation is the fact that interest rate spreads on trade credit are typically high,

---

[13] For a macroeconomic analysis of bankruptcy law, see J Suarez and O Sussman (2006) 'Financial Distress, Bankruptcy Law and the Business Cycle', Working Paper, CEMFI and the University of Oxford, 2006.

[14] By recovery rate we mean realization in liquidation divided by the face value of the loan.

[15] See Hart (n 7 above).

reflecting both the stake and the risk exposure of the trade creditors towards the distressed company.

2. Are there coordination failures and excessive liquidations?

In the entire sample there is virtually no evidence of coordination failures. We do not find any case where dispersed trade creditors initiate liquidation (as we would observe had the creditors' run hypothesis been valid). In the vast majority of cases the bank makes the decision to force the firm into liquidation; in the remainder, either the owners themselves or the Crown as a preferential creditor initiates the process.

We interpret the results as follows. The seniority and the high collateral to loan ratio place the bank in a clear leadership position in the distress game. The trade creditors have much to lose from liquidation (note their next-to-zero recovery rates) and much to gain from rescue (which happens in two-thirds of cases). Their best response is not to precipitate liquidation, and perhaps even expand their lending, in the hope that the bank will avoid liquidation. This is what we actually observe in a majority of cases.

This interpretation of the evidence carries an important lesson. The institution of seniority is not a random or arbitrary arrangement. Rather, it is a market mechanism that has evolved in order to resolve a problem of crucial economic importance: how to stabilize the company's debt structure, particularly during a period of financial distress when psychological factors such as anxiety and fear increase the likelihood of coordination failures. It is not a perfect solution, for as we have observed, it may come at the expense of providing banks with sufficient incentives to invest in the rescue of the distressed company.

It is interesting to note that the English system also avoids another coordination failure mentioned above, litigation. By and large, receivers are appointed out of court, and unless an action or default is challenged, the process can be completed without any court intervention. Indeed, in our entire sample there was only one case where the company challenged the appointment of a receiver; that case was dismissed after a short court hearing. Again, this is not a surprising result: in a system characterized by simple and highly standardized rules, where the court's role is limited to strict enforcement, there is only a weak incentive to litigate.

So far we have taken it for granted that liquidation is a 'bad thing'. Obviously, this is not the case, for the economic cost of avoiding the liquidation of a loss-making company can be as high as liquidating a viable one. Moreover, 'liquidation' is a concept that applies to the firm's legal personality rather than to its economic reality. Indeed, a third party may buy the assets of a wound-up company and deploy them immediately into the same function, carrying on the old relationships with workers, suppliers, buyers, etc. Hence, the legal personality may be put to rest with little interruption to the economic activity of the assets and the real personalities involved; that would still count as liquidation, though the economic cost may be small.

Bearing in mind the reservations above, we turn next to an international comparison of liquidation rates—in bankruptcy. A study by Davydenko and Franks[16] finds that 'piece-meal liquidation' (where operations cease and the assets are sold off) is less frequent in the United Kingdom than in France and Germany.[17] This is a somewhat surprising result since France has a much less creditor-friendly bankruptcy code than the United Kingdom, and has provisions that are supposed to encourage a sale as a going concern.

This evidence provides another important lesson. Insolvency law defines the rules, but the outcome is not easily predictable. The outcome is determined by how the players choose to react to the rules and by their reaction to the anticipated reaction of other players. There is no one-to-one relationship between the professed intentions of the system designer and the actual outcome. The English system is all about ensuring that if the creditors obtain a liquidation right, they will be able to exercise it. The French system is all about giving the courts the power to block the creditors from exercising their liquidation rights to the benefit of the company as a going concern. And yet, the outcome may frustrate the intention. English banks may be given the incentive to liquidate the company at the point where the assets can still be redeployed, while a French company's distress may be prolonged to the point that no going concern value is left.

3. Are UK corporate bankruptcy procedures fair?

There is little doubt that power and money is not evenly distributed in English insolvency. At the same time it is clear that since this uneven allocation is a result of a voluntary transaction, the parties have put themselves in this position in expectation of other advantages; for example, in exchange for bank control in distress, the owners obtain lower cost credit to develop their business out of distress.[18] One also has to remember that some of those who seek 'protection' in distress[19]—officers of the company or trading partners—may be well-off

[16] S Davydenko and J Franks, 'Do Bankruptcy Codes Matter?: A Study of France, Germany and the UK', Working Paper, London Business School, 2005.

[17] Franks and Sussman (n 11 above) report a going-concern rate of 44 per cent among English receiverships.

[18] See Davydenko and Franks (n 16 above) for evidence that French firms are more borrowing-constrained than British ones.

[19] US Chapter 11 is indeed more generous to the trade creditors who recover (on average) 27 per cent against 3 per cent in the United Kingdom. In some cases the trade creditors are fully paid by secured creditors even before formal proceedings start; see the case of Flagstar Companies, Inc, Harvard Business School, 1998, by Stuart Gilson.

individuals (unlike the workers, whom we shall discuss briefly in Part D below). And yet, the idea that English insolvency is 'unfair' is widespread.

An ethical-philosophical analysis of the proposition above falls outside of the scope of this chapter or its authors' expertise. We would like to point out, however, that recently markets have adjusted to provide a remedy to the trade creditors' problem. Trade creditors are frequently insuring their trade credit with specialized trade insurers (or equivalently, the trade creditors sell the receivables to these specialized 'factors'). Often, such a transaction requires that the trade creditors 'retain title' over the goods supplied. Being able to coordinate the debts contracted by many suppliers provides the insurer with greater bargaining power against the banks, which enables them to offer the insurance at more competitive rates (or equivalently, pay a higher price for the receivables). This provides a case where markets have adjusted to provide a more level playing field.

C. Enterprise Act 2002

We start this section by describing what the Act did not include: in spite of lengthy discussions at the DTI/Treasury Working Party (reflected in the final report) the Act did not introduce a provision for supra-priority finance. That would have required a significant deviation from the policy of freedom of contracting, for it would require court involvement to dilute a creditor's collateral or seniority, and redistribute those rights to another creditor in return for fresh funding.

At the same time the Act did try to tip (gently) the balance of power away from the floating charge holder in favour of the company and its unsecured creditors. Hence, the Act partially abolished the institution of administrative receivership (for charges created post-September 2003), allowing instead, the holder of a qualifying floating charge to appoint an administrator out of court,[20] as indeed previously any other creditor could, although it involved an application to the court. In the same vein, the Act seeks to make the administrator accountable to creditors other than the appointing floating charge holder. For example, the administrator owes a duty of care to the other creditors and has to make his decisions about the timing of asset-selling (if any) accordingly. According to Stevens 'this change in the duties owed by most office holders which results from the partial abolition of administrative receivership is to be welcomed, and is probably the most important change to corporate insolvency law made by the

[20] Already before the Enterprise Act 2002, administration was an option available to the floating charge holder.

Enterprise Act 2002'.[21] The administrator is also required to set out proposals for 'achieving the purpose of administration' to the registrar of companies and to every creditor (providing their address is known) within eight weeks of the appointment. The administrator must organize a creditors' meeting within 10 weeks, unless he thinks creditors can be paid in full, or if he feels that the objectives of administration cannot be carried out (for example, there is no hope of rescuing the company as a going concern). This contrasts strongly with the administrative receiver who owed virtually no duty of care to the creditors generally.[22]

Administrative receivership is being phased out. Somewhat surprisingly, this process has proved relatively fast. The number of appointments of administrative receivers has declined from 1,261 cases in 2003 to 864 in 2004, whereas the number of administrators appointed under the new Enterprise Act was 1601 in 2004. The same trend continues into 2005; in the first three-quarters of the year administrative receiverships declined to 451 appointments while administrators' appointments increased to 1,677.[23] One implication of these statistics is that in many cases the holders of floating charges are content with the appointment of an administrator because they have the power to appoint an administrative receiver.

How much of a difference the new Act will make is hard to gauge. If the objective is to change the balance of power in distress, one has to remember that the floating charge holder—the bank—is still the senior creditor, and still appoints the officer who executes the procedure, regardless of title. Since the relationship between the administrator and the bank may be ongoing, there is a limit to how much the former can disappoint the latter and still be appointed for another job. It is also too early to know which (if any) of the duties of the administrator towards the unsecured creditors is material, and which one is of a bureaucratic nature; only time and additional empirical work will resolve this question.

Lastly, the new Act has—for all practical purposes—cancelled the preferential rights of the Crown (for charges created post-September 2003).[24] The proceeds from this abolition of Crown preference are supposed to accrue to unsecured creditors. That takes us to our next topic.

---

21 R Stevens, 'Security after the Enterprise Act', ch 7 above, Part E.

22 See Stevens (n 21 above) for further discussion of these issues.

23 Source of data: Department of Trade and Industry <http://www.insolvency.gov.uk/otherinformation/statistics/insolv.htm>.

24 See Stevens (n 21 above) for more discussion of this issue.

D. The *Spectrum* Decision

Although, initially, the floating charge was 'a mere popular term . . . [with] no distinct legal meaning',[25] it has quickly acquired a prominent position within the English insolvency system. From an economic point of view, the absence of a 'distinct legal meaning' is not a problem, as long as the parties have a reasonably good idea about the causal relationship between certain words used in the contract and the allocation of rights in default. Indeed, one may apply the Coase theorem once again in order to argue that even if the contract is actually ambiguous—or, indeed, even when explicit contradictions are present—the parties may still bargain out of court a settlement that would avoid the need for a costly litigation to resolve the ambiguity. The system may work efficiently as long as the results of this bargaining process are predictable.[26]

Indeed, the *Spectrum* litigation was not motivated by a conceptual difficulty regarding the precise definition of the floating charge, but rather by the need to deal with an opportunity for tax-arbitrage.

Due to statutory intervention, the preferential creditors are junior to the fixed charge but senior to the floating charge. Hence, in the case of default the Crown's preferential claim on the liquidation value could be analysed theoretically as if it was a tax. For more than 25 years, companies such as Spectrum had freely contracted debentures that allowed the chargor to use the assets in normal course of business—as if they were a floating charge—and yet prevented the Crown from exercising seniority over the liquidation value by nominally categorizing the security as 'fixed'. The House of Lords' decision has closed that gap by ruling that in order to qualify as fixed, a charge needs to specify some material restrictions on the rights of the chargor to use the object that is charged. The House of Lords then develops a legal theory that would, hopefully, help to determine what would qualify as a sufficient restriction for the purpose of a fixed charge.

Since the Enterprise Act 2002 has eliminated Crown preference, it has also eliminated the tax-avoidance element of the fixed charge. At the same time, the combined effect of the elimination of the Crown's preferential position and the restrictions imposed on the fixed charge by the *Spectrum* decision have actually increased the amount available to the other class of preferential creditors,

---

25 *Re Yorkshire Woolcombers' Association Ltd* [1903] 2 Ch 284, 294–5, per Romer LJ.

26 For a more elaborate argument and some real-world examples, see O Sussman, 'The Economics of the EU's Corporate-insolvency Law and the Quest for Harmonization by Market Forces', Working Paper, University of Oxford, 2006.

namely employees' debt.[27] We analyse next the basic economic rationale for any provision made on behalf of the employees.

Interestingly, the legal literature is not entirely clear about the motive for that provision. One reason, given by Davies is that since the debenture holders resemble equity holders in some sense 'it has been thought unjust that they should obtain priority over employees (one of the categories of the preferential creditors) who have priority to the shareholders in liquidation'.[28] This fairness argument echoes some old decisions such as the case of *Re London Pressed Hinge Co Ltd*.[29] There, Buckley J describes the situation where upon liquidation 'there is nothing for anyone but the debenture holders' as an 'injustice which is now of frequent occurrence'.[30]

Another argument suggested by Davies (although he seems sceptical about it) is efficiency-based: that both the employees and the company could *ex ante* benefit from a contract that gave the former more rights in distress. For example, jobs could be made more attractive by such a contract. That such a contract is not written is a market failure that results from some legal-technical reasons. It is then the role of the State to intervene and fill in the gap that has been created by 'contractual incompleteness'.[31]

Regardless of the precise motives, we believe that a more efficient way to provide for employees' debt would be to grant them a certain proportion of the liquidation *value* rather than identify a certain *asset* within the pile of assets that a liquidated company leaves behind. Obviously, such an arrangement would avoid the need for a legal-technical distinction between charges. One has to remember, however, that the banks would quickly learn how to adjust their policy and time liquidation to the point where they would still realize close to 100 per cent recovery rates net of the fraction that belongs to the employees, thereby increasing the liquidation rate. Such policy thus stands in contrast to other objectives of recent reforms. It may also explain why the employees have so far accepted a junior position in distress; like the trade creditors they have a high stake in rescue and are willing to bear a high risk in order to improve rescue prospects.

Lastly, *Spectrum* provides an important insight into the mechanics of a freedom of contracting system. First, the House of Lords ruled that the parties in this case had no right to categorize a certain debenture as a fixed charge. Hence,

[27] Previously, the Crown had the lion's share of the amount available for preferential creditors; see Franks and Sussman (n 11 above).

[28] P Davies, *Gower's Principles of Modern Company Law* (6th edn, 1997) 371.

[29] [1905] 1 Ch 576. [30] ibid 580.

[31] Note, however, that it is a common practice in the shipping industry for crews to obtain a maritime lien over a ship in order to secure payment of salaries; see Sussman (n 26 above).

freedom of contracting does not imply an exemption from statutory doctrine, even if that doctrine is implied only indirectly. In this particular case, the implication was so indirect that it took the law 25 years to reach a comprehensive conclusion. Secondly, the decision still expressed a commitment to freedom of contracting. It states explicitly, that the parties do have the right to charge book debts by a fixed debenture, provided that the material constraints on the use of the asset, ie book debt, are satisfied. Thirdly, *Spectrum* is a good example of the legal uncertainties that might emerge under freedom of contracting, because the courts may change their interpretation of a contract even when that contract was used for a long time, and even when the cost of the reinterpretation is significant to some parties. That it took so long to resolve the matter gives an idea of the slow pace at which a freedom of contracting system evolves, and the cost implied by this sluggish change. Some may argue that the main advantage of a statutory system is that it achieves the same goals more speedily, with less uncertainty and at a lower cost.

E. Conclusion

Achieving economic efficiency in financial distress is a problem of great complexity. Although it is quite easy to identify the players and the mechanisms through which they interact, or even to predict winners and losers as a result of a certain changes in contractual instruments, it is far more difficult to quantify the losses and the benefits. The above-mentioned facts regarding repeated amendments to insolvency law seem to suggest that no country so far has found the Holy Grail.

In absence of a textbook solution, one is forced to make a strategic choice: should we 'leave insolvency to the market' or should the State take over? The latter policy may be implemented either through a strictly enforced codified procedure or by granting the courts the power to review the creditors' contractual rights and block them if they feel that the rights conflict with the common good. Traditionally, English law has largely allowed the market to operate and has largely left the administration of the procedures to the parties themselves. In our view, there is no compelling argument at hand—either theoretical or empirical—that proves this policy is wrong. Though some would allege that this policy is outdated, others will regard the idea of a 'privatized bankruptcy' system as modern and even radical.

So far, the changes in the Enterprise Act 2002 have not dramatically altered the English system. At the same time, changes taking place elsewhere may create greater incentive to do so. The greater integration of European financial markets and the recent attempt to harmonize insolvency laws across the EU could pose more significant challenges. If Europe turns into a federalist legal system with effective competition across jurisdictions, the rules of the game might change significantly. At the same time, the fundamental questions will remain the same: whether insolvency law is a commercial instrument or an instrument of public policy. As emphasized elsewhere,[32] harmonization is not necessarily inconsistent with the notion of freedom of contracting. The logical arguments and the empirical evidence that might be brought both for and against freedom of contracting remain as relevant as ever.

[32] See Sussman (n 26 above).

12

THE LAW COMMISSION'S PROPOSALS FOR THE REFORM OF CORPORATE SECURITY INTERESTS

Michael Bridge

A. Introduction

After two consultation documents,[1] against a background of quite severe time pressure on consultants and the Law Commission itself, the Law Commission has now issued its Report on Company Security Interests ('the Report').[2] In this chapter I shall assume a general familiarity with the recommendations of the Law Commission.[3] The interests of brevity also rule out a close analysis of the progress of individual proposals through the two consultation papers prior to their final disposition in the Report. In addition, I shall not address all the recommendations contained in the Report but shall focus mainly on those that go to the heart of security and its location in the body of private and commercial

[1] *Registration of Security Interests: Company Charges and Property other than Land* (Law Com Consultation Paper No 164, June 2002); *Company Security Interests: A Consultative Report* (Law Com Consultation Paper No 176, August 2004).

[2] *Company Security Interests* (Law Com No 296, Cm 6654, August 2005) (hereinafter 'the Report').

[3] For a debate on the merits of the Law Commission's proposals (prior to the final Report) between the Law Commissioner in charge of the project and a leading critic of the proposals, see R Calnan, 'The Reform of the Law of Security' (2004) 3 JIBFL 88; R Calnan, 'The Reform of Company Security Interests' (2005) 1 JIBFL 25; and HG Beale, 'Reform of the Law of Security—Another View' (2004) 4 JIBFL 117. See also, G McCormack, *Secured Credit under English and American Law* (2004) ch 4; MG Bridge, R Macdonald, R Simmonds, and C Walsh, 'Formalism, Functionalism and Understanding the Law of Secured Transactions' (1999) 44 McGill Law Journal 567; MG Bridge, 'How Far Is Article 9 Exportable? The English Experience' (1996) 27 Canadian Business Law Journal 196.

law. The most notable omission in the coverage of this chapter is the introduction of a third means of 'perfecting' a security interest, namely, the taking of 'control' over 'collateral',[4] in addition to the long-recognized means of registration and the taking of possession. Control is to certain forms of intangible property what possession is to tangible property, though, as conceived by the Law Commission, it is not a true equivalent of possession.[5] As soon as it is realized that, under the Law Commission's proposals, control can be exercised by more than one creditor, it becomes clearer that control is not so much a means of perfecting, in the way that taking possession is, as an exemption from perfection requirements. Control had no part to play in the original Article 9 of the Uniform Commercial Code; it was introduced only in recent times.[6] It may fairly be said that Article 9 was not devised with modern capital markets in mind but rather was designed to cater for relatively small-scale commercial and retail transactions. The immediate post-war years, when Article 9 was conceived and executed, were not marked by the liberation of the capital markets.

1. Terminology

From this opening paragraph, with its reference to security interests, control, perfection, and collateral, all terms taken from the Report, it looks as though the Law Commission is in the process of redesigning the lexicon of the law dealing with company charges and pledges. Yet, interestingly enough, it is also placating its commercial and professional constituency by retaining traditional words and concepts in the draft Regulations[7] while using expressions inspired by Article 9 in the text of its Report. The Commission's evident desire not to excite the legal and banking communities unduly after its strenuous consultation exercises of the last few years, along with the continuing battle it will undoubtedly face if its proposals are not in the coming years to be whittled away to nothing, is understandable and is a subject that can wait for another day.

[4] See Part 5 of the Report.

[5] Possession at common law, if not joint, cannot be taken by two parties adversely to each other: see MG Bridge, *Personal Property Law* (2002) 19. Control therefore cannot have the visibility of possession that dispenses with the need to register as a substitute for the taking of possession.

[6] See the Uniform Commercial Code (UCC) §§ 9–104ff (as introduced in the 2000 edition of Article 9, where it was borrowed from UCC § 8–106). Control also serves as a means of attachment under the same provision (UCC § 9–104). Attachment has been dispensed with in the Law Commission's final proposals: see Part F below.

[7] Company Security Regulations 2006 (hereinafter 'the draft Regulations'), appended to the Report. See for example Pt 2, which is entitled 'Registration of Charges and Sales of Receivables'. Although 'receivables' may be something of a neologism for English law, the antiquated character of 'book debts' makes a compelling case for abandoning traditional terminology at this point.

2. The legal environment

One of the principal aims of this chapter is to comment on one aspect of the project that has always troubled me. It is this. Unlike Article 9, the Law Commission's project is much more narrowly contained. The Uniform Commercial Code (UCC) is exactly what it purports to be: it is a code of American commercial law, or at least a major part of it. I recall hearing John Honnold in the late 1970s describe the UCC as a tie-in sale: it was the attractions of Article 9 that sold the rest of the project to the legal and commercial community. It was conceived in a legal world not troubled by debates as to the substantive fusion of law and equity, presumably because fusion had already occurred or was quietly occurring.

The Law Commission's project is much more closely defined: for good pragmatic reasons it is confined to security granted by companies and not by individuals and partnerships;[8] it is remote from the law of title transfer, which has created for the Commission some problems in dealing with outright purchasers of collateral; it is also quite separate from insolvency law—though here it should be noted that the separation of state and federal powers in the United States enforces a similar division in that country; and above all, the Law Commission is not dealing with sale, letters of credit, negotiable instruments, securities, and the other matters that fall within the UCC. In one respect the Law Commission's project is more complex than Article 9. The UCC does not deal with interests in land, except when it comes to ordering priority between a security interest in personalty that becomes a fixture and a security interest in the land where the fixture is situate.[9] In contrast, the Law Commission has entered into the field occupied by the separate registers, building upon the history of registration of charges over land in the Companies Register and the practice of taking equitable charges and mortgages over registered land without separately registering them in the Land Registry, by making recommendations in respect of company property including land.[10] Reconciling the company charges register and the various asset registers has not been the least of the problems that the Law Commission has had to face.

3. External developments

There can be few commercial legal subjects more important than the taking of real security. Risk, together with its avoidance (where possible) and quantification, should by now have become deeply engrained in the minds of commercial

[8] This was due to its terms of reference and to the need to keep an eye on the legislative timetable in the coming years. Whilst a slot for companies legislation could be anticipated, a slot for major reform of the law of security interests could not. The absence of parliamentary time for the reform of private law is a long-standing reproach to the coherence and health of English private law. The continuing existence of the Bills of Sale Acts 1878–91 is the clearest possible expression of the needless survival of bad and antiquated law.

[9] UCC § 9–334.

[10] See pp 86–90 of the Report.

lawyers.[11] Restrictive laws on the taking of security are being replaced across the world. The European Commission has already marked out the taking of security over moveables as an integral part of its project on contract law[12]—this bland description is deliberate, as long as the European Commission keeps its cards close to its chest. The restructured economies of Eastern Europe are reshaping their commercial and insolvency laws, taking inspiration from a model law proposed by the European Bank of Reconstruction and Development.[13] This model law draws upon the thinking that underpins Article 9. And there are of course other instruments such as the Cape Town Convention,[14] which deals with security over particular types of mobile equipment, and the United Nations Convention on the Assignment of Receivables in International Trade 2001. The extensive American academic debate[15] on the taking of security, and the reasons why debtors grant this, shows little evidence of engagement with this dynamic world of practical action. Its general failure to engage with empirical evidence[16] detracts from the persuasive effect that its theoretical observations might otherwise have.

4. Modernization

In the light of these international developments, it is quite understandable that the Law Commission should be seeking to modernize the law of company security interests. Whether it is a matter of compulsion, in the form of a future European directive or regulation on security, or of voluntary commitment, in the

[11] MG Bridge, 'The Future of English Private Transactional Law' [2002] Current Legal Problems 191, 213.

[12] See, for example, the Communication from the Commission to the European Parliament and the Council, *A More Coherent European Contract Law[:] An Action Plan* (Brussels, 12 February 2003, COM (2003) 68).

[13] See <http://www.ebrd.com/country/sector/law/st/core/modellaw/modellaw.pdf>; L Mistelis, 'The EBRD Model Law on Secured Transactions and Its Importance on Collateral Law Reform in Central and Eastern Europe and the Former Soviet Union' (1998) 5 Parker School Journal of East European Law 455; G McCormack and F Dahan, 'The EBRD Model Law on Secured Transactions: Comparisons and Convergence' [1999] Company Financial and Insolvency Law Review 65.

[14] UNIDROIT Convention on International Interests in Mobile Equipment 2001.

[15] For an extensive list of articles, see G McCormack, *Secured Credit under English and American Law* (2004) 3–4, fn 10, who comments: 'The literature is truly enormous and a lot of contributions seem to consist of assertions or attempts to demonstrate that most previous contributions to the debate have been flawed'. Leading articles include: T Jackson and A Kronman, 'Secured Finance and Priority among Creditors' (1979) 88 Yale Law Journal 1143; A Schwartz, 'A Theory of Loan Priorities' [1989] Journal of Legal Studies 209; R Scott, 'A Relational Theory of Secured Financing' (1986) 86 Columbia Law Review 901; SL Harris and C W Mooney, 'A Property-Based Theory of Security Interests' (1994) 80 Virginia Law Review 2021; L LoPucki, 'The Unsecured Creditor's Bargain' (1994) 80 Virginia Law Review 1887.

[16] H Kripke, 'Law and Economics: Measuring the Economic Efficiency of Commercial Law in a Vacuum of Fact' (1985) 133 University of Pennsylvania Law Review 929. For an example of engagement with empirical evidence, see R Mann, 'Explaining the Pattern of Secured Credit' (1997) 110 Harvard Law Review 626.

form of adopting a convention that is drafted in accordance with the concepts of Article 9, it is better to harmonize at leisure, in the light of the wisdom and experience of one of the world's leading financial centres, than under compulsion and stress. Legislation enacted in London is likely to be more suited to the needs of a major financial centre than legislation enacted in Brussels.[17] The existing uncodified law of security in this country, posited on the distinction between law and equity, cannot serve as a model for European integration, whereas UK legislation along the lines of the Law Commission's proposals, especially the broader ones entertained before its final report, could be. It should not be forgotten, moreover, that there is the matter of a statutory embarrassment to clear up: this is the unimplemented Pt IV of the Companies Act 1989.[18] The sooner this failed effort to reform the law is excised from the statute book, the better.

Whatever incentive there may be for the Law Commission to propose major structural changes to the law, it nevertheless does not have the impetus that lay behind the formulation of Article 9. The proponents of that instrument had to deal with a proliferation of separate registration statutes[19] and a restrictive decision of the Supreme Court—*Benedict v Ratner*[20]—that made it extremely difficult to take a charge over future property because of the barriers it erected against the chargor's beneficial enjoyment of receivables and their proceeds. English law has for 150 years had under another name the enterprise charge, though its initial existence as a floating charge over the corporate undertaking has long since been modified so as to become a residual floating charge tucked in behind as many fixed charges over company property as the law permits. Not the least consequence of the decision of the House of Lords in *Re Spectrum Plus Ltd*,[21] however, is that the floating charge is revived as a genuine security interest over what, for very many companies, is their most important asset—receivables—instead of acting just as the trigger that enables the chargee to appoint out of court an administrative receiver or an administrator.

5. Scope

The specific subjects that I wish to cover in this chapter are the following: the continued existence of the floating charge; the relationship of security law to

---

[17] This is because of the restrictive tradition of the civil law on the taking of non-possessory security and because an instrument dealing with security generally, or even security in general commercial cases, will be applied to more than just the capital markets.

[18] A subject worthy of consideration is the responsibility of the executive to implement the will of Parliament.

[19] Dealing with different types of interest, such as chattel mortgages, conditional sales, and trust receipts.

[20] 268 US 353 (1925).

[21] [2005] UKHL 41, [2005] 2 AC 680, reversing [2004] Ch 337, CA.

insolvency law; the failure to recognize the purchase money security interest and the concomitant decision not to include quasi-security devices; the decision, however, to include general assignments of receivables; the dating of priority from filing notice of a charge and not as at present from its creation (subject to the 21-day rule); the related matter of treating filing as a positive priority point, instead of treating the failure to file as defeating a priority entitlement that would otherwise exist; the proposed abolition of the Registrar's conclusive certificate in consequence of the adoption of notice filing; and the congruence of the treatment of outright purchasers of collateral with the treatment of such purchasers under the general law of *nemo dat quod non habet.* Apart from the omission of control, this list by no means exhausts the topics dealt with by the Law Commission.

B. The Continued Existence of the Floating Charge

1. Role of the floating charge

It scarcely needs to be said that the contribution of the floating charge to the financing of corporate businesses was one of the outstanding achievements of nineteenth century equity lawyers. Indeed, had it not been for the restrictive decision of the US Supreme Court in *Benedict v Ratner,*[22] as hostile as it was to the floating charge, much of the impetus behind the reform of personal property security law in the United States would not have existed. Yet, despite the sentimental attachment of many in the legal profession to the floating charge,[23] it has been apparent for decades that it is a weak security[24]—though it comes into its own as a precondition to that most powerful of remedies, the out-of-court appointment of an administrator or administrative receiver[25]—and greatly inferior to the fixed charge. The practice has arisen of using it only as a sweeper to pick up collateral that cannot be encompassed within a fixed charge or series of fixed charges, a category that has now grown in significance in consequence of the House of Lords' decision in *Spectrum.* The weakness of the security largely stems from its statutory subordination to preference creditors[26] and now to unsecured creditors availing themselves of the fund created under s 176A of the Insolvency Act 1986 (as amended). The main purpose of the floating charge in modern times has been to entitle the chargee to appoint an administrator or administrative receiver out of court, with all of the advantages that that process entails.

[22] 268 US 353 (1925).

[23] 'The floating charge is viewed as enormously important . . .': para 3.164 of the Report.

[24] And although, for practical purposes, it will, in consequence of *Spectrum,* be the only generally available security over receivables, it will for priority purposes be a weak security.

[25] Enterprise Act 2002, Pt 10.

[26] Insolvency Act 1986, s 386 and Sch 6 (as amended by Enterprise Act 2002).

2. Continuing need for floating charges

The Law Commission, in its first consultative document,[27] plainly had difficulties in dealing with the floating charge but had resolved them by the time of the second consultative document.[28] There is no need in an Article 9 scheme of security to recognize any distinction between fixed and floating charges, or indeed any distinction between legal and equitable interests. That is perhaps its most striking feature for an English lawyer. Priority issues between secured creditors can be resolved according to the first-past-the-post scheme of priority as laid down (subject to the primary exception of the purchase money security interest in Article 9) in such legislation. In its Report, however, the Law Commission states that it has retained the distinction between floating and fixed charges.[29] So far as the Law Commission cannot ignore the retention of that distinction in insolvency legislation, where the rights of preference and unsecured creditors come into play, its stance is understandable. There is less justification for persisting with the distinction where a property conflict arises between chargees and outright purchasers.[30] The Commission's continuing attachment to the distinction between fixed and floating charges is all the more understandable in the light of the evident difficulty the Commission faced in dealing with consultees who might not fully have understood the purport of its proposals, or who might have had concerns about the reverberating consequences of those proposals.

Yet, on closer examination, the proposals of the Commission amount to a disregard of the distinction between fixed and floating charges. This is because the two charges are treated equally in a first-past-the-post priority system and because the Law Commission is not directly concerned with the intersection of security and insolvency. As between an earlier floating charge and a later fixed charge, both registered (or, to use the language of Article 9 and the Law Commission, 'filed') and in that order, the floating charge will outrank the fixed charge.[31] In consequence, there is no need to insert a negative pledge clause in the floating charge or rely upon the current practice of smuggling that clause into the particulars of charge so as to fix those searching the register with actual notice of restrictions on the company chargor's authority to deal with its assets. This ordering of priority appears to be predicated upon all floating charges containing restrictive clauses: what has become of the case, if it exists in practice at all, of the later fixed charge over a narrow collateral base that is permitted

[27] See n 1 above. [28] See paras 2.56ff of the Consultative Report, n 1 above.

[29] See paras 3.158 and 3.173 of the Report. cf para 2.57 of the Consultative Report ('under the notice-filing scheme the distinction between fixed and floating charges will in practice disappear').

[30] See Part G below, 'The Rights of Outright Purchasers of the Collateral'.

[31] See para 3.180 of the Report and reg 24(3) of the draft Regulations.

under the terms of the earlier floating charge?[32] Can this be treated as the equivalent of a priority agreement between two secured creditors ousting the default priority rule? Regulation 34 on the permissibility of voluntary subordination is somewhat terse and, whilst probably allowing for implied subordination, is not sufficiently certain to put the matter beyond doubt.[33]

A similar example of the distinction between fixed and floating charges being of no consequence, provided the charge is filed, concerns execution creditors. The issue of whether a floating charge has crystallized[34] will no longer arise under the Commission's proposals. A floating charge will, by virtue of its perfection by filing, prevail against the rights of execution creditors.[35] One area where the distinction between fixed and floating charges at first sight remains of significance is the rights granted to outright purchasers of the collateral, an expression that I prefer for present purposes to 'transferees', which is not fully defined in the draft Regulations.[36] Assuming the case of a charge over tangible personalty that has been filed, a fixed chargee prevails over the purchaser in the case of an unauthorized disposition[37] whereas a floating chargee does not, unless the transferee knew that the transfer was in breach of the terms governing the floating charge.[38] Nevertheless, the distinction that ought properly to be borne in mind is not that between fixed and floating charges but that between authorized and unauthorized dispositions, authority for present purposes including apparent authority. A floating chargee is contractually authorized to dispose of the collateral in the ordinary course of business in the absence of special restrictions. Even where there are such restrictions, the floating chargee has the apparent authority to dispose of the collateral in the ordinary course. In consequence, the rights of transferees could have been stated to identical effect in the draft Regulations without mention of the distinction between fixed and floating charges.

The treatment in the draft Regulations of fixed and floating charges as identical for priority purposes helps to obviate any need for the concept of attachment,

[32] *Re Automatic Bottle Makers Ltd* [1926] Ch 412, CA.

[33] See reg 34(1): 'These Regulations do not preclude subordination by a person entitled to priority'. The Australian Corporations Act 2001 is more explicit. Apart from priority agreements (s 279(2)(b)), the Act reverses the statutory priority rule in the case of 'any consent (express or implied) that varies the priority' (s 279(2)(a)).

[34] *Evans v Rival Granite Quarries Ltd* [1910] 2 KB 979, CA.

[35] See the Law Commission's recommendation at para 3.204 of the Report, together with regs 20(1), (4) and 24(11). A reading of the draft Regulations alone might not convince everyone that the order of priority between an execution creditor and a floating chargee whose registered floating charge has not crystallized has been reversed.

[36] See reg 29(3)(b) (' "transferee" does not include chargee, pledgee or buyer of receivables').

[37] See reg 29(1). [38] See reg 29(2).

which is dispensed with in the Report.[39] The approach of the Commission goes part way to the functionalism of Article 9,[40] though of course the exclusion of quasi-security from the proposals blocks the complete acceptance of a functionalist philosophy that looks to the practical purpose rather than the conceptual bases or names of proprietary devices.

C. The Relationship of Security to Insolvency Law

1. Floating charges in insolvency legislation

This matter is substantially dealt with by reference to the Law Commission's proposed retention of the distinction between fixed and floating charges which, as we have seen, is presentational rather than substantive. The practical need to distinguish the two types of charge does not lie within the draft Regulations themselves. There seems to be no reason why the distinction cannot be retained in insolvency legislation for the purposes of insolvency law, but abandoned in company charges legislation for the purposes of security.[41] The proposed abolition of the closed list of registrable charges,[42] which at present requires *all* floating charges to be registered, in favour of filing with exceptions,[43] would make this permissible. The approach adopted by the Law Commission is nevertheless understandable. The law of security and the law of insolvency are so intertwined that any attempt to reform the one but not the other is fraught with major difficulties. Three further points concerning the floating charge and insolvency can however be taken. The first concerns s 245 of the Insolvency Act 1986; the second, the rights of preference creditors and s 176A unsecured creditors[44]

39 'With the simplified scheme that we now recommend we have found it unnecessary to employ "attachment" ': para 3.6 of the Report.

40 Hence, the inclusive non-definition of charge in reg 2(3) (' "charge" includes a mortgage'), which reproduces the language of Law of Property Act 1925, s 205(1).

41 For the view that the distinction should not be retained for either purpose, see R Goode, 'The Case for the Abolition of the Floating Charge', ch 2 above, and L Gullifer and J Payne, 'The Characterization of Fixed and Floating Charges', ch 4 above.

42 In Companies Act 1985, s 396.

43 See reg 2(1)(a). The major exception is perfection by control. Financial collateral arrangements are effective without either registration or control: see reg 36(1). This accommodates the Directive on Financial Collateral Arrangements (Directive 2002/47/EC of 6 June 2002 [2002] OJ L168/43), transposed by the Financial Collateral Arrangements (No 2) Regulations 2003, SI 2003/3226.

44 Section 176A of the Insolvency Act was added by the Enterprise Act 2002. It provides for the payment to unsecured creditors of a prescribed part of a company's 'net property', which includes assets the subject of a floating charge. The regulations implementing s 176A define this prescribed part as consisting of 50 per cent of the first £10,000 and 20 per cent of the remainder of the company's net property, but then cap the prescribed part at £600,000. See the Insolvency Act 1986 (Prescribed Part) Order 2003, SI 2003/1730.

in the light of *Spectrum*;[45] and the third, the apparent increase in circular priority problems consequent upon the proposal to order priority between fixed and floating charges in order of filing.

2. Late floating charges

Section 245 of the Insolvency Act 1986 renders invalid a floating charge on the company's undertaking or property, granted within one year of the onset of insolvency (two years in the case of connected persons), except to the extent of the consideration provided by the chargee at the same time as or after the grant of the charge. No similar invalidity extends to fixed charges or even a series of fixed charges that in their totality cover a substantial part of the company's undertaking. It is difficult to understand why the scope of s 245 is so limited, since it does extend to floating charges over less than the whole of the company's undertaking. The decision in *Spectrum*, nevertheless, restricting as it does the scope of fixed charges, diminishes the force of this adverse comparison between fixed and floating charges. Those consulted by the Law Commission favoured the extension of s 245 to all charges, as the Law Commission provisionally recommended,[46] but in the event no changes are recommended to s 245. The reason given[47] seems a very odd one, namely, the decision of the Law Commission to retain the distinction between fixed and floating charges. The confinement of s 245 to floating charges does not require the distinction between fixed and floating charges to be drawn elsewhere. Any argument that the Law Commission has enough to do to reform the law of company charges, without going through insolvency legislation as well, is more compelling than the reason given. All of this assumes that the matter of s 245 falls within the Law Commission's terms of reference.[48] As far as these go, it is barely arguable that s 245 is concerned with 'priority' and the final heading of 'recommendations for reform' ought surely to be interpreted in the light of what precedes it, where no mention at all is made of insolvency. Indeed, the Law Commission itself acknowledges that the reform of insolvency law lies outside its terms of reference,[49] which makes its reasoning on s 245 all the more curious. It is apparent at various stages in the Report that the Commission must have been frustrated by the limits in respect of insolvency law imposed by its terms or reference.[50]

---

45 [2005] UKHL 41, [2005] 2 AC 680, reversing [2004] Ch 337, CA.

46 See para 3.146 of the Consultative Report (n 1 above).

47 See para 3.84 of the Report.

48 These are set out in para 1.15 of the Report.

49 See para 3.167 of the Report ('Reform of insolvency law in its own right is outside our terms of reference').

50 See, for example, paras 3.167–3.168 of the Report and the recommendation for revising the Insolvency Act 1986 in para 3.187.

3. Unsecured and preference creditors

As for the rights of preference creditors and s 176 A creditors,[51] the current law imposes a major practical distinction between fixed and floating charges. Only floating chargees are subordinated to these categories of non-secured creditors.[52] At first glance, the need in insolvency cases to retain the distinction here seems incontrovertible. Yet the same effect can be achieved by granting these non-secured creditors a special priority over stock-in-trade and accounts receivable, since the decision in *Spectrum* would seem to make the prospects of a fixed charge over such collateral impossible. (But one should never underestimate the ingenuity of the commercial draftsman.) Indeed, the Law Commission recognizes that the rights of preference and s 176A creditors could be defined by reference to stock-in-trade and accounts receivable, as well as other assets which the company is permitted to dispose of free of the charge.[53] Chargees would therefore have a powerful incentive to retain control over the disposition of collateral so far as they are able to do so. The Law Commission's shift of focus from the nature of the charge to the nature of the collateral strikingly shows how the substance and outcomes of the present law can be replicated in a radically different instrument and ought therefore to allay much suspicion and doubt that inevitably is attendant upon legal innovation.[54]

A final point about fixed and floating charges is this. The power of a chargee to appoint an administrator out of court,[55] which requires there to be a floating charge, ought surely to exist also where there are just fixed charges over at least substantially the whole of a company's property (though, again, the outcome in *Spectrum* might render it in practice unnecessary to pursue this line of reasoning, since the difficulty of taking a fixed charge over book debts would in practice mean that a chargee could not take just fixed charges over substantially the whole of a company's property). The utility of the continued existence of the floating charge is far from evident. Nevertheless, the points made above about the size of the Law Commission's project, as well as its proper scope in the light of the Commission's terms of reference, retain their force here too.

4. Circular priority

The circular priority issue that arises as a result of the Law Commission's

[51] See n 43 above.

[52] Insolvency Act 1986, ss 40 and 175 and Sch B1, para 65(2) (as inserted by Enterprise Act 2002); Companies Act 1985, s 196.

[53] See paras 3.165–3.170 of the Report. See also the discussion of this point in L Gullifer and J Payne, 'The Characterization of Fixed and Floating Charges', ch 4 above.

[54] The Law Commission did not in the end pursue the proposal to shift the emphasis from the nature of the charge to the nature of the collateral: see paras 3.165–3.175 of the Report.

[55] Insolvency Act 1986, Sch B1, para 15, as inserted by the Enterprise Act 2002.

recommendations concerns floating charges that are filed before fixed charges. For insolvency purposes, the fixed chargee ranks ahead of preference and s 176A creditors, but these latter creditors rank ahead of the floating chargee who ranks ahead of the fixed chargee by virtue of the first to file rule. The Law Commission's proposals increase the likelihood of such circularity though the Commission believes this will be uncommon.[56] The effect of the *Spectrum* decision, which renders it exceedingly difficult to take a fixed charge over circulating assets, coupled with secured creditors' desires to take a fixed charge wherever they possibly can, diminishes the likely incidence of such circularity problems. The Law Commission nevertheless recommends a revision of the Insolvency Act 1986 to allow the prior-ranking floating chargee to succeed to the position of the fixed chargee qua preference and s 176A creditors.[57]

Difficulties in the way of such a solution are certainly presented by the present law, as the decision in *Re Portbase (Clothing) Ltd*[58] demonstrates, largely as a result of the mandatory language of s 175(2)(b) of the Insolvency Act 1986.[59] Nevertheless, if the agreement in *Re Portbase (Clothing) Ltd*, by which the fixed chargee ceded priority to the floating chargee, had taken the form of an exchange of priorities,[60] in the sense of fixed and floating chargees each having a power of attorney to collect on behalf of the other recoveries to be held on trust by the collecting party, the strange advancement in *Re Portbase (Clothing) Ltd* of preference creditors ahead of both fixed and floating chargee[61] could have been avoided. The priority agreement in *Re Portbase (Clothing) Ltd* took the simpler and ultimately unsuccessful form of a fixed chargee subordinating itself to a floating chargee and was not cast in the form suggested above. The alternative approach here suggested would also dispense with any need to consider *how*, whether by subrogation or otherwise, circularity can as a matter of general principle be resolved. Nevertheless, although an amendment to the Insolvency Act 1986 is unnecessary to avoid the outcome in *Re Portbase (Clothing) Ltd*, it is needed to deal with circular priority issues that arise out of the Law Commission's proposal to rank earlier floating charges ahead of later fixed charges, which happens where the chargees themselves have not entered into a priority agreement to the same effect.

---

[56] See para 3.183 of the Report. [57] See para 3.187 of the Report.

[58] *Re Portbase (Clothing) Ltd* [1993] Ch 388.

[59] 'Preference debts . . . have priority over the claims of holders of debentures secured by, or holders of, any floating charge created by the company, and *shall be paid accordingly* out of any property comprised in or subject to that charge' (emphasis added).

[60] It is not suggested here that a priority position is an item of property that, moreover, is transferable.

[61] The effect of the priority agreement was that the preference creditors were promoted from second to first position.

D. The Purchase Money Security Interest

1. Purpose of purchase money security interests

The purchase money security interest, which was so prominent at the consultation stage of the project, has no part to play in the Report and the draft Regulations.[62] Before considering the reason for this omission, it is worth recalling the nature and purpose of this type of security interest. The main ideas behind an abandonment of the first-in-time approach, so as to grant a super-priority to certain chargees who file later than earlier chargees, are, first, that the later chargee adds new collateral to the company's asset base so that any charge taken is not at the expense of the earlier chargee. If a later chargee advances credit to the debtor so that the debtor may purchase equipment, the purchase price of the equipment does not come from assets of the debtor charged to an earlier chargee, whose charge is therefore not watered by the later charge. Indeed, the equipment in this example may generate additional receivables and thus positively enhance the security of the first chargee. A second reason for the grant of this super-priority is that it obviates the risk of a situational monopoly, by which the company is in thrall to the earlier chargee and is dependent upon the willingness of that chargee to make further advances or enter into a priority agreement with a later chargee in response to a condition imposed by the latter for the grant of additional credit. The idea here is that it is not healthy for the company to be dependent upon a single line of secured finance, especially where further finance will not be made available from that source.

2. Title retention

Now, the disappearance of the purchase money security interest appears to be due completely to the exclusion in the Report of quasi-security in the form of title retention.[63] The present law, which ensures that an effective retention of title prevails over the rights of even a prior chargee, amounts to a covert recognition of the purchase money security interest. This is because, first, assets the subject of a retention of title do not vest in the buyer/chargor so that they might be encumbered in favour of a chargee, whether an existing or a future chargee. Moreover, the absence of any requirement that a true retention of title device be registered as a charge underlines the primacy of the title retainer's position. Had retention of title clauses been brought within the general filing scheme, as was earlier proposed by the Law Commission at the consultation

[62] See para 1.29 of the Report. 'Registration and priority of title-retention devices . . . will be considered further in future reports': ibid.

[63] Note the way the two issues are bracketed together in para 1.29 of the Report.

stage, a way would have had to be found to preserve the present priority advantages of the title financier. The architects of Article 9, seeking not to effect a complete overturning of established priorities, found a way to preserve the existing priority of title-based financiers, even of ordinary sellers supplying on retention of title terms, by means of the concept of the purchase money financier.

In English law, apart from retention of title, there is a lingering recognition of this super-priority in the case of competing mortgages or charges,[64] though it is hardly significant in practice. The Law Commission's proposals do not allow for a super-priority in such cases. Nevertheless, it is unlikely that the absence of a super-priority will make much difference to the practice of secured credit, except perhaps in smaller, informal dealings, given the recognition of priority agreements and the common use of such agreements in practice.

It is a matter of regret that quasi-security, in the face of implacable opposition from the City of London Law Society and the financial leasing industry, has been dropped from the Law Commission's proposals.[65] One of the great merits of public registration is its transparency and the information it gives to those dealing with the company debtor. If this argument remains good for charges, then it is good for title retention too, so long as registration does not impose onerous burdens upon title retainers (which the Law Commission's proposals would not do).[66] The argument that everyone knows that equipment is the subject of a financial lease or similar transaction proves too much: it could also be made in the case of conventional security for those company debtors who lack the financial muscle to resist the giving of security.

[64] *Re Connolly Bros Ltd (No 2)* [1912] 2 Ch 25, CA, reinforced by *Abbey National Building Society v Cann* [1991] 1 AC 56, HL.

[65] This is not to say that the extension of the Law Commission's scheme to title retention would not have been without its technical difficulties. For example, if title retention had been re-characterized as a charge, this would have had knock-on consequences under the Insolvency Act 1986 (as amended by the Enterprise Act 2002). A floating chargee seeking to appoint an administrator out of court and having, as required by para 15 of Sch B1 to the 1986 Act, to notify the holders of prior floating charges (which would inevitably be the type of charges held by title retainers), might have found this no easy task in the case of title retainers.

[66] The burden of filing online will be significantly less than the current paper burden, the cost of using the system will be less and the cost of setting up the new system will be quite modest: see Part 2 of the Report. The cost of filing in New Zealand is low enough to be described as nominal: ibid para 2.09.

E. General Assignments of Accounts Receivable

1. General assignments: an exceptional case

With the exclusion of quasi-security, the Law Commission's proposals are now confined to security properly so called, with this exception. The exception concerns the general assignment of accounts receivable (though the expression 'general assignment' is avoided) which, in the case of individuals, have to be registered under bills of sale legislation further to s 344 of the Insolvency Act 1986. With the support of the factoring industry, the Law Commission proposes that such transactions be brought within the filing net (though they are not to be treated as charges *eo nomine*), even if the receivables are discounted (that is, sold)[67] instead of charged. The distinction between a charge and a discounting arrangement can be whittled away to nothing by means of recourse agreements[68] and clauses returning any surplus[69] to the assignor. A dogmatic insistence here on the distinction between discounting and charge would therefore be most unwelcome, especially now that the Law Commission has abandoned an earlier tentative proposal to include in secondary legislation a restatement of rights and duties of debtor and creditor.[70]

2. Survival of the rule in *Dearle v Hall*?

As a result of its filing and priority proposals, the Law Commission would, to a degree at least, dispense with the rule in *Dearle v Hall*.[71] Under this rule, a second chargee, without notice of the first charge at the time the second charge is given, will take priority over the first chargee by notice of the assignment to the debtor before the first chargee does so. This departs from the first-in-time rule in that notice to the debtor is not required to complete the equitable assignment of a debt.[72] The rule in *Dearle v Hall* would nevertheless not disappear entirely. It would survive subliminally, in that priorities between two secured creditors, each exercising control over cash, would be determined according to which of them is the first to notify the account debtor.[73] There is another possible area of survival, so far as a priority conflict might arise between an assignment within the statutory scheme and one that stands outside the

[67] *Chow Yoong Hong v Choong Fah Rubber Manufactory* [1962] AC 209, PC; *Lloyds & Scottish Finance v Cyril Lord Carpet Sales Ltd* [1992] BCLC 609, HL.

[68] By which the assignee may claim reimbursement from the assignor in the event of non-payment by the debtor.

[69] A discounting arrangement will involve the creation of a retention fund on which the factor can draw in the event of, for example, bad debt.

[70] See Part 5 of the Consultative Report (n 1 above) and para 1.26 of the Report.

[71] (1828) 3 Russ 1, 38 ER 475.

[72] *Gorringe v Irwell India Rubber and Gutta Percha Works* (1886) 34 Ch D 128.

[73] See reg 40(8)(a).

scheme. An exception to the filing requirement exists in the case of small-scale discounting of receivables,[74] but this exception does not in terms save the rule in *Dearle v Hall* for those cases where there is a conflict between a registered charge or registered general assignment, on the one hand, and a small-scale assignment that in the insolvency sense is exempt from the registration requirement. A literal reading of the draft Regulations[75] leads to the conclusion that an unregistered assignment that is exempt from registration is defeated by a registered one. If this indeed is what the draftsman intended—which seems unlikely—then it is consonant with a policy to encourage voluntary filings of exempt transactions. It is nevertheless perfectly possible to read the regulations in a way that treats the exemption of an assignment from registration as dealing only with its opposability to an administrator or liquidator in insolvency proceedings (see reg 20).[76] However extensive the abolition of the rule in *Dearle v Hall*, the Law Commission's proposed priority rule has the great merit of freeing factors from the need to notify each and every account debtor if they are to obtain the best available priority position. They can rely instead upon a single advance filing free from the restrictions on tacking contained, as far as mortgagees and chargees are concerned, in the current law.[77]

3. Clauses prohibiting assignments

Another matter relating to the assignment of receivables may be mentioned here. It concerns clauses prohibiting assignment that under existing law are effective as between account debtor and assignor,[78] and therefore also as against assignee, yet do not preclude the assignee from laying claim to the proceeds in the event of the assignor's insolvency. The Law Commission proposes that a prohibition of assignment should be ineffectual against an assignee,[79] thus following a lead to be found in modern personal property security legislation in the United States and Commonwealth, as well as in the United Nations Convention on the Assignment of Receivables in International Trade 2001.[80] As important as this rule is in the case of global assignments, this interference with freedom of contract does not suit every taste.[81] The rule against prohibition has, from the assignee's point of view, the great merit of protecting it from the proceeds of receivables being frittered away in the hands of an assignor who has been paid by the account debtor. A proprietary interest by way of security in those proceeds in the hands of the assignor is only as good as the value of

[74] See reg 20(2). [75] See reg 24(2), (3). [76] See reg 24(2), (3).

[77] *Hopkinson v Rolt* (1861) 9 HLC 514, 11 ER 829, HL; Law of Property Act 1925, s 94.

[78] *Helstan Securities Ltd v Hetts CC* [1978] 3 All ER 262; *Linden Gardens Trust Ltd v Lenesta Sludge Disposals Ltd* [1994] 1 AC 84, HL; *Don King Productions Inc v Warren* [2000] Ch 291, CA.

[79] See para 4.40 of the Report and reg 35(5). [80] See Article 9.

[81] Note however the quite narrow definition of receivables in reg 2(3).

proceeds, or proceeds of proceeds, still in the assignor's hands when formal insolvency proceedings concerning the assignor take place. The assignee is not therefore protected to a sufficient degree by the imposition of a trust on the proceeds of receivables in the assignor's hands.[82]

F. The Dating of Priority and the Effect of Registration

1. Dating priority from registration

Under the present law, priority dates from the creation of a charge and not from its registration. That gives rise to the notorious invisibility problem in that, since chargees have 21 days within which to *preserve* their existing priority by registration,[83] the use of that grace period prevents competing financiers and other interested parties from discovering the current state of affairs of the company chargor by examining the Companies Register.[84] The Law Commission proposes that priority should date from perfection,[85] for example by filing, rather than from creation.[86] This is to be commended because it creates an incentive for the chargee to get on with the business of filing and informing the business and legal communities. It is congruent with further proposals of the Commission, which remove the existing statutory duty on the company chargor to register and thus also the criminal penalty arising from the failure to register.[87] The removal of this absurdity makes explicit something that the banking community has always understood, namely, that it is the business of the chargee to file and to do so with dispatch.

2. Tacking and future advances

The Law Commission's proposals have a number of consequences. For example, they make it intellectually and practically inevitable that current restrictions on tacking[88] in respect of future advances have to be abolished. The effect of these restrictions is that further discretionary advances by a senior chargee may not be tacked on to an earlier charge so as to give such advances priority over intervening advances from a junior chargee. Under the Law Commission's proposals, a single filing can preserve a priority position no matter how many further

---

[82] *Barclays Bank plc v Willowbrook International Ltd* [1987] BCLC 717.

[83] Companies Act 1985, s 395.

[84] It also takes registry staff an average of a further five days to enter the charge upon the register: see para 2.17 of the Report.

[85] An expression that the Law Commission largely eliminates from the Report and the draft Regulations: para 3.6 of the Report.

[86] See para 3.155 of the Report.

[87] Companies Act 1985, s 399(3).

[88] See n 77 above.

advances are made, whether or not pursuant to previous commitment.[89] Difficulties arising in this respect from bank overdrafts under the present law[90] would be eliminated. These difficulties arise because the application of the rule in *Clayton's Case*[91] to a current account results in the retirement of debt as payments are made into that account. Further drawings on the account create new debt which is subordinate to advances made by an intervening creditor, in view of the absence of any right on the part of the bank to tack these later overdraft advances to the original overdraft advance. The proposed abolition of tacking restrictions would encourage further resort to priority agreements between secured creditors, in which connection the Law Commission's express recognition of priority agreements (called subordination agreements)[92] assumes a particular significance.

3. The disappearance of 'attachment'

Again, the Law Commission's proposals[93] facilitate the disappearance from the draft Regulations of the concept of attachment, in that priority does not date from creation. Under the present law, a charge cannot be said to have been created—and thus effective for priority purposes—if the debenture has not yet been executed or if all of the charged assets are future assets.[94] The opportunity to file even in advance of entry into the security agreement, proposed by the Law Commission,[95] also avoids any prejudice accruing to the secured creditor if there is a short delay between the conclusion of a security agreement and the subsequent act of filing. A further beneficial consequence of priority dating from filing is that the tedious difficulties presented by applications to register outside the 21-day period[96] under existing law would disappear. The Commission's proposals in this area represent a major improvement on the present law and would seem to be relatively uncontroversial.

4. Effect of registration

As for the effect of registration, two points can be made. First, the doctrine of constructive notice in *Wilson v Kelland*[97] can be laid to rest. The present law is laid out so that, as against named classes of interested parties, a failure to register

---

[89] See para 3.151 and draft reg 33(6) of the Consultative Report (n 1 above).

[90] *Deeley v Lloyds Bank Ltd* [1912] AC 756, HL.

[91] *Devaynes v Noble* (1816) 1 Mer 529, 35 ER 767.

[92] See reg 34. [93] See para 3.6 of the Report.

[94] A prudent lender taking a charge over a bank account, for example, will make sure that the account contains at least a nominal amount at the time of registration of the charge.

[95] See paras 3.86ff of the Report and reg 6(1)(a).

[96] See, for example, *Re Ashpurton Estates Ltd* [1983] Ch 110, CA; *Re LH Charles & Co Ltd* [1935] WN 15.

[97] [1910] 2 Ch 306.

renders the charge subject to defeasance against those classes. Since the classes thus named in s 395 of the Companies Act 1985 do not include purchasers of the company's property, factors under discounting arrangements may not take objection to a competing chargee's failure to register.[98] There is no established link between those classes entitled to object to a failure to register and those who, under the doctrine of constructive notice laid down in *Wilson v Kelland*, are fixed with notice of a charge once it has been registered. The better view, however, is that factors and other outright purchasers of the collateral are not fixed with constructive notice of a registered charge. This view assumes that those who do not register, or procure the registration of, a charge are not expected themselves to examine the register, no matter how aware as a class they might be of the existence of that register. The lack of clarity in the present law on a matter of such importance is regrettable.

5. Constructive notice

Now, the creation of an uncertain structure of constructive notice in *Wilson v Kelland* by a puisne judge[99] nearly 90 years ago is hardly a satisfactory matter. The priority system proposed by the Law Commission dispenses altogether with any need to resort to a doctrine of constructive notice (though it took the Ontario legislator rather a long time to discover this):[100] this is recognized in clear terms by reg 19. Chargee A ranks ahead of chargee B, not because the latter could, if it had examined the register, have detected the existence of A's charge, but because, under the first-in-time rule, A was the first to register. This is an altogether simpler way to proceed.[101] The inclusion of general assignments of accounts receivable within the Law Commission's filing proposals has the great merit of including factors within this simple first-in-time system. This system, moreover, works so as to advance a second chargee who knows of the existence of an earlier unregistered charge. This is implicit in the language of reg 24(2) and in the explicit statement of a different rule for outright purchasers.[102] It accords with existing law[103] and, in its favour, is supported by arguments based on the integrity of the register that have found favour in jurisdictions with modern personal property security systems. That said, the evangelical fervour

---

[98] *Pfeiffer Weinkellerei-Weinenkauf GmbH & Co v Arbuthnot Factors Ltd* [1988] 1 WLR 150.

[99] Eve J.

[100] The original Personal Property Security Act 1967 (brought into force in 1976) contained a provision that registration amounted to constructive notice of the security interest.

[101] But since such legislation does not give rise to a title register, such an approach does not work in the case of conflicts between chargees and outright purchasers.

[102] See reg 28(1). But why should the reasoning in the Report at para 3.214, based on the avoidance of fraud, not also apply to a later chargee?

[103] See *Re Monolithic Building Co* [1915] 1 Ch 643.

with which the integrity argument is sometimes made ought to give any supporter of this approach some misgivings.

6. The registrar's conclusive certificate

The second point on the effect of registration concerns the conclusive effect of the registrar's certificate in *National Provincial Bank and Union Bank of England v Charnley.*[104] Put simply, one of the baneful effects of that rule is that the position of the chargee depends upon the contents of the debenture delivered to Companies House rather than upon the particulars of charge delivered with it and the appearance of those particulars on the register for third parties to see. Those examining the register can never have full confidence that what they see will be what they get. Given the opportunities for mistakes and oversight presented by Companies House staff laboriously having to check particulars against the debenture, it is no wonder that the response from consultees favoured a system of notice filing[105] that places responsibility for filing on the chargee and protects the position of the chargee to the extent only that the chargee has accurately entered the necessary information on the register. It is hardly a credit to the present system that a chargee taking responsibility for registration can visit the consequences of its own negligence in failing to record accurately the particulars of charge upon innocent third parties misled by what they see on the register. But that is what *Charnley* decided and the abolition of the conclusive registration rule is to be welcomed for that reason alone.

7. Notice filing and further information

The introduction of notice filing does of course raise interesting questions about how an interested third party can discover details of a charge over and above the limited details provided on the register. The obvious person to seek the information is the debtor, who is looking for additional financing. There seems to be no provision in the draft Regulations for the debtor to obtain the necessary information from the existing chargee and in a form acceptable to the third party.[106] It is not easy to see the reason for this omission but it may possibly be a casualty of the abandonment of rules concerning the rights and duties of debtor and secured creditor.

G. The Rights of Outright Purchasers of the Collateral

I exclude from this Part the rights of those, like factors, who discount receivables, in that their position is approximated by the draft Regulations to that of

[104] [1924] 1 KB 431, CA. [105] See para 2.1 of the Report.
[106] cf draft reg 18 in the Consultative Report (n 1 above).

chargees. The paradigm case to be borne in mind is the outright purchaser of tangible personalty like equipment. During the early stages of the Law Commission's consultation, its tentative recommendations on the rights of outright purchasers were somewhat discordant with the existing law on title transfer. In the result, there is still some cause for concern arising out of the Report. There has however been some shift in the Commission's stance, dictated by the supposed retention of the distinction between fixed and floating charges, which can be summarized as follows.

1. Outright buyers and unregistered charges

Draft reg 28 embodies the Law Commission's recommendation that an outright buyer to whom delivery is made should take free of an unregistered fixed charge so far as the buyer lacks knowledge of its existence. A similar provision is made for floating charges: the relevant knowledge provision here goes to the existence of restrictive clauses in the debenture disabling the company from selling in the ordinary course of business.[107] As regards floating charges, the Commission's recommendation is declaratory of existing law in that the company is licensed by the chargee to dispose in the ordinary course. That constitutes either an actual authority or, if restrictions are not apparent to third parties, an apparent authority to dispose.

There remain nevertheless some concerns about the case of the fixed charge, in respect of the delivery requirement. Two issues present themselves here: first, whether delivery should be required at all, and secondly, if so, whether it has to be physical delivery or might instead be constructive delivery, as where the seller remains in actual possession but attorns to the buyer. Taking first the general delivery requirement, it is by no means obvious that a transaction taking place in good faith should be ineffective to transfer title if delivery does not take place. A failure to take delivery might in some instances betray the absence of good faith, but that is a different matter. The outright buyer may be at risk when it comes to subsequent dealings with the collateral by the company seller with a second buyer, but our concern here is with the position of an earlier chargee.

The second point is the more difficult one, largely because it is not entirely clear what type of delivery the Law Commission has in mind. The formulation in the regulations that the buyer of tangible collateral '*takes* possession or delivery' (emphasis added)[108] appears to point towards physical and not merely constructive delivery. An argument in favour of physical delivery is that the chargee may be misled as to the effect of its charge against alienated assets remaining in

[107] See para 3.221 of the Report.

[108] See reg 28(1)(b).

the company chargor's possession. Nevertheless, if no further advances are made by the chargee, there would seem to be no loss accruing to it as a result of the chargor's misleading, continuing possession. And even if further value is given, the charge will in all probability extend instead to the proceeds of disposition in the chargor's hands. If that disposition has taken place in good faith, it is likely to yield market value or something approximating to it. The notion of ostensible ownership based upon possession, which in the past inhibited security bills of sale, has long been exploded. If nevertheless delivery were to extend to include constructive delivery, as it does in the general law of sale and personal property, in the form of an attornment by the company seller,[109] the continuing necessity of delivery, over and above a good faith requirement (here, articulated in terms of a lack of knowledge of the charge by the buyer),[110] seems even more redundant. Moreover, an earlier chargee would be as easily misled by the attorning company's continuing actual possession as by a non-attorning company's actual possession.

2. Outright buyers and registered charges

Draft reg 29, so far as it deals with registered fixed charges, gives rise to greater concern. It provides that an outright purchaser takes subject to the charge and therefore embraces such purchasers within the community of those who can be expected to examine the register. Even though a fixed charge is most unlikely to include stock-in-trade, there will inevitably be cases of equipment being purchased by buyers (for example, surplus vehicles formerly used by sales representatives) where the buyer acting in good faith and giving full value will not have examined the register. The fixed chargee—who, let us remember, has only an equitable interest under existing law—may also have a charge over the proceeds of sale of that vehicle. In that event, a clear windfall gain occurs. So far as the buyer is caught by the registered charge, it looks like constructive notice of that charge under another name and constructive notice of the contents of the register has been repudiated by the Law Commission.[111] The Law Commission's proposal in reg 29 reverses the bona fide purchaser doctrine in subordinating legal to prior equitable interests. For all practical purposes, it transforms the chargee's equitable proprietary interest into a legal interest. It also tilts the law further in the direction of protecting property rights and against the protection of commerce, even though English law already favours property interests, when these collide with the needs of commerce and the protection of good faith buyers, to a greater extent than almost any other legal system.

[109] *Gamer's Motor Centre (Newcastle) Pty Ltd v Natwest Wholesale Motor Auctions* (1987) 163 CLR 236; *Four Point Garage Ltd v Carter* [1985] 3 All ER 12.
[110] See reg 28(1). [111] See Part F, Section 5 above.

The Law Commission's proposal, as embodied in reg 29, highlights the difficulty of moving forward with radical sectoral reform that is philosophically at odds with the surrounding legal environment. If the Law Commission's project on title transfer reform[112] leads to a rebalancing of the present law in favour of good faith purchasers, then reg 29 will look out of line with recommended changes in title transfer law to the above effect. Furthermore, if a vital doctrine of equity is to be set aside by statutory instrument, this has important implications for the future of equity and its relationship with the common law. It might fairly be said of this issue that it reinforces a rather important point about the relationship between equity and the common law, namely, that it can survive in its present form only within an uncodified, or substantially uncodified, legal tradition.

H. Conclusions

In view of the unenthusiastic response of the legal profession to previous consultation documents, which a critic might fairly say is in places complacent, it has to be asked whether there is truly a need for a revision of the law. It is submitted that there is, not just as to the substantive content of what the Law Commission is proposing, but also as to its presentational aspect. The Commission's incidental recommendation that there be a further project aiming to restate the law relating to security is also to be welcomed.[113] Those who have participated in international gatherings will be acutely aware that the absence of a presentable package of English commercial law is a major hindrance to its international influence. This is one of the major planks supporting Roy Goode's call for a codification of English commercial law.[114] One cannot leave the Law Commission's Report without feeling that its articulation has been hampered by two major constraints, namely, the exclusion from the Commission's terms of reference of insolvency law and the lifting of security from a broader environment of commercial law that contains elements that do not quite fit the proposals forthcoming from the Commission. The Commission's reference to a future project dealing with the law of title transfer[115] is both indicative of this handicap and to be welcomed in its own right.

Above all, one looks at the Report and sees the enormous work and progress

---

[112] See the Ninth Programme (Law Com No 296, Cm 6654, August 2005) para 1.66.

[113] See para 22 of the Summary of the Report.

[114] See, for example, RM Goode, 'Insularity or Leadership? The Role of the United Kingdom in the Harmonisation of Commercial Law' (2001) 50 ICLQ 751.

[115] See para 21 of the Summary of the Report.

made by the Law Commission working to severe deadlines over a short period of time. That is most impressive and stands as a great credit to the common law team of the Commission. Nevertheless, it must be asked whether this is the best way to conduct law reform and whether the Law Commission, at least when working unaided, is a suitable vehicle for large-scale, structural legal reform. It does not have the resources to conduct major research. Might it not be better for work to be done, not necessarily by the Law Commission but rather through the academic and professional legal communities, towards a restatement of commercial law—no restatement is ever just a restatement—so that in future years a body like the Law Commission or the Department of Trade and Industry will not find itself working from a standing start to achieve the near impossible? If the creation of a body like the American Law Institute were feasible, then that body would assist in such a project and would do much to break down the barriers between academic and practising lawyers. The Law Commission's own fruitful efforts in bringing academics and practitioners together in the cause of promoting its work in the field of company charges itself holds out promise for the future of such a venture.

INDEX